ORAL READING

LIONEL CROCKER, Ph.D.
Denison University

LOUIS M. EICH, Ph.D.
University of Michigan

ORAL READING

Discussion and Principles and an Anthology of Practice Materials from Literature Classical and Modern

SECOND EDITION

Englewood Cliffs, N. J.
PRENTICE-HALL, INC.

L. C. Cat. Card No.: 55-7942

First printing .... *May, 1955*
Second printing ...... *May, 1956*
Third printing ..... *March, 1960*
Fourth printing ... *October, 1961*
Fifth printing .... *April, 1964*

PRINTED IN THE UNITED STATES OF AMERICA

63881-C

Preface

It is gratifying to have a text meet with enough favor by one's colleagues to warrant a second edition. It is particularly encouraging in the field of oral reading because it means that educators are rediscovering the value of this fine old tool in the field of liberal arts and general education.

Several major changes have been made in the new edition. Three new chapters have been written to emphasize the importance of aspects of oral reading that were present in the first edition, but were not singled out for special attention. The aesthetic basis of oral reading is now treated in a chapter by itself. The various relationships of the reader to the aspects of oral reading have been brought together and enlarged. And, since so much of the student's time in a class in oral reading is spent in listening, it seemed necessary to expand that material.

The minor changes are almost too numerous to mention. We are proud, however, to call attention to the reprinting of Robert Hillyer's "On Reading Verse Aloud." Not often do poets treat of this art. And a few of the new faces appearing in the anthology are those of Arthur Miller, Herman Wouk, Dwight D. Eisenhower, Wallace Stevens, Marianne Moore, Dylan Thomas.

Teaching aids have been increased. For example, at the end of each chapter the teacher will find interesting projects to challenge the student's serious attention to the art of reading aloud. More than seventy projects are listed throughout the text. We teachers of speech often say that the library is the heart of the liberal arts college. This is certainly true for classes in oral interpretation. No anthology could possibly contain enough materials to satisfy the appetites of the teacher and the student of reading aloud effectively. The lists of books in the extensive appendices have been reworked and enlarged with many items.

Some of the chapters have new titles with relevant materials added. Many of these changes were made at the suggestion of friends of the text. Other changes such as the ones in the chapter on radio and television have been necessitated by events.

THE AUTHORS

Contents

PRINCIPLES

CHAPTER

I. Importance, Nature and Function, 1

II. Some Aesthetic Considerations, 22

III. The Provinces of the Reader, the Actor, and the Speaker, 50

IV. Tools of Understanding and Appreciation, 61

V. Words, Words, Words, 94

VI. Voice and Speech, 122

VII. Some Problems in Technique, 150

VIII. Reading Narrative Prose, 171

IX. The Reader's Relationships, 181

X. The Public Recital, 195

XI. Choral Reading, 210

XII. Radio and Television Reading, 224

XIII. The Reader Himself, 240

XIV. Listening to a Selection, 253

ANTHOLOGY

PART

I. Essays, Speeches, Reports, 273

II. Narrative Prose, 291

III. Narrative Poetry, 302
IV. Lyrical Poetry, 330
V. Stories with Dialogue, 393
VI. Plays, 413
VII. Dramatic Monologues, 441

APPENDICES

I. Novels Suitable for Readings, 445
II. Plays Suitable for Readings, 447
III. Suggested Reading in the Field of Oral Reading, 450
IV. Suggested Reading in Radio and Television, 452
V. Suggested Reading in the Field of Choral Reading, 453
VI. Suggested Reading in the History of Oral Reading, 455
VII. Suggested Reading in the Field of Literary Criticism, 457
VIII. Suggested Cuttings from Shakespeare, 459
IX. Suggested Readings from the Bible, 461
X. Great Speeches for Oral Reading, 463
XI. Anthologies of Materials for Oral Reading, 465
XII. Terms of Versification, 467
XIII. The Notebook, 472

Selections in the Text

Conrad Aiken	*Bread and Music*	330
Dean Alfange	*My Creed*	273
Sherwood Anderson	*I'm a Fool*	393
Matthew Arnold	*Dover Beach*	330
W. H. Auden	*As I Walked Out One Evening*	331
Sir James Barrie	*The Will*	413
Henry Ward Beecher	*Naturalness*	52
	On the Voice	145
Bible	*Beatitudes*	217
	The Prodigal Son	291
	Psalm XXIII	333
	Psalm CVII	335
	The Song of Songs	335
William Blake	*The Tiger*	336
Rupert Brooke	*The Soldier*	337
Elizabeth Barrett Browning	*Sonnets from the Portuguese, XIV, XLIII*	337
Robert Browning	*An Incident of the French Camp*	302
	Boot and Saddle	41
	Home Thoughts from Abroad	338
	How They Brought the Good News from Ghent to Aix	70
	Meeting at Night	83
	My Last Duchess	441
	My Star	57
	Paracelsus	245
	Parting at Morning	339
	Prospice	339
	The Patriot	442
William Cullen Bryant	*To a Waterfowl*	340

Edmund Burke	*The Judgment of a Representative*	273
Robert Burns	*Honest Poverty*	341
Lord Byron	*To Thomas Moore*	342
Madison Cawein	*Deserted*	343
	The Man Hunt	343
	Snow	345
Russell H. Conwell	*Acres of Diamonds*	74
Winston Churchill	*Dunkirk*	274
T. A. Daly	*Mia Carlotta*	459
Emily Dickinson	*I Never Saw a Moor*	345
Dwight D. Eisenhower	*Our Great Team*	274
T. S. Eliot	*The Hollow Men*	346
Ralph Waldo Emerson	*Days*	349
	Self Reliance	278
William Faulkner	*The Sound and the Fury*	45
Frances Frost	*The Storyteller*	349
Robert Frost	*Birches*	303
	Stopping by Woods on a Snowy Evening	350
	The Pasture	305
	The Death of the Hired Man	305
John Galsworthy	*Told by the Schoolmaster*	402
Wolcott Gibbs	*On Candida*	99
Alice Hamilton, M.D.	*Words, Lost, Strayed or Stolen*	118
Philip Hamburger	*On Robert Frost*	238
Learned Hand	*The Preparation of Citizens for Their Political Duties*	278
William Ernest Henley	*Invictus*	350
O. Henry	*A Service of Love*	406
Robert Herrick	*To the Virgins to Make Much of Time*	351
Robert Hillyer	*On Reading Verse Aloud*	280
Thomas Hood	*I Remember, I Remember*	351
A. E. Housman	*When I Was One-and-Twenty*	352
William James	*The Social Value of the College Bred*	286
Robinson Jeffers	*The Excesses of God*	353
Ben Jonson	*Song to Celia*	353
John Keats	*A Thing of Beauty Is a Joy Forever*	354
	When I Have Fears That I May Cease to Be	355

Charles Kingsley	*Young and Old*	355
Rudyard Kipling	*Gunga Din*	309
	Tommy	311
Charles Lamb	*The Old Familiar Faces*	356
Sidney Lanier	*A Ballad of Trees and the Master*	356
Charles Laughton	*The Laughton System*	269
Winifred Letts	*The Spires of Oxford*	357
Abraham Lincoln	*Gettysburg Address*	287
	The Second Inaugural	288
	Private Enterprise	289
Vachel Lindsay	*A Negro Sermon: Simon Legree*	218
	John Brown	313
	The Congo	315
	General Booth Enters into Heaven	316
Henry Wadsworth Longfellow	*The Rainy Day*	358
Amy Lowell	*A Lady*	358
	The Bombardment	292
James Russell Lowell	*The Fountain*	359
Archibald MacLeish	*Ars Poetica*	24
Edwin Markham	*Lincoln, The Man of the People*	360
Herman Melville	*Moby Dick*	258
Edna St. Vincent Millay	*God's World*	361
	Lament	362
Arthur Miller	*"Requiem"* from *Death of a Salesman*	433
John Milton	*When I Consider How My Light Is Spent*	363
	L'Allegro	41, 363
Marianne Moore	*In Distrust of Merits*	363
Thomas Moore	*Orator Puff*	141
	Oft, in the Stilly Night	365
Christopher Morley	*To a Post-Office Inkwell*	366
Ogden Nash	*Frailty, Thy Name Is a Misnomer*	318
St. Paul	*Whatsoever Things Are True*	38
Plato	*The Death of Socrates*	294
Edgar Allan Poe	*Annabel Lee*	367
	To Helen	37
Alexander Pope	*An Essay on Man*	368
Nathan M. Pusey	*Religion's Role in Liberal Education*	116

Ernie Pyle	*Men Show Devotion to a Loved Officer*	296
Edwin Arlington Robinson	*Calvary*	369
	Miniver Cheevy	319
	Richard Cory	216
Christina Rossetti	*Song*	56
Carl Sandburg	*Chicago*	369
	Grass	370
Sir Walter Scott	*The Lay of the Last Minstrel*	371
	Marmion	320
Robert W. Service	*The Shooting of Dan McGrew*	321
	The Cremation of Sam McGee	324
Eric Sevareid	*The Adjective*	93
William Shakespeare	*Hamlet*	435
	Henry V	90
	Julius Caesar	67, 434
	Othello	438
	Romeo and Juliet	440
	Sonnets	371
	The Merchant of Venice	262, 438
Percy Bysshe Shelley	*To a Skylark*	374
	Threnos	40
Edward Rowland Sill	*The Fool's Prayer*	327
Lillian Smith	*Ten Years from Today*	96
Robert Southey	*After Blenheim*	33
Stephen Spender	*In Railway Halls*	376
Sylvia Stallings	*What Word for Spring?*	376
Wallace Stevens	*Peter Quince at the Clavier*	377
Robert Louis Stevenson	*The Celestial Surgeon*	113
	The House Beautiful	379
John Steinbeck	*The Grapes of Wrath*	410
Sir John Suckling	*The Constant Lover*	380
Sara Teasdale	*Barter*	381
Alfred, Lord Tennyson	*Break, Break, Break*	381
	Flower in the Crannied Wall	382
	Ulysses	382
	Crossing the Bar	383
	In Memoriam	69, 383
	Of Old Sat Freedom on the Heights	385
	The Eagle	386

George R. Tweed	*I Learned to Read on Guam*	242
John V. A. Weaver	*Moonlight*	386
Walt Whitman	*Beat! Beat! Drums!*	388
	For You, O Democracy	389
	I Hear America Singing	389
	O Captain! My Captain!	388
	Out of the Cradle Endlessly Rocking	72
	The Wound Dresser	328
	Vocalism	387
John Greenleaf Whittier	*Dear Lord and Father of Mankind*	390
William Wordsworth	*Composed upon Westminster Bridge*	391
	It Is a Beauteous Evening, Calm and Free	391
	London, 1802	392
	The World Is Too Much with Us	62
Herman Wouk	*The Caine Mutiny*	298
Elinor Wylie	*Golden Bough*	392

ORAL READING

Boston Herald

Robert Frost speaking and reading to 15,000 people on the Boston Commons on June 14, 1954 in connection with The Boston Art Festival.

Wide World Photo

I could write volumes on the subject of my public speaking adventures. My friends seem to think that I have had more than my fair share of fun—jaunts around the world, expeditions to far countries, association with many of the world's leaders and glamorous figures, and so on. Well I owe it almost entirely to public speaking.

As I look back on it now, if given the chance to do it all over again, and if obliged to choose between four years in college and two years of straight public speaking, I would take the latter, because under the proper direction, it could include most of what one gets from a four year Liberal Arts course, and then some.

I can think of nothing that is more likely to add cubits to your stature than well-rounded training in public speaking, combined with plenty of practical experience. *Letter from Lowell Thomas to the Author.*

CHAPTER I

Importance, Nature and Function of Oral Reading

I. IMPORTANCE
- A. In Business and Professions
- B. In General Education
- C. In Speech Education
- D. In Self-Development
- E. In Meeting Human Need
- F. In Radio and Television
- G. The Two Arts Unite

II. NATURE
- A. Oral Reading Thoroughly Practical
- B. Thinking the Thought
- C. Reading as if Speaking
- D. Reading to an Audience
- E. Art Conceals Art

III. FUNCTION
- A. Individually
  1. Forming Your Taste
  2. Improving Your Speech
  3. Developing Your Leadership
- B. Socially
  1. Enlarging Your Sympathies
  2. Nourishing the Class Discussion

IV. SUMMARY

V. PROJECTS FOR CHAPTER I

I. IMPORTANCE

A. *In Business and Professions*

Too long we have thought of reading from the printed page as an art exercise only, and not long enough have we thought of this method of communication as an important medium for the exchange of ideas in the day-by-day work of the world. Next to direct face to face public speaking there is no communicative act so widely practiced as reading from the printed page to an audience. Unless we think twice, we are very likely to think of oral reading as confined largely to the reading of poetry and literary prose, and yet how often in the actual everyday world is poetry read aloud? How often is drama read aloud to others as a solo performance?

On the other hand, are not most speeches at business conferences read? And it is due to a lack of understanding on how to read from the printed page that most speeches are poorly read. The dismal process goes something like this: A busy business man with little or no experience in public address will employ someone to write him a speech. On the appointed day he will proceed to pull it out of his pocket, take off the paper clip, adjust his glasses, and stumble through it. Because he did not personally write the address, he will read to himself, apparently fascinated by many of the ideas he finds there. He will get twisted up in a style that is not his own. Sentences will elude him. There will be little or no contact with the minds and hearts before him. He finishes the ordeal no less glad than the people before him. One dare not call it an audience for few, if any, listened.

Clarence Belden Randall, President of the Inland Steel Company, declared recently,

> This is an age of ideas. Business men are probably the most inarticulate group God ever placed in one calling. And the free enterprise system will fail in favor of the avalanche of attacks upon it unless we have young men, not only to understand it, but who can get up on their hind legs and say something about it. It makes absolutely no difference how much you know, if you can't tell somebody about it and be persuasive, it won't do.[1]

And be persuasive! This cannot be done by a reader who mumbles to himself, who fails to project his ideas, who fails to make contact with the people before him. Some speakers seem to think that an audience will be impressed by a manuscript. Quite the contrary! Instead of thinking the speaker learned and wise because he has a manuscript, the audience will think him unprepared. Listen to what Harold Cooke Phillips, a manuscript preacher, says about mastering the manuscript:

> The sermon is as a rule finished by Saturday forenoon, that is, as far as writing it goes. But now I must get the sermon off the paper and into myself, "soak in it," as Spurgeon, I believe, put it. When a manuscript gets in the preacher's way it usually means that the sermon is on the paper rather than in the preacher. So I read and mark up

[1] Commencement Address at Denison University, Granville, Ohio, June 8. 1953.

what I have written again and again, not in order to memorize it necessarily, but in order that what is on the paper may be felt and become a part of me.[2]

What magic is there in a piece of paper? As a matter of fact, the manuscript may be the worst kind of a block between the speaker and his audience. The audience wants the personality of the author to glow again through his words and not be smothered in an unintelligible flood of words.

B. *In General Education*

Grayson Kirk, President of Columbia University, speaking before the National Education Association, declared that, "Beyond the inculcation of certain basic skills such as mathematics and the use of language, both spoken and written, the primary purpose of education is to widen the mental horizons of the student. Except for certain technical or vocational courses of study, the primary purpose of a school is not to increase earning power but to enrich the human spirit."[3] Those of us who teach oral reading know that the discipline develops skill in the use of language, both written and oral, and that it does enrich the human spirit. The Harvard report on *General Education in a Free Society* states that general education should develop the abilities (1) to think effectively; (2) to communicate thought; (3) to make relevant judgments; and (4) to discriminate among values. Oral reading can be so taught as to develop these four desirable traits in the student. As the student puts his mind alongside the minds of some of the great thinkers, whether they are essayists, poets, dramatists, he has the opportunity to sharpen his ability to think. Oral reading permits the student to get back to the selection itself instead of reading what others say about the selection, and, in so doing, he has to formulate some ideas of his own about the selection. This gives him intellectual independence. This brings him face to face with literary criticism. Instead of skimming over a work in

---

[2] Harold Cooke Phillips, "How I Prepare My Sermons," in *Here Is My Method,* ed. Donald Macleod (Westwood, N. J.: Fleming H. Revell Company, 1952), p. 127.

[3] Grayson Kirk, "The Three Additional R's of Education," *Vital Speeches,* XX, No. 20.

order to pass a written examination, the student must come to grips with it and discover how he can read this intelligently to others.

For example, to become master of the parable, "The Prodigal Son," to appreciate all its implications and applications, to understand its rich symbolism and religious overtones, to read some of the sermons that have been preached on the parable, to wonder why the parable has lived through the centuries, to read what the commentaries say about this parable, to listen to such oral interpreters as Walter Hampden read it, is to make the parable an exercise in thinking, in communication, in making relevant judgments, in discriminating among values, and in enriching the human spirit.

In many institutions oral reading has made a firm place for itself in the general education curriculum. Garff B. Wilson has given this picture of the place oral reading has come to occupy at the University of California:

> In recent years, the University of California has witnessed a phenomenal growth of its courses in the Oral Interpretation of Literature. In 1941, 4 members of the Speech Department were teaching this subject; in 1949, 12 instructors were assigned to it. In 1941, 13 classes in Oral Interpretation were offered; eight years later, 38 classes were being given. In 1941, about 340 students were enrolled in these courses; in 1949, there were more than 1,000. During this eight year period, the enrollment in the University increased 30%; the enrollment in Oral Interpretation courses increased 300%.
>
> This remarkable growth is a result not only of good teaching and wise departmental leadership; more especially it has resulted from the adoption of an approach to Oral Interpretation which serves the ideals of a liberal arts college and furthers the aims of general education. The experience at California may be useful to other Departments of Speech where Oral Interpretation has not yet attained the standing it deserves.[4]

C. *In Speech Education*

Oral reading is an integral division of the present-day Department of Speech, which includes, in addition, speech correction, theatre, radio and television, speech pedagogy, rhetoric, and public

[4] Garff B. Wilson, "The Growth of Oral Interpretation at the University of California," *The Speech Teacher,* I, 187.

address. In fact, some of the oldest departments in the country, such as the ones at the University of Michigan under Thomas C. Trueblood and Northwestern University under Robert Cumnock, are direct outgrowths of oral interpretation, which was called, during the last quarter of the nineteenth century, elocution, a term which has much to recommend it, but which fell into disrepute due to abuse. Oral reading has its roots deep in the history of communication. One of the classics in the history of speech education is *Lectures on Elocution,* 1763, by Thomas Sheridan, father of Richard Brinsley Sheridan. Richard Whately in 1828 wrote an essay that has had much influence in bringing about a pragmatic approach to the problems of oral reading, and it is found in Part IV of his *Elements of Rhetoric,* called "Elocution."[5] And James Rush gave us helpful concepts in the use of voice, such as quality, pitch, time, and force, in his *The Philosophy of the Human Voice,* 1827.[6]

Oral reading is an aid in speech correction, acting, and radio and television,[7] and, as has been pointed out, is a direct aid to public speaking. It is a wide open field for scholarly investigation. Both master's and doctor's degrees are earned today with emphasis upon oral reading. In a current issue of *Speech Monographs* one finds theses for the master's degree on such interesting subjects as "The Concept of Aesthetic Distance in Oral Interpretation" and "Scholarship and Milton—a Study in the Method of the Oral Interpreter." A doctoral dissertation on "An Experimental Study of Training in Oral Reading on Silent Reading Skills" indicates some of the implications of the study of oral reading.

D. *In Self-Development*

There is a good deal of sense in the thought that no idea is really ours until we vocalize it. To formulate the idea in words in

---

[5] See James A. Winans, "Whately on Elocution," *Quarterly Journal of Speech,* XXXI, 1.

[6] For the history of the subject see Mary Margaret Robb, *Oral Interpretation in American Colleges and Universities* (New York: H. W. Wilson Company, 1941).

[7] See Sara Lowrey, "Interpretative Reading as an Aid to Speech Correction, Acting and Radio," *Quarterly Journal of Speech,* XXXI, 459.

one's throat is an important step in entering the experience detailed in the selection. To grasp the idea, to hold the idea, to phrase the idea in order to communicate the idea develops one's power over language. The study of a passage for oral reading imposes the necessity of knowing as much as possible about the author, about the ideas expressed, about the emotions underlying the selection, and the import of all the words. This knowledge aids the student in his grasp of the world outside himself, of indirect experience, of the life of the mind. For example, what student's thoughts about death are not enlarged when he is brought face to face with Plato's account of the death of Socrates? And what student's appreciation of the beauties of nature are not enhanced by a contemplation of Keats's "Endymion"? A student may get some help in his own personal development by a quiet perusal in his study of these masterpieces, but he will get much more if he makes them a part of himself so that he can share them with others. The fact that it is one thing to read to oneself and quite another to read aloud to someone else is borne out in the following experience of F. Fraser Bond who had his career as a writer halted by cataract. He had to depend upon readers and this is a record of his experience:

> I employed students at first, but not for long. Students, by and large, are not sufficiently practiced in reading aloud. Their eyes had a way of skipping ahead of their voices so that their tardily spoken syllables lagged behind their visual interest and made no sense. They might just as well have been reading Chocktaw. In despair, I turned to young actors. This change proved highly successful.[8]

Emotional and spiritual sensitivity is developed through oral reading. Hiram Corson in his little classic, *The Voice and Spiritual Education,* reminds us of this spiritual value:

> Special stress is laid upon the importance of spiritual education as the end toward which all education should be directed, and as an indispensable condition of interpretative reading. Such education is demanded for responding to, and assimilating, the informing life of any product of literary genius; without it mere vocal training avails little or nothing. By the spiritual I mean man's essential, absolute being; and I include in the term the emotional, the susceptible or impressible, the

[8] *Saturday Review,* February 3, 1954, p. 14.

sympathetic, the instinctive, the intuitive,—in short, the whole domain of the non-intellectual, the non-discursive.[9]

And it has been shown that students of oral reading become more aware of the communication of feeling on the part of a speaker than do students of mathematics, students with speech problems, and junior high school groups of both higher and lower socio-economic status. This super-sensitivity by students of oral reading was discovered by Paul L. Pfaff when he tried to determine the degree to which a listener can identify the feelings of a speaker when the speaker is not seen and does not use syntactical means of communication.[10]

E. *In Meeting Human Need*

Closely associated with the student's development of his own spiritual sensitivity is the development of his ability to satisfy the spiritual craving of his fellow men. We want communion with each other. Way down deep in each of us there is an essential loneliness which can be satisfied by the eternal truths of the great poets and prose writers whom the oral reader is called upon to interpret. Often the test of the reader's success is in the extent to which he binds us together. Sincerity, courage, hope, unselfishness, kindliness, nobility, self-sacrifice, gentleness—emotions and actions that are found in the lasting literary works of our culture help bind us humans together. At the Boston Festival held in 1954 Robert Frost read his poems to 15,000 people one evening on the Boston Commons. This vast audience listened quietly to his poetry so full of courage and wisdom and serenity. They found spiritual nourishment in his statement on courage: "The human virtue that counts most is courage—courage to act on limited knowledge; courage to make the best of what is here and not whine for more." Charles Laughton declared that one of the reasons people like to hear him and others read in public is that for the moment they

---

9 Corson, Hiram, *The Voice and Spiritual Education* (New York: Macmillan, 1896).

10 Pfaff, Paul L., "An Experimental Study of the Communication of Feeling Without Contextual Material," Ph.D. Thesis, U. of Southern California, *Speech Monographs,* XXI, 155.

are all bound together, that they momentarily lose their sense of being alone.[11]

F. *In Radio and Television*

Robert Montgomery, the actor, spent many hours with President Dwight D. Eisenhower teaching him how to keep his personality from being lost in the manuscript he was to read over TV. He taught him to fold his arms, to prop himself up on his desk in a half-sitting, half-standing position, how to smile as the cameras approached him, how to read as if he were talking directly to his audience. The reactions to this address were most favorable. Successful emcees on TV, like Arlene Francis, often owe their success on radio and TV to their years in the theatre where they have been taught how to project the written word to the audience. One writer in describing the behavior of Arlene Francis before the cameras puts it this way:

> She has no compunction about whipping out her spectacles, without which she cannot read, in front of millions of viewers. But on TV, vivacity gets higher marks than visages. When she talks, in a voice that has been described by the unkind as a cultured bray, she gestures with her head, her arms, and her eyebrows; her laugh is one of those welcome, old fashioned yocks. Perhaps her forte is that she always looks alert. She radiates a warmth that could only come from an interest in everybody and everything. Suspicious souls might consider it merely the trained "projecting" of a skilled actress, but anyone who has spent a couple of minutes sunning his ego anywhere in Miss Francis's vicinity believes otherwise. She genuinely likes people and desperately wants everyone to like her—a very marketable combination when transmitted electronically.[12]

Knowing how to project, knowing how to make the words come alive, is necessary for the radio and TV reader. The same intimate tone which has been advocated for the radio reader is advocated for the TV reader. One or two or three people may be seated before the screen. The reader is likely to think that he is reading to millions. Perhaps he is when the people are counted in the aggregate but this larger audience is made up of people in small

[11] *The Atlantic,* June, 1950.

[12] *Newsweek,* July 19, 1954, p. 50.

groups in their homes. Arthur Godfrey is often praised for his contact, his rapport with his audience. Is it not this closeness, this intimacy which he has developed that makes for his success?

For the student of speech, radio and TV are important as possible job opportunities. In the June 21, 1954 issue of *Time* the following data emphasize this growing field: "In Chicago, researchers of Columbia College (a speech school with a radio and TV department) queried 182 TV executives on the future of television. They estimated that 1) the industry might create as many as 37,000 new jobs in the next five years, 2) there will be twice as many stations on the air in 1960 as there are now, 3) color TV is not likely to enlarge substantially the number of people working in the industry." And in the August 9, 1954 issue of *Time* the story of Ken Nordine and his success in TV is told. The story is of interest because it illustrates how the daily compromise with perfection is mastered by one idealist. (Courtesy TIME Magazine. Copyright Time Inc. 1954.)

DOUBLE LIFE

Ken Nordine is a fortunate fellow who enjoys double rewards for living a double life. Over national TV hookups, as a smooth-talking pitchman for deodorants, detergents and such (Stopette, Pamper Shampoo, Tums), he earns, he figures, about $80,000 a year. But Nordine has his real fun and finds his real fans on his own show, which pays him practically nothing.

Chapter & Verse. Once a week, over WNBQ in Chicago, tall, hollow-cheeked Ken Nordine recites poetry to a late evening audience. Perched on a stool, with a stepladder full of books beside him, the 34-year-old Iowan reads earnestly in a subdued, husky voice, glancing from page to camera like a casual host reading to guests in his library. What distinguishes Nordine's shows from others like it is the flashing telephone by his side. He has adapted the disk jockey's request-format for poetry and made it work. When he finishes a poem, he picks up the telephone, listens to a new request from a viewer, and makes small talk while he leafs through his library to find the poem or passage wanted. *Now for Nordine* is broadcast after peak viewing hours, yet hundreds of listeners try to phone in every week. Those who fail to get through send in requests by mail. Last week he read, by request: Alexander Pope's "Ode on Solitude," Robert Frost's "Mending Wall," Elizabeth Barrett Browning's "How Do I Love Thee?", Carl Sandburg's "Clean Curtains," *I Corinthians 13.*

Although *Now for Nordine* is only a few weeks old, Nordine himself is no stranger to experimental television. For more than a year he has been frightening and delighting Chicago audiences with eerie readings of classic horror tales such as Poe's *Pit and the Pendulum,* Lovecraft's *Rats in the Walls*. He calls this show *Faces in the Window,* plays weird music as he reads and scares his listeners with a bagful of simple but effective tricks. For a story where a man is hanged, he had the camera turn slowly back and forth to suggest a corpse swinging on a rope. Trick lights and a turtle-neck sweater make his cadaverous face appear to float in air, and sometimes a zoomar lens moves in until only one glittering Nordine eye fills up the television screen.

The Big Money. Nordine keeps his programs simple because he has no time to rehearse. Each week he records commercials for more than a dozen radio and TV sponsors, acts on soap operas, announces local shows, narrates for Chicago's growing TV film industry.

Nordine's own shows are unsponsored, but he has no intention of making them slick enough to sell. Says he: "Television tries to show off too much. I just want to sit down with people and read poetry." On the practical side, he also wants to stay in Chicago and keep on reading commercials. Thanks to tape recording, he can get his slice of the big-money network shows that originate on the East and West coasts.

G. *The Two Arts Unite*

In reading aloud the two arts of speaking and writing unite. Radio and television have served to jog us out of our false acceptance of writing and of print as forces more powerful than the spoken word, for the truth, of course, is that the written language is but the crystallization of the spoken. What is written had to exist in speech before it was ever put down. The return to an emphasis upon the spoken word is salutary. It will make better writers of us all, and we will better understand the written word. Nicholas Murray Butler had this in mind when he said: "The idea is prevalent that the best way to improve the written English of students is to compel them to write constantly and on all sorts of subjects. This is a fallacy. . . . The best way in which to teach students to write good English is to teach them to read good English." [13] We have all had the experience of comprehending, by reading aloud, passages that are difficult to understand when read

[13] Quoted by Algernon Tassin, *The Oral Study of Literature* (New York: Knopf, 1923).

silently. The voice brings out the meaning, through emphasis, thus showing the correct relationship of the words.

Amy Lowell [14] points out that Shakespeare is fortunate in having had his poetry read aloud for the past three hundred years. Who would not much rather see a play of Shakespeare's than read it to himself, silently? Most poets are not so fortunate as to have their poetry read constantly aloud; yet in composing it, they aimed at the ear. Vachel Lindsay barnstormed the country, reading his poetry aloud to anyone who would listen, and Robert Frost and Edna St. Vincent Millay have made their poems live by reading them before thousands of their fellow Americans. Fortunately, one can get phonograph records of many of the modern poets reading their own works; and, indeed, poetry needs to be read aloud. Can there be any doubt of such necessity for poems like "The Congo," by Vachel Lindsay; "The Barrel Organ," by Alfred Noyes; "The Lady of Shalott," by Tennyson?—to cite just a few examples of poems that literally seem to sing themselves, wherein the melody created by reading the poem aloud is indispensable to its enjoyment and appreciation. Novelists of the stature of Thomas Hardy and Lafcadio Hearn testify that in writing they kept in mind the possibility of their sentences being read aloud.[15] Brander Matthews [16] has pointed out how, in writing, Mark Twain chose to reproduce the spoken idiom, and so did not encumber his pages with words long dead and gone. Mark Twain's language is the living speech of all those who have English for their mother tongue.

II. Nature

A. *Oral Reading Thoroughly Practical*

We want to think of the work done in oral reading classes, then, as a thoroughly practical activity, inasmuch as its benefits will be apparent not only in the classroom, but also in extracurricular activities, in the vocations of later life, and in social affairs. It is this practical aspect that we wish to emphasize throughout this

[14] Gertrude Johnson, "Poetry as a Spoken Art," *Studies in the Art of Interpretation* (New York: Appleton-Century-Crofts, 1940), p. 153.

[15] See Lionel Crocker, "The Voice Element in Prose," *Quarterly Journal of Speech,* XII (April, 1926).

[16] Brander Matthews, *Essays on English* (New York: Scribner's, 1921), p. 249.

book. Training in reading as a practical accomplishment has lagged behind training in public speaking. Excellence in public speaking is now quite generally accepted as a necessary qualification for success in public life in a democracy. Perhaps oral reading has lagged behind public speaking because the former has been thought of as a parlor accomplishment. But reading from the printed page, as the radio daily reminds us, plays a vital part in American life; we must all learn to do it better.

Thinking the content is the basis of good public speaking, and it must be the basis of public reading as well. All artificiality must go. We need to give new meaning to the term *reading in public.*

Oral reading is the process of getting the meaning (thought and emotion) from the printed page and translating it into symbols of voice and action which will communicate to the listener a meaning approximating that intended by the author. Thus oral reading is a process of creation and re-creation. The reader creates when he makes the truth on the page live again through his personality and he re-creates when he expresses through voice and action what the author intended to communicate to the audience. Oral reading involves the technique of impression (analysis) and the technique of expression (projection).

B. *Thinking the Thought*

More than a hundred years ago Whately [17] called attention to the only true way of reading aloud, which is, to understand the sense of what one is reading. How simple, yet how difficult! The reader must first of all be interested in communicating the sense and emotion of what he is reading to his audience. In writing of the death of Little Nell, it has been pointed out, Charles Dickens became more interested in wringing tears from his readers than in describing the death of Little Nell; consequently, some of his worst writing appears in those scenes. The reader who becomes more interested in the technique than he is in the sense of what he is reading is headed for artificiality. But to be interested in the sense one must, first of all, understand what it is, and that

[17] Richard Whately, *Elements of Rhetoric* (7th ed.; London, 1846), pp. 348–353. See also James A. Winans, "Whately on Elocution," *Quarterly Journal of Speech,* XXXI, 1.

is not easy. What did the author intend to say? For example, take these lines from Macbeth:

> Will all great Neptune's ocean wash this blood
> Clean from my hands? No—this my hand will rather
> The multitudinous seas incarnadine,
> Making the green one red.
>
> —ACT II, Sc. ii.

Thomas Sheridan has pointed out that if, in reading these lines, we phrase the words *green one,* the passage makes no sense; but that if, divining the author's intention that the attribute *green* stand for the substantive *ocean,* we pause in our reading after *green* and then phrase the two words *one red,* we get a meaning that is truly Shakespearean.[18] But the reader must himself comprehend the sublimity of Shakespeare's idea in order to communicate that sublimity to his listeners. Again it is evident that *ex*pression cannot exceed *im*pression.

On every hand the college student is confronted with books that exhort him to learn "How To Read Better And Faster." He is taught how to skim, how to read a page at a time, and how to read a book in a day.[19] Should there not also be some place along the way where the student is taught how to ponder over what he reads, how to separate the wheat from the chaff? When the student spends a week on one selection, living with it, digging deep into the emotion as well as into the intellectual content of the passage, he gets something that fast reading can not possibly give him. Such passages become a very part of him. If great poetry and prose cost the writer much in time and effort, how can we expect the reader to absorb all they have to give him without a commensurate amount of time and effort? Ellen Glasgow reminds us: "Although a sort of fiction may be written without a formula or a method, I doubt if the true novel has ever been

---

[18] This illustration is taken from Thomas Sheridan's *Lectures on Elocution* (London, 1787).

[19] See Edna Euphemia Gilbert, "An Experimental Study of the Effects of Training in Oral Reading on Silent Reading Skills," Ph.D. Thesis, University of Wisconsin, 1950, abstracted in *Speech Monographs,* XVIII, 207. See also William B. McCoard and Samuel N. LeCount, "Oral Reading Evaluation of Good and Poor Silent Readers," *Speech Monographs,* XVIII, 288.

created without the long brooding season." Poets who write a poem a day may not be difficult to comprehend, but most of the poetry college students are called upon to read is not so ephemeral.

Does the emphasis we have laid upon "thinking the thought" in reading aloud imply that there is no necessity, as well, for a technique of voice and body? Of course not! Many hours must be spent in improving voice, posture, articulation, vocabulary, and facility for grouping words. A few years ago Sherwood Anderson lectured on our campus. As he talked to the audience he teetered back and forth on his toes and heels; he played with his glasses; he seemed embarrassed. He must have felt that he was not doing a very good job of lecturing, for he told his audience that for years he had been training the creative impulse to go down his finger tips to the keys of the typewriter, and that now he found it a different thing to send the impulses down to his voice and have his voice obey. Just as the fingers had to be trained to hit the right keys, so must the voice be trained to register the right modulation, the right quality, the right inflection.

C. *Reading as if Speaking*

One of the commonest criticisms of radio speaking is this: "He sounds as if he were reading his address." Similarly, one frequently hears the following comment on the radio reader or actor: "It certainly is obvious that he is reading his lines from a manuscript or book." For us, who know that practically all material presented on the radio *is* read from paper or book, such criticisms take on additional significance. For they use the term "reading" in a disparaging sense. The truth is that the effective speaker on the air is really the effective *reader;* his secret lies in *reading* as if he were *speaking*. When I asked Lowell Thomas for a word of advice to offer to those eager to emulate his success, he said just that: "Tell them to read as if they were speaking." The good actor reads his lines from the printed page or from memory as if he were speaking them for the first time. Nor is this practice peculiar to broadcasting; indeed, it should hold true whether the speaker is visible or invisible to his audience, whether he is using a manuscript or is free from it. Recall any speech by one of the past masters of the art: the late Franklin Delano Roosevelt, Winston Churchill, Thomas Dewey. There was a manuscript and the eyes were on it most of the time, but the manner was that of conversation. In the same way an effective reader, presenting a poem or play from a book, raises his eyes often and holds the attention of the audience as closely as if he were making a speech to them. The technique is slightly different, *but the effect is the same.* Joseph Jefferson, the famous comedian, who played *Rip van Winkle* approximately five thousand times, made the lines of his rôle sound, each time, as if he had never spoken them before. He was *reading or speaking from memory,* from the pages of his mind; but, as do all good actors and readers, he sounded completely spontaneous. He spoke with abandon.

D. *Reading to an Audience*

If you have studied public speaking, you surely have heard a great deal about communication, directness, conversational mode, and audience contact. But not even in public speaking is the application of these principles more essential than in *reading* to an audience; reading, for example, selections such as those we have suggested at the end of this chapter. In the past there has been entirely too much reading to himself by the individual engaged, supposedly, in reading to others. Certainly, we have all had the painful experience of attempting to listen to a reader who buries his face in his book and to whom the presence of listeners means, apparently, nothing. Could anything be duller? In *your* reading, be direct. Communicate. Make contact. Feel that the audience is listening. Share the ideas with the audience, read *with* them. Look up from the book occasionally. Be so familiar with the selection that you can do this with impunity. Make use of those fine instruments of expression and communication, the eyes. Do you recall how Coleridge describes the effect of the hand and eyes on attention in "The Rime of the Ancient Mariner"?

> He holds him with his skinny hand,
> "There was a ship," quoth he.
> "Hold off! unhand me, grey-beard loon!"
> Eftsoons his hand dropt he.

He holds him with his glittering eye—
The Wedding-Guest stood still,
And listens like a three years' child:
The Mariner hath his will.

To be sure, such reading demands preparation, a price that lazy students will not pay. It is more difficult than speaking to an audience because, in the latter situation, no book or manuscript acts as a barrier between the speaker and his audience. The reader, on the other hand, desiring the advantages of the clearer exposition and more graceful expression possible to one reading from a manuscript, must pay the price of extra effort to make the physical presence of the manuscript fade from the consciousness of his audience.

E. *Art Conceals Art* [20]

Much of the charm of the stage production of *Our Town,* by Thornton Wilder, was in the easy way Frank Craven played the part of the narrator. It was as if he had walked in off the street and told us the story. It all looks so easy. Jack Benny's radio shows seem perfectly fresh, as if they were being done for the first time, and yet we know that they have been in rehearsal for hours on end. We, as readers, must give that same impression of freshness. After we have mastered the technique, after we have set the pattern, then we can act with abandon within that form. If we can catch the inspiration of the moment and live the part we are reading, as if for the first time, then we shall surely put the reading over. There must be no straining after effect. Restraint is the key to good speaking as well as to good writing; and indeed, to all the arts. The painter does not leave his paint brush sticking out of the canvas; neither should the reader show us his technique. You may have had to look up the pronunciation of a word, but that fact should be apparent to no one. The amateur always has you sitting on the edge of your seat, worrying whether

[20] For collateral reading on this section see Sara Lowrey and Gertrude E. Johnson, *Interpretative Reading* (New York: Appleton-Century-Crofts, 1942), chap. v, "Illusion in Interpretative Reading," p. 168.

or not he will get through; the professional lets you sit back in your seat and relax, for you know he will. Spontaneity built on technique—that is what we are after. Remember the lines of Robert Browning:

> . . . he sings each song twice over,
> Lest you should think he never could recapture
> That first fine careless rapture!

III. Function

A. Individually

1. Forming Your Taste

One thing your college education should do for you is to help you form a standard of taste in all fields of endeavor. In this course we are interested in literature. We remember that Goethe, who wrote *Faust*, quit college because he did not find teachers who had standards of judgment. The ability to judge wisely is a worthwhile accomplishment. Pope, you will recall, in his *Essay on Criticism*, declared that he valued the ability to judge even above the ability to write:

> 'T is hard to say, if greater want of skill
> Appear in writing or in judging ill;
> But, of the two, less dangerous is the offense
> To tire our patience, than mislead our sense.

This course will help you to appreciate what others have thought good in the past. Your judgment has to pass before the bar of the classics. If you do not like the classic, it is you who are wrong, and not the classic. You must, through careful study, discover why the work before you *is* a classic. Why have men and women through the years cherished this work of art? Faith enters into forming a literary taste. You must have faith that others have found something valuable in the selection that does not appeal to you, and faith that, if you study the selection carefully, you too will find why it has become a classic.[21] Your literary taste will

---

[21] See Arnold Bennett, *Literary Taste* (London: Hodder and Stoughton, n.d.), p. 33.

dictate what books you enjoy in the years to come, what magazines you subscribe for, and what prose and poetry you read. Your taste will gather about you friends in the flesh and friends of yesteryear.

2. Improving Your Speech

Your ability to think will be improved, because speech and thinking are so closely related. You will learn how to organize ideas carefully, because in preparing a selection to read you will analyze the organization of a master of discourse. You will add many new words to your vocabulary, for in reading aloud you will have to understand all the words you read and know how they are pronounced. Ordinarily, one's silent reading vocabulary is far larger than one's speaking vocabulary. By reading from the printed page you will make many words, heretofore known only by sight, part of your active speaking vocabulary. You will gain in fluency, for you will pick up words and phrases of writers of merit who have learned how to express their thoughts. By close association with grammatical English, your own English will tend to became more acceptable grammatically. You will be required to use distinct articulation without affectation. You will be asked to read with enough vigor to be heard easily, and yet not so loud as to be unpleasant. You will be encouraged to read deliberately, at a pace neither too fast nor too slow. Your voice quality will improve as you read and reread passages to secure the proper nuances.

3. Developing Your Leadership

Oral reading, like public speaking, necessitates standing out from the crowd. Poise and self-composure are requisite that a student may stand for any length of time before a group without getting fussed and reading hastily, with the thought only of rushing through the assignment and getting it over with. To be able to read and know that others are listening to every shading, every pause, every emphasis of one's voice gives one a sense of self-confidence. To be able to read passages of great emotional power and not give way one's self to the emotion demands self-mastery. Every college student should aim at being a person of consequence in his community. The ability to read effectively from the printed page will be a long step in that direction.

B. *Socially*

1. Enlarging Your Sympathies

One cannot ponder over Elizabeth Barrett Browning's sonnets without enriching one's conception of what true love is. Authors who have penetrated the depths of emotional experience help one enlarge one's own sympathies. Poets who lack this insight are defective. Stephen Spender, in speaking of the need of emotional power by the poet, says: "On the whole English poets before the war suffered from lack of contact with the hardest conditions of life, and they tended to live in a kind of intellectual vacuum." True poetry combines sense and emotion—it is not one or the other alone. You may find the poet expressing thoughts you have had; and he may do you a great service by putting into words emotions you could not capture and express. The poet who can verbalize experience enriches you immeasurably.

And, of course, the sympathies you have developed thus far will find expression in the selections you read. You may know something of love; you may know something of death. The reading of literature of power will be shallow until one matches the poet's sensitiveness with a reader's insight. Hiram Corson has expressed himself on the need for an inner capital of emotional power in the reader: "Some of the best readers I have ever known have been of the former class, who honestly voiced what they had sympathetically assimilated, and did not strain after effect. But it seems that when one sets out to read, with no interior capital, he or she, especially she, is apt to run into all kinds of extravagances which disgust people of culture and taste. The voice instead of being the organ of the soul is a betrayer of soullessness." [22] We gain experience both by direct contact with life and by indirect contact, through reading. Truly, "Reading maketh a full man."

---

[22] Hiram Corson, *The Voice and Spiritual Education* (New York: Macmillan, 1896).

2. Nourishing the Class Discussion

H. M. Kallen,[23] in the concluding paragraph of his review of *Philosophy in American Education: Its Tasks and Opportunities,* states: "And if this is the case with education, how can it not be with philosophy? I do not think that I am merely pleading for my own house when I say that of all discourse, philosophy is the most natural and most generous which youth falls into in its congregations by day and its bull-sessions by night. Could but the classroom find a way to nourish and refine what there grows! But to the everyday heart of everyday youth the classroom shuts out and cuts off." The class in oral reading *does* find a way to nourish and refine what grows in the student's discussion. The ideas of the authors are taken up and considered from all angles. What did the author mean? What is the best way to bring out the point in the selection? The give-and-take of a class in oral reading during the period of discussion is educational, for it helps each student to appreciate the contribution of his fellows. Oral reading is a course that obliges the student to react to ideas every time he appears on the platform. The student can not convey to his fellow students ideas he does not have. In a class in oral reading the student comes to realize his mental self. As he reads aloud from the selections, he finds himself discussing religion, politics, philosophy, theology, economics, education. The class in oral reading is what Professor Kallen has been looking for.

IV. Summary

Anyone can read! Are you sure? Is not effective reading from a manuscript one of those skills possessed by the very few? To be sure, anyone can hem and haw his way through a passage. But how many effective radio speakers can you count? Don't you usually turn off your radio when a speech is coming up, especially when it is to be made by an untrained speaker? How many teachers have you had who could read effectively? I was pleased, in reading J. Donald Adam's column in *The New York Times Book Review* for February 17, 1946, to run across this sentence: "There came to mind a teacher of high school days who by his communicated enjoyment of the poetry he read aloud quickened

[23] *The Saturday Review of Literature,* XXVIII, No. 48, p. 60.

my own appreciation." Would that there were more teachers who could do this! And it is interesting that William Lyon Phelps calls attention to one of his teachers who could read effectively from the printed page: "The art of reading aloud is so great an art that one may spend many years in developing and perfecting it; sympathetic and intelligent reading is often the most illuminating interpretation and criticism. . . . When I was a graduate student at Harvard more than forty years ago, I learned more of the meaning of Shakespeare by hearing Professor Child read dialogue, than I did by most of the explanatory and critical notes."[24]

This course offers you an unusual opportunity for growth. The richer our lives are, and the more vivid our responses when we come into the class, the greater is going to be our appreciation. The more we get from what we read, the more we have to appreciate what we read. May I beg you not to expect any miracles in this course. If a miracle happens, it will be because you work hard.

V. Projects for Chapter I

1. Present a 30-minute reading from one of the best selling novels of the day.

2. Present a reading of "Trifles" by Susan Glaspell.

3. Discuss this definition of interpretative reading: "Interpretative reading is the process of audible and visible suggestion by means of which a complex of intellectual, imaginative, and emotional meanings, under the dominance of the author's language and intention, is translated through the artistic behavior of the reader for the aesthetic enjoyment of an audience." Margaret Mary McCarthy, "Interpretative Reading Behavior: A Study of Selected Factors," Ph.D. Thesis, University of Wisconsin, 1950, *Speech Monographs,* XVIII, 208.

4. Discuss, "The poetical, like the rhetorical, utterance persuades those who come in contact with it, and thus affects social action." Wilbur Samuel Howell, "Literature as an Enterprise in Communication," *Quarterly Journal of Speech,* XXXIII, 417.

5. Read Chapter I, "The Reader as Artist," from Holbrook Jackson's *The Reading of Books* (New York: Scribner's, 1947). Bring book to class and discuss. Be prepared to read excerpts aloud.

6. Prepare a reading of "The Twelve Pound Look" by Sir James M. Barrie.

---

[24] Foreword to *Poet's Gold* by David Ross (New York: The Macaulay Company, 1933).

CHAPTER II

Some Aesthetic Considerations

I. PHILOSOPHIES OF COMPOSITION
   A. Realism
   B. Imagination
   C. Expression
   D. Impressionism
   E. Communication
   F. Integration

II. FACTORS OF LITERARY COMPOSITION
   A. Intrinsic
      1. Unity
      2. Harmony
      3. Variety
      4. Contrast and Comparison
      5. Balance and Proportion
      6. Rhythm
      7. Meter
   B. Extrinsic
      1. Universality
      2. Individuality
      3. Suggestiveness
      4. Aesthetic Distance

III. SUMMARY

IV. PROJECTS FOR CHAPTER II

I. PHILOSOPHIES OF COMPOSITION [1]

A. *Realism*

Should the artist stick close to the facts and language of everyday living? Should a work of art be an imitation, or a copy, or a reproduction of what the author sees about him? Should the artist represent the dialogue of everyday life with no selectivity? Thomas Wolfe tells us he used to listen to and record actual conversations to discover how people really talked. Should the artist represent the interesting and significant, the essential, or the ideal aspects of life and nature? Should the artist have a peep hole on life and report everything he sees? Are *Main Street* and *Babbitt* by Sinclair Lewis examples of this theory of art? Are some of Carl Sandburg's poems, like "Halstead Street Car," slices of life?

[1] The student is referred to any book on aesthetics for a detailed treatment of these theories. A helpful book is Hunter Mead, *An Introduction to Aesthetics* (New York: Ronald, 1952).

B. Imagination

Does the author create without imitating or representing? Does he create a work of art that has little or nothing of himself in it? Is it what we might call a work of pure imagination? The work might have its inception in life, but the artist creates a character or a plot that never existed in life itself. The author is not interested in communicating any message to anyone, yet the work is read, recited, and remembered with enjoyment through the generations. Think, for example, of Daniel DeFoe's *Life and Strange Adventures of Robinson Crusoe,* Dante's *Inferno,* Milton's *Paradise Lost,* Coleridge's "The Rime of the Ancient Mariner," Hemingway's *The Old Man and the Sea.* From your knowledge of literature can you list other examples that fit into this category?

C. *Expression*

Does the artist write primarily to express himself? Is the poet or novelist concerned with putting himself on paper? Is the pleasure and enthusiasm within the author's own mind his reward and his inspiration? Is the lyric poem an outpouring of the soul? This theory of art reached its highest expression in the nineteenth century and became known as the Romantic Movement. It is interesting to go through the poems of that period and note the personal pronouns. The artist reacts to the stimulus of the outside world in such poems as "I Wandered Lonely as a Cloud" and expresses his personal enjoyment. Genêt in his "Letter from Paris" (*The New Yorker,* August 21, 1954, p. 70) in commenting upon the passing of Colette describes her peculiar contribution to French letters. (Note particularly the reference to the civilized omission of self-expression in current French literature.)

> In her writings, she even transferred to French readers her love for nature and for animals, domestic or roaming the hills. Tastes such as these had been absent—in an almost too civilized omission—from French literature until she brought her Burgundian girlhood to Paris and put her rural sensibilities on paper. She had a sensual harvest fullness in her writing and in her person, and a profound feeling for love springing up or being mowed down. She was indifferent to moral calculations, and composed her novels and stories with her informed instincts rather than by building any formal plot, and thus left behind her

pages that are uniquely feminine and the work of a master, in which the perceptions of her five senses were made permanent through her genius for the exactitudes of the French language.

D. *Impressionism*

It is difficult to express this theory of art in one word. Should an author render and not report, making no comment, not injecting himself into the scene? Should he let the reader form his own picture, his own story, his own conclusions? Is this a doctrine of impersonality or anonymity? Is the style implicit in the subject? Is this a rebellion against the idea that "style is the man"? Is this a philosophy rebelling against the nineteenth century artist pouring out his soul? Is this the sort of thing Archibald MacLeish has in mind when he says:

Ars Poetica [2]

ARCHIBALD MACLEISH

A poem should be palpable and mute
As a globed fruit

Dumb
As old medallions to the thumb

Silent as the sleeve-worn stone
Of casement ledges where the moss has grown—

A poem should be wordless
As the flight of birds

A poem should be motionless in time
As the moon climbs

Leaving as the moon releases
Twig by twig the night-entangled trees,

Leaving, as the moon behind the winter leaves,
Memory by memory the mind—

A poem should be motionless in time
As the moon climbs . . .

---

[2] By permission of and arrangement with Houghton Mifflin Company, the authorized publishers.

A poem should be equal to:
Not true

For all the history of grief
An empty doorway and a maple leaf

For love
The leaning grasses and two lights above the sea—

A poem should not mean
But be.

E. *Communication*

Does the author want an audience? Is the author always conscious that he is trying to say something to his fellow men both now and in the future? Is art the communication of emotion? Does William Faulkner have the desire to communicate? What does he mean by these words in the Nobel Prize speech?

I decline to accept the end of man. It is easy enough to say that man is immortal simply because he will endure; that when the last ding-dong of doom has clanged and faded from the last worthless rock hanging tideless in the last red and dying evening, that even then there will still be one more sound: that of his puny inexhaustible voice, still talking. I refuse to accept this. I believe that man will not merely endure: he will prevail. He is immortal, not because he alone among creatures has an inexhaustible voice, but because he has a soul, a spirit capable of compassion and sacrifice and endurance. The poet's, the writer's duty is to write about these things. It is his privilege to help man endure by lifting his heart, by reminding him of the courage and honor and hope and pride and compassion and pity and sacrifice which have been the glory of his past. The poet's voice need not merely be the record of man, it can be one of the props, the pillars to help him endure and prevail.

Should literature attempt to propagandize, teach, moralize? Should literature criticize the social scene, evaluate it, influence it? The student can think of literary productions that do these things. Think of *Uncle Tom's Cabin, Death of a Salesman, Darkness at Noon, The Crucible, Grapes of Wrath.* Do you agree with I. A. Richards when he states, "Those artists and poets who can be suspected of close separate attention to the communicative aspect tend (there are exceptions to this, of which Shakespeare might be one) to fall into a subordinate rank"? [3]

F. *Integration*

As the student has thought of these five theories of artistic productions, it probably has occurred to him that no one of the theories is entirely satisfactory. When one is trying to set forth one theory, he seems to be on the borderland of one of the other theories. The artistic process seems too complicated to be explained by any one theory, therefore should not the student of oral reading be an eclectic and use what he can of these various theories or philosophies of art to help him understand the selection he is reading? In his analysis he may well ask himself such questions as these: Does not the author attempt to represent life so that it will be recognizable? Does he not try to select, idealize, invent characters and situations, symbols and figures of speech that will make his work of art stand out as an individual creation, but at the same time universalize his creation so that all men will find something in it? Does the author not try to say his piece in such a way that it will convey more than it actually does so that the reader will translate it into his own experience, but at the same time not make it so intimate that the reader is led to think that it is an actual occurrence, thus giving his production aesthetic distance? And no matter how much the artist may protest to the contrary, does he not secretly hope that someone someplace, sometime will understand him, that he will communicate?

II. Factors of Literary Composition

A. *Intrinsic* [4]

1. Unity

Edgar Allan Poe in his "The Philosophy of Composition," which every student of oral reading should know, declares "I prefer commencing with the consideration of an *effect*." Here is a controlling

[3] I. A. Richards, *Principles of Literary Criticism* (New York: Harcourt, Brace, 1928), p. 27.

[4] I am indebted to *Literature as a Fine Art* by C. C. Cunningham (New York: Ronald Press, 1941) for the terminology of this section.

purpose that gives unity to the composition. The choosing of such symbols as the raven, the marble bust, and the chamber all contribute to the unified effect.

The classical unities of time, place, and action can be found to lesser or greater extent in most compositions. (If the student has not read Aristotle's *Poetics,* he should.) For example, read Ring Lardner's *Hair Cut* and see how unity is achieved, or read J. M. Barrie's *The Will.*

The mind likes order, and superior compositions have the impact of superior unity. Consider the unity of the controlling idea, the unity of the sub-ideas, the unity of the organization, the unity of the style, such as the choice of words, phrases, sentences. Consider the unity of the figures of speech. If a simile is used, is it integrated with the composition? Does the opening sentence in such a sonnet as Elizabeth Barrett Browning's "How Do I Love Thee?" prepare the way for unity of composition?

In analysis the reader will look for key words, key phrases, key sentences, key figures of speech, key moods, key attitudes so that he can emphasize these in presenting the unified effect desired by the author.

2. Harmony

A factor that is important in achieving unity of effect is a sense of congeniality of details. In a work, whether it be a painting, a piece of sculpture, or a written composition, the student will find a fitness of the means. A sculptor may create a human figure that combines all the perfections of the human form: he may have to use several models. It is said that Millet inserted the church in the background of his picture called "The Angelus" after he had painted the two figures leaning on their hoes because it seemed to harmonize with the total idea. A study of Carl Sandburg's "Chicago" will reveal a consistency of imagery, word choice, repetition, assonance with the over-all theme of strength. Max Perkins, the editor, spent hours with Thomas Wolfe and his manuscripts, in selecting, sifting, cutting, trying to achieve a harmonious effect.

Lincoln is said to have been more pleased by Edward Everett's comment that the *Gettysburg Address* came nearer to the heart of the occasion in three minutes than his own address did in three hours than by any other compliment he received on the address. A reader, who is reading his own address, may seek to achieve a harmony of audience, occasion, and idea. For example, a reader who employs humor out of harmony with the occasion jars on the sensibilities of his audience.

The student in analyzing a selection should try to discover what tools the writer employs in securing his over-all satisfying result.

3. Variety

The importance of variety in delivering a selection has been treated elsewhere in the book. Here we want to call attention to variety within the selection itself. Think of the various ways in which a poet may secure variety. He may use among other things different meters, rhythms, rhyme schemes, line lengths. For example, Edgar Allan Poe in "The Raven" composed his first line with eight feet, the second with seven and a half, the third with eight, the fourth with seven and a half, the fifth with the same, the sixth with three and a half. In *The Ring and the Book* Robert Browning holds attention by having various people tell the same story. The playwright may use different scenes to bring out character. The essayist may use opinions, examples, facts, and reasons to develop his theme. In an argument, the writer may relieve the audience by changing from statistics to illustrations. In music, the composer may get variety by using solo voices and choruses. Similarly in choral reading the chorus may introduce variety by solo and group work.

In preparing a selection for oral presentation, the student should keep a critical eye on the devices used to introduce variety. For example, how does Robert Frost introduce variety in "The Death of the Hired Man," or what variety of imagery is employed by Stephen Spender in "The Express" to give the illusion of motion?

4. Contrast and Comparison

Within a composition an artist will employ opposites in order to make his theme strike home. Robert in *Beyond the Horizon* is pictured as a weakling more sharply because he is pitted against his stronger brother Andy. In *Picnic* by William Inge, the two sisters, Millie and Madge, are opposites and promote the theme of the play. Robert Browning in the last few lines of "My Last Duchess" has the Duke speak with more affection of a piece of bronze than he does of his wife. The reader will not fail to note and bring out this contrast. Georgia Harkness in her book *Toward Understanding the Bible* points out the contrast in the Books of Revelation.

> There is vivid dramatic contrast, in the visions that follow, between the terrors that stalk the earth—strife, famine, invasion, death, fire, flood, hail, earthquake, drought, pestilence, war—and the mighty chorus of adoration and worship of Christ, the Lamb who was slain for our redemption. The contrast appears also with great poignancy in the description of the utter destruction that will fall upon Rome, which the author identifies with Babylon, "the beast," a "great harlot" drunk with the blood of the saints, and the blessedness of the new heaven and the new earth which God has in store for his faithful ones. The main motif of the book is summed up for the individual in "Be thou faithful unto death, and I will give thee the crown of life;" and for all society in
>
> The kingdom of the world has become the kingdom of our Lord and of his Christ, and he shall reign for ever and ever.[5]

In the parable of "The Good Samaritan," the Samaritan who bound up the stranger's wounds is contrasted with the priests who went by on the other side. In the parable of "The Prodigal Son," the "fatted calf" is contrasted with "a kid." The interpreter who fails to bring out this contrast misses the poignancy of the elder brother's complaint: "And he answering said to his father, Lo, these many years do I serve thee, neither transgressed I at any time thy commandment: *and yet thou never gavest me a kid,* that I might make merry with my friends. But as soon as this thy son was come, which hath devoured thy living with harlots, *thou hast killed for him the fatted calf.*" Read this sentence and bring out by means of your voice the distinction the elder son is making.

In the following passage from St. Matthew 7:24–27, note how the meaning is brought out by means of contrast and comparison:

> Therefore whosoever heareth these sayings of mine, and doeth them, I will liken him unto a wise man, which built his house upon a rock:

[5] Georgia Harkness, *Toward Understanding the Bible* (New York: Scribner's, 1954), p. 103.

And the rain descended, and the floods came, and the winds blew, and beat upon that house; and it fell not: for it was founded upon rock.

And everyone that heareth these sayings of mine, and doeth them not, shall be likened unto a foolish man, which built his house upon the sand:

And the rain descended, and the floods came, and the winds blew, and beat upon that house; and it fell: and great was the fall of it.

By discovering all the contrasts and comparisons in a passage, you prepare the way for your voice to bring these out by subtle modulations, pauses, and emphases.

A method of heightening comparison and contrast is the use of figures of speech. Language is greatly enriched by means of simile, metaphor, metonymy, and synecdoche. The power of the simile and the metaphor lies in the relation of things wholly unlike each other save in one thing, a comparison between two objects that are alike only in the point of comparison. This is the force of both metaphor and simile; the two figures differ from one another, however, in form and color. If we say, "The Lord is *like* a shepherd," we are using a simile; but when the psalmist sings, "The Lord *is* my shepherd," he is using a metaphor to express the same conception of the Lord, that of a shepherd caring tenderly for his flock. The metaphor is more vigorous and more spontaneous than the simile; it is less self-conscious. The simile is less striking, less emotional, and more intellectual than the metaphor. The simile sees resemblance; the metaphor ignores differences and identifies one object with another.

Metonymy and synecdoche are related to metaphor and simile, all being forms of comparison. Metonymy (literally, "name-change") is the substitution of one thing to represent another. It is the use of one word for another it suggests, as the effect for the cause, the cause for the effect, the sign for the thing signified, the container for the thing contained. Shakespeare uses metonymy in making *light* stand for *life* in the following lines from *Othello:*

Put out the light, and then put out the light:
If I quench thee, thou flaming minister,
I can again thy former light restore,
Should I repent me; but once put out thy light,
Thou cunning'st pattern of excelling nature,

I know not where is that Promethean heat
That can thy light relume.
—Act V, Sc. 1.

Synecdoche (literally, "receiving together") is the figure of speech in which a part represents the whole. When, in "Recessional," Kipling speaks of Britain holding dominion over "palm and pine" he suggests the vast extent of the British Empire—pine being a northern tree, and palm a flora of the tropics. The reader must be aware of the significance of figures of speech. In this poem, certainly, the substitution of the vivid and the particular *palm* and *pine* for the prosaic and the general *south* and *north* contributes much to the total effect.

5. Balance and Proportion

The literary artist, whose works we are to interpret, like other artistic workers, uses these two principles. He omits or modifies anything which will throw his composition out of balance. In prose the author is careful to bring out his main intention by the amount of materials and space he spends in elaborating a point. If the author goes off on excursions into irrelevancies, we hold him to account for a lack of proportion. In a book on presidents of the United States, we would expect the author to spend more time on Lincoln than on Polk. Balance and proportion show grasp.

Within the composition balance and proportion help give a sense of rhythm to the entire composition. Scene is balanced against scene as in *Beyond the Horizon.* Character is balanced against character as in "The Prodigal Son." Idea is balanced against idea as in the parable of the house built on the rock and the house built on the sand. Unit is balanced against unit as in Romans 12. Sentence is balanced against sentence as in Robert Frost's:

And nothing to look backward to with pride,
And nothing to look forward to with hope.

Here is another tool for the analyst to use in readying a selection for oral presentation. What use did the author make of balance and proportion?

6. Rhythm

A part of our response to poetry is our enjoyment of its *rhythm,* the swing of it, that which helps to bring out its melody and music. All good speech is rhythmical, good prose has rhythm, but it is in poetry that we find it in most marked and largest measure. Rhythm in poetry at once implies meter and metrical arrangement. *Meter* is the mechanics of rhythm, part of the composition process, the technical disposition of short and long, of light and heavy syllables.[6] Rhythm, on the other hand, is the response this technique arouses in the reader himself. Rhythm is determined by meter, but the meter should not dominate the rhythm to such an extent as to submerge the meaning. If I read these two lines from Tennyson's "Guinevere" in this way:

But *when* the *queen* im*mersed* in *such* a *trance*
And *moving* *thru* the *past* un*con*scious*ly*

it is obvious that I am not thinking the meaning. I am merely performing an exercise in scansion. Yet there *is* strong rhythm in those lines, and that rhythm is determined by the meter; but by meter whose artificial regularity of beat is modified by the natural inflections of speech:

But when the *queen* im*mer*sed in *such* a *trance*
And *moving* thru the *past* un*con*sciously

It is the rhythm of poetry that is so often essential to the expression of the mood. Note the long sweeping sounds Shelley chose for his "Dirge":

Rough wind, that moanest loud
Grief too sad for song;
Wild wind, when sullen cloud
Knells all the night long;
Sad storms, whose tears are vain,
Bare woods, whose branches strain,
Deep caves and dreary main,—
Wail, for the world's wrong!

In contrast, note the abrupt staccato rhythm of "After Blenheim":

---

[6] Read "Poetry and Drama" by T. S. Eliot in *The Atlantic,* CLXXXVII, No. 2 (February, 1951).

It was a summer evening;
  Old Kaspar's work was done,
And he before his cottage-door
  Was sitting in the sun;
And by him sported on the green
  His little grandchild, Wilhelmine.

She saw her brother Peterkin
  Roll something large and round,
That he beside a rivulet,
  In playing there, had found,
She ran to ask what he had found,
  That was so large and smooth and round.

Old Kaspar took it from the boy,
  Who stood expectant by;
And then the old man shook his head,
  And with a natural sigh,
"Tis some poor fellow's skull," said he,
  "Who fell in the great victory."

—SOUTHEY.

Often this rhythm is quite marked even in blank verse, as in the famous lines:

All the world's a stage,
And all the men and women merely players:
They have their exits and their entrances:
And one man in his time plays many parts,
His acts being seven ages.

—WILLIAM SHAKESPEARE.

Tennyson was supreme at conveying mood through rhythm and meter:

Break, break, break,
  At the foot of thy crags, O Sea!
But the tender grace of a day that is dead
  Will never come back to me.

Longfellow, too, understood this principle very well indeed. Note the difference in rhythm, even though the metrical arrangements are much the same, between the expression of the *joy* of the wooing in "Hiawatha" and the intimation of the *sadness* and *terror* of winter in "The Famine." After Hiawatha has won Minnehaha, the poet says:

Pleasant was the journey homeward;
All the birds sang loud and sweetly
Songs of happiness and heart's-ease.
From the sky the sun benignant
Looked upon them thru the branches.

Now note the contrast in "The Famine":

O the long and cruel Winter!
O the cold and cruel Winter
Ever thicker, thicker, thicker
Froze the ice on lake and river,
Ever deeper, deeper, deeper
Fell the snow o'er all the landscape.

Our modern poets are, as a rule, less interested in the regular meters than were the so-called classical poets. Yet the rhythm of modern poetry is often quite marked, even when the style seems almost conversational. Robert Frost's poetry illustrates this fact very well. You remember these lines from "The Pasture."

I'm going out to clean the pasture spring;
I'll only stop to rake the leaves away
(And wait to watch the water clear, I may);
I shan't be gone long.—You come too.[7]

Among modern American poets, the late, lamented Vachel Lindsay is famous for the superb rhythm and ballad-like sweep of his poetry. You will recall the opening lines from "The Congo."

Fat black bucks in a wine-barrel room,
Barrel-house kings, with feet unstable,
Sagged and reeled and pounded on the table,
Pounded on the table,
Beat an empty barrel with the handle of a broom,
Hard as they were able,
Boom, boom, BOOM,
With a silk umbrella and the handle of a broom
Boomlay, boomlay, boomlay, BOOM.[8]

---

[7] From *The Collected Poems of Robert Frost* (New York: Henry Holt and Company). By permission of the publishers.

[8] From Vachel Lindsay, *Collected Poems*. By permission of The Macmillan Company, publishers.

Perhaps a note should be added under the topic,[9] "Rhythm of Poetry," on the troublesome problem of the carry-over line. First, some examples:

All that I know
Of a certain star
Is. . . .

—ROBERT BROWNING.

With blackest moss, the flower-plots
Were thickly crusted, one and all.

—ALFRED LORD TENNYSON.

On either side the river lie
Long fields of barley and of rye.

—ALFRED LORD TENNYSON.

There she weaves by night and day
A magic web with colors gay.

—ALFRED LORD TENNYSON.

Now, it is obvious that we do not want a rat-ta-tat pause at the end of each line. But it is also obvious that these lines are poetry, not prose. It is not, "On-either-side-the-river-lie-long-fields-of barley-and-of-rye," or "All-that-I-know-of-a-certain-star-is-." The poet has gone to the trouble of breaking up his material into lines of verse, poetic units, often rhymed. We can see this on the page; but how is the oral reader to indicate the line arrangement? Often—not always, but often—he can do so by a sound pause, a welling-up of the rhythm that carries the last syllable of one line over into the beginning syllable of the next. At any rate, try it!

Rhythm in literature,[10] as in music, depends on the recurrence of stress and accent. English is a language of pronounced and varied word accent. It takes only a moment's thought to confirm that statement for one's self. Words of more than one syllable have at least one accent. Words of two syllables, like *laughter, silver, blessed,* accent the first syllable; words like *between, suppose, receive* accent the second syllable; and words like *wayward, rose-lipped, childhood* accent both syllables. In words of three syllables, like *popular, musician, promenade,* the accent is on a

---

[9] See Robert Hillyer's "On Reading Verse Aloud," p. 280.

[10] In connection with this section read Bliss Perry, *A Study of Poetry* (Boston: Houghton Mifflin, 1920), chap. v, "Rhythm and Meter."

different syllable in each case. A word like *glorify* has a primary accent on the first and a secondary accent on the third syllable. *Consolidate* has four syllables, with the primary accent on the second and the secondary accent on the fourth syllable. It can readily be seen that English is hospitable to an infinite number of accentual combinations.

When we combine words into sentences we retain the individual word accents, but superimpose upon them a sentence or phrase accent. In the sentences, "Where is Mary? Mary is in school today," the accents are placed in accordance with the meaning the reader supposes the words to convey. So, in the sentence, "Mary walked home from the village today," we could vary the accent and, in so doing, vary the shade of meaning. If we accent *walked,* we mean that Mary did not ride, or go in some other way. If we accent *Mary,* we point out the fact that we do not mean some other girl. This word or phrase accent organizes the sentence into patterns that bring out the meaning. These patterns, or phrasings, are groupings of words into sense units. Such phrases are set off by pauses, either before or after. On the printed page the pause is usually indicated by punctuation, but the oral reader will find that punctuation is not a complete guide to the use of the pause.

To a certain extent all speech is rhythmical and is grouped in phrases. Robert Green Ingersoll paid much attention, some critics feel too much attention, to the rhythm of his speech. Consider the following passage:

> The laugh of a child will make the holiest day more sacred still. Strike with hand of fire, O weird musician, thy harp strung with Apollo's golden hair; fill the vast cathedral aisles with symphonies sweet and dim, deft toucher of the organ keys; blow, bugle, blow, until thy silver notes do touch and kill the moonlit waves, and charm the lovers wandering 'mid the vine-clad hills. But know your sweetest strains are discords all, compared with childhood's happy laugh—the laugh that fills the eyes with light and every heart with joy. O rippling river of laughter, thou art the blessed boundary between beasts and men; and every wayward wave of thine doth drown some fretful fiend of care. O laughter, rose-lipped daughter of Joy, there are dimples enough in thy cheeks to catch and hold and glorify all the tears of grief.

We find the phrase as a rhythmical unit in poetry as well. Often it is synonymous with the line, as in this example from Edgar Allan Poe:

To Helen

EDGAR ALLAN POE

Helen, thy beauty is to me
  Like those Nicaean barks of yore,
That gently, o'er a perfumed sea,
  The weary, wayworn wanderer bore
  To his own native shore.

On desperate seas long wont to roam,
  Thy hyacinth hair, thy classic face,
Thy Naiad airs have brought me home
  To the glory that was Greece,
And the grandeur that was Rome.

Lo! in yon brilliant window-niche
  How statue-like I see thee stand,
  The agate lamp within thy hand!
Ah! Psyche, from the regions which
  Are holy land!

But more often the phrase is not synonymous with the line. It may end somewhere within it, as in the following lines from Pope's *Essay on Criticism:*

True ease in writing comes from art, || not chance,
As those move easiest || who have learned to dance.
'Tis not enough no harshness gives offense;
The sound || must seem an echo of the sense.

The pause marked by the double bar (||), which is called the caesural pause,[11] is occasioned when a phrase is not synonymous with the line; it is a rhythm break, usually a sense pause, about the middle of a verse.

Irregularity is characteristic of the rhythms of prose.[12] This is to be expected, because these rhythms originate in everyday

[11] See Appendix XII for the terms of versification.

[12] The student of rhythm will find two articles by Fred Newton Scott of interest. See "The Most Fundamental Differentia of Poetry and Prose" and "The Scansion of Prose Rhythm" in *The Standard of American Speech and Other Papers,* ed. Clarence DeWitt Thorpe (New York: Allyn and Bacon, 1926).

speech, which is infinitely varied. Robert Frost, in particular, tries to capture these accents of everyday speech in his poetry. Rhythms depend upon the unbroken succession of one phrase to the next, like water cascading over a falls. And yet students of rhythm have detected three rather distinct patterns:

1. *The phrases are similar, though not identical in length:*

With malice toward none
With charity for all

—LINCOLN.

Whatsoever things are true,
Whatsoever things are honest,
Whatsoever things are just,
Whatsoever things are pure,
Whatsoever things are lovely,
Whatsoever things are of good report;
If there be any virtue,
If there be any praise,
Think on these things.

—ST. PAUL, *Epistle to the Philippians.*

2. *They are often parallel in structure.* Similar thoughts are expressed in similar language:

From America, they will get ships.
From America, they will get planes.

—F. D. ROOSEVELT.

3. *The phrases make frequent use of cadence.* When we come to the end of a phrase we drop the voice. The word *cadence* comes from the Latin *cadere,* "to fall." Note the cadence in the following sentences from President Eisenhower's radio and television address of April 5, 1954:

It is very important that you and I value the spiritual things that they had in mind when they founded this country. For example, the things that announce the rights that every single individual has in this country; his equality before the law; his right to worship as he pleases, think as he pleases and talk as he pleases just so long as he does not trespass on the rights of others.

Cadenced verse, or free verse, is built on the rhythm of phrase. Its unit is the strophe, which is composed of a number of phrases subtly balanced so as to constitute a complete cadence, as in the following poem:

The Grass [13]

CARL SANDBURG

Pile the bodies high at Austerlitz and Waterloo.
Shovel them under and let me work—
I am the grass; I cover all.

And pile them high at Gettysburg
And pile them high at Ypres and Verdun.
Shovel them under and let me work.
Two years, ten years, and passengers ask the conductor:
What place is this?
Where are we now?
I am the grass,
Let me work.

You are no doubt familiar with the Psalms and have been struck by their beauty. The Psalms are often classed with free verse. They are made up of phrases spoken in parallel, one clause being balanced against another of similar structure.[14]

7. Meter

As the term suggests, we apply this term only where the rhythm can be definitely measured. You have noticed that in the preceding section we have discussed various effects of rhythm. Prose, split prose, as used in *Beach Red* [15] and *On a Note of Triumph,*[16] free verse, and bound verse all have rhythm; but only bound verse has meter. The regularity of the recurrence of accents makes for the fundamental difference between prose and bound verse. In metrical passages there is a norm; in unmetrical passages there is no norm.

In literature meter is predominantly duple or triple; that is, the

[13] From *The Cornhuskers,* by Carl Sandburg (New York: Henry Holt and Company, 1918). By permission of the publishers.

[14] See Mary Ellen Chase, *The Bible and the Common Reader* (New York: Macmillan, 1944).

[15] Peter Bowman, *Beach Red* (New York: Random House, 1945).

[16] Norman Corwin, *On a Note of Triumph* (New York: Simon and Schuster, 1945).

accent falls on every second or third beat. Duple meter is either iambic (re *peat*) or trochaic (*mass* ive), as the accent falls on either the second or the first syllable. The iamb is found very commonly in speech and for that reason it is the unit of meter most used in English poetry. In Robert Frost's "The Death of the Hired Man," note the iambic stress:

"Be kind," she said.
She took the market things from Warren's arms
And set them on the porch, then drew him down
To sit beside her on the wooden steps.[17]

And in Shelley's "Threnos," the iambic stress is used:

Threnos

PERCY BYSSHE SHELLEY

O World! O Life! O Time!
On Whose last steps I climb,
Trembling at that where I had stood before;
When will return the glory of your prime?
No more—Oh, never more!

Out of the day and night
A joy has taken flight:
Fresh spring, and summer, and winter hoar,
Move my faint heart with grief, but with delight
No more—Oh, never more!

The trochaic stress is a sprightly meter. And when the first syllable is heavily emphasized, the rhythm takes on the character of an incantation, as in the lines from the "Witches' Song" in *Macbeth:*

Double, double, toil and trouble;
Fire burn and cauldron bubble.

The tripping character is illustrated in Milton's lines from "L'Allegro":

Haste thee, nymph, and bring with thee
Jest, and youthful Jollity,
Quips, and Cranks, and wanton Wiles,

[17] From *The Collected Poems of Robert Frost* (New York: Henry Holt and Company). By permission of the publishers.

Nods, and Becks, and wreathèd Smiles,
Such as hang on Hebe's cheek,
And love to live in dimple sleek;
Sport that wrinkled Care derides,
And Laughter holding both his sides.
Come, and trip it as you go
On the light fantastic toe.

Triple meters are not so common in English literature as the duple meters. You are no doubt familiar with triple meters such as the dactyllic (*mer* ci ful) and the anapaestic, which is the reverse of the dactyllic with the accent falling on the third syllable. Triple meters give a long swing to the verse, which may be very graceful. It is common to find trochees and iambs mingled with the triple meters.[18]

Poems descriptive of riding employ triple meters. Consider the following example:

Boot and Saddle

ROBERT BROWNING

Boot, saddle, to horse, and away!
Rescue my castle before the hot day
Brightens to blue from its silvery gray,
  Boot, saddle, to horse, and away!

Ride past the suburbs, asleep as you'd say;
Many's the friend there, will listen and pray
"God's luck to gallants that strike up the lay—
  "Boot, saddle, to horse, and away!"

Forty miles off, like a roebuck at bay,
Flouts Castle Brancepeth the Roundheads' array:

[18] Van Wyck Brooks in his *New England, Indian Summer* (New York: Dutton, 1940), p. 326, has an interesting comment on Emily Dickinson's employment of rhythm and meter. "She liked the common hymn-metres, and the metres of nursery-jingles, which had been deeply ingrained in her mind as a child, and she seemed to take a rebellious joy in violating all their rules, fulfilling the traditional patterns while she also broke them. She was always experimenting with her rhymes and rhythms, sometimes adding extra syllables to break up their monotony, sometimes deliberately twisting a rhyme, as Emerson did, for the sake of harshness, to escape the mellifluous effect of conventional poems. Many of her pieces were like parodies of hymns, whose gentle glow in her mind had become heat-lightning. For Emily Dickinson's light was quick. It was sudden, sharp and evanescent; and this light was the dry light that is closest to the fire."

Who laughs, "Good fellows ere this, by my fay,
"Boot, saddle, to horse, and away!"

Who? My wife Gertrude; that, honest and gay,
Laughs when you talk of surrendering, "Nay!
I've better counsellors; what counsel they?
"Boot, saddle, to horse, and away!"

B. *Extrinsic*

1. Universality

Wherever people live together there is an experience that is a universal experience. Love and hate, joy and sorrow, goodness and evil, life and death, nature and art are a few of the subjects that are written about in literate societies. Faulkner can write about Oxford, Mississippi, and have a world audience. Billy Graham can preach in Berlin to 100,000 Germans in English and have his sermons translated and hold his audience. All of Shakespeare's plays have been translated into Japanese.

Undoubtedly there are many references in Shakespeare the Japanese do not understand, but surely they would understand the universality of Portia's speech on the quality of mercy, or the universality of Othello's jealousy, or the ambition of Macbeth. Particularly would the Japanese enjoy the descriptions of nature in King Lear, for Japanese poetry is concerned largely with nature. Different cultures tend to write about different things. Western civilization writes its poetry largely about love and death.

It is the universal in the artistic experience that draws us together. We like to sit with 5,000 others and enjoy the same artistic thrill. The 15,000 who gathered to hear Robert Frost read his poetry at the Boston Festival in the Boston Commons were together experiencing an aesthetic thrill. How delighted we are when we are reading a poet like Keats or a philosopher like Emerson and find a universal expressed. We feel that we are kin to them. On a lecture course poets reading their own poetry draw better houses than do lecturers speaking on other subjects because the poet deals more with universals. The poet expresses our ideas better than we can express them ourselves. The poet helps to bridge the gulf between the one and the many.

2. Individuality

Although we like to sense the universality of a theme, we want to realize it through an individual such as we ourselves are in our everyday life. We want to hear about other individuals. William Faulkner, a recent reviewer has pointed out, found his universals in the particular.

> In his earlier work, the two decades of books that won him fame in this country and Europe, Faulkner did all his writing in the context of his own very special world, the 2,400 square miles of Yoknapatawpha County. Like Anthony Trollope's Barsetshire, Yoknapatawpha has become immortal, because it is a mirror for so many others. Faulkner entered, as only the very best writers can, to the heart of his characters—even of the land and weather. They came alive in his exaggerated, rhetorical style. He made their pride, pity, love, anguish, glory, and endurance into universals.[19]

Robert Frost similarly has written about New England, and has uttered such universals about home as the following in "The Death of the Hired Man,"

> "Home is the place where, when you have to go there
> They have to take you in."
> "I should have called it
> Something you somehow haven't to deserve."

through individuals that we recognize as very much like ourselves. Truth is individualized. It is as Phillips Brooks would express it, "truth through personality."

In another sense themes are individualized. Truths are so spoken as to be identified with certain authors. Artists feed on each other's work and often say pretty much the same things, but there is that something which makes the product of each different. As James Russell Lowell put it:

> Though old the thought and oft expressed
> 'Tis his at last who says it best.

Take, for example, Lincoln's great phrase at the conclusion of *The Gettysburg Address* "and that government of the people, by the people, and for the people, shall not perish from the earth." The content of this definition of democracy was often expressed

[19] *Newsweek,* August 2, 1954, p. 49.

before Lincoln. Students have traced a similar phrasing back to Daniel Webster who said on January 26, 1830, "The people's government, made for the people, made by the people, and answerable to the people." John Marshall described our government as "Government over all, by all and for the sake of all." The abolitionist preacher Theodore Parker said on May 29, 1850, in a speech on the "American idea" before the New England Anti-Slavery Convention in Boston: "A democracy—that is a government of all the people, by all the people, for all the people." On September 29 of the same year Theodore Parker used the identical expression in a sermon. Lincoln was a reader of Theodore Parker's sermons. The phrase now belongs to Lincoln because he said it better.

As you analyze a selection preparatory to sharing it with others try to look for those signs of individuality that make it belong to this particular author and to him only. How does Hemingway differ from Faulkner? How does Robert Frost differ from Carl Sandburg? How does Edna St. Vincent Millay differ from Sara Teasdale? These are thought-provoking questions and lead the student to the individuality of the artist.

3. Suggestiveness

How often you and I have had our thoughts sent reeling by some bit of poetry, by a sermon, by a lecture. The parables in the Bible are filled with suggestiveness and remain a quarry for sermons after thousands of years. Henry Ward Beecher in preaching on the parable of The Prodigal Son takes the phrase "took his journey into a far country" as meaning a far country psychologically, not geographically. What vistas of thought this opens up! In his *Yale Lectures on Preaching* (first series), p. 223, this great preacher recognizes the value of unleashing the associations of the audience.

A respectable source of failure is conscientious thoroughness. It is true that it is the office of the preacher to furnish thought for his hearers, but it is no less his duty to excite thought. Thus we give thought to breed thought. If, then, a preacher elaborates his theme until it is utterly exhausted, leaving nothing to the imagination and intellect of his hearers, he fails to produce that lively activity in their minds which is one of the best effects of right preaching; they are merely recipients. But under a true preaching, the pulpit and the audience should be carrying on the subject together, one in outline, and the other with subtle and rapid activity, filling it up by imagination, suggestion, and emotion.

What Beecher has said of preaching is also true of other forms of literary composition. Robert Browning in the opening stanza of "Love Among the Ruins" awakens our imaginations:

Where the colored end of evening smiles,
    Miles and miles
On the solitary pastures where our sheep
    Half-asleep
Tinkle homeward thro' the twilight, stray or stop
    As they crop—
Was the site once of a city great and gay,
    (So they say)

Impressionism in writing carries the idea of suggestiveness to its greatest extent. Japanese painting using chiefly outlines instead of details often suggests a mountain scene, a waterfall, a snow scene. The beholder of such art is called upon to fill in the details for himself. John Steinbeck in the Prologue to *Sweet Thursday* comments on this technique in an interesting fashion:

"Well, I like a lot of talk in a book, and I don't like to have nobody tell me what the guy that's talking looks like. I want to figure out what he looks like from the way he talks. And another thing—I like to figure out what the guy's thinking by what he says. I like some description too," he went on. "I like to know what color a thing is, how it smells and maybe how it looks, and maybe how a guy feels about it—but not too much of that." [20]

An interesting example of rendering a scene is found in William Faulkner's *The Sound and the Fury*. Notice that the author is careful not to interpolate or inject a word into the dialogue. He leaves it entirely to the reader as John Steinbeck would like to have it:

"Hush, Benjy." Caddy said. "Go away, Charlie. He doesn't like you." Charlie went away and I hushed. I pulled at Caddy's dress.

"Why, Benjy." Caddy said. "Aren't you going to let me stay here and talk to Charlie awhile."

[20] John Steinbeck, *Sweet Thursday* (New York: Viking, 1954), p. vii.

"Call that nigger." Charlie said. Charlie came and put his hands on Caddy and I cried more. I cried loud.

"No, no." Caddy said. "No, no."

"He can't talk." Charlie said. "Caddy."

"Are you crazy." Caddy said. She began to breathe fast. "He can see. Dont dont." Caddy fought. They both breathed fast. "Please. Please." Caddy whispered.

"Send him away." Charlie said.

"Yes." Caddy said. "Let me go." Charlie went away. "Hush." Caddy said. "He's gone." I hushed. I could hear her and feel her chest going.[21]

4. Aesthetic Distance [22]

The oral reader in reading various types of materials comes face to face with the problem of the extent of participation on the part of his audience in what he is reading. If it is a story or speech or sermon, he no doubt will want to have the audience feel that they are sharing in the ideas. He will use all the means of contact at his command to enter into the thinking and feeling of his hearers.

But when the reader is engaged in reading a lyric poem, for example, where the listener will be a non-participator, a beholder, he will employ those means that will give the listener a sense of detachment. H. S. Langfeld in his book *The Aesthetic Attitude* described aesthetic distance in this way: One standing safely on the bow of a ship could contemplate the raging sea as a thing of beauty, but let the sea start to inundate the ship and the beholder could no longer view the sea as something detached from himself. Now he is intimately concerned with what the sea is doing.

How can the oral reader employ aesthetic distance in reading? How can he build up the illusion? One of the most important ways is that of keeping the eyes averted, by reading to the back wall, by knowing that the audience is present but by not recognizing them as such. Another means is in the employment of gestures that are not too direct. The speaker, the debater, uses direct, appealing gestures, gestures that make contact with the audience

[21] William Faulkner, *The Sound and the Fury* (New York: Random House, 1946), The Modern Library, p. 66.

[22] One of the most illuminating articles on aesthetic distance is that of Edward Bullough, "Psychical Distance as a Factor in Art and an Aesthetic Principle," in *The British Journal of Psychology,* eds. H. R. Rivers and C. S. Myers (Cambridge: Cambridge University Press, 1912), V, 88.

when he wants them to participate in what he is saying. The reader uses less definite but more suggestive gestures.

Part of the preparation for reading will be in deciding whether the reading is to be one in which the audience participates or one in which it listens with detachment.

The composition one is reading must be studied for those elements which help to keep it at a distance from the direct experience of the audience, those intrinsic techniques that keep it out of step with everyday living. The artistry of the reader will come in emphasizing these elements without making the audience too conscious of them. For example, think of the intrinsic elements in the sonnet. To begin with, there are three different types: English, Italian, and Spenserian. The fourteen lines are sometimes broken up into three quatrains and a couplet and sometimes into an octave and a sestet. Usually, we must have in mind a single theme which will adapt itself readily to (1) a simple statement, (2) a variation on that theme by metaphor, contrast, or comparison, (3) a secondary variation clearly subordinated to the first, and (4) either a restatement with the effect of a climax or an anticipation of the main idea. The fourteen lines in the English sonnet are put into these divisions: first quatrain, a statement of the idea; second quatrain, metaphorical variation on the idea; third quatrain, secondary variation on the idea; couplet, a compact, memorable summing up of the idea. Furthermore, consider the elevated language and the intricate rhyme scheme of the sonnet that tend to remove it from the mundane. The rhyme scheme of the Italian octave is fixed, and will permit no liberties: a b b a a b b a. Yet there are various rhyme schemes for the Italian sestet, the two most common of which are c d e c d e and c d c d c d. Enough has been pointed out about the sonnet to show that it has within it intrinsic elements that inevitably give it aesthetic distance.[23]

On the other hand a public speech, which has a low or a nonexistent aesthetic distance, tries to ape the speech of everyday. It uses the I, you, we. It may even use slang; it certainly uses the colloquial or vernacular idiom. Whatever organization the speech has is kept as simple as possible so that the audience can follow

[23] See Troy Caswell, "The Concept of Aesthetic Distance in Oral Interpretation," unpublished M.A. Thesis, University of Oklahoma, 1953.

the idea with little or no difficulty. The ideas of the speech are usually centered on immediate problems that are of pressing importance and need to be solved. Thus, the more the audience participates in the speech situation, the better.

But how should the Bible be read? Is it just another book? Is it the voice of God? How can the reverence that most of us feel toward the Bible be respected? Bliss Perry records a conversation with Professor J. W. Churchill, who held the chair of Homiletics at Andover Seminary, which suggests that a detached attitude helps the reader to create the impression that the Bible is the voice of God. "He never read in public from the Bible except when he was preaching, and I remember his saying to me that 'a clergyman should always read the Bible as if he were himself listening to its message as well as conveying it to the congregation'; a counsel of perfection which is violated every Sunday." [24]

III. Summary

Not every student can take the time to elect a course in the philosophy of composition. This chapter was written to stimulate the student's thinking and reading in this field. And it is hoped that the ideas expressed here will form the basis of profitable class discussions. Man does not want only to do; he wants to know why. Theory develops from practice; practice develops from theory. Most classes in speech, including oral reading, neglect theoretical considerations because the student is eager to get before the class and practice. But we must discuss theory for it is through theory that often we learn the better way. Certainly a liberally educated person not only knows the techniques of communicating his native tongue, but he also knows the theories that underlie those techniques.

IV. Projects for Chapter II

1. Give a short talk on one of the following themes:
   (a) Expression cannot exceed impression.

[24] Bliss Perry, *And Gladly Teach* (New York: Houghton Mifflin, 1935), p. 76. Students especially interested in reading the Bible aloud should be familiar with S. S. Curry, *Vocal and Literary Interpretation of the Bible* (Boston: The Expression Company, 1923).

(b) Read as if you were talking.
(c) Think the thought.
(d) Don't read to the book.

2. Give a short talk in which you illustrate your conception of *universality* and *individuality* in literature.

3. In reading a poem show how aesthetic distance can be maintained or broken.

4. From your experience, what intrinsic techniques are most widely employed? Illustrate.

5. Look through *Speech Monographs* and select an M.A. thesis that bears on oral reading and have your instructor send for it for you through the inter-library loan service. Give a report on this in class.

6. Get acquainted with one of the philosophers on the theory of art and give a short talk on him to the class. Emphasize particularly what he says about literature.

7. Discuss the following:

> The first question that inexperienced readers are likely to ask about a poem is "What does this poem mean?" Such a question implies that a poem contains a central thought which equals the whole meaning of the poem and that the reader goes through the poem simply to get to the end for the sake of the little nugget of wisdom that the poem may contain. The implication that a poem can be equated with its central thought is not true. On the contrary, one reads a poem in much the same way that he watches a baseball game. Every bleacher fan is a participant in the game in the sense that he identifies himself with the players. He is thrilled with a neatly executed double-play, becomes excited whenever a home run is hit, and quarrels with the umpire over a close decision. Although he may be interested in the outcome, it is the process of the game itself, the experience of watching it develop play by play that counts. To read poetry for thought alone is like going to a baseball game to watch the scoreboard instead of the game. The final score is no more the whole game than the central thought is the whole meaning of a poem.[25]

---

[25] Norman C. Stageberg and Wallace L. Anderson, *Poetry as Experience* (New York: American Book Company, 1952), p. 3.

CHAPTER III

The Provinces of the Reader, the Actor, and the Speaker

I. NATURALNESS VS. TRAINING

II. THE "BE NATURAL" CONCEPT

III. SPEAKING, READING, AND ACTING

IV. PROVINCE OF READING

V. DIAGRAM OF RELATIONSHIPS

VI. RELATION TO AUDIENCE
- A. Public Speaking and Acting
- B. Reading and the Audience
  1. Prose
  2. Lyric Poetry
  3. Dialogue
  4. Dramatic Monologue

VII. SUMMARY

VIII. PROJECTS FOR CHAPTER III

I. NATURALNESS VS. TRAINING

This chapter is an attempt to compare and contrast the art of the reader, the actor, and the speaker, and to determine in this way the relationships of the three phases of platform and stage performance. Manifestly, all three types of speech are forms of art involving definite skills and techniques acquired by study, observation, and experience. We may pride ourselves on our insistence upon *naturalness*, but if we use the term to deceive ourselves into believing that no technique is involved, no "special way of doing the thing," we must be very gullible indeed. The public speaker is an artist, as are the actor and the reader. The construction of his address so that it is easy for the audience to follow, with an introduction, body, and conclusion; the skillful choice of illustrations; the use of an animated style of delivery—these devices are *natural* no doubt, but they are also *art*.

One cannot escape from the fact that the effective speaker is an artist. Books on acting sometimes advocate "living the part." This does not mean, however, that an actor is to become so completely absorbed in the rôle of, let us say *Macbeth,* as to lose all consciousness of the fact that he is on the stage before an audience. One feels sorry for the other actors in such a situation. No, indeed; the actor playing Macbeth must be located at a certain place on the stage at a certain time or chaos would result. He must cross in front of another actor in a carefully rehearsed manner at an exact moment in the progress of the play. Nothing can be left to chance. Technique is necessary in every department of play production.

II. The "Be Natural" Concept [1]

In the case of the reader, books sometimes say that all he need do is to think the thought and feel the emotions implicit in a passage and all the outward manifestations of voice and body will take care of themselves. But suppose the voice is wholly inadequate to express that thought and that emotion? Suppose the voice is high and thin, when the accurate expression of the thought and the emotion in question requires a low and heavy quality of voice? No, the voice becomes a responsive instrument fit to express ideas adequately only after training and experience. "Be natural" would be good advice only if one were "naturally good."

We would all smile, unless we shuddered, if a surgeon were to walk into an operating room for a delicate operation and the young internes, who had come to watch the operation, leaned over the rail of the amphitheatre and said, "Just be natural, Doc." We all realize that it takes something more than just being natural to perform an operation. Similarly, it takes more than a nonchalant attitude to be able to stand before a group and read intelligently. Is it not true that it is natural for man to have his capacities trained? Indeed, if we mean by "being natural" that one has had his capacities disciplined, then we can agree that all the reader need do is to be natural before the group. Henry Ward Beecher brings out the point that by training we arrive at our second nature:

---

[1] See W. M. Parrish, "The Concept of 'Naturalness,'" *Quarterly Journal of Speech,* XXXVII, 448.

But, besides that, what power there is in posture, or in gesture! By it, how many discriminations are made; how many smooth things are rolled off; how many complex things men are made to comprehend! How many things the body can tongue when the tongue itself can not well utter the thing desired! The tongue and the person are to co-operate; and having been trained to work together, the result is spontaneous, unthought of, unarranged for.

Now, to the real natural man—and the natural man is the educated man; not the thing from which he sprang—how much is to be added! Many a man will hear the truth for the pleasure of hearing it; and so there must be something more than its plain statement. Among other things, the voice—perhaps the most important of all, and the least cultured—should not be forgotten. How many men are there that can speak from day to day one hour, two hours, three hours, without exhaustion, and without hoarseness? But it is in the power of the vocal organs, and of the ordinary vocal organs, to do this. What multitudes of men wear themselves out because they put their voice on a hard run at the top of its compass!—and there is no relief to them, and none, unfortunately, to the audience. But the voice is like an orchestra. It ranges high up, and can shriek betimes like the scream of an eagle; or it is low as a lion's tone; and at every intermediate point is some peculiar quality. It has in it the mother's whisper and the father's command. It has in it warning and alarm. It has in it sweetness. It is full of mirth and full of gaiety. It glitters, though it is not seen with all its sparkling fancies. It ranges high, intermediate, or low, in obedience to the will, unconsciously to him who uses it; and men listen through the long hour, wondering that it is so short, and quite unaware that they have been bewitched out of their weariness by the charm of a voice, not artificial, not prearranged in the man's thought, but by assiduous training made to be his second nature. Such a voice answers to the soul, and it is its beating.[2]

III. Speaking, Reading, and Acting [3]

Granting, then, three distinct forms of the spoken art—speaking, reading, and acting—employing three somewhat different techniques, let us attempt to differentiate among them. Probably

[2] "Lecture on Oratory," as quoted in Lionel Crocker, *Henry Ward Beecher's Speaking Art* (New York: Fleming H. Revell, 1937), p. 220.

[3] For a discussion of the relation of reading to acting, see Rollo Anson Tallcott, "Teaching Public Reading," *The Quarterly Journal of Speech Education,* IX, 53.

we shall find as much overlapping as distinction. In the diagram on page 54 we have listed a number of types of speaking and reading. There is, we believe, a progression from what we call extempore speaking to the realm of acting; the term *acting* being used in its usual sense to describe the assumption of rôles by a group of actors in an especially costumed stage production.

By extempore speaking we mean the type of public speaking in which the line of thought has been planned, but in which the actual choice of words is left to the time of delivery of the speech. Wendell Willkie was known as an extempore speaker. Certainly, such speaking belongs squarely under the caption, "Public Speaking." Here, too, we would be inclined to place declamation. We use the word *declamation* to designate a memorized rendition of an address or part of an address by, usually, a well-known orator. No doubt you have heard declamation contests, in which such selections as Bryan's *Cross of Gold,* Webster's *Liberty and Union,* and Lincoln's *Gettysburg Address* were presented.

IV. Province of Reading

From extempore speech and declamation we move out of the realm of public speaking proper, and into the outskirts of the province of reading. The similarities are very close, however, in such reading as that of reports, essays, newspaper editorials, and radio speeches. Here we have, very markedly, the manner and atmosphere of public speaking. The reader tries to communicate very directly with his audience, as if he had no manuscript in front of him. When we come to the narration of simple stories, the nature of the material changes. "Storytelling" is more definitely in the province of reading, although the reader is just as anxious to be direct and to get his material across to his listeners as is the public speaker. Further progression into the province of reading is accomplished when poetry is read or recited. Such material we think of as squarely in the province of reading. When we get to the reading of stories with dialogue and to the oral reading of plays, in the reading of which some impersonation is used, we are edging toward the realm of acting, which is finally reached when the actor reads the lines of a specific rôle in a play. We note, therefore, that somewhere between the rather definite regions of

V. Diagram of Relationships

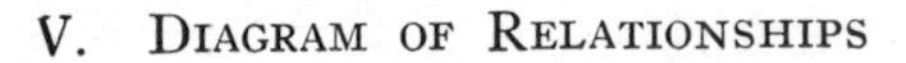

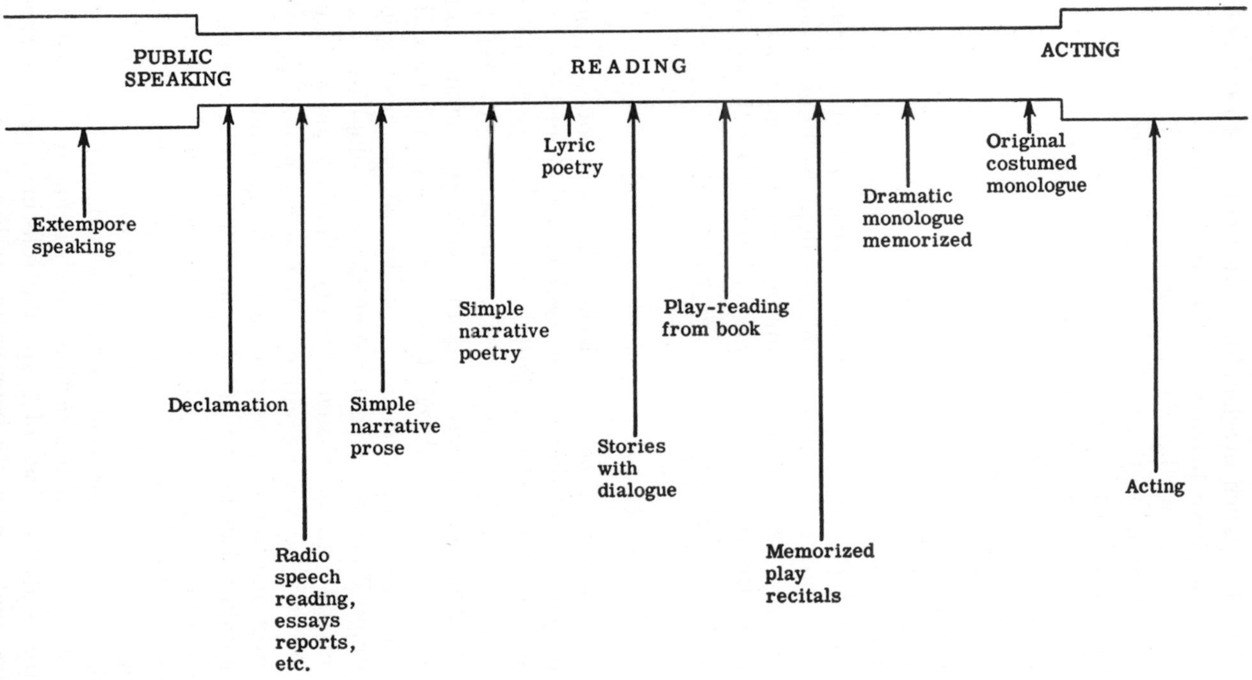

PUBLIC SPEAKING

READING

ACTING

Extempore speaking

Declamation

Radio speech reading, essays reports, etc.

Simple narrative prose

Simple narrative poetry

Lyric poetry

Stories with dialogue

Play-reading from book

Memorized play recitals

Dramatic monologue memorized

Original costumed monologue

Acting

the speaker and the actor or, rather, occupying most of the space between the two is the province of the reader. As the diagram indicates, it is a wide and varied area.

VI. Relation to Audience

A. *Public Speaking and Acting*

Perhaps we can best make the differentiation clear on the basis of *relation to the audience.* In extempore speaking we have the closest objective connection between speaker and audience. It is: "Ladies and Gentlemen, I am going to talk to you today about ———." The speaker keeps his eyes on the audience, he talks *with* the audience. At the opposite extreme from the speaker is the actor. Theoretically, he has no concern with the audience. His business is with the other actors. Thus, Bassanio talks to Portia in *The Merchant of Venice,* Rosalind to Orlando in *As You Like It.* We know, however, that the audience *is* a matter of very great concern to the actor. Again the matter of "naturalness" is to the fore. It may be natural to the rôle an actor is playing to speak so softly that only his fellow actors can understand him, but such a method would irritate the audience located at some distance from the stage. No, the actor must speak so as to be understood by all; he must face toward the audience, for the most part, so the audience can see his expression. It is communication, but of a different kind from that achieved by the speaker.

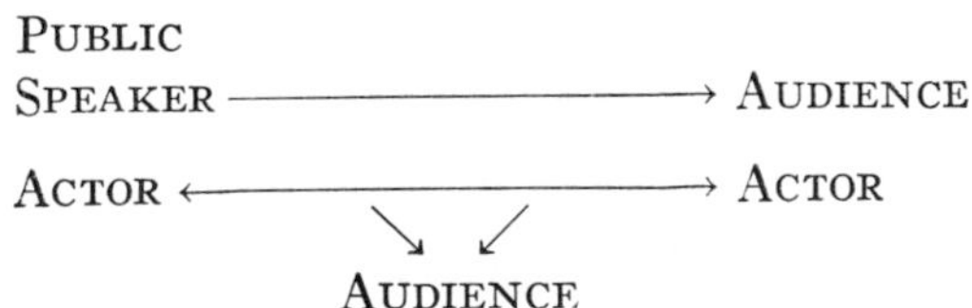

B. *Reading and The Audience*

1. Prose

When we come to the extensive province of the reader, we have to deal with numerous types of material. In reading aloud a letter before a committee, a newspaper editorial to others, an essay from a book, an original address, etc., we strive to establish communication just as objective and direct as that sought in extempore speaking. True, we may be reading words originally written by others, whereas the extempore speaker composes his own speech; but the effective reader from manuscript or book makes the words in a very real sense his own. Except for the presence of the book or paper between the reader and his audience, there is really no difference in the two methods. We might start out with "Ladies and Gentlemen" or any other form of direct address. In declamation, meaning by that the memorized presentation of a speech of some orator, we are again in the realm of reading, reading from a mental photograph of the speech presented. And again we wish the closest communication with the audience we can attain. In this case not even a book or manuscript is in the way. In reading simple narrative prose, as exemplified in Chapter VII, and in reading narrative poetry, we continue this method.

2. Lyric Poetry [4]

When we come to lyric poetry, however, there is a subtle change in the relationship of the reader to his audience. Take the following poem, for example:

Song

CHRISTINA ROSSETTI

When I am dead, my dearest,
  Sing no sad songs for me;
Plant thou no roses at my head,
  Nor shady cypress tree:
Be the green grass above me
  With showers and dewdrops wet;
And if thou wilt, remember,
  And if thou wilt, forget.

I shall not see the shadows,
  I shall not feel the rain;
I shall not hear the nightingale
  Sing on, as if in pain;

[4] For collateral reading the student might enjoy Robert Hannah's, "The Oral Interpretation of Lyric Poetry," *Quarterly Journal of Speech,* XV, 374.

And dreaming through the twilight
  That doth not rise nor set,
Haply I may remember,
  And haply may forget.

Now, obviously, one would not say, "Ladies and Gentlemen: 'When I am dead my dearest, Sing no sad songs for me.' " The reader is not addressing the audience, but an imaginary individual, possibly "in his mind's eye."

Another example:

My Star

ROBERT BROWNING

All that I know
  Of a certain star
Is, it can throw
  (Like the angled spar)
Now a dart of red,
  Now a dart of blue;
Till my friends have said
  They would fain see, too,
My star that dartles the red and the blue!
Then it stops like a bird; like a flower, hangs furled:
  They must solace themselves with the Saturn above it.
What matter to me if their star is a world?
  Mine has opened its soul to me; therefore I love it.

These poems, like so much fine lyric poetry, deal with sacredly intimate and personal concerns. Doubtless, Christina Rossetti and Robert Browning were thinking of very definite personalities when they wrote these poems, personalities that had meant a great deal in their lives. The object of the oral reader of these poems is to arouse similar thoughts and recollections of definite individuals and personalities in the minds of his listeners. He is communicating with the audience, as directly as in making a speech, but the facial expression, particularly the expression of the eyes, and the general "set" of the body may well be different from those used in the latter activity. This type of lyric poetry, intensely subjective, introspective, and personal in mood, is the most difficult to read. We believe it represents spoken reading at its highest spiritual and intellectual pitch. In our diagram such reading has been placed in the center of the province of the reader.

3. Dialogue [5]

As we come to dialogue in prose and poetry and to plays read aloud, we are still in the realm of reading, but we are fast approaching the province of the actor. We begin to impersonate another, not so fully as the actor does but, still, to some extent to assume a personality distinct from our own. The *degree* of this impersonation, how far toward acting we may go, is again a graduated process. The actor given the rôle of a feeble old man would dress the part. He would wear a wig, he would paint in the wrinkles, he would totter along on a cane, his legs would wobble, his back would be stooped, his head and hands would shake, his voice would be tremulous and would crack. This might be the *acting impersonation.* The *reader,* in the generally accepted sense (with an exception to be noted later), would not carry his impersonation to such a high degree. If he were reading a play, the old man might be one of half a dozen characters, each of whose parts he must voice in turn. Inasmuch as he must turn instantly from one part to the next, it would not be feasible for him to attempt any complete impersonation. If he is reading from the script, just a bit of portrayal in voice is perhaps all that is necessary. The reader who is presenting a play from memory may well carry his characterization further, with quite a pronounced vocal coloring and, in the case of the old man, with a suggestion of a stoop and of weakness at the knees. This type of impersonation is often carried too far. Yet it is impossible to draw a line that will measure off exactly where the artistic ends and the inartistic begins. Tastes differ so decidedly in these matters. What offends some seems perfectly all right to others. Extremes one *can* avoid. For example, there should be little movement; for the most part the reader should sit or stand in one position. Certainly, wholesale floundering about the platform would be a violation of good taste. We can simply restate the old saying: "Entertain the many but do not

---

[5] For collateral reading, see Phidelah Rice, "The Art of Impersonation in Play Reading," *Studies in the Art of Interpretation,* ed. Gertrude E. Johnson (New York: Appleton-Century-Crofts, 1940).

make the judicious few grieve by such entertainment." It is better to err on the side of too little impersonation than on that of too much. At any rate, with some degree of impersonation, we are drawing close to the realm of acting.

4. Dramatic Monologue

In the dramatic monologue, where the author represents a definite individual as speaking, a considerable degree of impersonation may be indulged in, so far as voice, gesture, and facial expression are concerned. Always, of course, there should be restraint and control. Browning has given us the finest examples of the dramatic monologue, and we shall study some of his monologues later in this text. Again, we repeat, we are drawing closer to acting. Some would say we are in that region, but we could protest that the *reader* of the dramatic monologue is still *reading*.

In recent years, Ruth Draper, Cornelia Otis Skinner, and others have been very successful with costumed original monologues. Simple properties are employed, such as a shawl, a coat, a hat, comb and brush, et cetera. Chair and table may be used. On the merits of this form of entertainment the opinion of the experts will never be unanimous. The art will, no doubt, always be objectionable to some. We, the authors of this book, are quite liberal in such matters. We admit without question that we have derived considerable pleasure from these monologists. But their *forte* is a highly specialized form of entertainment and, above all, it must be well done to be done successfully. Certainly we would be justified, in mapping out our chart of relationships, in putting the original monologist next door to the actor.

VII. Summary

Spoken reading, in summary, is an enormous province, extending all the way from (and overlapping somewhat) extempore speaking, with many and variegated gradations, up to (and partially including) the realm of acting. All these types of reading will be dealt with later in this text. Suffice it to state at this point that in all types of reading we are communicating, we are attempting to get some material across to an audience.

VIII. Projects for Chapter III

1. How does another text on oral interpretation treat the subject matter of this chapter?

2. Read and report on a book on acting, such as Michael Redgrave, *The Actor's Ways and Means* (New York: Theatre Arts, 1954). Try to keep in mind the distinctions that have been made in this chapter.

3. Find reviews of performances by Ruth Draper or Charles Laughton or Cornelia Otis Skinner and make a report in class. Does the reviewer say anything that would be helpful to the beginner?

4. Listen to a television broadcast of a speech in which the speaker is obviously reading and make a list of all the distractions that you can discover.

5. Read and report on Hiram Corson's *The Voice and Spiritual Education* (New York: Macmillan, 1896).

6. Present a reading of Ernest Hemingway's *The Old Man and the Sea.* Cut it to fit the time limits.

7. Bring to class a series of comic strips and read them as if you were reading them to children.

CHAPTER IV

Tools of Understanding and Appreciation

I. Special Rhetorical Devices
   - A. The Central Idea
   - B. Main and Subordinate Ideas
   - C. Climax
   - D. Assertion and Implication

II. Units of Discourse
   - A. Parts of Speech
     1. Nouns
     2. Verbs
     3. Adverbs
     4. Adverbial Modifiers
     5. Adjectives
     6. Thought Connectives
   - B. Vehicles of Thought and Emotion
     1. The Sentence
     2. The Paragraph

III. Types of Discourse
   - A. Exposition
     1. Explanation
     2. Interpretation
     3. Criticism
   - B. Description
   - C. Argumentation
   - D. Narration

IV. Psychological Means
   - A. Mood and Attitude
   - B. Sound and Sense
   - C. Imagery

V. Summary

VI. Projects for Chapter III

Up to this point in your education for communicating with others, you have studied many of the tools to be set forth in this chapter, but you have studied them with the thought of writing out your ideas so as to enter into the minds of others through their *eyes*. Now you are asked to use these tools to analyze and appreciate what you are going to read aloud for the *ears* of others. It is one thing to contemplate the aspects of a tool which you are going to use yourself in writing, and it is quite another to figure out how this tool was used by a successful writer so as to read his composition better to others. In this chapter you are going to be reminded of much that you already know, but it will be with a different approach and emphasis. For example, if you know that a writer used certain words to produce certain effects, you will not carelessly pass over these words when you read aloud. This chapter should increase your awareness and appreciation of how writers achieve their effects. Much more could be written about each one of the tools, but only that which is pertinent to reading aloud from the printed page effectively has been singled out to bring to your attention.

I. Special Rhetorical Devices

A. *The Central Idea*

As the first step in your approach to the interpretation of any piece of prose or poetry, read the entire selection through for the complete idea expressed. Before starting your analysis get the fun or thrill this first impression will give you. Read for enjoyment, first, for that is what you want to give your audience when you read to them. In this way you will prevent the details from obscuring the whole; the trees will not obscure the woods. Concentrate on the passage. Read it silently and as quickly as you can to get the total effect.

For example, read the following poem by Wordsworth. (You really should memorize this sonnet.)

> The World is too much with us; late and soon,
> Getting and spending, we lay waste our powers:
> Little we see in nature that is ours;
> We have given our hearts away, a sordid boon!
> This sea that bares her bosom to the moon;
> The winds that will be howling at all hours,
> And are up-gathered now like sleeping flowers;
> For this, for everything, we are out of tune;
> It moves us not.—Great God! I'd rather be
> A pagan suckled in a creed outworn;
> So might I, standing on this pleasant lea,
> Have glimpses that would make me less forlorn;
> Have sight of Proteus rising from the sea;
> Or hear old Triton blow his wreath'd horn.

The general impression you get of the idea of this poem is that we do not half appreciate the beauty around us because we are slaves to materialism. *Things* are in the saddle. This is the central idea. Everything in the poem contributes to emphasizing it. But now if we go back and read this poem again, carefully, we appreciate at once that reading is a highly active and synthesizing process. A whole is composed of parts, and the effect of the whole is built up from the sum of the parts. What relation do these parts bear to one another? We do not simply absorb the words from the page one by one, individual and distinct. Each word takes on certain meanings, these meanings often become associated with other ideas already in the mind, and the whole process becomes extremely complicated and full of life. The first word of importance is "world." At once we perceive that the ordinary definition of the word is insufficient. We see that by the word "world" the poet signified the whole mass of material things, and immediately into our minds rushes a great stream of associated ideas: money, refrigerators, Fords, Buicks, Wall Street, the stock exchange, tanks, machine guns, streamline trains, millionaires, love of the things of this world. It is this world of material things that is "too much with us." It is with us "late and soon." "Getting and spending" is the complete life cycle of too many of us. The pay check so hardly won is soon spent. Perhaps we think of specific examples of some whose life consists solely of accumulating money and then squandering it on mink coats and champagne. In our chase after the almighty dollar, the finer things of life, particularly a knowledge of the birds, the trees, the flowers, have all but lost their hold upon us. "Little we see in nature that is ours." We do not possess anything in Nature because we have not been willing to pay the price of understanding her. Perhaps our own guilt, our own overindulgence in worldly things, troubles our consciences. What is the matter with us? "We have given our hearts away, a sordid boon!"

The context of the passage may give you the meaning, and you may feel that you get its full import with no need of outside aids; but use a dictionary anyway. Exactly what does "sordid boon" mean? In the study of the poem we have been considering, you may need a dictionary of classical mythology to find out who Proteus and "old Triton" are.

B. *Main and Subordinate Ideas*

Study each sentence for the relationship of the ideas. What is the dominant idea? Are there any key words that suggest the leading thought? What are the contributing ideas? Grammatically, the distinction may be made clear by means of independent and dependent clauses. In the following sentence (one of the most beautiful ever written) from the *Second Inaugural Address,* by Abraham Lincoln, note the relationship of the subordinate phrases to the main verb, *strive on:*

> With malice toward none; with charity for all; with firmness in the right, as God gives us to see the right, let us strive on to finish the work we are in; to bind up the nation's wounds; to care for him who shall have borne the battle, and for his widow, and for his orphan—to do all which may achieve a just and lasting peace among ourselves, and with all nations.

To emphasize this relationship, let us rewrite Lincoln's thought, expressing it in several independent sentences:

> Let us strive on to finish the work we are in. Let us strive on to bind up the nation's wounds. Let us strive on to care for him who shall have borne the battle, and for his widow, and his orphan. Let us strive on to do all which may achieve a just and lasting peace among ourselves and with all nations. Let us strive on to do all this with malice toward none. Let us strive on to do this with charity for all. Let us strive on to do all this with firmness in the right, as God gives us to see the right.

Such a study gives us a respect for the compactness of Lincoln's style. Say his version of the sentence aloud and note how the voice attempts to bring out the qualifying nature of those parts of the sentence that precede and follow the verb. Such an analysis insures against a careless rendering of a well-written passage. One of the side values of a carefully taught course in oral reading appears precisely at this point. To a generation of college students who know little or no formal grammar, a course in oral reading can stress the importance of the structure of a sentence and show how structure is related to meaning.

Besides key words look for topic sentences, usually to be found at the opening of paragraphs. And often, in carefully constructed articles, the main ideas are set forth in the introduction and repeated in the conclusion. The writer follows the tried-and-true technique of telling the audience what he is going to say, saying it, and then recapitulating what he has said.

Repetition may give you the relationship of ideas. The author may repeat the same words or, more subtly, the same thought. Be on the watch for all forms of repetition. In poetry the refrain is commonly used to emphasize, to bring out, the main point. You may have noticed that some prose selections have refrains as well. Robert G. Ingersoll, in his greatest lecture, *The Liberty of Man, Woman, and Child,* keeps repeating the refrain: "It is a question of intellectual development." Russell H. Conwell, in his *Acres of Diamonds,* reiterates his central idea: "Where there is a need there is a fortune."

Transitional words and sentences are helpful to one trying to see the relationship between ideas. Words like *however, now, then, but, so;* and phrases like *to be sure, on the other hand, in the next place* help the author carry his audience with him. Look for these, and when you read them, give them the proper vocal treatment. Transitional sentences look forward and back. They are valuable to the interpreter, for they help him keep in mind the forward marching of ideas from one point to the next. The voice can indicate whether there is more to follow when the point is made. A falling inflection generally indicates a completeness of thought.

Be on the alert for internal and final summaries. The author uses these means to acquaint you with what he thinks important.

C. *Climax*

Frequently the author employs contrast and comparison in minor climaxes to prepare the audience for the major climax. The latter word, like so many terms we employ in rhetorical theory, comes from the Greek; it means, literally, *ladder.* How expressive the term is! We ascend and descend from one climax to another. The reader must know where the highest point in the selection is. If he does not know where it is, because of faulty preparation, he is likely to stumble over it unawares and miss its significance, thus losing the meaning of the selection. The shading necessary to bring out the major climax will be missing. Details will swallow it up.

Climax in art is man's attempt to find a meaning in life, a reflection of his desire to see things come to fruition, to bring the scattered implications of life to a point, to give importance to existence, to "get some place." The lives of most of us are pretty much the same day in and day out, humdrum and devoid of contrast; and so, in poetry and drama we try to experience the thrill that comes in the presence of *climax*.

The cumulative effect of climax may be found in a single sentence, where it is usually built up from units of three.[1] For example, Shakespeare uses three members thus: "You blocks, you stones, you worse than senseless things." But we find four members in this sentence from Cicero's oration against Verres: "To bind a Roman citizen is an outrage; to scourge him is an atrocious crime; to put him to death is almost a parricide; but to put him to death by crucifixion—what shall I call it?" Turn this sentence around and you will understand the meaning of anticlimax.

In cutting a novel or a play for reading, the reader must be careful to use the minor climaxes to build up to his major climax. Tempo, volume, pitch, all help us in building up the minor climaxes in preparation for the dénouement. A play, for example, must be so studied that the climaxes of sentences, paragraphs, speeches, whole scenes and acts are known, in order that the reader may carry his hearer with him on a mounting wave of interest and excitement to the peak of the play's action. The reader's *ex*pression of the effect the author has achieved by the use of climax cannot exceed the *im*pression it has made upon him.

D. *Assertion and Implication* [2]

What does the author whisper? What are the overtones of the writer? You may remember the final lines, the climax, of Robert Frost's "Stopping by Woods on a Snowy Evening":

> The woods are lovely, dark and deep,
> But I have promises to keep,
> And miles to go before I sleep,
> And miles to go before I sleep.[3]

The first time the poet says the line, "And miles to go before I sleep," he is imparting geographical information, he is making an assertion; but the second time he says it, he implies, he whispers,

[1] The student of climax would be interested in studying A. D. Conkey's unpublished Ph.D. thesis, "A Study of Climax," University of Michigan.

[2] For another treatment of this subject, see Algernon Tassin, *The Oral Study of Literature* (New York: Knopf, 1929).

[3] From *The Collected Poems of Robert Frost* (New York: Henry Holt and Company). By permission of the publishers.

that it is something more than miles he has to cover. The lines become metaphorical. The reader who employs the same tone and mood and tempo for the repetition of the line as for its first statement shows that he has missed the poet's implication, his hidden meaning. Is there an unpleasant duty the lover of the woods must perform? Are his words spoken with a sigh? What sort of promise is involved? Is the distance a spiritual distance? There have been countless interpretations of these haunting lines. Robert Frost himself, commenting upon them in a lecture, said whimsically that he had to end the rhyme scheme (which is a difficult one) *someway* and that this seemed the easiest way to do it!

In H. C. Bunner's poem, "One, Two, Three," the first line reads: "It was an old, old, old lady." Now the first *old* is an assertion, it is informative; but the other *olds* are filled with implication. The interpreter must divine the significance of the repetition. Was the old, old lady kindly, loving, gentle, thoughtful? All this may be whispered by the poet's art; the reader must hear the whisper and make his audience hear it as well.

Let us take another familiar example. Marc Antony tells the Roman mob that Brutus is an honorable man, but by his ironic repetition of the line he introduces overtones that the words, in themselves alone, do not possess:

> But Brutus says he was ambitious;
> And Brutus is an honorable man.
> He hath brought many captives home to Rome,
> Whose ransoms did the general coffers fill;
> Did this in Caesar seem ambitious?
> When that the poor have cried, Caesar hath wept;
> Ambition should be made of sterner stuff:
> Yet Brutus says he was ambitious;
> And Brutus is an honorable man.
> You all did see that on the Lupercal
> I thrice presented him a kingly crown,
> Which he did thrice refuse. Was this ambition?
> Yet, Brutus says he was amibtious;
> And, sure, he is an honorable man.
>
> —Act III, Sc. ii.

Read this selection over several times and bring out a different meaning each time you say the word *honorable*.

Look for this "repetition with a purpose." Every sentence contains old as well as new material. The repeated material takes on new meaning in relation to the new. The context will supply part of this meaning, but the hidden implications should not escape the reader. In reading the passage the tone of the voice should make clear the words and phrases repeated for effect. The emphasis that was given a point the first time it was read should be missing. A new vocal interpretation is imperative.

What are the connotations of the passage? What does the imagination suggest? Talk over the selection with your classmates and with the teacher. Not only must we comprehend the obvious mood and thought of the poem and interpret them to the audience; we must, as well, stimulate the audience's imagination to listen for the overtones. Remember the words of Keats in the "Ode to a Grecian Urn":

> Heard melodies are sweet, but those unheard
>   Are sweeter; therefore, ye soft pipes, play on;
> Not to the sensual ear, but, more endear'd,
>   Pipe to the spirit ditties of no tone.

II. Units of Discourse

A. *Parts of Speech*

1. Nouns

Our understanding the meaning of an author, "the harvest of the quiet eye," will be improved if we look for his nouns, his names of things, his substantives. What is the author talking about? He will tell you in his choice of nouns. What are the subjects of his sentences? If we discover these subjects, we stand a better chance of stirring up in the listener the thought that the author is trying to convey. How important it is for the interpreter to get a clear idea of what the author is considering, what he is going to join together with his verbs, what his verbs are going to do to his subjects. The author's nouns are his relatively stable elements, those things that the writer and the reader, the interpreter, and the listener have a fairly adequate idea of. In the rest of the sentence the author tells what is to be done with these elements he has named. For example, if the author mentions *world,* we have a fairly good idea as to what he has in mind. Here are three poets starting their thoughts with the word *world:*

> The *world* is too much with us.
>
> —WORDSWORTH.

> The *world* stands out on either side
> No wider than the heart is wide.
>
> —MILLAY.

> O *world,* thou choosest not the better part.
>
> —SANTAYANA.

The importance of the noun is seen in the fact that it can stand alone as a sentence, and it sometimes does effectively. The verb, however, always must have a subject.

2. Verbs

Writers use various parts of speech to secure their effects. Verbs, for example, denote activity and change. The omission of the verb in the principal clauses of Canto XI of Tennyson's *In Memoriam* adds an element of calm that could not otherwise be secured.

> Calm is [4] the morn without a sound,
> Calm as to suit a calmer grief,
> And only thro' the faded leaf
> The chestnut pattering to the ground;
>
> Calm and deep peace on this high wold,
> And on these dews that drench the furze,
> And all the silvery gossamers
> That twinkle into green and gold:
>
> Calm and still light on yon great plain
> That sweeps with all its autumn bowers,
> And crowded farms and lessening towers,
> To mingle with the bounding main;
>
> Calm and deep peace in this wide air,
> These leaves that redden to the fall,
> And in my heart, if calm at all,
> If any calm, a calm despair;

[4] The only verb of a principal clause in these five stanzas is the second word of the first line, *is.*

Calm on the seas, and silver sleep,
And waves that sway themselves in rest,
And dead calm in that noble breast
Which heaves but with the heaving deep.

In the poem "The Fountain,"[5] by James Russell Lowell, the absence of verbs is deliberate so as to produce the effect of smoothness and suggest the rhythm of a leaping fountain. On the other hand, note the effect of such verbs as *sprang, galloped, cried, undrew, echoed, shut, sank, turned, shortened, set, rebuckled, chained, drew, crew, dawned, came out, broke, leaped* in giving urgency to the poem that follows. Note, particularly, how the power of the verb *galloped* is woven into the context of the piece. Isn't this artistry at its zenith!

How They Brought the Good News From Ghent to Aix

ROBERT BROWNING

I

I sprang to the stirrup, and Joris, and he;
I galloped, Dirck galloped, we galloped all three;
"Good speed!" cried the watch, as the gate-bolts undrew;
"Speed!" echoed the wall to us galloping through;
Behind shut the postern, the lights sank to rest,
And into the midnight we galloped abreast.

II

Not a word to each other; we kept the great pace
Neck by neck, stride by stride, never changing our place;
I turned in my saddle and made its girths tight,
Then shortened each stirrup, and set the pique right,
Rebuckled the cheek-strap, chained slacker the bit,
Nor galloped less steadily Roland a whit.

III

'Twas moonset at starting; but while we drew near
Lokeren, the cocks crew and twilight dawned clear;
At Boom, a great yellow star came out to see;
At Düffeld, 'twas morning as plain as could be;
And from Mecheln church-steeple we heard the half-chime,
So, Joris broke silence with, "Yet there is time!"

---

[5] See p. 259.

IV

At Aershot, up leaped of a sudden the sun,
And against him the cattle stood black every one,
To stare thro' the mist at us galloping past,
And I saw my stout galloper Roland at last,
With resolute shoulders, each butting away
The haze, as some bluff river headland its spray:

V

And his low head and crest, just one sharp ear bent back
For my voice, and the other pricked out on his track;
And one eye's black intelligence,—ever that glance
O'er its white edge at me, his own master, askance!
And the thick heavy spume-flakes which aye and anon
His fierce lips shook upwards in galloping on.

VI

By Hasselt, Dirck groaned; and cried Joris, "Stay spur!
Your Roos galloped bravely, the fault's not in her,
We'll remember at Aix"—for one heard the quick wheeze
Of her chest, saw the stretched neck and staggering knees,
And sunk tail, and horrible heave of the flank,
As down on her haunches she shuddered and sank.

VII

So, we were left galloping, Joris and I,
Past Looz and past Tongres, no cloud in the sky;
The broad sun above laughed a pitiless laugh,
'Neath our feet broke the brittle bright stubble like chaff;
Till over by Dalhem a dome-spire sprang white,
And "Gallop," gasped Joris, "for Aix is in sight!"

VIII

"How they'll greet us!"—and all in a moment his roan
Rolled neck and croup over, lay dead as a stone;
And there was my Roland to bear the whole weight
Of the news which alone could save Aix from her fate,
With his nostrils like pits full of blood to the brim,
And with circles of red for his eye-sockets' rim.

IX

Then I cast loose my buffcoat, each holster let fall,
Shook off both my jack-boots, let go belt and all,
Stood up in the stirrup, leaned, patted his ear,
Called my Roland his pet-name, my horse without peer;

Clapped my hands, laughed and sang, any noise, bad or good,
Till at length into Aix Roland galloped and stood.

X

And all I remember is—friends flocking round
As I sat with his head 'twixt my knees on the ground;
And no voice but was praising this Roland of mine,
As I poured down his throat our last measure of wine,
Which (the burgesses voted by common consent)
Was no more than his due who brought good news from Ghent.

And note the comparative absence of verbs in the following poem by Walt Whitman:

Out of the Cradle Endlessly Rocking [6]

WALT WHITMAN

Out of the cradle endlessly rocking,
Out of the mocking-bird's throat, the musical shuttle,
Out of the Ninth-month midnight,
Over the sterile sands and the fields beyond, where the child leaving his bed wandered alone, bareheaded, barefoot.
Down from the showered halo,
Up from the mystic play of shadows twining and twisting as if they were alive,
Out of the patches of briers and blackberries,
From the memories of the bird that chanted to me,
From your memories, sad brother, from the fitful risings and fallings I heard,
From under that yellow half-moon late-risen and swollen as if with tears,
From those beginning notes of yearning and love there in the mist,
From the thousand responses of my heart never to cease,
From the myriad thence-aroused words,
From the word stronger and more delicious than any,
From such as now they start the scene revisiting,
As a flock, twittering, rising, or overhead passing,
Borne hither, ere all eludes me, hurriedly,
A man, yet by these tears a little boy again,
Throwing myself on the sand, confronting the waves,
I, chanter of pains and joys, uniter of here and hereafter,
Taking all hints to use them, but swiftly leaping beyond them,
A reminiscence sing.

---

6 From *Leaves of Grass* (Philadelphia: David McKay, 1900). By permission of the publishers.

Note Walt Whitman's use of the *-ing* participle to secure his pleasing effects: *rocking, leaving, twining* and *twisting, risings* and *fallings, beginning, yearning, revisiting, twittering, rising, passing, throwing, confronting, taking, leaping.*

3. Adverbs

In his poem "Bridge of Sighs," Thomas Hood depends upon the adverb ending in *ly* for his haunting effect. This poem lives on in the memory partly through the poet's use of such adverbs as *tenderly, slenderly, constantly, instantly, scornfully, mournfully, gently* and *humanly*, and so on.

4. Adverbial Modifiers

Sometimes the author uses the adverbial modifier to color an entire sentence. Such a modifier shows the author's attitude toward the thought expressed. The reader is thus given a clue to the interpretation of the idea. Such modifiers are: *to be sure, I am sure, in fact, all things considered, fortunately, certainly, undoubtedly, surely, of course, obviously, clearly, therefore, thus, nevertheless.* The unusual mobility of the adverbial modifier accounts for part of its power in expression. Note what the position of the adverbial modifier in the last verse of the Twenty-third Psalm does to the sense:

> *Surely* goodness and mercy shall follow me all the days of my life: and I will dwell in the house of the Lord for ever.
>
> Goodness and mercy shall *surely* follow me all the days of my life: and I will dwell in the house of the Lord for ever.
>
> Goodness and mercy shall follow me all the days of my life *surely:* and I will dwell in the house of the Lord for ever.

By putting the *surely* at the opening of the verse do we get a sense of confidence that underwrites the entire thought that we do not get when we put it elsewhere in the verse?

5. Adjectives

Watch the author's use of adjectives, for often the vague is made definite, is brought into focus, by means of modifications. A thorough comprehension of the adjective's function is the key to the understanding of all modifying elements—verbals, phrases, and clauses. Adjectives modify nouns, or noun-like words or groups of words. When we modify we change the meaning. Let us quote a paragraph from Russell H. Conwell's *Acres of Diamonds* and note the use of adjectives:

> The man who purchased Al Hafed's farm led his camel out into the garden to drink, and as the animal put his nose into the *shallow* waters of the *garden* brook Al Hafed's successor noted a *curious* flash of light from the *white* sands of the stream. Reaching in, he pulled out a *large black* stone containing a *strange* eye of light. He took it into the house as a *curious* pebble, and putting it on the mantel that covered the *central* fire, went his way and forgot all about it. But not long after, that *same old* priest came to visit Al Hafed's successor. The moment he opened the door he noticed the flash of light. He rushed to the mantel and said:
>
> "Here is a diamond! Here is a diamond! Has Al Hafed returned?"
>
> "O no, Al Hafed has not returned, and we have not heard from him since he went away, and that is not a diamond. It is nothing but stone we found out in our garden." [7]

One is impressed by the fact that there are not many adjectives in this selection. (Henry Ward Beecher said that adjectives steal away the power of the noun.) Two of the adjectives help to give the passage its air of mystery: *curious* (used twice) and *strange*. And note how much depends upon the adjective *shallow*. The listener must get the image of a *shallow* stream in order to understand how the man can see and pick up in his hand the stone with the *strange* eye of light. Note also that Conwell is careful to contrast the *white* sands with the *large black* stone. Careful authors use adjectives with intent. Study this passage for the modifying elements.

In the following quotation from Arthur M. Schlesinger, Jr.'s review of *Mr. Lincoln's Camera Man: Mathew B. Brady,* by Roy Meredith, note the effect of the word order used—the placing of the adjectives *after* the noun: "The Civil War is the first modern war as much because of photography as of the iron-clad warship

---

[7] As quoted in Agnes Rush Burr, *Russell H. Conwell and His Work* (Philadelphia: John C. Winston Company, 1926), p. 408.

or the captive balloon. Brady's camera realized war no longer as a romance in oils, but as human experience, lucid, gray and awful."[8]

6. Thought Connectives

Prepositions, conjunctions, relative pronouns, and adverbs are the mortar of a passage. And the nouns, adjectives, and verbs may be thought of as the bricks. But a structure would not stand long if built of bricks with no mortar. We have all received telegrams with the connectives left out, to save space, and we have often had to puzzle over the meaning. Usually the meaning was not clear until we supplied the thought connectives. How dependent we are on thought connectives can be illustrated by omitting them from the first sentence of the Declaration of Independence:[9]

. . . the course of human events, becomes necessary one people dissolve the political bands have connected them another, assume the powers the earth the separate equal station the laws nature nature's God entitle them, a decent respect the opinions mankind requires they should declare the causes impel them the separation.

When, in the course *of* human events, *it* becomes necessary *for* one people *to* dissolve the political bands *which* have connected them *with* another, *and to* assume *among* the powers *of* the earth the separate *and* equal station *to which* the laws *of* nature *and of* nature's God entitle them, a decent respect *to* the opinions *of* mankind requires *that* they should declare the causes *which* impel them *to* the separation.

An audience would have difficulty in making head or tail of the first passage. Connectives bind the words into sentences. Good reading will bring out the connections of thought. Sometimes the connective words suggest what is going to come; sometimes they look back at what has already been said. The importance of connectives is emphasized when we consider the difference of opinion that has developed over whether Lincoln said "of the *people,* by the *people,* and for the *people*"; or whether he said "*of* the people, *by* the people, and *for* the people."

---

[8] *The New York Times Book Review,* February 10, 1946, p. 22.

[9] See James C. Fernald, *Connectives of English Speech* (New York: Funk and Wagnalls, 1904).

B. *Vehicles of Thought and Emotion*

1. The Sentence

The author, who writes in English, records his speech in sentences. The sentence is a unity, a unit of discourse. The sentence may consist only of the noun, but usually it consists of the noun and verb, or subject and predicate. An example of such a sentence, a simple sentence, is: "Jesus wept." (John 11:35.) When we write more than one assertion into a sentence we have a compound sentence. Think of Winston Churchill's "We shall go on to the end, we shall fight in France, we shall fight on the seas and the oceans." When we put one principal assertion and one subordinate assertion into a sentence, we have a complex sentence. Heywood Broun wrote such a sentence, "Anger and vengeance are attributed to God because these are failings which we ourselves experience and can therefore understand."

It is helpful to the oral reader to understand that sentences can be classified into four groups: interrogative (questions); declarative, whether indicative or subjunctive (reports, opinions, affirmations, denials, comments, remarks, judgments, propositions); exclamatory (ejaculations); and imperative (commands).

In analyzing a passage to read aloud we can usually identify what type of sentence we are reading by the marks of punctuation. Conscious writers are careful and discriminating in their use of punctuation. The oral reader must be certain that he understands just why the writer used the comma, the semicolon, the colon, the dash, the exclamation point. Punctuation by structure is logical; it serves to indicate and help the sense of what is being said. It marks off the process of thought, outlines the steps of argument, and controls the expression in the interests of meaning.[10]

In the management of the word, the phrase and the sentence, the author shows his power over his means of communication. Hemingway learned through his apprenticeship in journalism how to make his sentences short and clean. He writes in vigorous English, eschewing the encumbering adjective. He knows the truth of Henry Ward Beecher's admonition, "Don't whip with a switch that has leaves on, if you want to tingle." William Faulkner

---

[10] For an excellent discussion on the interpretation of punctuation the student is referred to S. H. Clark's *Interpretation of the Printed Page* (Chicago: Row, Peterson and Company, 1915).

writes of the trials and tribulations of the lowly people of his home county and has found through the richness and majesty of words and his long, circuitous, punctuationless sentences the means of elevating his stories to sublimity. His style, so bothersome at first, is a means of making his reader slow up, feel and reconsider, ponder, hear on the inner ear. After a few pages the rhythm gets beneath the surface of the page into one's soul and the reader is lost, captured by the author.

2. The Paragraph

Another unit of discourse, which is made up of sentences, is the paragraph. Usually a writer leads off his thought in each paragraph of a composition by what is called a topic sentence. This section of this chapter will be so developed. However, sometimes the writer may bury his topic sentence in the body of the paragraph, or he may omit it altogether. If on scanning a piece of writing you discern that the writer has used a topic sentence to introduce each paragraph, you can run through the article and get a fairly good idea of the meaning by reading the opening sentence of each paragraph.

Now the writer in developing his paragraphs may use several different means. He may use examples, analogies, testimonies, reasons, facts, statements and principles, definitions and specific instances. In analyzing a paragraph for oral presentation, it will help you to identify the means of amplification.

Now take a look at the order of the sentences. How are they arranged? Can you discover a pattern? The author may use such devices as these: (1) Climax, less to greater value. (2) Known to unknown. (3) Deductive—general to the particular. (4) Inductive—specific to general. (5) Story form. (6) Story form mingled with description. (7) Description.

Finally, take a look at the way the writer weaves his materials, his sentences, together by means of transitions. Does he use any or all of these three: (1) Does he repeat the key word of the previous sentence? (2) Does he use a reference word? (3) Does he use a transitional expression, *like, moreover, but, likewise, at the same time, to this end, consequently, indeed, for instance, in brief, meanwhile, near by?*

III. Types of Discourse

In reading prose orally it is helpful to realize what type we are dealing with. The rhetorician has divided prose into four categories: exposition, argumentation, description, and narration. Sometimes the first two are thought to be rhetorical, and the second two, poetic.

A. *Exposition*

In attempting to help an audience appreciate a piece of expository prose, it is helpful to discover whether the author is concerned with (1) explanation, (2) interpretation, (3) criticism.

1. Explanation

Does the author explain how something is made, how it works, the genesis of an idea, how it came into being, does it exist, when did it occur? Explanation tends to be technical and factual. What are the logical details?

2. Interpretation

Does the writer have a sympathetic attitude toward the subject expounded? Does he answer the question, "What does it mean?" Does the author give play to his own personal whims, his own personal point of view? Does it reveal insight? What are the emotional details? When Shelley writes on "The Defense of Poetry" do we not have interpretation?

3. Criticism

When the author appeals to external, or objective, standards rather than personal feelings and personal impressions, we have criticism. When we seek to answer, "How well does it fulfill its intended function?" "Does the piece make complete use of the medium?" "Does it make unique use of the material?" "Does it make perfect use of the medium in the effort to fulfill the artistic purpose of sympathetic representation?" we are indulging in criticism.

B. *Description*

We have the phrases: "It beggars description" or "It is beyond description." By these statements we mean that we can not use words with sufficient skill to make the listener see in his mind's eye what we have seen. Yet authors do try to describe, to evoke images. What the author describes may be actual or imaginative. For example, a college catalogue may give such data as the number of buildings, the nature of the courses, and so on and the reader would get a fairly good factual idea of the institution. But a college student in describing his college to another individual might give his feelings, his impression, his reactions. The first description of the college will be technical and the second suggestive.

There are six methods that authors use in the process of description which are helpful to the oral reader as he analyzes a passage preparatory to reading it aloud. Ask these questions as you analyze description:

1. Does the author have a single purpose?
2. Does he maintain a point of view?
3. Does he follow a definite and natural outline?
4. Are the details selected in accordance with the purpose of the description?
5. Are the details well arranged and subordinated?
6. Are appropriate terms, phrases, and other helps to vivid presentation chosen?

C. *Argumentation*

Argumentation is a process of advancing reasons. We use reasons to establish a proposition. The author may want to convince us of a new idea, or to instill in us a new belief in the place of an old one. As you analyze an argumentative passage ask yourself these questions:

1. What is the exact purpose of the author?
2. Can you find the proposition-sentence?

3. Can you find the main points to support the proposition?
4. Does the author use facts, reasons, opinions, and examples to convince?
5. Does the author follow any particular plan of organization?
6. What devices does the author employ? Does he go from the known, the accepted, to the unknown? Does he show there is a trend? Does he use contrast and comparison? Does he show a need? Does he offer a plan to meet the need?
7. Does the author refute opposing arguments?

D. *Narration*

The reader of a story is going to do a better job for the listener if he understands the following outlines of simple and complex narratives. First, is the narrative simple or complex?

By simple is meant that the action pursues its course from start to finish without check or delay. Unity, sequence, and climax are the essentials of simple narrative as they are of all narrative. A simple narrative must begin at a definite point of time and in a definite place; it must develop its subjects in a series of incidents; it must come to a fitting conclusion. Thus there are the following elements present in the simple narrative: (1) a setting, (2) beginning of an action, (3) a course of action, (4) the conclusion. (5) the characters, (6) purpose of the writer.

Complex narrative differs primarily from simple narrative in that some obstacle is interposed to check the forward movement of the action. The characteristics, then, of complex narrative are: (1) the obstacle, (2) the plot, (3) the characters, and (4) suspense.

The plot has three distinguishing characters which the reader must keep in mind; (1) the beginning, (2) the climax, (3) the conclusion. In analyzing the conclusion decide whether it is: (1) tragic, (2) pathetic, (3) cheerful, or (4) humorous.

Some of the important helps to narration which the reader should note are: (1) description, (2) contrasts of characters, (3) contrasts of scenes, (4) transitions from scene to scene, (5) conversations which have point and purpose, (6) conversation which is in character, (7) actions which reveal character.

IV. Psychological Means

A. *Mood and Attitude*

The sound of words can help create a mood. For example, Vachel Lindsay's poem, "The Congo," is vivid with the contrasts created by his use of tone color.[11] Tennyson was a master of tone color, as we see in his poem:

> Break, break, break
> On thy cold gray stones, O Sea!
> And I would that my tongue could utter
> The thoughts that arise in me.

Notice the effect of the long *o* sound in *cold,* and *stones,* and *O.*

A poet who excels in the choice of words to produce mood through sounds is Edgar Allan Poe. It is interesting that he has left us an essay, "The Philosophy of Composition," in which he describes how he composed "The Raven." In this essay he tells us how he happened to choose the word *nevermore* [12] to give tone coloring:

> These points being settled, I next bethought me of the *nature* of my *refrain.* Since its application was to be repeatedly varied, it was clear that the *refrain* itself must be brief, for there would have been an insurmountable difficulty in frequent variations of application in any sentence of length. In proportion to the brevity of the sentence, would, of course, be the facility of the variation. This led me at once to a single word as the best refrain.
>
> The question now arose as to the character of the word. Having made up my mind to a *refrain,* the division of the poem into stanzas was, of course, a corollary: the refrain forming the close to each stanza. That such a close, to have force, must be sonorous and susceptible of protracted emphasis, admitted no doubt; and these considerations, inevitably led me to the long *o* as the most sonorous vowel, in connection with *r* as the most producible consonant.
>
> The sound of the refrain being thus determined, it became necessary to select a word embodying this sound and at the same time in the fullest possible keeping with that melancholy which I had predetermined as the tone of the poem. In such a search it would have been absolutely impossible to overlook the word "Nevermore." In fact, it was the very first which presented itself.

---

[11] See Davis Edwards, "The Real Source of Vachel Lindsay's Poetic Technique," *Quarterly Journal of Speech,* XXXIII, 182.

[12] Note Percy Bysshe Shelley's use of *never more* in his "Threnos."

What, one must always ask oneself in interpreting a selection, is the mood of the passage? Is it sad, gay, ironical, satirical, explanatory, concessive, exclamatory, triumphant, defiant, challenging, sombre? One of the commonest faults in reading is failure to grasp the *feeling* of a passage. The inexperienced reader attacks every selection in the same colorless manner. No doubt his inability to distinguish varying emotional tones is due to lack of experience in the business of living itself, or to a lack of imaginative insight. The amateur actor often reveals his inexperience by failing to grasp the "feeling" of a scene. He has not developed the ability to enter upon it at the right emotional pitch. He lets the pitch down. The next time you go to the theatre, note how the professional actor, on the contrary, enters directly into a scene keyed, from the beginning, to the proper emotional pitch.[13]

An aid to grasping the emotional tone of any selection is knowledge of the circumstances under which it was written. What is the author's general outlook on life? Clarence Darrow was a fatalist; Robert G. Ingersoll an agnostic; Harry Emerson Fosdick is a Christian preacher. In the preliminary reading for background the reader may gain some hints as to the emotion that should accompany the reading of a particular passage.

To develop range of emotional feeling, practice reading the same passage in different moods. Read it laughingly; read it with tears. Note also how the mood is reflected in your posture and gesture. In the sister art of singing, note how the concert artist (Leonard Warren, for example) assumes a posture in keeping with the song he is going to sing.

We must *understand* a passage to render it in the proper mood. An interesting illustration is to be found in Abraham Lincoln's study of Shakespeare. F. B. Carpenter, who lived for six months in the White House while painting a picture of the reading of the *Emancipation Proclamation,* tells the following anecdote. Lincoln is speaking:

> The opening of the play *King Richard the Third* seems to me often entirely misapprehended. It is quite common for an actor to come upon the stage, and, in a sophomoric style, to begin with a flourish:—

[13] See Paul L. Pfaff, "An Experimental Study of the Communication of Feeling Without Contextual Material," a doctoral dissertation, University of Southern California, abstracted in *Speech Monographs,* XXI, 155.

Now is the winter of our discontent
Made glorious summer by this sun of York,
And all the clouds that lowered upon our house,
In the deep bosom of the ocean buried!

Now this is all wrong. Richard, you remember, had been, and was then, plotting the destruction of his brothers to make room for himself. Outwardly, the most loyal to the newly crowned king, secretly he could scarcely contain his impatience at the obstacles still in the way of his own elevation. He appears upon the stage, just after the crowning of Edward, burning with repressed hate and jealousy. The prologue is the utterance of the most intense bitterness and satire.[14]

B. *Sound and Sense* [15]

In order to have sound echo sense, and so the more vividly impress his words upon the reader's memory, the writer employs many rhetorical and psychological devices. He may use onomatopoeia, choosing words like *crash* and *bang* and *slushy;* and alliteration, which is the repetition of the same sound at the beginning of two or more consecutive words or of words near one another. Or he may employ words whose sounds contribute in more subtle ways to the mood of the passage. Look for the marks of these tools in prose. You will find that their use is not so obvious there as it is in poetry. For an example of a poet's use of rhyme, alliteration, and onomatopoeia to reinforce his sense, let us take Robert Browning's "Meeting at Night":

Meeting at Night

ROBERT BROWNING

The gray sea and the long black land;
And the yellow half-moon large and low;

---

[14] F. B. Carpenter, *Six Months at The White House with Abraham Lincoln* (New York: Hurd and Houghton, 1867), p. 51. For collateral reading see W. M. Parrish, *Reading Aloud* (New York, Ronald Press, 1941), chap. v, "Interpretation of Attitude."

[15] For collateral reading on this section, see DeWitt H. Parker, "The Asthetics of Poetry" and "Prose Literature," *The Principles of Aesthetics* (New York: Silver, Burdette and Company, 1920). The advanced student might also like to read Fred Newton Scott, "Vowel Alliteration in Modern Poetry," *The Standard of American Speech and Other Papers* (New York: Allyn and Bacon, 1926). See also Kenneth Burke, *The Philosophy of Literary Form* (Baton Rouge: Louisiana State University Press, 1941), "On Musicality in Verse."

And the startled little waves that leap
In fiery ringlets from their sleep,
As I gain the cove with pushing prow,
And quench its speed i' the slushy sand.

Then a mile of warm sea-scented beach;
Three fields to cross till a farm appears;
A tap at the pane, the quick sharp scratch
And blue spurt of a lighted match,
And a voice less loud, through its joys and fears,
Than the two hearts beating each to each!

Notice first the difficult rhyme scheme, *a b c c b a*. The memory enjoys the recall of the sound of *land* when it hears the word *sand*. The anticipated joy of repetition is thus accomplished.

Now notice the repetition of the *l* sound in such words as *long, black, land, yellow, large, low, startled, little, leap, ringlets* and *sleep*. (Notice, too, that the *l* sound is not used with such intent in the second verse.) Moreover, one can hear the sucking of the sand as the boat is beached in such sounds as *pushing, quench,* and *slushy*. The repetition of the *s* sound is noticeable in words like *ringlets, sleep, speech,* and *sand*.

In the second verse the *s* sound is continued in such words as *sea-scented* and *cross*. Then come the masterful phrases that catch the sense in the sound: *tap at the pane, quick sharp scratch, blue spurt*. And in the last line the very words themselves pulse with the rhythm of beating hearts.

Often the student asks, "Did Shakespeare, or did Browning, or did any other poet think of all these minutiae as he wrote, or are we reading into the poem something that did not occur to the poet?" Perhaps the best way to answer this question is to point to the craftsmanship of A. E. Housman. In his review of *A Shropshire Lad,* William Rose Benét [16] reveals how Housman struggled for the most perfect expression of his ideas and emotions of which he was capable. Examination of one line alone will show how a finished technique, such as Housman possessed to a superlative degree, often improves upon the sound, sense, and rhythm of

[16] William Rose Benét, "The Passion for Perfection," *The Saturday Review of Literature,* February 2, 1946. Mr. Benét's article is a review of *A Shropshire Lad,* by A. E. Housman, with notes and bibliography by Carl J. Weber (Jubilee Edition; Waterville, Maine, 1946).

spontaneous utterance. Before this particular line was revised, it read, "And cloudy shadows racing." After Housman worked over it, it became, "And cloud-led shadows sailing." Let us examine this second version, first of all for improvement in sense. By changing one syllable of the line, Housman was able to create a majestic figure of speech: that of shadows being led by the clouds. Then, by changing *racing* to *sailing,* he applies another stimulus to the imagination—the clouds are likened to ships that ride majestically through the blue. The urgency of the word *racing* is eliminated. Now note the improvement in rhythm. The *a* in *racing* is shorter than the *a* in *sailing.* Thus the pace of the line is slowed down to suggest the movement of clouds through the sky. The introduction of the syllable *-led* for the syllable *-y* introduces another *d* into the line and checks its pace still further. There are now four *d*'s in the line. The improvement in sound is evident. In the revised line we have three *l*'s and four *d*'s. The final sounded *s* of *shadows* blends into the initial unsounded *s* of *sailing.* Thus did Housman improve sense, sound, and rhythm.

C. *Imagery* [17]

Attention has just been called to the difference in the imagery created by the use of the word *racing* instead of the word *sailing* to describe the motion of cloud-shadows. There is a difference in the image of movement as well as in that of sight. Let us go back a moment to the poem "Meeting at Night," by Robert Browning, and study the images in that masterpiece. Sight images of the land, the moon, the waves, the cove, the boat, and the sandy beach are given to us in the first verse. The second verse provides us with visions of the beach, the three fields, the farm, the lighted match. Then we *hear,* in the first verse, the beaching of the boat, the *tap at the pane,* the *quick sharp scratch,* the sound of the human voice. The smell image is in the word *sea-scented.* The image of action is in such phrases as *leap in fiery ringlets, three fields to cross, a tap at the pane, the quick sharp scratch.* And there is a strong tactile, or touch, image in the two hearts *beating each to each.*

---

[17] The student would be benefited by a study of "Imagery in Poetry" in Fred B. Millett's *Reading Poetry* (New York: Harper, 1950).

The reader's imagination is so important in working up a selection that we must consider the matter in some detail. Begin by putting yourself in the place of the author. Consider the author your friend; remember that your friend received his impressions through his various senses, and that if you are going to recreate the passage, you too must awaken your memories of past events through sense images. See it! Hear it! Taste it! Feel it! Smell it! —in your imagination.

We are living in a picture age. The moving pictures draw their nightly multitudes. *Life* can not get enough paper to satisfy its millions of readers. *Esquire* caters to the demands of the public by mirroring life in the flesh. *Time* employs pictures in every column of newsprint, to enhance the eye appeal of the page, and always uses an attractive picture of a famous contemporary on its cover. Advertisers demand pictures and cartoons to enable them to get into the consciousness of their readers. *The Saturday Evening Post* accompanies its articles with pictures. If the oral reader is to compete with the visual picture, he must develop his ability to conjure up the latter *in the audience's imagination* by the words he uses. But first of all, the reader himself must see the picture.

In the following opening paragraph, written a few years ago by columnist Thomas L. Stokes, note how the writer attempts to awaken response in the *experience* of his reader. Let us quote the paragraph and then go over it sentence by sentence to see if we can experience more deeply the pictures Mr. Stokes is painting.

> PARIS, March 14.—One sunny afternoon you are in Washington, at the airport. The next evening you are looking down on the scattered lights of Paris, not the flaming, brilliant Paris of old, but a lady without her jewels. But still it is Paris, the end of the line. The plane hovers, then descends into the darkness. Everybody aboard is relieved. For hours we have been waiting for this. We get set for the final landing, for that thump. It comes, a good, honest thump of solid earth.

Let us take the first image, "One sunny afternoon you are in Washington, at the airport." Here is the image of warmth. A spring day in March. Can you recall the first early days of spring? Do you feel the sun on the back of your neck?

Note the scene: Washington at the airport. The setting is always given in good writing and speaking. Now with a little exercise of your imagination you can see yourself at the airport ready to board the transatlantic liner. You may never have been on such a liner, but you have seen pictures of them in the newspapers and in the movies. You read in the light of your experience, whether direct or indirect. Can you picture yourself waiting in line to climb the ladder to get into your seat? Now the point is, that if you prepare yourself to read this selection by going over this scene in your imagination, your voice will then suggest to the listener the warmth of the sun on the back of your neck, the air liner glistening in the sun with the ladder attached to the open door. Only a second is needed to see all this in the theatre of the mind.

Then with lightning speed the author has you hovering over Paris. What better word could have been chosen than the word *hover?* In order to give you the sensation of *speed,* the author puts you over Paris in the second sentence. How can you evoke the scene? Well, you have seen many movies of Paris. You have seen many interiors of planes in the movies, or you may have examined such an interior at an air show. You have the makings of knowing *how* it feels to hover over Paris in an airplane at night. All you need do is to weave the odds and ends of direct and indirect experience together actually to feel yourself there, in the plane. Note the splendid descriptive phrase of Mr. Stokes', "scattered lights of Paris." Well, being in this place with Mr. Stokes is something like the reverse of standing upon the earth and looking up at the stars. You are up there looking down at the earth and its scattered lights. You might imagine that someone points out the light on the Eiffel Tower, or shows you the lights over the bridges of the Seine. Mr. Stokes is writing for millions who have never been to Paris, for you and me. He must arouse our imaginations.

The author knows the power of contrast and comparison; the past and the present are contrasted. And note with what skill, by means of a metaphor, Mr. Stokes tries to make you sense the war mood of Paris, "a lady without her jewels." How jewels do set off a dress or a beautiful throat!

Suddenly the writer changes the picture. He wants you to conjure up a different mood. He wants you to feel the joy of coming to the end of a journey. We have all experienced this emotion of elation that comes with journey's end. Even though the trip across the Atlantic was but a few hours, it has been long. Cramped up in a plane, flying through the dark with its hazards, seeing the ocean dashing beneath us, stopping to refuel at the Azores—we are glad our flight is over, and that we are soon to be on the ground. Can you capture this sense of relief?

Can you picture yourself in the plane as it circles over Paris, waiting for the signal to land? Can you hear the communications officer talking to the official on the ground? Can you feel the plane losing altitude? You know what it is like to go down in an elevator and feel the pressure on your ears as you descend. Can you project your experience into the printed page and make it come to life? Mr. Stokes is eager for the reader to feel the emotion of completion, of joy at coming to the end of a journey, and so repeats the thought.

Then comes the climax—landing. The "thump" (what an excellent word that is!) of hitting the earth. The pleasure of being back on the earth again is given utterance in those words, "a good, honest thump of solid earth." It is not so much what is asserted as what is implied. Perhaps as a child you went up in a Ferris Wheel—and were immensely relieved when the ride was over and you stumbled out of your swaying seat on to the solid earth.

And now let us examine the image of *touch*. Have you ever gone barefoot? Of course you have! The delight of the following few sentences from Rollo Walter Brown's "Portrait of My Mother" (*The Atlantic,* October, 1944) comes from their evocation of the sense of touch or, as it is sometimes called, "the tactile image":

> When we were in our Sunday best and there had been heavy summer rains that had left the hill and hollow roads gutters and loblolly, she insisted that we pick our way along the roadside so that our shoes would not be all mud when we reached the church. Although I hit upon the less genteel way of carrying my shoes and socks and enjoying the elemental feel of the soft mud squashing up between my toes, and then washing my feet in the cool water below a spring within sight of the church, putting on my shoes, and appearing as mudless as if I had walked all the way on Fifth Avenue, I did accept her principle of making as decent an appearance as circumstances would allow.

Can't you feel the mud squashing up between your own toes in your imagination, the cool water on your feet? Try to substitute yourself for Mr. Brown and see yourself, in your mind's eye, putting on your shoes as you sit on the bank of the spring. Do you see the little white church on the brow of the hill above the spring? And now imagine an immaculate self walking up the spotless reaches of Fifth Avenue, before the shining window displays.

Again, let us consider an author's employment of the image of *smell.* Can you recall the smell of stale tobacco smoke? Have you trained your imagination sufficiently to be able to conjure up olfactory images at will? For most of us, sight images are the most potent. But authors depend upon the experience we have gained through the use of our sense of smell to quicken our imaginations. Can you, for example, evoke "the bouquet of a room much lived-in" as A. J. Cronin describes it in *The Green Years:* [18]

> I entered a strange, interesting, dreadfully untidy room. The high brass bed in the corner, with its patchwork quilt and lop-sided knobs, was still unmade; the bearskin hearthrug was rumpled; the towel on the splashed mahogany washstand hung awry. My eye was caught by a black marble timepiece of the "presentation" variety lying upon its side on the littered mantel-piece with its inside in pieces beside it. I felt a queer smell of tobacco smoke and past meals, a blending of complex and intricate smells, forming, as it were, the bouquet of a room much lived-in.

The reader must develop his sensitivity to all images. It stands to reason that if the reader does not get the full import of what the author intends to convey, he can not make the listener get it. With faulty preparation students will try unsuccessfully to re-create passages that have not fully captured their imaginations. These students read the words but do not receive the images those words are intended to create.

Have you developed your ability to conjure up images of *taste?* In his essay, "Portrait of My Mother," Rollo Walter Brown speaks of his mother's excellence as a cook. Try to taste as well as see the following images: "In addition to the everyday cooking done in a household, she made all sorts of jellies of the clearest colors and the most trembling consistency, grape marmalade, blackberry and raspberry jam, strawberry preserve, peach butter, the special Ohio kind of apple butter, melting cakes with deep icing, mincemeat of her own proportioning that all the neighbors bought ravenously from her as long as she would sell." Linger over these words long enough to recall the *taste* each image con-

[18] Little, Brown & Company, 1944.

jures up, and distinguish, with a connoisseur's palate, among them. Recall the difference between the taste of peach butter and that of strawberry preserve. Can you do it? Draw upon your memory until you make your mouth water.

Is your imagination trained to *hear?* When you read the following sentence from a sermon by Harry Emerson Fosdick, can you picture the scene and hear the words being uttered from the platform? Dr. Fosdick said: "Centuries afterward a boy on the Cornell campus wandered into a religious meeting out of curiosity just as the words were being spoken, 'Seekest thou great things for thyself? Seek them not.' It was the turning point of that boy's life, as it had been, long before, of Baruch's, and with some importance to Christianity withal, because that boy was John R. Mott." Is your imagination so trained that you enter easily into that picture? Can you see the speaker on the platform? Can you hear him directing the question to his audience? Can you see young Mott standing there listening?

Or test your ability to conjure up the sound images in the following passage from Amy Lowell:

> Slowly, without force, the rain drops into the city. It stops a moment on the carved head of Saint John, then slides on again, slipping and trickling over his stone cloak. It splashes from the lead conduit of a gargoyle, and falls from it in turmoil on the stones in the Cathedral square. Where are the people, and why does the fretted steeple seep about in the sky? Boom! The sound swings against the rain. Boom, again! After it, only water rushing in the gutters and the turmoil from the spout of the gargoyle. Silence. Ripples and mutters.[19]

Analyze this passage for every one of the sound images and see if you can hear those sounds in your imagination.

Let us remember that the listener can make a theatre out of his mind; we have the phrase "the mind's eye." The reader deals with the image making power of the listener's mind and the skilful reader will help the listener see, and feel, and taste, and hear, and touch in the theatre of his mind. Charles Laughton usually begins his lecture-recitals by reciting this well known passage from *Henry V:*

> O, for a Muse of fire, that would ascend
> The brightest heaven of invention;

[19] See p. 292 for this selection.

A kingdom for a stage . . .
. . . But pardon, gentles all.
The flat unraised spirits, that hath dared,
On this unworthy scaffold, to bring forth
So great an object. *Can this cockpit hold*
The vasty fields of France? or may we cram
Within this wooden O [stage] the very casques
That did affright the air at Agincourt?
O, pardon! . . .
And let us, ciphers to this great accompt,
On your imaginary forces work:
Suppose, within the girdle of these walls,
Are now confined two mighty monarchies,
Whose high, upreared and abutting fronts
The perilous narrow ocean parts asunder.
Piece out our imperfections with your thoughts;
Into a thousand parts divide one man,
And make imaginary puissance:
Think, when we talk of horses, that you see them,
Printing their proud hoofs i' the receiving earth:
For 'tis your thoughts that now must deck our kings,
Carry them here and there; jumping o'er times;
Turning the accomplishment of many years
Into an hour-glass . . .
Thus with *imagined wing* our swift scene flies,
In motion of no less celerity
Than that of thought. . . .
. . . O, do but think,
You stand upon the rivage, and behold
A city on the inconstant billows dancing . . .
. . . Follow, follow!
Grapple your minds to sternage of this navy . . .
Work, work your thoughts, and therein see a siege:
Behold the ordnance on their carriages . . .
. . . Still be kind,
And eke out our performance with your mind.

V. Summary

Study the passage you intend to read aloud over a period of time. Keep coming back to it. Do not hasten the process of absorption. If the selection is to challenge your listeners, it must necessarily have much meat to it. You will not be able to digest its full significance in one reading. This warning needs to be sounded many times for the benefit of students who think that no preparation for the class in oral reading is necessary. "Why, I've read ever since, and even before, I went to school," the lazy student says. And the teacher says, "But how?"

A hasty perusal of the selection on the way up the stairs to the classroom will not do. Reading to the group with his eyes glued to the book he has opened, perhaps, for the first time, the unprepared student is afraid he will miss the next word. The emphasis is poor. The eye contact is nil. A mispronounced word disturbs the rhythm of the passage. Not appreciating the full flavor of a phrase, the reader does not permit the audience to experience what the author intended to give them. Struck by a new meaning in one of the sentences, a meaning that had not occurred to him in his cursory preparation, he stops to ponder, and in this impromptu awareness of the hidden meaning loses the pulse of the passage. His grasp of the selection as a whole is ruined. And as Goethe said, "Alas! the spirit-bond is gone." If, on the other hand, the selection had been studied and read many times beforehand, and the fragments of beauty had been absorbed into the total impression, the reader would have been able to compel his audience to grasp the selection in its entirety.

Prepare or fail! Even when you are permitted to use the book, you should be able to look up from it when important phrases are voiced. The eyes are important in holding attention. Use them to full effect; gaze directly at your audience when you wish to emphasize the importance of what you are saying. Be so well versed in your selection that you can do this without fear of the consequences. What would you think of a singer who worried about the next note in a phrase? If you are unprepared, the audience will not give itself to you.

VI. Projects for Chapter IV

1. Secure copies of *Pleasure Dome* by Lloyd Frankenburg (Boston: Houghton Mifflin, 1949) and work out exercises for the entire class using this book. The following poets are represented in the volume: James Stephens, T. S. Eliot, Marianne Moore, E. E. Cummings, Wallace

Stevens, Ezra Pound, William Carlos Williams, Ogden Nash, W. H. Auden, Dylan Thomas, Robert Lowell, and Elizabeth Bishop. Each student might give a lecture recital on one of these poets.

2. Secure a copy of Philip Wylie's *Generation of Vipers* (New York: Rinehart, 1942) and work out a reading from it.

3. Prepare a cutting from "The Sermon" found in *Moby Dick* by Herman Melville.

4. Prepare for reading in class one of the shorter selections from Irving J. Lee's *The Language of Wisdom and Folly* (New York: Harper, 1949).

5. This is an exercise for seven students. Each student will take a chapter from Fred B. Millett's *Reading Poetry* (New York: Harper, 1950) and talk about it and read from it in class. The chapters are: 1. The Substance of Poetry, 2. The Structure of Poetry, 3. Rhythm in Poetry, 4. Sound-Pattern in Poetry, 5. Imagery in Poetry, 6. Figures and Symbols in Poetry, 7. Directions for the Analysis of a Poem.

6. Eric Sevareid makes the following comment on the adjective. What does he mean? Do you agree? Can you give examples?

> Historians looking back on this particular age will have to have some handy label for it. They may, of course, call it the age that destroyed civilization; but we have a suspicion that they might call it the age that destroyed the adjective. Since the adjective is of ancient lineage and is a basic tool in our trade, its decline fills us with a certain sense of sadness. We understand how an old-fashioned woodworker must feel these days, with all the machine-made plastic stuff around. You know how it is with many of these glamorous-looking plastic things—they get busted and nobody can repair them. That is what is happening with adjectives today—they're getting busted all over the place. The only difference is that people go on using them, not realizing that they are busted.[20]

7. Prepare a reading of "Three Hebrew Children in the Fiery Furnace" (Daniel 3), with particular emphasis on the rhythm of the passage.

---

[20] Eric Severeid, *In One Ear* (New York: Knopf, 1952).

CHAPTER V

Words, Words, Words

I. Language and Experience
- A. Word and Thought
- B. Imagery
- C. Symbols
- D. Total Meaning
- E. Associations
- F. World of Words
- G. Words and Things

II. The Referent
- A. Three Classes of Labels
  1. Names
  2. Collections
  3. Abstractions
- B. Examples of Clearness and the Referent
  1. Keats
  2. Franklin Delano Roosevelt
  3. Lowell Thomas
- C. Examples of Obscurity and the Referent
  1. Milton
  2. Dylan Thomas
  3. Robert Browning

III. Order of Words

IV. Definition
- A. By the Context
- B. By Derivation
- C. By Negation
- D. By Examples

V. Changes of Meaning

VI. Connotation and Denotation

VII. Phrasal Patterns

VIII. Summary

IX. Projects for Chapter V

I. Language and Experience [1]

Long before you learned to read you could speak. You were initiated into the realm of English sounds in your cradle. Gradually, with the help of your parents, you began to attach significance to those sounds. Your own first attempts to reproduce them —your *mama* and *dada,* for instance—may have been intelligible only to your family and to you, but they sufficed for a language until people outside the family began to come into your life. Then you had to drop your familiar language for a more widely

[1] For collateral reading on this section, see S. Hayakawa, *Language in Action* (New York: Harcourt, Brace, 1941).

accepted set of sounds standing for things and ideas. Even though *wawa* plainly and unmistakably *meant* water to you and to your mother, you had to change it to *water* if you wanted the neighbors to understand you. The process was slow; probably you still retain some words or sounds that are known only to you and your immediate family; or, perhaps, words or phrases having a particular meaning within your own family group.

In learning to read in school your job was to translate sound language into eye language. In some schools children are taken to local points of interest to see for themselves what words mean. For example, a class goes to the post office and there sees a canceling machine. Then, when the youngsters read about the canceling machine the next day, they have a visual image to which unfamiliar words can easily be related. There comes a time, however, when children cannot get direct experience—as when they begin the study of geography—and must depend upon the printed page alone. Every new idea now has to be interpreted in terms of old ideas. How big is England? The answer is in terms of the United States, the conception of whose size, in turn, has previously been grasped in terms of a particular community, city, county, or state. So, gradually, more and more of the information the child acquires is the fruit of indirect experience. One can see how easy it was to distort the textbooks in Germany and Japan.

A. *Word and Thought*

The printed word is meant to be an expression of thought; but it is a mere symbol, and therefore must remain forever inadequate—Wordsworth spoke of the "sad incompetence of speech." Lytton Strachey said, "In a single sentence, a hundred elusive meanings obscurely palpitate." So, when you set out to read from the printed page, you will have to attempt first of all to find out what the author really meant. We want you to learn to interpret language of fact as well as language of emotion in this course, and to become able to read directions for performing a chemical experiment as effectively as you present a piece of imaginative literature.

Both tasks have their difficulties, and the first is by no means the easier of the two. If you have ever had to "write up" a scientific experiment, you have no doubt been impressed with the difficulties involved in putting into words so complicated a procedure. A reader who would hope to read such a description effectively must have grasped every detail of the performance, and his voice must reveal his grasp. No doubt you have noticed that written reports often employ diagrams to explain obscure points; the oral reader has no such resources.

B. *Imagery*

We want you to develop your power to evoke images in the minds of your listeners. Now, no two people can read a piece of imaginative literature and get the selfsame pictures from it. Your visualization of the writer's words will not be identical with that of any other person. When I read *The Return of the Native,* by Thomas Hardy, I saw in my imagination the fields of a farm near Howell, Michigan, which I visited as a child. Your experience of the world outside yourself and your interpretation of that experience are not the same as mine. And the symbols you have used to represent that outside world are not the symbols that I have used. Or, put the other way, the symbols may be the same, but the things for which they stand are very apt to be dissimilar. For instance, to one person the word *sorority* may symbolize a hateful world of snobs; to another it may have none but its literal meaning, *sisterhood.*

C. *Symbols*

As your experience widens, you will have to adopt new symbols to give it expression. When the state of modern Palestine was created, Hebrew was adopted as one of its official languages. Obviously, however, there were no words in ancient Hebrew for many modern inventions, so symbols from other languages had to be pressed into service to express these new ideas. Lillian Smith, author of *Strange Fruit,* in an address on the crumbling of segregation in the South declares that the South, freed from race hatred, will need a new vocabulary to express the new relationships between the races.[2]

Our second job is a very important one also. And I stress it here

[2] "Ten Years from Today," *Vital Speeches,* XVII, No. 21.

because it is so easy to forget it. We must give back to our people, white and colored, in this time of severe change, *something equal to or better than* that which has been taken away from them. We must not let people feel cheated, if it can possibly be helped, when great change takes place. When old defenses are torn down within an individual's personality without building up new defenses, that personality is likely to collapse into mental illness. When such change takes place in a culture, there will be great trouble unless we build up new defenses as the old go down.

Our South has been through one hard and terrible reconstruction. We do not want to go through another. And it is not necessary—for our people have already demonstrated their capacity for change—*if we remember* that we must give our people new beliefs, new images of themselves to substitute for the old "Superior white" and the old "Heart frustrated Negro," new outlets for their frustrations, new and creative outlets. (I am assuming that segregation is going to be as hard psychically for many Negroes to give up as it is going to be for many whites.)

It is a tremendous responsibility, an awesome and fascinating job for our writers and speakers and teachers and leaders: to find new words for old, to create new images of ourselves without which we cannot live sane lives, to help men fall in love with new ideals, to find new outlets for the old hates and humiliations.

If we fail—we, the preachers, the editors, the writers and teachers—new and perhaps far less wise leaders will take our place. The vacuum will be filled. New words are going to be on the people's tongues. What these words are depends upon *us*.

The good people, the wise people, the talented ones, failed Germany in her time of great change. Great writers—and Germany could claim some of the world's most distinguished—were not the ones who said words that created substitutions for the psychic defenses which the Germans lost in their defeat in the first world war. Germany's poets and novelists and preachers and teachers could have filled this void but they failed to do it. So Hitler filled it. He was the one who found words for the wounded German people. It was *his* images of "the German" that the people hugged to their minds. No writer in the South after the Civil War, except George Washington Cable, tried to give new images to our people. He gave us good words, but our people did not listen because only the one man spoke them. During Russia's great change, the new words were given the people by the communist party. It was communism and the communist leaders who gave the people the image of themselves that they now have; Mao and his fellow-communists are doing the same for China.

The poets, the wise men, the talented were mute. They withdrew to their ivory towers and let the demagogues of the world take over the most precious task, the most important to the human being in time of change: that of giving him images of himself to live by, images created out of words.

What a sad and tragic thing this will be in our South if those who are gifted with words stay silent!

What words to use? What images to substitute for the old? While no writer or artist or speaker can tell others what to say, I think we can judge the rightness of our words, our feelings and acts, by checking and doublechecking them with the shape that the world's future is taking, and checking that future with man's old dream of himself as a unique and "sacred" and free person.

Radio and television are new businesses involving unfamiliar and even unique techniques and processes. It was necessary, therefore, to develop a standard set of terms that workers in these fields might use to communicate with one another. Recently Sponsor Services Inc. published a new edition of their *Television Dictionary Handbook,* listing 2,200 TV terms. Here are some of the terms: *dinky inkie*—the smallest of incandescent spots; *drooling*—padding a show with unimportant talk; *idiot sheet*—printed reminder sheets out of camera range; *whip shot*—very fast pan shot that usually blurs scene; *woof*—"on the nose" or O.K.

Just as new industries have to develop a new vocabulary, so you, in your contact with new ideas, should acquire the vocabulary necessary to express them. Kipling was once discovered by a friend, lying flat on his stomach on his front porch, reading the dictionary. When asked why he was reading such an uninteresting book, he replied that he was "reading for words." Henry Ward Beecher was often found reading books of doubtful literary value for the vocabulary they contained. To increase one's grasp of the language, a conscious attempt must be made.

Pause over words long enough to see how they are made up. Take, for example, the word *synthesis.* Here we have the word *thesis,* from the Greek root meaning to place, or set, plus the prefix *syn,* together. So the process of placing ideas together is a *synthesis.* Now the word *antithesis* is made up of the same word, *thesis,* plus the prefix of opposite meaning, *anti.* A dictionary can be a lot of fun for the student of reading.

D. *Total Meaning*

And, on the other hand, a dictionary may not always be helpful. Language, the English language in particular, is filled with expressions that defy definition. A foreigner has difficulty with such phrases as, "I'll be tickled pink," or, "I'd be tickled to death." So also words in certain combinations are hard to define. For example, the phrases "yellow streak," "sugar daddy," and "It's up to you" have meanings, by association, at which it is impossible to arrive by learning merely the literal definitions of the words. The foreigner who attempts to grasp the meaning of these phrases starts by tearing them apart. Success, by this method, is utterly impossible. Such expressions have a *total meaning* that transcends their component parts. Goethe calls this "the spirit-bond":

To understand the living whole
They start by driving out the soul;
They count the parts, when all's done
Alas! the spirit-bond is gone.

Compositions have total meanings. Everything adds up to what? If the reader lets this total intent escape him, he can not possibly portray what the author had in mind. In the following comment on Olivia de Haviland in *Candida,* Wolcott Gibbs shows how the actors failed to get Shaw's intent: [3]

"Candida" is, to be honest, a very hard piece for actors to execute successfully. The heroine, whose husband is a pompous English cleric and whose admirer is alleged to be a young poet, is obliged to decide which of the two needs her more, or—better, perhaps—which of their lives would be more likely to be wrecked if she chose the other. It is a part that calls for a great deal of humor and sympathy (Katharine Cornell was once admirable in it), and if it is done, as it was last week, with neither of these qualities and with no apparent understanding of what was on the author's mind, it can easily be a disaster. Morell, the pastor, and Marchbanks, his adolescent rival, are also key figures, and if actual weakness and latent strength are transposed in them—another unfortunate effect obtained at the National—the play is practically without any meaning.

[3] *The New Yorker,* May 3, 1952, p. 66.

E. *Associations*

The use of words in certain combinations that have old and familiar associations always stirs up in the mind a recollection of the source of those associations. To one who knows the Bible, a phrase like "house of many mansions" is redolent with meaning. Phrases from Shakespeare, quotations from poets and orators that creep into the writings of others have a manifold meaning for those who recognize them. T. S. Eliot has written much of his poetry for the intelligentsia: his poetry contains allusions that only the very well-read understand.[4] We often hear a student say of an article or speech, "It went right over my head." What the student means is that he has no experience with which to match, and so interpret, the experience of the writer or speaker. But should Lincoln's *Gettysburg Address* be a frequent source of quotation in a speech or article, such phrases as "a new birth of freedom"; "of the people, by the people, and for the people"; and "full measure of devotion" would stir a responsive chord in any American. Such gems are given a new setting by the careful author, and so they glow with a new brilliance. Horace praises this skill in a poet:

> In words again be cautious and select,
> And duly pick out this, and that reject.
> High praise and honor to the bard is due
> Whose dext'rous setting makes an old word new.

The preacher who interweaves Biblical phraseology in his prayers and sermons arouses associations in the minds of his congregation that make his pulpit discourses doubly effective.

F. *World of Words*[5]

The world in which we live has a dual nature; it is at once a world of experience and a world of ideas. Demosthenes said that he learned words through experience, rather than experience through words. The college student, for the most part, reverses

[4] The student would find the discussion of T. S. Eliot in *Reading Poems* by Wright Thomas and Stuart Gerry Brown (New York: Oxford, 1941), p. 716 illuminating.

[5] J. Donald Adams has an interesting essay on words in *Literary Formulas* (New York: Duell, Sloan and Pearce, 1951).

that process; he is largely concerned with interpreting the word-symbols of other men's experience. There are, of course, exceptions: the student of medicine, for example, pursues a course of study that lies half in the world of experience, the laboratory, and half in that of words, the textbook. The laboratory and later the hospital ward provide the student with direct contact with reality, and clarify its relationship to his study of textbooks and medical journals. But for all this emphasis on the actual and the practical, the theoretical and verbal aspects of the subject are not neglected. During his freshman year the student usually wears out his medical dictionary in acquiring a vast new vocabulary.

G. *Words and Things*

It is important, then—particularly important for those of us who do not have the medical student's direct contact with reality—to remember that the word is not the thing. We must continually beware of identifying words with things. This danger of the projection of ideas, of the substitution of the symbol for the thing signified, lies always in wait for those who deal with words. The snare has been accomplished when we hear the fallacy, "Simon Legree was well named, for he was so cruel"; or, "Pigs are rightly named, for they are such dirty animals." Children who have had their mouths washed out with soap for saying a "dirty word" are likely to identify the word with the object. They become as afraid of the symbol as of the thing.

Raymond Moley once pointed out that any executive who is denied direct access to facts begins to deal with *words* as though they were facts:

> No one who has seen an executive at work over a long period has failed to see that as his power increases, he has less access to the true facts or true opinions of those who see him. In the crowded day of a President of the United States, almost every caller wants something. Those necessitous visitors are not going to say unpleasant things, however true. The President's comments and opinions are greeted with enthusiastic acquiescence. After some years of this, the President may think things are true merely because he says them. The windows of an executive's mind have a way of slamming shut.[6]

[6] *Vital Speeches,* X, No. 21.

Newspaper commentators as well are likely to fall into this error of living exclusively in a world of words. The best of them realize this danger, and go out "to see for themselves." If you follow the movements of Kaltenborn, Lowell Thomas, and Fulton Lewis, Jr., you know how industrious they are in keeping in contact with the world of things.

II. The Referent [7]

The object in the real world to which the word, label, or symbol refers is called the *referent.* When the speaker and the audience agree as to what a particular referent is, no difficulty arises. In the attempt to arrive at this desirable state of affairs paraphrase often proves helpful, and for this reason: that it simplifies or elucidates the problem of finding the referent. Paraphrase is concerned with the expression of an author's meaning in simpler or more familiar language.

A. *Three Classes of Labels*

1. Names

When we point out, or designate a definite object by a particular symbol, we do not leave much room for ambiguity. When the poet or any other writer speaks of tables, or handles of brooms, or silk umbrellas, we have a fairly definite idea of what he means by them.

In the following stanza from "Up at a Villa—Down in the City," Robert Browning labels common objects, and we follow him without much difficulty:

But the city, oh the city—the square with the houses! Why,
They are stone-faced, white as a curd, there's something to take the eye!
Houses in four straight lines, not a single front awry;
You watch who crosses and gossips, who saunters, who hurries by;
Green blinds, as a matter of course, to draw when the sun gets high:
And the shops with fanciful signs which are painted properly.

As a student of language you may be familiar with the classification of this mode of expression as the *concrete.* In addition, it

[7] See C. K. Ogden and I. A. Richards, *The Meaning of Meaning* (New York: Harcourt, Brace, 1923). See also Leonard Bloomfield, *Language* (New York: Henry Holt, 1933), chap. ix, "Meaning."

has been found helpful to establish two other classifications as an aid to the analysis of the difficulties we experience with language. The other two are *collections* and *abstractions*. Ambiguity creeps into our language as we move from one class to another.

2. Collections

When Kipling sang of the "white man's burden," he was lumping together a large portion of the human race and calling it "white." Who and what constitutes the "white race"? You can see how ambiguity creeps in. When we allow emotion or prejudice to take over the controls from the intellect, blindly lumping individuals in general categories—"the yellow race," "isolationists," "fascists"—we take a tailspin into obscurity. What is a "fascist"? We are extremely likely, moreover, to assign individuals and things to groups to which they do not belong. The latter is done consciously, of course, as well as inadvertently. Haven't you heard unscrupulous advertisers claim: "Many doctors agree that *this* (the advertised brand) is the best complexion soap"? The thoughtful person asks, "Which doctors?" Be on guard against this fallacious "appeal to experience"; learn to recognize and analyze the nature of the *collection*.

3. Abstractions

Such words as *liberty, beauty, justice, love* are nebulous terms. Almost any meaning can be read into them: the referent is not clear. As Edmund Burke said, there is no such thing as "abstract liberty." John Keats wrote, "A thing of beauty is a joy forever." One who reads that line must provide, from his own experience, a referent for the term, "thing of beauty." Keats' own referents are implied in the sights and sounds the poem goes on to list.

Thomas Erskine employs an abstraction when he declares: "Liberty, herself, the last and best gift of God to his creatures, must be taken just as she is; you might pare her down into bashful regularity, and shape her into a perfect model of severe, scrupulous law, but she would then be Liberty no longer; and you must be content to die under the lash of this inexorable justice which you have exchanged for the banners of freedom." And yet, we must not forget that men die for liberty, justice and freedom, even though they be—glorious—abstractions!

Ambiguity may be heightened or lessened by means of one word. A single word can change the complexion of an entire sentence—consider, to take the most obvious example, the difference that the inclusion or omission of a negative can make. Franklin Delano Roosevelt often wrote as many as twelve revisions of an address. He wanted to avoid ambiguity.

The process of abstracting, the consciousness of abstracting, it has been pointed out, is the basis of modern literary thought. Don Geiger says, "This consciousness prepares for an understanding of the nature of literature which is of great importance to the oral interpreter, helping him verify his intuition that oral interpretation is a valuable means of coming to understand literature." [8]

B. *Examples of Clearness and the Referent*

1. Keats [9]

With Keats the conception of what was poetical was almost always directed to the specific and concrete. He changed the following line ("Eve of St. Agnes"):

> A *drooping* lamp was flickering *here and there*

to

> A *chain droop'd* lamp was flickering *by each door*

and it can easily be seen that the second line is more vivid.

Endymion begins with the abstraction

> A thing of beauty is a joy for ever

but Keats goes on to define for the reader the things of beauty, such as,

> Such the sun, the moon
> Trees old and young, sprouting a shady boon
> For simple sheep; and such are daffodils

[8] See Don Geiger, "Modern Literary Thought: The Consciousness of Abstracting," *Speech Monographs,* XX, No. 1, March, 1953.

[9] For an interesting discussion of this aspect of Keats see Walter Jackson Bate, *The Stylistic Development of Keats* (New York: The Modern Language Association of America, 1945), p. 2.

With the green world they live in; and clear rills
That for themselves a cooling covert make
'Gainst the hot season.

2. Franklin Delano Roosevelt

Not by accident did the late President Roosevelt achieve his preeminence as a radio orator. His manuscripts were most carefully prepared. In the first draft of his *Fireside Chat* of April 28, 1938, he wrote: "Today I sent a message of far-reaching importance to the Congress. I want to read to you tonight certain passages from that message, and to add certain observations by way of simplification and clarification." But later he revised those lines, and so made his message simple and more direct: "Therefore, I have today sent a message of far-reaching importance to the Congress. I want to read to you tonight certain passages from that message, and to talk with you about them."

3. Lowell Thomas

Painstakingly, Lowell Thomas goes over the scripts written for him by his staff to make the words more meaningful. The radio script he was given to read at the time the children of London were being evacuated began as follows: "The parents were down to the station to see their kids off to the country." How much more tender was the version Lowell Thomas gave his listeners: "The parents were down to the station to see their little ones off to the country."

C. *Examples of Obscurity and the Referent*

1. Milton

Obscurity as a device to make the reader linger over a passage and to try to find the meaning is not to be despised. Does not William Faulkner do this in his long sentences? If the writer rewards us with a heightened meaning by the employment of obscurity we do not feel cheated. It is only when the writer uses obscurity to hide his poverty of thought that we rebel. Edmund

Burke calls attention to the use of obscurity by Milton in heightening the effect of death:

> The other shape
> If shape it might be call'd that shape had none
> Distinguishable, in member, joint, or limb;
> Or substance might be call'd that shadow seem'd;
> For each seem'd either; black he stood as night;
> Fierce as ten furies; terrible as hell;
> And shook a deadly dart. What seem'd his head
> The likeness of a kingly crown had on.[10]

2. Dylan Thomas

Concealment and disclosure, suspense and surprise underlie much of the poetry of Dylan Thomas. Try reading without any help the "Altarwise" sonnets, such as can be found in Elder Olson's *The Poetry of Dylan Thomas,* and you will run into difficulty because of the ambiguity of the referent. The modern symbolic poet, Elder Olson points out, is seldom content with symbols used by all of us every day but invents his own or borrows from unexpected sources. To quote Elder Olson, "What Thomas wanted was for the reader to begin with the idea that he *might* be speaking literally; to declare something a symbol or a metaphor only after it was evident that it could not be a literal expression; to find out, in that case, what kind of symbol or metaphor it was; and so go, eventually, *from the text,* to Thomas' meaning. This is the right way to read Thomas, and the right way to read anything; and it is the only right way." [11]

3. Robert Browning

Browning is said to have declared that he had not written his poetry as a substitute for a lazy man's cigar. That Browning is often obscure cannot be denied. But for an energetic, alert reader these obscurities often disappear and the reader is rewarded by the insight of Browning. Some of the more common obscurities are

[10] *The Works of Edmund Burke,* "On the Sublime and the Beautiful" (New York: Harper, 1846), p. 56.

[11] Elder Olson, *The Poetry of Dylan Thomas* (Chicago: University of Chicago Press, 1954), p. 62. See also Edith Sitwell, "Dylan Thomas," *The Atlantic,* February, 1954, p. 42.

due to (1) the elision of many of the smaller words of relationship which the reader can supply; (2) Browning's frequent use of parentheses and digressions; (3) casual references to little known facts of history and biography, but these can be ignored without ruining the dramatic effect. It adds little to the appreciation of the "Incident of the French Camp" to know the history of the storming of Ratisbon, and a knowledge of the geography of the country between Ghent and Aix adds nothing to the appreciation of "Good News"; and (4) Browning's style and form are not stereotyped and each new poem is a challenge to the reader's understanding and appreciation.

How difficult it sometimes is to find the referent of a word or phrase may be judged from the following quotation from Hiram Corson, on the meaning of a line from Robert Browning's poem, "My Last Duchess":

> It may be of interest, and of some value to many students of Browning's poetry, to know a reply he made, in regard to the expression in *My Last Duchess,* "I gave commands; then all smiles stopped together."
>
> We were walking up and down the great hall of the Palazzo Rezzonico, when, in the course of what I was telling him about the study of his works in the United States, I alluded to the divided opinion as to the meaning of the above expression in *My Last Duchess,* some understanding that the commands were to put the Duchess to death, and others, that she sank slowly and uncomplainingly away. He made no reply, for a moment, and then said, meditatively, "Yes I meant that the commands were that she should be put to death." And then, after a pause, he added, with a characteristic dash of expression, and as if the thought had just started in his mind, "Or he might have had her shut up in a convent." This was to me very significant. When he wrote the expression, "I gave commands," etc., he may not have thought definitely what the commands were, more than they put a stop to the smiles of the sweet Duchess, which provoked the contemptible jealousy of the Duke. This was all his art purpose required, and his mind did not go beyond it. I thought how many vain discussions take place in Browning Clubs, about little points which are outside of the range of the artistic motive of a composition, and how many minds are occupied with anything and everything under the sun, except the one thing needful (the artistic or spiritual motive), the result being "as if one should be ignorant of nothing concerning the scent of violets, except the scent itself." [12]

---

[12] Hiram Corson, *An Introduction to Robert Browning's Poetry* (Boston: D. C. Heath, 1889), Note to Third Edition.

III. Order of Words

Not only words themselves, but the order in which they are written, is important for meaning. Probably no English poet has ever taken more pains over a poem than did Thomas Gray. His famous *Elegy* was on his mind and heart and hands for fully seven years, for he began it at Stoke Poges in 1742, when he was twenty-six, worked upon it at Cambridge, and finished it, again at Stoke, in June, 1750, when he was thirty-four. It is said that the line, "The ploughman homeward plods his weary way," cost Gray endless thought. And well it might, because it is capable of many variations without injury to rhyme or sense:

1. The weary ploughman plods his homeward way.
2. The weary ploughman homeward plods his way.
3. The ploughman, weary, plods his homeward way.
4. The ploughman, weary, homeward plods his way.
5. Weary the ploughman plods his homeward way.
6. Weary the ploughman homeward plods his way.
7. Homeward the ploughman plods his weary way.
8. Homeward the ploughman, weary, plods his way.
9. Homeward the weary ploughman plods his way.
10. The homeward ploughman, weary, plods his way.
11. The homeward ploughman plods his weary way.

But this is unusual. Not many sentences can be written so that altering the order does not alter the sense. Note what happens when we change the sentence from "I'd like to see that" to "That I'd like to see!" Does sarcasm, satire creep into the expression? Note what happens to the sentence from Romans 10:15, "How beautiful are the feet of them that preach the gospel of peace, and bring glad tidings of good things!" when we say, "The feet of them that preach the gospel of peace, and bring glad tidings of good things are beautiful." Does not the idea of the beautiful suffuse the entire sentence when it comes first?

W. Somerset Maugham in *The Summing Up* tells us that he took care with the order of his words in a sentence. He studied Swift especially for word order and sentence structure, but came to the realization that what was natural at the beginning of the eighteenth century was most unnatural for the twentieth. The natural order in English is not the natural order in other languages. In English we say, "A white horse." In French it would be "A horse white." In English we would say, "I have had a good time." In German we would say, "I have a good time had." Remember, an author uses word order to convey his meaning.

Note in the following excerpt from Edna Ferber's best selling novel *Giant* how words are piled on top of each other, single words, words in groups, long words, short words in order to evoke the kaleidoscopic effect of the emotion of returning home. Practice reading it in various ways.

Leslie was in a state of chills and fever as the Southwest receded, then the Midwest was left behind and the train approached the Eastern Seaboard. Her father. The lovely rambling old shabby house. Lacey. Apple trees in bloom. Rich green grass in the meadows. Her mother. In exactly that order of her longing. The safari wound its way out of the train to the station platform in such a brouhaha of squeals shrieks chatter laughter tears Spanish English and Southern sweet talk that Leslie only tardily became aware of the actual presence of her sister Leigh. Lady Karfrey. "Leigh!" Her surprise was less than completely joyous. "Is Alfred with you?" She hoped not, she wanted only her own dear family for this home-coming.[13]

IV. Definition[14]

Now, as you attempt to find out what words mean, you become concerned with *definition*. Unless you have given some thought to the matter, you will no doubt be surprised to find that there are many different ways in which a word can be defined.

In the following passage from *Tarawa,* by Robert Sherrod, it is unlikely that you will have any difficulty in understanding what is meant. You have never experienced the events described, but your imagination can give you a fairly good representation of them:

Lines of corpsmen are bringing in the bodies as fast as they can find stretchers and wade into the shallow water. One Marine is brought in who has suffered the greatest indignity of all. His head has been blown off completely. His left arm is gone, and only a few shreds of skin hang on his shoulders. I thought I had become inured to anything, but I am nauseated by this sight. I turn to the big red-bearded Marine gunner

[13] Edna Ferber, "Giant," *Ladies' Home Journal,* October, 1952, p. 85.

[14] See Kenneth Burke, *A Grammar of Motives* (New York: Prentice-Hall, 1945), chap. ii, "Antinomies of Definition."

who is standing beside me and say, "What a hell of a way to die!" The gunner looks me in the eye and says, "You can't pick a better way." [15]

A. *By the Context*

There is one word in this passage that might cause you a little difficulty if you saw it by itself—that is the word *inured*. But because it is surrounded by other words, the meaning of which you know, you gather that it means *used to* or *hardened to*. The dictionary definition ("to accustom to something hard or painful; harden; habituate") would tell you the same thing. But in this case it was unnecessary to look the word up in the dictionary, because the *context* gives you its meaning.

We depend upon the context in everyday matters. A young man starting out to learn a trade does not carry a dictionary with him, but he soon learns, from the context of the conversation in which the terms of the trade are used by his fellow workers, what those terms mean. Again, we have all had the experience, at one time or another, of being asked the meaning of a difficult or ambiguous word; whereupon we asked, in turn, "How is the word used?" Much of the difficulty a foreigner has in translating English expressions into his own idiom lies in his inability to derive the meaning of an unfamiliar term from the context of the passage in which it is used. Instead, he looks up the word in the dictionary, and very likely obtains for it a meaning which, although perfectly correct, does not exactly fit the context.

B. *By Derivation*

If you are a student of biology, you may know, through actual physical contact with the instrument, what a microscope is; but even if you do not, a realization that the term comes from two Greek words meaning to see (*skopein*) the small (*mikros*) would reveal that instrument's function. Similarly, in coming across the word *passion* in the phrase *Passion Week,* you have a deeper understanding of its significance if you know that it is derived, ultimately, from the Latin *pati, passus,* to suffer. The word *photograph* takes on new meaning when we realize it comes from two words meaning *light* and *write*. Photography, then, is the art of

---

[15] *Time Magazine,* March 13, 1944, p. 102.

writing (i.e., producing images) on sensitized surfaces by the action of *light*.

C. *By Negation*

Another way in which we frequently arrive at the definition of a word is by ruling out what that word does *not* mean. If we do not know what a French horn is, but do know the names of the other instruments in the brass section of an orchestra we can discover by negation, in other words, by the process of elimination, what a French horn is. Here again we are trying to fasten a term to a fact of experience.

We are familiar with this means of definition from the use we make of it in solving such word puzzles as occasionally appear in *The Saturday Evening Post,* and other magazines. By means of eliminating the terms we do know from the ones we do not, we finally guess the meanings of words formerly unknown to us.

D. *By Examples*

We also define by means of examples. When we are confronted with terms the meanings of which are hazy or indefinite in our minds, we frequently use illustrations to make them clear. If you were asked to define a college or a university you would probably answer by naming a particular college (Oberlin) or university (Chicago) as a concrete example or embodiment of the term. If you should ask me what a comic strip is, I might reply by mentioning one or two, such as "Blondie" or "Boots and Her Buddies." If you were asked what is meant by iambic or trochaic stress, it is likely that you would illustrate these meters in order to answer the question. So, when you are attempting to recreate the meaning of a poem, it is often helpful to illustrate from your own experience or from the experience of others what is meant.

V. Changes of Meaning

Words change their meaning through the years. Some words gain new meanings while still retaining the old, for as new inventions come into use, the old terms are pressed into double duty to interpret the new experience. A glance at the page of an unabridged dictionary will reveal how many definitions a word can have. On the other hand, some words pass out of daily use, and become archaic. Still other words remain in use but take on different meanings. By way of illustration, take the word *wretch.* In Shakespeare's time it was one of the strongest terms of endearment in the language; its use implied deep affection, touched with a dash of pity. So in *Hamlet,* Act II, Scene II, the Queen says of her son: "But look where sadly the poor *wretch* comes reading." Again in *Othello,* Act III, Scene III, the hero, speaking of his beloved Desdemona, exclaims in a rapture of tenderness: "Excellent *wretch,* perdition catch my soul, but I do love thee!" Today, however, the word has lost its connotations of tenderness; and the pity is likely to be strongly tinged with contempt. The effective reader is a student of words and follows their history with deep interest.

The fact that words do change their meanings necessitates, from time to time, new translations of the Bible. This point was emphasized by a reviewer of the *Revised Standard Version of the New Testament:*

> A foremost aim, in previous revisions as in this one, has been to eliminate from the text the archaisms of 1611. Words wear out with use; meanings shift; idioms disappear. Many such things in the "King James" were no longer familiar; and when the popular reader guessed at what was said, the guess was not only apt to be wrong but sometimes it was ridiculous or even profane. In dealing with this problem the translators of 1881 and 1901 were not thoroughgoing, consistent, or sometimes even in good taste. All this the present version has made every effort to correct.[16]

VI. Connotation and Denotation

When we point out an object, we are *denoting.* "This is a typewriter; that is a chair." The *denotation* of a word is its actual meaning. When, on the other hand, the use of a word suggests or implies ideas that are in addition to its actual meaning, that word is said to have a *connotative* force.

De Quincey had some such division of labor for words in mind when he distinguished between the *literature of knowledge* and the *literature of power.* John Keats, student of medicine that he

[16] *The New York Times Book Review,* February 10, 1946, p. 5.

was, might have produced literature of knowledge; as a poet, he created, instead, undying literature of power. In order that the student of medicine may be able to denote with exquisite clarity, he never ceases to name, to denote. Penicillin is but one of the many new words that have been added to the medic's vocabulary in the past few years. The purpose of denotation is to promote agreement on meaning. Two people can agree exactly on what is meant by a standard, pica type, 1954 Royal typewriter. Connotative words or phrases, on the other hand, are subject to a wide variety of interpretations. No two people could possibly get the selfsame ideas from a reading of Robert Louis Stevenson's poem, "The Celestial Surgeon":

If I have faltered more or less
In my great task of happiness;
If I have moved among my race
And shown no glorious morning face;
If beams from happy human eyes
Have moved me not; if morning skies,
Books, and my food, and summer rain
Knocked on my sullen heart in vain:—
Lord, thy most pointed pleasure take
And stab my spirit broad awake;
Or, Lord, if too obdurate I,
Choose thou, before that spirit die,
A piercing pain, a killing sin,
And to my dead heart run them in!

Ideas are set going in your head by the words of this poem. What ideas, is dependent upon your past experience. The poet speaks of books. What books? Something you have read lately? A "pointed pleasure"—what is that? Undoubtedly, part of our liking for the poem is due to the fact that we can read so much of ourselves into it. Vagueness, suggestion, that leave much to the imagination, can be as much a source of beauty as are clarity and definition.

VII. Phrasal Patterns [17]

The fact that passages of prose seem to fall naturally into phrasal patterns has probably not escaped you. These patterns are

[17] For another discussion of this idea see pp. 153, 234.

not alike. In fact, their chief characteristic seems to be their variety. But these patterns do help the reader to grasp the thought. The pauses that create the design seem to be written or spoken into the very fabric of the piece. Daniel Webster's well-known line: "Liberty and union, now and forever, one and inseparable!" breaks up easily into well-defined phrasal units. The *Gettysburg Address* falls into patterns. The pauses are written into the address no less than are the words. These patterns appeal to us; we like them. Their rhythms stir up in us the responses the speaker wishes to arouse. The variety of rhythm in this masterpiece is another reason why we enjoy it: its melody is never dull or monotonous. One can stand on the deck of an ocean liner and watch the rolling of the sea for hours because of the never-ending variety of its rhythm. The beginner in writing and speaking tires his audience by the monotony of his delivery, because he has not yet learned to vary his rhythmical patterns. Just as one has to be educated to appreciate the complicated rhythms of orchestral music, so one has to be trained to hear and to reproduce the intricate rhythms of good prose and poetry.

A magnificent example of prose rhythm is to be found in the Authorized or King James Version of the thirteenth chapter of I Corinthians. You may remember that the mother in *A Tree Grows in Brooklyn* reads from the Protestant Bible rather than from the Douay Version because, she says, she likes the rhythm of its language. The King James translation is the work of masters of English prose.

In order to show how the changing of a word or a phrase can affect the rhythm of a passage, let us study several verses from the famous homily on Charity in different translations. First, consider these three verses from the King James Version (I Cor. 13):

1. Though I speak with the tongues of men and of angels, and have not charity, I am become as sounding brass, or a tinkling cymbal.

8. Charity never faileth; but whether there be prophecies, they shall fail; whether there be tongues, they shall cease; whether there be knowledge, it shall vanish away.

12. For now we see through a glass darkly; but then, face to face: now I know in part; but then shall I know even as also I am known.

Now consider the version of Edgar Goodspeed in his *An*

American Translation. Say these verses aloud and note the difference in rhythm:

1. If I can speak the languages of men and even of angels, but have no love, I am only a noisy gong or a clashing cymbal.
8. Love never dieth out. If there is inspired preaching, it will pass away. If there is ecstatic speaking, it will cease. If there is knowledge, it will pass away.
12. For now we are looking at a dim reflection in a mirror, but then we shall see face to face. Now my knowledge is imperfect, but then I shall know as fully as God knows me.

And now, in order that the shift in rhythm may be even more pointedly shown, consider this translation of Weymouth:

1. If I can speak with the tongues of men and of angels, but am destitute of Love, I have but become a loud-sounding trumpet or a clanging cymbal.
8. Love never fails. But if there are prophecies, they will be done away with; if there are languages they will cease; if there is knowledge, it will be brought to an end.
12. For the present we see things as if in a mirror, and are puzzled; but then we shall see them face to face. For the present the knowledge I gain is imperfect; but then I shall know fully, even as I am fully known.

Finally, the 1946 *Revised Standard Version of the New Testament* translates these verses in the following manner (you will note here an attempt to keep some of the beauty of rhythm of the King James Version):

1. I speak in the tongues of men and of angels, but have not love, I am a noisy gong or a clanging cymbal.
8. Love never ends; as for prophecy, it will pass away; as for tongues, they will cease; as for knowledge, it will pass away.
12. For now we see in a mirror dimly, but then face to face. Now I know in part; then I shall understand fully, even as I have been fully understood.

Compare these four versions. Which do you like best? Why?

In reading prose, keep your ear tuned to the way the phrases fall into patterns. The design of these patterns is governed by the thought being expressed. Take, for example, a paragraph from an article by President Nathan M. Pusey of Harvard University,

"Religion's Rôle in Liberal Education" and note how its very definite phrasal patterns emphasize its meanings:

What every young person seeks in college, from liberal education—whether or not he has articulated this—is self-discovery. What he wants most to know is what it means to be a human being, what is expected of him as such, what the world is and what are the options in it that lie before him, and how he is to get on with others. In short, the really burning question that faces someone trying to live through his mind is *what is he to do with his life?* What such a person wants—what we all want—is a meaning that becomes a motivating force in our lives. And when we ask this question, whether we are conscious of it or not, we have begun to think religiously, and have begun to ask of God. I see no reason not to admit that this is so.[18]

Is this the way you phrase it?

What every young person seeks in college
from liberal education
whether or not he has articulated this
is self-discovery.
What he wants most to know is
what it means to be a human being,
what is expected of him as such,
what the world is and
what are the options in it that lie before him,
and how he is to get on with others.
In short,
the really burning question
that faces someone trying to live through his mind is
what is he to do with his life?
What such a person wants
what we all want
is a meaning
that becomes a motivating force in our lives.
And when we ask this question,
whether we are conscious of it or not,
we have begun to think religiously,
and have begun to ask of God.
I see no reason
not to admit that this is so.

---

[18] From "Religion's Role in Liberal Education" by Nathan M. Pusey in *Religion and Freedom of Thought* by Perry Miller, Robert L. Calhoun, Nathan M. Pusey, and Reinhold Niebuhr, copyright 1954 by the Union Theological Seminary, reprinted by permission of Doubleday & Company, Inc.

In passages that are difficult to comprehend, try to arrange the words in rhythmical patterns. It is said of Lyman Abbott that he used to write with his pen in one hand while gesturing with the other. This practice helped him to mark off his phrases into understandable units.

VIII. Summary

Experienced writers work hard to make their meaning clear to the reader. An understanding of some of the devices they use, pointed out in this chapter, will aid you in grasping the meaning of the passage you are trying to read to others. Every moment you spend in analysis beforehand will make it easier for your listener to comprehend the meaning of the author. It is a truism that unless you understand the passage yourself you cannot make your listener understand it. Unless you understand the implications, the hidden meanings, the whisperings of the author, you will not pause in the right places; your inflection will be artificial and meaningless. A word spoken in one key, one tone of the voice, can mean something entirely different when transposed into another. Make sure you understand the meaning of the author yourself; only then can you make your audience hear the true progressions and modulations of his harmonies.

IX. Projects for Chapter V

1. Read and report orally upon one of the chapters in Irving J. Lee's *Language Habits in Human Affairs* (New York: Harper & Brothers, 1941). Be prepared to read aloud a few paragraphs to the class.

2. Read and report orally upon one of the chapters in Irving J. Lee's *The Language of Wisdom and Folly* (New York: Harper & Brothers, 1949). Be prepared to read aloud a few paragraphs to the class.

3. Read and report orally upon one of the early chapters in C. K. Ogden and I. A. Richards' *The Meaning of Meaning* (New York: Harcourt, Brace & Company, 1927). Be prepared to read aloud a few paragraphs to the class.

4. Read and report orally upon one of the chapters in S. Hayakawa's *Language, Meaning and Maturity* (New York: Harper, 1954). Be prepared to read a few of the paragraphs to the class.

5. Read and report orally upon Edgar Allan Poe's "The Philosophy of Composition." This essay may be found in a number of books. See

Rollo Walter Brown's *The Writer's Art* (Cambridge: Harvard University Press, 1924).

6. The style of Adlai Stevenson's speeches has been admired. Make a study of a few of them found in *Vital Speeches* and make a talk about it in class.

7. Read and report orally upon one of the chapters in Stuart Chase's *The Power of Words* (New York: Harcourt, Brace & Company, 1954).

8. Be prepared to read the following essay to the class. Can you think of other words that are being similarly misused?

Words Lost, Strayed, or Stolen [19]

ALICE HAMILTON, M.D.

Words have always been of great interest to me, and their misuse gives me a sense of more than discomfort: of actual indignation, as if a friend were being mistreated. I cannot claim to be a writer, but then a music critic is not a musician, nor an art critic a painter. I am a reader, so I feel I have a right to criticize authors, journalists, editorial writers, who, to my mind, are doing violence to the English language by surrendering precious words to base uses or by substituting cheap words for valuable ones.

Take some of the lost words. It is hard to see why the useful and simple "because," "since," "owing to," should have been lost, but apparently they have been pushed out by the would-be elegant "due to." This is no longer an adjective and does not have to qualify a noun; it is a preposition on its own, and its queer new use increases all the time, invading even the highbrow weeklies and the "slick" magazines. "Due to the fact that" is bad enough—such a cumbrous substitute for a simple "because" or "owing to"—but what are we to say to such sentences as these, which I have been picking up for a long time? "There were no homeless children due to a local wave of adoption." "He lost time from work due to drinking." "No accident can happen due to glaring headlights." "The amount of undernourishment is not large due to past plenty." "The man died soon after help came due to the injuries." Somehow "because" and "since" are rejected as lowbrow. The educated say "due to the fact that"; the uneducated, "on account."

Among the stolen words are some valuable ones, such as "advice" and "advise"—and that does seem a pity, when we have the perfectly good word "inform." We even have "tell," though I suppose no businessman's secretary could use words as simple as "tell" or "say." "Yours of the

[19] *The Atlantic,* September 1954. Copyright 1954 by the Atlantic Monthly Company, Boston 16, Massachusetts.

14th instant received and contents duly noted. In reply would advise . . ." But what shall we use when "advise" is completely surrendered to the business world? "Counsel"? But how formal. Business is also stealing another good word which it does not need but which we do. To be "interested" now is to be induced to buy or subscribe to something.

"Middle" seems to have strayed away, and its place is being taken by its brother "midst," which for some mysterious reason seems to impress itself on writers as more elegant. Webster says that "midst" implies a number of enveloping objects, as, in the midst of a forest; while "middle" is the part of an object which surrounds the center. But we do not keep to this rule, and "midst" is more and more pushing into the places formerly held by "middle," so that now we continually come across queer things such as these: "in the midst of the session"; "in the midst of the controversy"; even "in the midst of his life." Shall we come finally to "the midst years"?

"Satisfied" is straying, is pushing into the place long filled properly by "convinced" or even the lowly "sure." The result is sometimes startling. For instance: "The man's family is satisfied that he was murdered." Of course that may be literally true, but the family did not mean to tell the world so. Apparently the reporter who wrote about Bernt Balchen's unsuccessful rescue mission did not realize how callous was his statement that "Balchen is satisfied that none of the missing men is still on the ice."

The journalists have stolen another useful word which they do not need at all. "Argument" has a definite meaning and a dignified one. Then why make it take the place of "quarrel," "dispute," or even a "drunken brawl"? "The murder followed an argument in the saloon." What are we to use, for instance—if "argument" is lost—when scientists disagree about the atom bomb, or economists about a depression?

More amusing is the increasing rejection of "believe" and "think" in favor of "feel." Notice how often statesmen, journalists, commentators, tell you what the "feeling" is in the State Department, the Foreign Office, the Pentagon. Both American and English public men seem now to depend on their "feelings" about the most controversial questions. Does it show that we accept the dictum of the newer psychology that all our decisions are based on emotion, not on thought?

It is to me especially irritating to see the word "sick" straying so far into limbo, though it is not yet irreparably lost. Here we are slavishly following the English in rejecting it for "ill." The English seem to be too modest to use such coarse words as "vomit" or even "throw up," and to be "sick" in England is to do just that. I came across an amazing sentence in an English medical article. "The man was plainly very ill, but had not yet been sick." And just the other day I found this in an English novel: "I think I'm going to be sick. It's not anything I ate. It's that I have a delicate nervous system. Excitement makes me feel ill. I get sick with it."—"I should go and get it over."—"Be sick, you mean?"—"Yes, it's a wonderful feeling."

The trouble with "ill" is that it has so many bad associations: ill will; an ill wind; ill luck; ill used; "ill fares the land" and Annie of Lochroyen's tragic cry, "Oh woe betide my ill mother. An ill death may she die!" Yet more and more our newspapers avoid the vulgar "sick" and substitute "ill." Do not we all shrink a little when we read "an ill baby," "an ill woman"? And even the English could hardly say "a love-ill swain."

The word "obscene" has a definite meaning and there is no other word to take its place, but it is being stolen and made to serve as a simple hate-word. It is used to describe extreme cruelty, such as that of Buchenwald and Auschwitz, or the destruction of the Warsaw ghetto, even the Ku Klux Klan, the deliberations of the Politburo, the Dies Committee. Edna St. Vincent Millay used it to describe the Sacco-Vanzetti case; Borgese, the Fascist salute; Waldo Frank, the members of the Reichstag; the *Nation,* the Horst Wessel song. Mencken wrote that the Scopes trial was "so farcical it was almost obscene." Now, however detestable all these may be, we have no right to call them obscene and thereby rob ourselves of a useful word when we have no other to take its place.

English-speaking people have long prided themselves on having the word "home" in their language, while the Latins have to use some weak substitute like *chez soi.* But now we are letting "home" stray into low company so far that we are in danger of losing it altogether. This is because of our inveterate belief that if we put a nice word in the place of one we dislike ("mortician," for instance, the man who takes charge when we "pass away") we thereby change the thing we dislike to a likable thing. So we call an undertaker's establishment a "funeral home"; and all sorts of institutions for the sick, the insane, the delinquent, are called "homes" when there is and can be nothing homelike about them. When I lived at Hull-House, "home" was far from being a beloved word. A poor widow said to me, "I'll work my fingers to the bone before I'll let my children go to a home." The once beautiful word "asylum" is straying along the same down-path.

That brings us to the wickedest of steals, "disinterested." Think what a valuable word that is and how irreplaceable. The quality of disinterestedness is one of the finest of which human beings are capable, and there is no way to describe it in a single word except just that one. Yet out of sheer laziness we are letting it substitute for the perfectly adequate "uninterested," and this crime is being committed, not by the uneducated or the business world, but by "intellectuals" who know better. Editors ought to join a crusade against this unscrupulous steal and reject any manuscript that contains such outrages as: "The statement met with complete disinterest on the part of the assembly." "Unfortunately the man was disinterested and I came away depressed."

I will not go into the many forms of gobbledygook—legal, medical, business, sociological—that plague us. Bad as they are, they are read mostly by professionals only; they do not often invade literature. My own profession is pretty bad, but certainly less so than the legal. However, it is hard to understand why it has given up the good word "fever" and taken to using "temperature." You will hear not only a layman but a doctor ask, "Has he a temperature?" Well, if he has not he must have been dead a number of hours. And why should a patient be "ambulatory" instead of "up and about"? Why should we give up that convenient old word "bedfast"? Social workers have their own dialect and have rejected "poor." We may still use it provided it does not deal with physical poverty, but we must no longer speak of "the poor" except when we quote the Bible. We must say "underprivileged" instead—not "a poor child" but "an underprivileged preadolescent."

Changes in language that lead to greater clarity or conciseness or vividness—as some of our American slang does—are to be welcomed, but that is not true of any of the examples I have given. Maybe we need an "Académie américaine" to call a halt and rescue our lost, strayed, or stolen words.

CHAPTER VI

Voice and Speech[1]

I. Voice
- A. Breathing
- B. Phonation
- C. Resonance
- D. Quality

II. Speech
- A. Vowels
- B. Consonants
- C. Articulatory Problems
  - 1. Muscular Movement
    - a. The Tongue
    - b. The Lips
    - c. The Jaw
  - 2. Misplaced Sounds
  - 3. Processes of Articulation
    - a. Blending
    - b. Assimilation
    - c. Gradation
- D. Relaxation

III. Inflection

IV. Voice and Diction
- A. An Acceptable Diction
- B. An Agreeable Voice

V. Summary

VI. Projects for Chapter VI
- A. Correction of Common Faults in Vocalization Through Reading
  - 1. Monotony Due to Sameness in Pitch
  - 2. Weak Thin Voice
  - 3. Mumbling
  - 4. Too Loud a Voice
  - 5. Heaviness, Lifelessness, Lack of Flexibility
  - 6. Lack of Sense of Rhythm
  - 7. Too Slow Rate
  - 8. Too Rapid Rate
- B. List of Words for Pronunciation

We can best express the distinction between the two words *voice* and *speech* by saying that voice production, for the Japanese, is the same problem it is for the American; but that its use to produce intelligible utterance, in other words, speech, is different for each because of the language differences. The Japanese produces sound waves that result in *yama,* where we say *mountain;* and

[1] As collateral reading for this chapter the student might enjoy W. A. Aikin, M.D., *The Voice: An Introduction to Practical Phonology* (New York: Longmans, Green and Company, 1927). See also Elise Hahn, Charles W. Lomas, Donald E. Hargis, and Daniel Vandraegen, *Basic Voice Training for Speech* (New York: McGraw-Hill, 1952).

kodomo, where we say *boy.* Voice is the production of sound; speech, the articulation (joining together) of these sounds so that they become symbols of meaning to others. Let us first consider voice, under four headings:

I. Voice

A. *Breathing*

No doubt you have been told you should always "breathe from the diaphragm." What does this mean? Let us explain. Your lungs are encased in a rib cage, which can expand in three directions. This cage has as its base the diaphragm, a muscle attached to the sternum in front, to the rib arch at the side, and in the back to the spinal column at a point somewhat lower than its front attachment. The diaphragm, which is dome-shaped, rests on the upper organs of the abdominal cavity until inspiration takes place. Then it contracts, and in contracting pushes the abdominal organs down and forward, thus extending the waistline; the lower, or floating, ribs are raised at the same time. The diaphragm is the most important agent of inspiration. By its contraction the chest cavity is enlarged; whereupon the air pressure within the lungs is reduced to the point at which atmospheric pressure will force air in from the outside. In expiration the ribs fall back in place of their own weight; the elastic recoil of the distended lungs and body wall helps the contraction; and the muscles of the abdominal wall may be used to force the abdominal organs up against the diaphragm and lower surfaces of the lungs, thus producing the forced expiration needed for speaking and singing. In ordinary silent breathing we take breath in slowly and let it out quickly, each cycle being followed by a brief pause. But in speaking we take in breath quickly and expend it slowly. Silent breathing is involuntary; speech breathing, voluntary. It is the control of the breath to support the tone that is important to the reader in managing the rate and the force of speaking. In using the muscles of the abdominal region to control the outgoing breath, we say we are "breathing from the diaphragm."

If a reader gets excited, he is very likely to interrupt the normal breathing from the diaphragm and to begin to use shallow chest breathing. His breaths now become shorter and there is no muscular basis to provide him with the power needed for speaking. He may start using throat muscles to control the breath, and this is disastrous to the production of tone. Stage fright has been known to wreck the breath control of even the most experienced readers and speakers. Charles Reynolds Brown, former Dean of Yale Divinity School, confesses: ". . . I often find myself now all in a tremble when I am about to face an audience. I still have to go apart at times and put myself through a set of deep breathing exercises in order to gain poise and self-control before speaking" [2]

Watch a baby sleeping on his back and you will see that his breathing is waist-centered and not chest-centered. Watch the movement of a dog's flanks as it lies before the fire and you will find that most of the work in breathing is done by the diaphragm.

Practice saying *ah* softly, increasing the tone to the greatest volume you can give it, then gradually diminishing it to a whisper. Or try the following exercise, using two lines from Tennyson's "The Splendour Falls":

> Blow, bugles, blow, set the wild echoes flying.
> Blow, bugles; answer, echoes, dying, dying, dying.

Up to the words *answer, echoes,* use a strong ringing tone; but beginning with *answer,* use a lighter and lighter tone, till your voice dies away with end of the line. Try renewing the breath before each of the last three words, because to maintain the control necessary for sustaining light tones we need plenty of breath in the lungs.

Do this to test your breath control. Light a candle and blow the flame to the greatest possible distance without putting it out. Practice holding the candle at various distances from the mouth to increase your breath control. Hold one hand over the stomach and feel the contraction and expansion taking place there as you breathe.

Practice this: Place one hand just beneath the sternum and the other upon the small of the back. If the action in breathing is normal, you will feel an expansive movement, which is due to the contraction of the diaphragm. It will be stronger in front. To test the movement still further, call out your own name with considerable volume. Before uttering the word take a deep, full breath

---

[2] Charles Reynolds Brown, *The Art of Preaching* (New York: Macmillan, 1922), p. 83.

to bring into action the diaphragm, the great breathing muscle. Then, when the muscle is thoroughly contracted and giving the lungs strong support, utter your name. If the work is correctly done an outward pressure, both before and behind, will be distinctly felt.

Try this: Rest the thumbs on the hip bones and extend the fingers over the abdomen. Breathe out, toward the hands, and hold the breath for five counts; then let the air out in short, sharp shouts of *No!*, increasing the volume of each *No!* until the breath is spent.

B. *Phonation*

When you blow up a toy balloon, you have to be careful to pinch the neck of the balloon or the air will escape faster than you can force it in. Your thumb and forefinger serve as the *valve* on the balloon. Likewise, we must have a valve to control the entry and exit of air used by the lungs. The valve that holds the air in the lungs, or lets it escape, is called the *larynx*. The larynx rests on top of the *trachea,* the series of cartilaginous rings that extend from the pharynx into the lungs; you can feel its upper ridges with the fingers at the base of the throat. In the larynx are two folds of mucous membrane containing elastic tissue and muscle fibre, which operate like a valve to open and close the laryngeal cavity. These folds are the *vocal cords* or *lips*. If you place your hands together so that the wrists are against each other and extend the fingers, you have a picture of the V made when the valve is open. This V, or wedge-shaped cavity, through which the breath to and from the lungs must pass, is called the *glottis*. In ordinary breathing the vocal cords are relaxed and the glottis is freely open; for voice production, however, the vocal cords stretch moving closer together until their inner edges touch; whereupon they are thrown into vibration by the pressure of the outgoing breath, and thus set up the sound waves that we utilize in speech.

Above the vocal cords (which are represented by the thumbs in the gesture we have just described) is another set of folds or wedges, pointed upwards. These are the *false vocal cords*. Their major purpose is to prevent foreign particles, such as food, from falling through the opening. When the muscles of the throat constrict, these false folds sometimes spread and interfere with the normal production of sound from the true vocal folds, thus causing unpleasant voice quality.

Above the laryngeal section, near the base of the tongue, is the *epiglottis*. The epiglottis shunts food and water into the *esophagus*, the tube leading from the pharynx to the stomach.

How do the vocal folds vibrate? [3] Research is still being carried on to determine this. Do the folds vibrate alternately, in segments, together? How is the column of air set in motion as it passes the vocal lips? The sound waves, however produced, are changed into various patterns by the pharynx, the mouth, and the nasal cavities.

C. *Resonance*

We are all familiar with the different sounds it is possible to obtain by adjusting water to various levels in glasses and rubbing the tops of the glasses. In like manner, different tones are produced as the resonating chambers of the head, which are used for speech, are made smaller or are enlarged by means of various muscle movements. The nasal cavities stay pretty much the same, although the use we make of these cavities may vary. But we can change the size of the pharynx or the mouth at will. The soft palate, the tongue, and the jaw are used to regulate the size of these resonating chambers. In addition, the hard surfaces of the head—the teeth, the roof of the mouth, the jaw and other bones—serve as resonators as well.

We see the importance of the resonators to voice control when one of them is shut off. A cold in the head takes the ring out of the voice. Speaking through one's teeth with the mouth almost shut deprives the voice of the fullness of tone that the action of the mouth can give. Tightness in the pharynx or in the muscles controlling the jaw gives a brittle tone. These muscles must be relaxed.

Remember that the tone is supported by the muscles of the waist. Remember that the throat and mouth are parts of a tube through which the sound waves must pass. This concept will help you to keep these passages relaxed.

Increase the resonance of your voice by putting an *m* or an *n*

---

[3] The interested student will find Paul Moore, "Vocal Fold Movement During Vocalization," *Speech Monographs,* IV, 44, helpful.

before the vowel sounds and chanting *may, me, my, moe, moo.* Try this chant at different levels of your voice. Place your thumb and forefinger lightly on the bridge of your nose and see if you can feel the vibration as you speak.

Try these exercises:

a. Say *Mahmmmmm.* Put a strong hum on the end of this syllable.

b. Repeat three times on different pitches: *Mahmmmmm! Mahmmmmm! Mahmmmmm!*

c. In the following sentences, exaggerate the *m* and *n* sounds:

> "Show me the man who does not make mistakes, and I'll show you a man who does not do anything."
>
> —Theodore Roosevelt.

> "What is a cynic? A man who knows the price of everything, and the value of nothing."
>
> —Oscar Wilde.

> "The permanent vitality of a work of art does consist in its capacity for stimulating and transmitting pleasure."
>
> —Bliss Perry.

> "For the plain truth is that we here in America have written the greatest success story in human history. The plain truth is that on the record of performance we here in America have in a few years made socialism obsolete, shown that communism is nothing but a noisome stagnant pool of reaction."
>
> —Adlai Stevenson.

D. *Quality*

The individual, essential quality of your voice has been determined by nature. The size of your larynx, pharynx, mouth, resonating surfaces, and chambers can not be changed by you but you can change and improve your use of them. Exercises to improve resonance will improve your vocal quality. How interesting that the French call quality *timbre,* literally stamp, for your voice is your mark. Your friends recognize you by it. And the Germans have the word *klang-farbe,* literally tone color, which throws additional light on the question of what vocal quality is.

Students of voice have found it useful to distinguish eight different qualities of the voice. Listen to your own voice and see if you can recognize them when you use them.

1. *Normal.* The ordinary, predominant, characteristic quality peculiar to each of us, when the resonance is in the upper and back part of the mouth, has been called the normal. Other qualities are deviations from the normal.

2. *Orotund.* This word is derived from the two Latin words *os* (mouth) and *rotundus* (round). This quality has the purity of the normal but is deeper in resonance, and is greater in volume and strength. The reader employs this quality when he has a large room to fill with his voice. To produce the orotund open wide the cavities of the mouth, pharynx, larynx, and chest and so project and reflect the sound that it shall be clear and full. Radio and TV announcers employ the orotund quality.

3. *Oral.* This term is derived from *os* (mouth) and is a thin, weak, shallow quality with the resonance in the front part of the mouth. It is not full like the orotund. It is a front mouth tone and has little reinforcing vibration.

4. *Aspirate.* This term comes from *aspiro* (to breathe) and designates a breathy, whispered quality. The breath may be partly vocalized or wholly whispered.

5. *Guttural.* This quality explains itself. It is harsh and arises when one is choked with anger.

6. *Pectoral.* This term arises from *pectus* (breast) and is described as a deep, hollow, sepulchral quality. The ghost in *Hamlet* might use this quality.

7. *Nasal.* We are all familiar with this quality from listening to hillbillies. It is an impure, twanging quality that suggests laziness.

8. *Falsetto.* Andy Devine lets his voice break and outrun its natural compass.

II. Speech

A. *Vowels*[4]

The *vowel* is a speech sound uttered with voice or whisper and

[4] The student is referred to the opening pages of *Webster's New International Dictionary,* Second Edition, for a discussion of the sounds of spoken English.

characterized by the resonance form of the vocal cavities during its production. In American speech there are twenty-two vowel sounds. Of these, twelve are major vowel sounds; two are intermediate sounds not in general use; two are identified with *r;* and six are diphthongs. Of the major vowel sounds, one is an unaccented form of *u;* and two, *o* and *a,* also have diphthongal characteristics.

Vowels have been classified as *front, middle* or *back,* depending upon the place in the mouth where they are formed. If we bunch the tongue high in the front of the mouth, we get *e* as in *eve;* if we lessen the bunching, we go through the following series:

He	eve, meet, yield, ravine
is	pretty, been, English, myth
met	end, pet, said, many
there	sale, tale, male
at	cat, hat, man, sand
my	the first sound of the diphthong in *dine*

These front vowel sounds are easy to remember by recalling the nonsense phrase, "He is met there at my . . ."

The middle vowels are to be found in the two vowel sounds in *a*b*o*ve. The tongue lies flat in the mouth for the first vowel sound and is raised just a little for the second.

If we bunch the tongue high in the back of the mouth, we get the vowel sound in *who;* and as we lessen the bunching we get the following sequence:

Who	prudential, rudimentary, shoe, rule
would	foot, wolf, good, pull
throw	poetic, location, mosaic
water	talk, dawn, fault, trough
on	doll, undulate, connect
father	calm, ah, mama

These back vowels are easily remembered by means of the nonsense phrase, "Who would throw water on father."

Some of our problems in diction are caused by the substitution of front or middle for back vowels, and vice versa. Take *just* for example. Many students carelessly say *jist.* Why? Well, it is easier to say *jist* than *just.* You do not have to open your mouth to say it. The student who says *far* for *fire,* on the other hand, is substituting a back vowel for a front one. The student who says *feesh* for *fish* is substituting one front vowel for another. And the student who says *booshel* for *bushel* and *poosh* for *push* is substituting one back vowel for another.

Sometimes students tamper with their speech. One student of our acquaintance decided he did not like to say *class,* to rhyme with *mass,* so he substituted *clahs,* with *a* broad as in *fäther.* It is dangerous for students who from childhood have spoken one regional variant, like that of the Middle West, to decide that they do not like certain sounds in it and adopt others they like better. Conformity is the law of speech. The true purpose of speech is the conveyance of ideas; it must not call attention to itself.

We sometimes get aberrations of speech in the diphthongs, too.[5] The diphthong in the word *dine* must not be prolonged. The jaw should be relaxed. In the speech of some persons, you will note that the diphthong *ā,* normally heard in accented syllables when the sound is final, or before voiced consonants, as in *day,* is prolonged so that the sound becomes *dayee;* or is heard before voiceless consonants as well, as in *gate,* pronounced *gayeet.* There are regional dialects in which this practice is common.

The diphthong *ū* is, in the main, a combination of *y* or long *ō* and *o͞o.* The word *you* illustrates how we pronounce this diphthong. No word in English in which the *ū* sound is initial is without the *y* sound as an introduction. We say *yoonion* station, not *oonion* station. The *y* sound is also generally used after *b* (beauty), *c* (cube), *f* (few), *h* (human), *k* (kew), *m* (mute), *p* (pupil), *v* (view); frequently on the stage and by very precise speakers, after *s* (assume), *th* (enthusiast), *d* (duty), *t* (tune), *n* (new). General American speech permits a weakening of the *y* sound before *u* in such combinations as *lute, suit, flute, presume, illumine.* Usage must determine how strong and to what extent a speaker uses the *y* before *u.*

The diphthong *ou* commences with *ȧ* and finishes near *o͝o.* In such a word as *cow* we sometimes hear *că͝oo* or *cä͝oo,* instead of *cȧ͝oo.* We also hear this substitution in such words as *town* and *house* in some dialects.

The *oi* diphthong is usually pronounced correctly; but occasionally we hear *erl* for *oil.* Conversely, it is interesting to note

[5] A good companion book for this chapter is W. N. Brigance and Florence M. Henderson, *A Drill Manual for Improving Speech* (New York: Lippincott, 1945).

that the *oi* diphthong is sometimes substituted for the *ir* in *third* and *bird,* producing *thoid* and *boid.*

B. *Consonants*

A *consonant* is a speech sound characterized in enunciation by constriction of the breath channel, as distinguished from the *vowel,* which is identified by the resonance form of the vocal cavities.

Where are the consonants formed? This is a useful method of classification to employ in distinguishing sounds. You have no doubt noticed that many of the consonants are formed by the lips or by the lips and teeth. Six of the consonants represented in the following chart are so formed. And you have no doubt remarked as well that the tip of your tongue is very useful in consonant formation. In fact, nine of the consonants on the chart are formed by this portion of the tongue. As for the remaining consonants shown, the tongue blade is responsible for four, the back of the tongue for three, and the pharyngeal cavity for one.

CHART OF ENGLISH CONSONANTS ARRANGED ACCORDING TO PLACE AND MANNER OF FORMATION

	Bi-labial	Labio-dental	Tongue point	Tongue blade	Tongue back	Pharyngeal
Plosives	p , b		t , d		k , g	
Nasals	m		n		ng	
Fricatives		f , v	th ~~th~~	s , z sh , zh		h
Continuants			l			
Glides	w		r			
Affricates			ch , j			

If you will look at the consonant chart you will see that the consonants are further classified as *plosives,* or stops, wherein there is a brief pause caused by the tongue or lips constricting the breath channel; *nasal,* wherein the sound is emitted through the nose; *fricatives,* wherein the breath is forced through a small opening; *continuants,* wherein the sound is emitted in a generally unhampered flow through the mouth; and *glides,* which have already been discussed as diphthong elements. And then there are two instances of the *affricate,* which is defined as a stop followed by a slow separation of the articulating organs, so that the last part is a fricative. To this classification is added the pharyngeal *h.*

You have probably noticed that some of the consonants appear on the chart in pairs. This juxtaposition is to emphasize the fact that one of the pair is voiced and the other is breathed. In English the consonants *p* and *b, t* and *d, k* and *g, f* and *v, s* and *z, th* and *~~th~~, sh* and *zh, ch* and *j* illustrate this phenomenon of speech. In the word *papa* the *p*'s are formed in the same place—by the lips—as the *b*'s in *baby,* but they are breathed, whereas the *b*'s in *baby* are sounded. The foreigner studying English has difficulty in learning which consonants are sounded and which are breathed. He is likely to say *housses* instead of *houzes.* Similarly, careless speakers, even though English be their native tongue, say *priddy* instead of *pretty.* At the opposite extreme are the precisionists who, once their attention has been called to these distinctions, like those between *t* and *d,* put too much emphasis upon them. *Winter,* in their speech, becomes *win-t-er,* although the average American barely touches the *t* in pronouncing the word. When the Floating University stopped at Oslo, Norway, the Norwegian guide said, "Do you want to know how I knew you were Americans?" We said we did. He said, "You said it was *twenny* minutes past two. The Britisher would have said *twenty,* pronouncing the second *t.*" It is the observance of nice distinctions in these small matters of articulation that makes our speech noticeably good or noticeably poor. The ultimate aim of all speech training is to make the listener unmindful of speech. Speech is a means for the communication of ideas; it is not an end in itself.

The affricates *ch* and *j* are interesting. If you say the word *China* slowly, you will notice that the tongue goes to the roof of the mouth in the *t* position. The *t* is followed by an *sh* sound. The *ch* sound, then, is a combination of *t* and *sh;* analogous, in its shift from one consonant to another in the same syllable, to the diphthong in the domain of the vowel. The affricates, in fact, are sometimes termed "consonantal diphthongs."

The affricate *j* is the sounded partner of *ch,* which is breathed. In the word *edge* the *j* sound is a combination of *d* and *zh.*

C. *Articulatory Problems*

Having briefly reviewed the nature and function of vowels and consonants, let us now look at some of the problems that arise in putting the sounds together. We have already discussed a number of these problems, but there are others yet to be solved if we would improve our speech.

1. Muscular Movement

a. *The Tongue.* The secret of good articulation is quick contact and quick release of the articulatory organs. Poor diction is usually due to the inaccurate activity of the organs of the mouth, such as the tongue, the lips, and the jaw. Occasionally it happens that the defect in articulation is due to some malformation of these organs, but usually such difficulties can be compensated for by re-education. Society at large is beginning to realize the importance of good speech, and is instituting programs for speech education in the public schools.

There is an old adage to the effect that the tongue is the only instrument growing sharper with constant use. All those who speak and read aloud a great deal can well afford to pay attention to the exercise of the tongue, in order to make its movements as accurate as possible. The tongue is composed of seventeen different muscles, with the principal point of control located at the back. If you have never marvelled at the agility of the tongue, you should. Note how its muscular make-up permits its various contortions. Try these exercises to strengthen the muscles of articulation:

1. Try to touch the tip of the nose with the tip of the tongue.
2. Try to touch the ear with the tip of the tongue.
3. Bunch the tongue out of the mouth by pressing the tip against the upper teeth.
4. Bunch the tongue out of the mouth by pressing the tip against the lower teeth.

5. Touch the soft palate with the tip of the tongue.
6. Make the tongue stand on each of its sides, in turn.

b. *The Lips.* If you have ever examined with attention pictures of speakers or actors of renown, you have probably noticed the lines running from the corners of the nose to the corners of the mouth—evidence that the lip muscles have been well developed. The next time you go to the theatre or to a lecture to hear a well-known actor or speaker, sit down near the front. Note the activity of the lips. The average speaker would improve overnight if he started to use his lips as they should be used in speaking. Here are some exercises designed to strengthen the lip muscles:

1. Purse the lips and blow through them for thirty seconds. Time yourself.
2. Purse the lips; then sharply open the mouth as wide as you can and bring the lips back again together, sharply. Repeat five times.
3. Draw the upper lip down over the upper teeth as far as you can. Repeat five times.
4. Draw the lower lip up over the lower teeth as far as you can. Repeat five times.
5. Twist the mouth alternately to the left and the right. Repeat five times.

c. *The Jaw.* Exercise helps to develop the jaw muscles, too. Much of a poor reader's difficulty can be attributed to his failure to open his mouth when he reads; he tends, rather, to speak through his teeth. The tongue must then compensate for a lazy jaw. Normal articulation is thus altered to resemble the slightly muffled or lisping accents of the ventriloquist. Edgar Bergen, of course, purposely does not move his jaw, and makes his tongue do the work. Try these exercises to develop your jaw muscles:

1. Move the jaw up and down as far as you can and as fast as you can for thirty counts.
2. Move the jaw slowly from left to right.
3. Yawn, and feel the muscles pull.

2. Misplaced Sounds [6]

But not every difficulty arises from muscle movement. Much poor speech is due to mere carelessness in the production of words. We omit sounds that should be included, and we include sounds that should be omitted. A few of the commoner errors of this type will be listed here, but each student should watch his own speech carefully to discover the particular errors which he himself is prone to commit.

The *t* in *gentleman* and *university* is often omitted. The first *r* in *library* and *February* is sometimes carelessly dropped, as is the *a* in *realize* and *idea*. Several sounds are left out of *Saturday,* so that it is pronounced as *Sad'y*. The *wh* sound causes trouble because of the tendency to drop the *h*. Note that the *h* sound *precedes* the *w*. Say:

Not what we have, but what we use;
Not what we see, but what we choose—
These are the things that mar or bless
The sum of human happiness.

—RICHARD LOVELACE.

being careful to sound the *h*.

Here are some common words to which sounds are erroneously added to produce mispronunciations: *fillum* for *film; athaletic* for *athletic; larnynx* for *larynx; colyum* for *column; elum* for *elm; overhalls* for *overalls; preventative* for *preventive; incidentces* for *incidents*.

Furthermore, incorrect sound substitutions are sometimes made, as in the following words: *jist* for *just; git* for *get; Amarica* for *America; progum* for *program; libidy* for *liberty; reckonize* for *recognize; buhlieved* for *believed; anathing* for *anything; Warshington* for *Washington; unided* for *united; pitcher* for *picture; zoo-ology* for *zo-ology; becuz* for *because*.

These lists are not, of course, complete. Each student should prepare a list of his own careless mistakes in diction and make a conscious attempt to correct them. Habits of articulation picked up over a number of years are difficult to change because speech

[6] In connection with this section the student might enjoy reading R. C. Borden and A. C. Busse, *Speech Correction* (Boston: The Expression Company, 1925), chap. viii, "Defects of Carelessness."

is, ordinarily, a subconscious process. Success can only be obtained by constant vigilance in the detection and correction of errors.

3. Processes of Articulation

a. *Blending*. You have probably noticed that speech has a marked tendency toward short cuts and simplification. Intelligibility is the criterion. I have been teaching a couple of German refugees English conversation. The foreigner who is learning to speak English, even though he has a reading knowledge of the language, has a difficult adjustment to make—he must forget the *eye images* of the words. When these German students listen to conversation, they prepare themselves to *see,* in their mind's eye, the words as they appear in print, with neat white spaces marking off one word from the next. But when they *hear* these words, they do not recognize them, because of processes of speech called *blending, assimilation,* and *gradation*. From infancy, those of us who speak English as our native tongue have become used to the running together of sounds. Take the word *blending* itself. We do not say *blend ing,* in two distinct syllables; rather, we carry the sound of the *d* over to *blend* with the sound of *ing*. The same process works in the transition from one word to the next as in the transition from one syllable to another within the same word. Note the blending of sounds in the following sentence from Henry Ward Beecher: "A man's ledger does not tell what he is worth. Count what is in a man, not what is on him, if you would know whether he is rich or poor." The phrase *what is in a man* is run together, and so heard as *whatisinaman*. And, although we pause to enunciate the *not* distinctly, for emphasis, we blend the words that follow: *whatisonim*. Here the blending is carried so far as to drop the *h,* which is a weak sound in any case—in the Greek alphabet, from which our own is derived, there was no letter corresponding to the sound of the aspirate. Listen to the conversation about you, and note how often the *h* is omitted.

When we start reading from the printed page, we somehow get the mistaken idea that we must give every word the same time and stress. We "talk like a book." One reason why an audience may not like to listen to oral reading is that the reader, all too often, forgets this process of blending to which the ear has become accustomed. Memorized speaking often suffers from this same fault, for the speaker is likely to have memorized the words exactly as they appear on the printed page; consequently, his speech does not have the aural quality of ordinary conversation.

b. *Assimilation.* We may define this process as the conformation of a sound, usually a consonant, to a neighboring sound; as when the voiced *b* in *gooseberry* transforms the preceding *s* to a *z*. Such a process makes speech easier. If we pronounced the *s* as a breathed sound, we should have to stop short in the process of phonation and a hiatus would result. By voicing the *z*, however, we can continue without a break. Similarly, *issue* becomes, by assimilation, *ishu;* and *pumpkin* becomes *punkin.* If, in past tenses of verbs formed by adding *-ed,* the last sound preceding the suffix is voiced, we hear the *d,* as in *pleased.* But if the last sound is unvoiced, the process of assimilation transforms the *d* sound to a *t*. He *soaped* (*sōpt*) the windows.

English spelling was more or less frozen in the fifteenth century by the invention of printing. If spelling were logical, consistent, and scientific, it would follow spoken usage in this matter of assimilation. Obviously, it does not; we *say* "Grinnitch," but we *write* "Greenwich." Of course, assimilation can be carried too far, and so lead to careless speech. Then the phrase *did you eat* becomes *d'jeet.* Other examples of faulty speech due to assimilation are to be found in such expressions as *whatchadoin, lemme, ast, twelth, gimme.* In the observance or neglect of assimilation we find ourselves in one of the border states of linguistic usage. To go too far in one direction leads to pedantry; to go too far in the other, to carelessness.

c. *Gradation.* This name is given to the tendency for certain vowels and unaccented syllables in the English language to become obscure or neutral. Here again, too much attention paid to the spelling of a word in pronouncing it is a hindrance to good speech. Just as unskilled doctors often overtreat their patients, so unskilled teachers of oral reading often overemphasize every syllable. When we are cautioned to read as we speak, gradation is one of the principles we must observe. We pronounce the word *less,* when it appears by itself as an adverb, with distinct stress;

but when we find it in combination with another syllable, as in the word *useless,* we tend to pass over it very lightly.

Read the following sentence by Stevenson and note how, in doing so, you observe the principle of gradation: "So long as we love we serve. So long as we are loved by others I would almost say we are indispensable; and no man is useless while he has a friend."

We see this principle at work again in the pronunciation of the connective *and,* in combinations of words like *bread and butter*—the *and* becomes *'n*. Moreover, in the sentence, "If I had known that, I would not *have* gone," we say, "If I had known that, I would not *'ve* gone." The schoolboy who writes *of* for *have* in a sentence of this kind is making a mistake in spelling and in grammar, but not in phonetic transcription.

D. *Relaxation*

Part of the student's difficulty in developing a pleasing voice is the muscular rigidity present when he reads. His throat tightens. His mouth shuts. He speaks through his teeth.

How can you relax? Open up the throat by yawning. Loosen the muscles of the neck by dropping the head forward on the chest and then rotating the head slowly.

Relax the jaw by opening the mouth as wide as you can. Say *yah* as fast as you can, with the mouth opened as wide as you can get it. Alternately, open the mouth wide and suck in deep breaths through it.

Relax the tongue by a series of exercises, such as touching the soft palate with the tip of the tongue, sticking the tongue out of the mouth as wide as you can, turning the tongue over in the mouth.

Relax the lips by drawing them tight against the teeth and then puckering them to a fine point.

If you catch yourself tightening up as you start to speak, just say to yourself, "Relax!"

Practice reading aloud with a relaxed throat, tongue, mouth and lips. Read the following Psalm, using a relaxed vocal apparatus:

The Twenty-fourth Psalm

The earth is the Lord's and the fulness thereof; the world, and they that dwell therein.

For he hath founded it upon the seas, and established it upon the floods.

Who shall ascend into the hill of the Lord? or who shall stand in his holy place?

He that hath clean hands, and a pure heart; who hath not lifted up his soul unto vanity, nor sworn deceitfully.

He shall receive the blessing from the Lord, and righteousness from the God of his salvation.

This is the generation of them that seek him, that seek thy face, O Jacob. Selah.

Lift up your heads, O ye gates; and be ye lifted up, ye everlasting doors; and the King of glory shall come in.

Who is this King of glory? The Lord strong and mighty, the Lord mighty in battle.

Lift up your heads, O ye gates; even lift them up, ye everlasting doors; and the King of glory shall come in.

Who is this King of glory? The Lord of hosts, he is the King of glory. Selah.

III. Inflection

This word comes from the Latin verb *inflectere,* meaning *to bend,* a derivation which is expressive of the meaning the word should have for students of speech. We must "bend" or modulate every syllable of English. In song we do not modulate the syllables of our words, but we do so in speech. We can "bend" our voices up, and we can "bend" them down. This sliding up or sliding down on a syllable is called, naturally enough, the *slide.* The length of the slide often gives overtones to the meaning of a word. Try the following exercises to help you master the slide:

a. Start as low as your voice will allow and go up in pitch as far as you can on the word *up,* thus:

UP UP UP UP

b. Start as high as your voice will allow and come down in pitch as far as you can on the word *down,* thus:

c. When we use both the rising inflection and the falling inflection on the same syllable we have the wave which is used to express many different emotions, such as, surprise, wonder, doubt, sarcasm. Try it on such words as *so, well, yes, sure,* et cetera. This is also known as the compound stress.

Another means of modulating the voice is the *step.* The distance between the steps in the voice can affect the meaning of what is being said. We indicate our emotions by the way we employ them. We can, for example, express either deliberation or irritation merely by the length of the steps employed in uttering such a sentence as, "Well, I don't know." If we say:

Well,
I
don't
know . . .

we indicate that we are not quite so sure, but that we will give the matter thought. But if we say, without much if any employment of the step:

WELL, I DON'T KNOW!

we suggest a state of irritation.

Say this sentence from Edith Wharton—

> "There are two ways of spreading light:
> to be
> The candle or the mirror that reflects it."

according to the following step pattern:

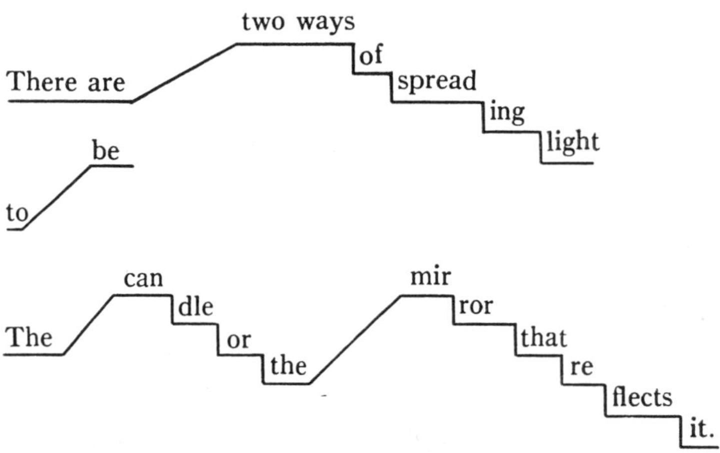

Here is an amusing poem by Thomas Moore satirizing an orator who had only two steps to his voice. Read the poem, making it clear what those two steps were:

Orator Puff

THOMAS MOORE

Mr. Orator Puff had two tones to his voice,
The one squeaking *thus,* and the other down *so;*
In each sentence he uttered he gave you your choice,
For one half was B alt, and the rest G below.
    Oh! Oh! Orator Puff
One voice for an orator's surely enough!

But he still talked away, spite of coughs and of frowns,
So distracting all ears with his *ups* and his *downs,*
That a wag once, on hearing the orator say,
"My voice is for war"; asked him "Which of them, pray?"
    Oh! Oh! Orator Puff,
One voice for an orator's surely enough!

Reeling homeward one evening, top-heavy with gin,
And rehearsing his speech on the weight of the crown,
He tripped near a saw-pit, and tumbled right in,—
"Sinking fund," his last words as his noddle came down.
    Oh! Oh! Orator Puff,
One voice for an orator's surely enough!

"Oh, save!" he exclaimed in his he-and-she tones,
"Help me out! help me out!—I have broken my bones!"
"Help you out!" said a Paddy who passed, "what a bother!
Why, there's two of you there; can't you help one another?"
    Oh! Oh! Orator Puff,
One voice for an orator's surely enough!

In conversation the average person speaks with pleasing modulation, but give him a script to read and the pull of the printed word exercises a strange compulsion which obliges him to drone on in a dead monotone from the beginning of a sentence to the end. The eye dominates the ear. All change of pace, melody, the dynamics of voice production are forfeited in the act of reading. To avoid this, practice listening to your own voice as you read. And, of course, make records of your voice and study them with a critical ear for its modulations.

IV. Voice and Diction

A. *An Acceptable Diction*

If your language is wholly acceptable to the ear of the public, you are indeed fortunate—and a *rara avis*. For most of us Americans have sounds and words in our speech and our vocabulary that are offensive to the general ear. The new hypocrisy, as far as speech is concerned, makes the college student prefer to be a "regular guy" than to speak with any suggestion of culture, if that implies attention to diction. If all Joe College's friends say "jist," Joe wants to say "jist" too. The same is true of "git." Teachers of speech wear out many pencils calling attention to just these two mispronunciations. Similarly, the long *u* in such words as *duty* and *duke* sound "sissy" to Joe if pronounced in the same way as the *u* in *putrid*. And yet, he would not dream of saying *boogle* or *moosic* for *bugle* or *music*. Make certain that this kind of inverted snobbism has no place in *your* speech.

Watch the *t* in such words as *pretty* and *beautiful:* It so easily becomes a *d*. Again, the *h* in *which* and *where* and *what* as well as in the other *wh* words is carelessly omitted by many people; they should remember that *wh* is really *hw*. It is helpful, too, in improving one's speech, to remember that there are only four *e's* in English that have the short *i* sound; these are illustrated by the words

English, been, pretty, breeches. Much of the time of the teacher of a class in oral reading is taken up with questions of diction such as these; pay heed to these discussions and correct your own speech so that it conforms to the norm of good diction in your area. Today it is generally agreed that although a good voice is a great asset, an "at-homeness" in the English language is still more important. We all know men, and some women, who possess splendid radio voices, but whose knowledge of English pronunciation and grammar is so faulty that they can not be trusted before the microphone.

B. *An Agreeable Voice*

Graham McNamee is typical of the radio announcers who first gained prominence in this new profession. Like Milton Cross, he had originally been trained for the concert platform. Singing lessons, though not absolutely necessary for the radio speaker, can be helpful in making the voice more agreeable. The microphone is especially friendly to the baritone or contralto voice, but it is possible for the bass and the soprano to achieve success in radio work as well; these voices, however, require more cultivation to develop their powers of expression. If the bass drags "in the mud" or drones like a bagpipe, he needs to lift his voice up, so that modulation can be brought into play. The soprano must develop her lower tones, in order to express a wide range of meaning.

In our impatience to master a new medium, we forget that the men who have reached the top in that medium often had serious problems to overcome. The following experience of Raymond Gram Swing should be of great interest to the beginner:

> Swing became, in 1925, chief of the London Bureau of the *Philadelphia Public Ledger.* The next nine years were perhaps the happiest of his life. He became recognized as one of the best of America's foreign correspondents. Suddenly in 1934, the *Ledger* liquidated its entire foreign staff. At 47, Swing was again out of a job.
>
> He had become a radio enthusiast and decided to find work in that field. One of his first moves in returning to the U. S. was to sample the rich fare of American radio. After an hour of suffering, he vowed that, even if he and his family had to starve, he would not speak over the radio with the bright glittering artificiality then thought proper even

for a news commentator. He would insist on speaking like a man. During 1934 and 1935 Columbia let him speak like a man, analyzing foreign affairs, but his appearances were infrequent and he was poorly paid. Finally, a vice president decreed that he would have to talk like a radio performer or get off the air. Swing got off the air.

For a while he earned a lean living as a free lance writer and contributing editor to *The Nation*. Hardened though he was by adversity, he was discouraged, until "a clergyman with a beautiful organ of voice" told him he could improve his radio delivery and still speak like a human being by the simple expedient of whispering ten minutes a day.

Swing whispered hoarsely and industriously every day for weeks. He made recordings of his voice, and for hours his long, lanky form was stooped before a phonograph, his features gaunt and somber as he studied the inflections of the voice that was to bring him fame. Within a few months he was hired by the Mutual Broadcasting System and his fortune began to improve.[7]

V. Summary

Most of us are not really conscious of the fact that we possess a voice, nor have we any idea that it should be a distinct part of our personality. We have spoken imitatively all our lives. We often hear daughters speaking exactly like their mothers, and sometimes boys who telephone for dates cannot distinguish between two sisters' voices. We tend to talk like those around us. Consequently, we go through life with thin voices, or throaty voices, or breathy voices. And yet there is no part of the personality that will improve so much with a little care as will the voice. Why, then, is this care so seldom given? Perhaps no one has ever told us that our diction is faulty and our voices poorly produced; so we continue to echo the speech errors of our associates, adding to them some all our own. Surely, however, it is worthwhile to spend a little time in this matter of speech analysis, for the way we speak undoubtedly affects the position in life we attain. As Shakespeare said in another connection: "Mend your speech a little, lest you may mar your fortunes."

And yet, having said all this, we hasten to add that nowhere is it so important for art to conceal art as in this attempt at speech

[7] *The Reader's Digest,* January, 1943. The article originally appeared in *The New Yorker.*

improvement. No one must ever suspect that we have studied hard and long to master good voice production, or that we have given painstaking attention to diction. Our speech drills must be like the pianist's five-finger exercises, which are to be inferred only from the perfection of his playing. Henry Ward Beecher, greatest of American preachers, testifies to the importance of drills in the formation of his own voice; but he too affirms that their purpose and result were to produce "not a rhetorical manner, but a flexible instrument":

If you desire to have your voice at its best, and to make the best use of it, you must go into a drill which will become so familiar that it ceases to be a matter of thought, and the voice takes care of itself. This ought to be done under the best instructors, if you have the opportunity; if not, then study the best books and faithfully *practice* their directions. It was my good fortune, in early academical life, to fall into the hands of your estimable fellow citizen, Professor Lovell, now of New Haven, and for a period of three years I was drilled incessantly (you might not suspect it, but I was) in posturing, gesture, and voice-culture. His manner, however, he very properly did not communicate to me. And manner is a thing which, let me remark, should never be communicated or imitated. It was the skill of that gentleman that he never left a manner with anybody. He simply gave his pupils the knowledge of what they had in themselves. Afterward, when going to the seminary, I carried the method of his instructions with me, as did others. We practiced a great deal on what was called "Dr. Barber's System," which was then in vogue, and particularly in developing the voice in its lower register, and also upon the explosive tones. There was a large grove lying between the seminary and my father's house, and it was the habit of my brother Charles and myself, and one or two others, to make the night, and even the day, hideous with our voices, as we passed backward and forward through the wood, exploding all the vowels, from the bottom to the very top of our voices. I found it to be a very manifest benefit, and one that has remained with me all my life long. The drill that I underwent produced, not a rhetorical manner, but a flexible instrument, that accommodated itself readily to every kind of thought and every shape of feeling, and obeyed the inward will in the outward realization of the results of rules and regulations.[8]

---

[8] *Yale Lectures on Preaching,* First Series (New York: J. B. Ford and Company, 1872), p. 134.

VI. Projects for Chapter VI

A. *Correction of Common Faults in Vocalization Through Reading*

1. Monotony Due to Sameness in Pitch

Pitch refers to the places on the musical scale of our speech notes. If too many of them are at the same level, or if there is constant repetition of the same speech melody or pattern, our voices will sound monotonous and sing-song. If you have been criticized for this fault, try reading the selections below. Do not be afraid to respond. Let yourself go! Abandon yourself to the mood. Listen to the sound of your own voice. Consciously strive for vocal variety, for ups and downs in pitch. Ask your instructor and your classmates if you are overcoming monotony. If possible, make a record of your voice on a recording machine at regular intervals, and note any improvement. Here are the selections to read:

a. Robert Service, "The Cremation of Sam McGee," p. 324.
b. Edna St. Vincent Millay, "God's World," p. 361.

These selections demand variety of pitch. Practice wide slides and long steps in rendering them.[9]

2. Weak Thin Voice

In reading the following selections, let the voice boom out. Open the mouth wide on the open vowels like ō, and o͞o, and ä as in *father*. Do not strain the throat, but be vigorous. Use your arms, sway your body, shout at the skies:

a. William Rose Benét, "Jesse James," p. 220.
b. Carl Sandburg, "Chicago," p. 369.
c. Alfred Lord Tennyson, "Break, Break, Break," p. 381.

3. Mumbling

If you are not understood because you are prone to mumble, work on the prose selections suggested at the close of Chapter I. In practicing these exaggerate enormously the distinctness of utterance. Make each syllable crystal clear by your enunciation. Overdo; the happy medium will come soon enough. What sounds exaggerated to you, with your

[9] The student may wish to go more deeply into the subject of speech melody. See Louise Zucker, "Psychological Aspects of Speech Melody," *Journal of Social Psychology*, February, 1946, p. 73.

own careless speech habits, will not sound exaggerated to other ears. Watch the "gonnas," the "jists," the "gits," and the weak labial sounds, as in *prob'ly.*

4. Too Loud a Voice

Over-distinctness, however, pedantic precision, is annoying; and so is the voice that is too loud, the "lion's roar," when such volume is quite inappropriate to the sentiments the reader is trying to convey. A great deal of declamatory speaking and debating is of this storm and castle type. Tone down the amount of volume in the following selections. See how gently and softly you can read them. Respond first to the tenderness of the sentiment. Cultivate a smooth-sounding voice:

a. Charles Lamb, "The Old Familiar Faces," p. 356.
b. Conrad Aiken, "Bread and Music," p. 330.
c. William Blake, "The Tiger," p. 336.
d. John Keats, "When I Have Fears," p. 355.

5. Heaviness, Lifelessness, Lack of Flexibility

If your reading lacks animation, it may be due to your inability to grasp the sense of the passage. Your imagination is not active enough in creating the scene for you. Kipling's *Barrack Room Ballads,* for example, demand changes in tempo, melody, and quality. Try saying the following selections in different keys. Go to the piano and strike a note; then begin the selection on that note:

a. William Ernest Henley, "Invictus," p. 350.
b. Edward Rowland Sill, "The Fool's Prayer," p. 327.
c. Vachel Lindsay, "The Congo," p. 315.
d. Rudyard Kipling, "Tommy," p. 311.
e. Rudyard Kipling, "Gunga Din," p. 309.

6. Lack of Sense of Rhythm [10]

If it has been pointed out to you that you seem to lack a sense of rhythm, the following suggestions may help you. Do you dance? Do you enjoy music? Listen to music on the radio and beat out the time with your foot or your hand. Feel a muscular response to the music. It may be helpful to join a choral verse-speaking group. Try reading the fol-

[10] The advanced student might like to read Richard D. T. Hollister's study, "Relation between Hand and Voice Impulse Movements," *Speech Monographs,* IV, 75.

lowing selections and respond to their swing. It is sometimes well to have one of your friends who possesses a good sense of rhythm read the selection, and then to imitate his delivery.

a. Vachel Lindsay, "General Booth Enters into Heaven," p. 316.
b. Robert Browning, "Prospice," p. 339.
c. Vachel Lindsay, "John Brown," p. 313.

7. Too Slow Rate [11]

If this is your difficulty, listen to radio commentators and study their rate of speech. See if you can discern any variation in the rate employed by Lowell Thomas as he narrates various parts of his program. Buy a record of John Barrymore's rendition of various passages from *Hamlet* and note how he changes his rate of speech to suit the changing thought. Imitate his reading. Memorize a particular passage thoroughly, so that you do not have to worry about the words, and then give the passage in the Barrymore manner. Practice the following selections, which demand a fairly rapid rate:

a. Robert W. Service, "The Shooting of Dan McGrew," p. 321.
b. Sir John Suckling, "Why So Pale and Wan?" p. 380.
c. Walt Whitman, "Beat! Beat! Drums!", p. 388.

8. Too Rapid Rate

Perhaps the commonest fault in reading is too fast a rate. This defect is no doubt due to the reader's lack of confidence in himself. Work up a feeling of security as you read. Believe that what you have to give your audience is of the utmost value to them. Read slowly and deliberately. Do not read "casually." *Think* every syllable. Try timing yourself in reading a selection. Read for three minutes and see how much ground you cover. Then slow down, and see if you can consume three minutes with about two-thirds of the material you previously read. Pause over words and phrases. Grasp the thought of the next sentence before you read it. In every way try to make yourself take more time. Try these selections:

a. Robert Louis Stevenson, "The House Beautiful," p. 378.
b. Wallace Stevens, "Peter Quince at the Clavier," p. 377.
c. Marianne Moore, "In Distrust of Merits," p. 363.

---

[11] Another article of interest to the advanced student on this subject is Jack C. Cotton's, "Syllabic Rate: A New Concept in the Study of Speech Rate Variation," *Speech Monographs,* IV, 112.

B. *List of Words for Pronunciation Drills*

acclimate
address
admirable
adult
advertisement
alias
allies
Alma Mater
alternate
amenable
anomaly
applicable
asked
association
athletics
attacked
bade
banquet
barbarous
blatant
bouquet
bravado
calliope
cerebral
chasm
chastisement
chiropodist
clique
column
combatant
comparable
corps
coupon
creek
cynosure
data
deaf
debut
decade
decadent
decorative
decorous
defect
deleterious
deluge
depot
despicable
desuetude
discretion
drama
dramatist
economic
economist
eczema
ego
either
eleven
envelope
err
erudition
esoteric
exponent
exquisite
extraordinary
facet
facetious
financier
forehead
formidable
frequented
gala
gallant
gamut
genuine
gesture
government
granary
gratis
grievous
grimace
guarantee
harass
height
heinous
hilarious
horizon
hover
illustrative
incognito
inexorable
infamous
infantile
inquiry
integral
inveigle
irrelevant
irreparable
isolate
issue
juvenile
lamentable
larynx
longevity
luxury
manor
medieval
mischievous
often
orchestra
parent
penalize
portentous
precedence
preferable
projectile
psychiatry
psychiatrist
pulpit
rabbinate
ration
regime
research
respite
resume
romance
saline
schism
senile
slough
solace
subtle
suggest
superfluous
theatre
toward
tremor
tribune
vaudeville
vehement
vehicle
vice versa
virile
viscount
vivacity
wandered
yacht
zoology

CHAPTER VII

Some Problems in Technique

I. Skill in Reading

II. Grouping of Words

III. Distinctness

IV. Communication

V. Distractions

VI. Variety

- A. Variety in Vocal Method
  1. Range of the Speaking Voice
  2. Steps and Slides
  3. Speech Patterns
- B. Variety in Tempo
  1. The Pause
  2. Change of Pace
- C. Variety in Volume and Force

VII. Bodily Action

VIII. Interpreting Emotions

IX. Summary

X. Projects for Chapter VII

I. Skill in Reading

As a preparation for oral reading, we cannot stress too strongly nor emphasize too highly the need to develop a capacity for thinking and feeling deeply. The reader should saturate himself with the ideas and moods of a piece of literature until he feels an impulse to share them with an audience; and then, in yielding to this impulse, should arouse in his listeners, by the way he handles his voice and body, ideas and associations similar to his own.

Of course, both voice and body must be trained to respond to such an impulse at a moment's notice. The voice must be a flexible instrument, developed to its fullest capacities, nor must the body fail to do its share in projecting the message. Through practice one must learn how to stand up before an audience, book in hand, and to feel relaxed and comfortable in that posture. One must train one's self to glance down at the book for the next phrase while speaking the words preceding it, without cramping one's vocal apparatus in doing so.

A reader who is scared stiff when he faces an audience, so scared, in fact, that the rhythm of his breathing is upset, can not get much variety of utterance. Here training and constant practice stand one in good stead in conquering that momentary flutter of fear that grips most speakers and readers when they appear before an audience. The oral reader must learn how to control himself before he can ever learn to control an audience. Edna St. Vincent Millay, for example, employed a regular routine of breathing exercises before she went on the platform. Nor is this piece of advice to be scorned: "Begin low, proceed slow; rise higher, take fire; when most impressed, be self-possessed; to spirit wed form, sit down in a storm."

We may understand a piece of literature ever so thoroughly; we may respond to it fully, mentally and emotionally; and still be unable to read it aloud in such a way as to convey its full meaning. Our voices, our bodies, may nullify our attempts to do so. It is the purpose of this chapter to examine some of the factors and skills involved in the successful practice of "speaking-reading."

II. Grouping of Words

As you read aloud, note the way in which you group your words, where you put your pauses. This principle of grouping or phrasing is of enormous psychological importance. The process of feeding the mind of the audience with exactly the right number of words at a time may make all the difference between lucidity and incomprehensibility, between being easy to listen to and being irritatingly choppy. It is this fault of poor grouping that is to be deplored, particularly, in the radio speech-reader, since there all must be accomplished by voice alone and no assistance from facial expression and gesture is possible.

But, granted this, the question inevitably arises: Are not the marks of punctuation a sufficient guide to grouping? It is easy to show that, in general, more pauses are necessary in what might be called oral punctuation than are indicated by the commas, semicolons, periods, et cetera, of the printed page. In fact, the chief defect of most oral reading is the tendency to run too many words together without a pause.

For example, consider a few sentences from Ernie Pyle's story of Captain Waskow (see p. 296):

In this war I have known a lot of officers who were loved and respected by the soldiers under them. But never have I crossed the trail of any man as beloved as Capt. Henry T. Waskow, of Belton, Tex.

Capt. Waskow was a company commander in the 36th Division. He had led his company since long before it left the States. He was very young, only in his middle twenties, but he carried in him a sincerity and gentleness that made people want to be guided by him.

It would be a young man in a hurry, with a good pair of lungs, who attempted to give the entire first sentence of this quotation in one breath. And even if such an agitated chap did accomplish that feat, he would merely succeed in ruining the emotional effect of the passage. Yet there *are* people under the false impression that, in reading aloud, they need pause only at printed marks of punctuation, and who, consequently, would be entirely unaware of the implied rests and half-stops in a sentence like this first sentence of Ernie Pyle's, which contains no commas, no dashes, no semicolons. Most assuredly, such reading is not conducive to ease in understanding the author's meaning.

Sometimes nervousness causes a student to sheer away at the mere thought of pausing. He must hear the sound of his own voice continuously or he becomes alarmed. To him let us say at once that pauses for grouping, although essential to the mental activity of one's listeners, are usually very brief; secondly, and this above all, that such pauses are not cessations of thought. Rather, they are points at which thinking is intensified. The listener thinks over what has just been said and prepares to relate it to what will be said next; at the same time, he integrates it with his own thinking and emotions. As someone has said, "When in a hurry, skip everything but the pauses."

Considerable variation is permissible in grouping. Two people may not group a passage in exactly the same way and yet give equally clear readings. The same person may not use identical grouping in repeating a selection. Taking such variability into consideration, the grouping of the Ernie Pyle quotation might well run something like this:

In this war / I have known a lot of officers / who were loved / and respected / by the soldiers / under them. . . . But / never have I crossed the trail / of any man / as beloved / as Capt. Henry T. Waskow, / of Belton, / Tex.

Capt. Waskow / was a company commander / in the 36th Division. He had led his company / since long before it left the States. / He was very young, / only in his middle twenties, / but he carried in him a sincerity / and gentleness / that made people / want to be guided / by him.

III. Distinctness

You know people who mumble their words in conversation. You have to "beg pardon" constantly. Annoying enough, isn't it? But when a speaker or reader does the same thing, you must multiply that annoyance by the number of people in the audience.

Many people seem to forget that public speaking and reading are *enlarged* conversation. It may be necessary to speak louder. It is certainly necessary to speak more distinctly, to enunciate more clearly. Press the *d*'s a bit more with the tongue, "pop" the *t*'s, pronounce the final *-ed* and *-ing*. Make the lips and tongue work a little more briskly on *make, add, can, win, go, have, at, fall, walking, sorry, people, dated.* Read the selections suggested at the close of this chapter, exaggerating the distinctness of your diction a little. It won't do you any harm! Of course, don't neglect the fine, warm vowel sounds in *father, far, eve, meat, iron, right, home, hold, use, news, boy, oil, house, mouse, moose, all, law.*

IV. Communication

We have stressed the importance of *communication* before in this book. We stress it again. Don't read to yourself when listeners are present: read to *them.* Hold the book or paper high enough so that you can look up occasionally at your audience. Get the head up so that the throat is not cramped. Now *share* the story of the Good Samaritan:

A certain man was going down from Jerusalem to Jericho; and he fell among robbers, who both stripped him and beat him, and departed, leaving him half dead. And by chance a certain priest was going down that way: and when he saw him, he passed by on the other side. And in like manner a Levite also, when he came to the place, and saw him, passed by on the other side. But a certain Samaritan, as he journeyed, came where he was: and when he saw him, he was moved with compassion, and came to him, and bound up his wounds, pouring on them oil and wine; and he set him on his own beast, and brought him to an inn, and took care of him. And on the morrow he took out two shillings, and gave them to the host, and said, "Take care of him; and whatsoever thou spendest more, I, when I come back again, will repay thee."

V. Distractions

When one is reading poetry, or dramatic literature, or any other literary form that does not require the close intimate contact that a public speech necessitates, the reader must be careful to build up an illusion that is out of step with reality. No one objects to a reader using the book if it has been mastered, but to have to stop and do more than refresh the memory of the material is like turning on a light in the middle of a movie. Anything that destroys the illusion, anything that brings us back suddenly to reality, anything that keeps us from enjoying the selection as a whole is a serious defect in technique. If the selection has become a part of the reader, if from beginning to end we feel we are in the hands of one who knows what he is doing, the feeling of being transported, of being carried away, is ours. The prepared reader has conceived of the reading as an entirety and every part falls into its proper place. There are no parts left over which the reader tries at the last moment to fit into the total picture to the discomfort of the listening audience. In short, if the reader maintains aesthetic distance, which has been defined by Edward Bullough as "putting the phenomenon, so to speak, out of gear with our practical, actual self; by allowing it to stand outside the context of our personal needs and ends . . . by cutting out the practical sides of things and our practical attitude toward them." [1]

Meaningless gestures, walking around the platform without purpose, playing with the clothes, standing too near the edge of the platform, half stumbling off the platform, all interfere with aesthetic distance. Is it not a distraction for the interpreter to sing the lines of T. S. Eliot's "The Hollow Men"?

Here we go round the prickly pear
Prickly pear prickly pear
Here we go round the prickly pear
At five o'clock in the morning.

---

[1] See Melvin M. Rader, *A Modern Book of Aesthetics* (New York: Henry Holt, 1935), p. 317.

VI. Variety

"Variety's the very spice of life," wrote the eighteenth-century English poet, William Cowper, and no truer word was ever written. Monotony is deadly in the ways of life, and particularly lethal in those of speech. Perhaps some of you have suffered under a college professor who drones on and on with deadly sameness in his lectures, and then wonders why his students are inattentive, why they fail to acquire the information he hands out to them. The fact is that the human ear just doesn't seem to function under a continuous bombardment of the same sound.

Halford E. Luccock, professor-emeritus of homiletics at Yale University Divinity School, gives a vivid description of vocal monotony:

> A related hindrance to delivery that really delivers the sermon to the mind of the hearer, is the reading voice. This is by no means the same as that of the clearly enunciated "boom-boom" of the synthetic voice. A voice may be natural; yet, if it has the monotonous pace that confined reading gives, it soon loses its grip. In an earlier day reading aloud was a king of indoor sports. Perhaps we have to our great loss allowed it to become a lost art. The fact is, however, that today few people like to be read to. Some radio studios do make a real effort, when they get the chance, to help the occasional speaker to get rid of the reading voice, which most nonprofessional speakers bring to the reading of a manuscript. There is a different cadence when one is reading, a steady drone which either irritates or puts to sleep, a draining out of excitement from the voice. To say this is not for a moment to forget that some of the most effective preaching done today in the United States is done by preachers with a complete typed manuscript in front of them. But such preaching is not reading. The reading voice never gets into it at all.[2]

Let us note some of the ways in which a speaker or reader can defeat monotony and keep his listeners alert and *actively* listening.

A. *Variety in Vocal Method*

1. Range of the Speaking Voice

Read aloud this stanza by Elizabeth Barrett Browning, noting the ups and downs of pitch:

---

[2] Halford E. Luccock, *In the Minister's Workshop* (New York: Abingdon-Cokesbury, 1944), p. 196.

What was he doing, the great god Pan,
Down in the reeds by the river?
Spreading ruin and scattering ban,
Splashing and paddling with hoofs of a goat,
And breaking the golden lilies afloat
With the dragon-fly on the river?

As you read, enter into the happy spirit of these lines; then note your speech melody. You are *talking* notes, not *singing* them; still, your vocal tones could be reproduced on a scale, perhaps in the graphic form illustrated below (see p. 157). But the vocal tones of no two persons are the same. Locate your own tones on the chart.

2. Steps and Slides

In these lines note the two types of tonal variety obtained through changes in pitch. First, there are *slides* from one pitch to another, called *inflections*. The slide is illustrated in the words *doing,* and *river*. There are also steps from one pitch to another, with a distinct break between the two notes. This is illustrated in the way we say *what was he.*

Vocal variety is possible then, by changes in pitch. These changes occur spontaneously as we think and feel the literature we are reading. The formal graphic representations of them are made merely to enable us to analyze what goes on unconsciously in order that we may be a bit more aware of the possibilities of the voice. But such a study need not make us artificial in its use. The primary purpose of the analysis is to emphasize how vocal variety in pitch serves to keep listeners alert, and appreciative of the mood of what is being read to them.

3. Speech Patterns

Be on guard against the monotony of a fixed speech pattern. It is extremely easy to fall into the sing-song type of delivery, to go up and down between the same two notes on the scale, in the same time interval, regardless of the selection one is reading. Preoccupation or inability to project the meaning may be the cause. The fixed pattern goes something like this:

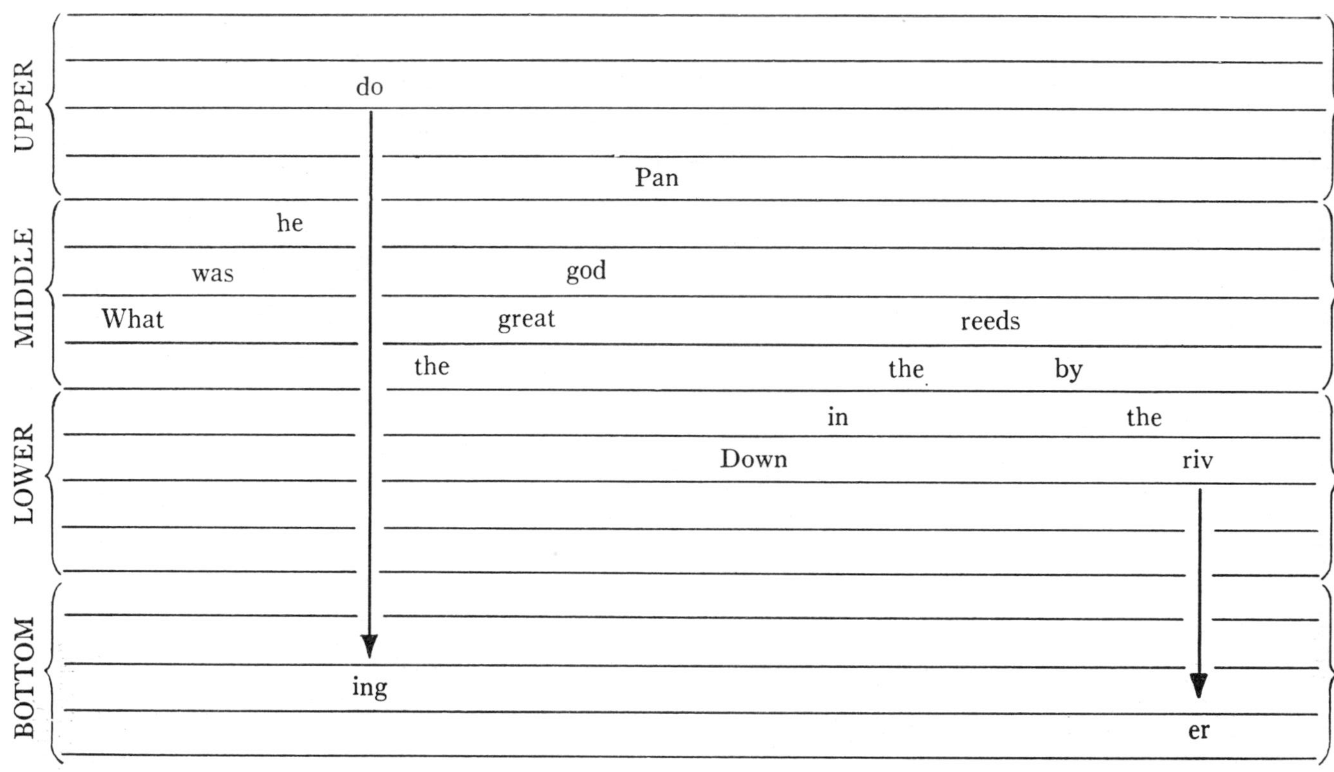

What was he doing, the great god Pan
Down in the reeds by the river?

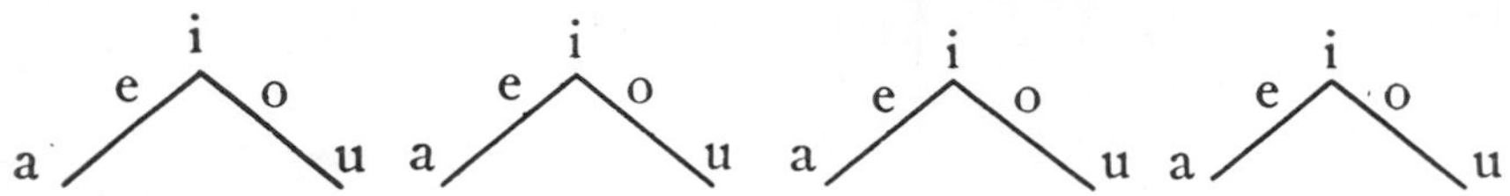

Whereas the monotony could be relieved by substituting a pitch pattern of greater flexibility:

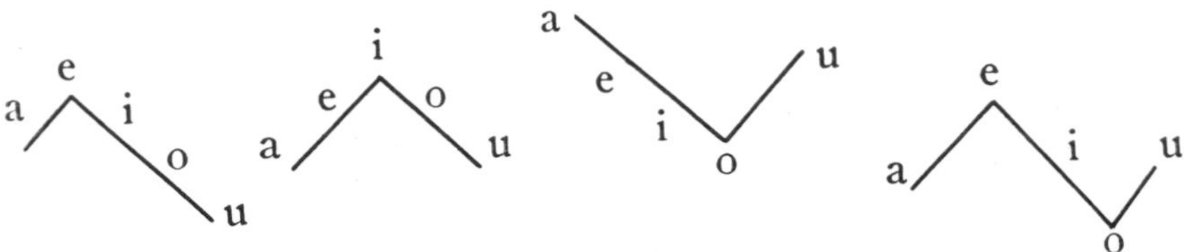

Another thing to be watched—and avoided—is the false cadence, a type of modulation so common to clergymen that it has been called the *preacher's cadence.*[3] Instead of dropping to a conversational note at the close of a sentence or phrase, the preacher drops to a note a little above or a little below it. This cadence is difficult to illustrate on paper, but if you will listen to an H. V. Kaltenborn broadcast, or to one of the radio evangelists who think that it is a "holy" tone, you will hear it. Your teacher will illustrate it for you. This cadence is not direct. It, too, shows preoccupation.

B. *Variety in Tempo*

Another method of obtaining variety is by change of *rate* or, as the musicians term it, *tempo*. The musician uses the term *adagio, andante, allegro, presto,* et cetera, in a more formal and regular sense than we use *slow, rapid, lightly, gay, very slow,* et cetera, but the analogy to music holds very well. The average layman is likely to become bored, even when listening to a musical masterpiece played by a great orchestra, if one particular tempo is sus-

[3] For a discussion of vocal problems faced by the preacher, see W. C. Craig and R. R. Sokolowsky, *The Preacher's Voice* (Columbus, Ohio: The Wartburg Press, 1944).

tained too long. When the tempo changes attention picks up immediately.

Again, we know how, in music, time and rhythm are governed by the emotion—sad or mournful, light or gay—that the music seeks to express. So it is in reading. Variety in rate is a necessity, from the standpoint of holding the attention of the listener, but we find writers, very generally, adjusting the range of tempo of their material to harmonize with the depth of thought or the sentiment involved. Naturally, in a deeply thoughtful essay, we expect that range to be limited to the slower measures. But do not, for that reason, sacrifice variety of pitch; the danger of a monotonous tone is all the greater in reading a serious, deliberate selection:

"What is truth?" said jesting Pilate; and would not stay for an answer. Certainly there be those that delight in giddiness, and count it a bondage to fix a belief, affecting free-will in thinking, as well as in acting. And though the sects of philosophers of that kind be gone, yet there remain certain discoursing wits which are of the same veins, though there be not so much blood in them as was in those of the ancients. But it is not only the difficulty and labor which men take in finding out of truth; nor again, that when it is found, it imposeth upon men's thoughts, that doth bring lies in favor: but a natural though corrupt love of the lie itself.

—FRANCIS BACON, *Of Truth.*

In a thoughtful but lighter vein, the oral reader uses a somewhat quicker tempo and, often, a great pitch range:

The test of real literature is that it will bear repetition. We read over the same pages again and again, and always with fresh delight. This bars out all mere jocosity. A certain kind of wit, which depends for its force on mere verbal brilliancy, has the same effect. The writers whom we love are those whose humor does not glare or glitter, but which has an iridescent quality. It is the perpetual play of light and color which enchants us. We are conscious all the time that the light is playing on a real thing. It is something more than a clever trick; there is an illumination.

—SAMUEL M. CROTHERS.

Note how the same principle of variation in tempo, according to the depth or lightness of the thought and mood, applies also to poetry. And observe, too, how the effectiveness of variety of pitch is demonstrated:

Tears, idle tears, I know not what they mean,
Tears from the depth of some divine despair
Rise in the heart, and gather to the eyes,
In looking on the happy Autumn-fields,
And thinking of the days that are no more.

—TENNYSON.

In contrasting fashion, read:

Who doth ambition shun,
And loves to lie in the sun
Seeking the food he eats,
And pleased with what he gets,
Come hither, come hither, come hither
    Here shall he see
    No enemy
But winter and rough weather.

—SHAKESPEARE.

Or watch the tone and tempo as you read these strong lines from Walt Whitman:

Afoot, and light hearted
I take to the open road.
Healthy, free, the world before me,
The long brown path before me
Leading,—wherever I choose.

Here it would be well to call attention to two important means of achieving variety of tempo: (1) the pause and (2) change of pace.

1. The Pause [4]

One of the most useful tools of expression in the reader's kit is the pause. The writer envies the reader this tool and tries in every way to employ it himself. He uses dots, dashes, parentheses, paragraphs, to arrest the attention for a moment and make his words sink in more deeply. All the reader need do is to cease speaking, and he can hold the listener in the hollow of his hand.

[4] The advanced student of oral interpretation might like to study Grant Fairbanks and LeMar W. Hoaglin, "An Experimental Study of the Durational Characteristics of the Voice During the Expression of Emotion," *Speech Monographs,* VIII, 85.

The pause is frequently used to point up a phrase, to call attention to something that the reader particularly wishes the audience to notice. In the following sentence from Russell H. Conwell's *Acres of Diamonds,* the pause before the word *moral* at the end of the sentence points up the pun. If the reader does not pause there, he gives the audience no time to grasp the play on words and smile in recognition: "These Arab guides always had morals to their stories although their stories were not always (pause) *moral.*"

Practice telling some funny stories that depend upon the last word or phrase for their effect. You will find plenty of these in *The Reader's Digest.* Before you say the catch word or phrase, make use of a deliberate pause. Sharpen your audience's appetite by putting them in a mood of expectancy.

Besides its use to point up a word or phrase, the pause is also used to give the audience time to reflect on what has just been said. Walt Whitman's poetry, which often is a category of images, one after another, needs long pauses after each word picture, in order that the audience may identify and examine the image just evoked. Carl Sandburg's "Chicago," likewise, is a series of such pictures. The wise reader of this poem will give his audience time to conjure up each picture. Only careful preparation on his part, however, will show him where these pauses should be made. If the audience is not allowed to reflect on one idea before the reader goes on to the next, they will lose the thread of the argument, and wander off in a revery of their own at the expense of the new ideas yet to be presented.

Again, the reader can make use of the pause to get his bearings for the next scene or mood of the passage. He can grasp the significance of what is coming next, and see its relation to the whole idea, the central theme.

The pause is also useful in building up the mood of the passage. Emotion consumes time. You will remember that Antony, in his famous oration over the dead Caesar, says:

> Bear with me;
> My heart is in the coffin there with Caesar,
> And I must pause till it come back to me.

A sense of the struggle that the mastery of emotion demands must be communicated to the audience. Time must be given them to sound the depths of the emotion being portrayed. A strikingly dramatic instance of the emotional effect the pause can create was witnessed when the National Association of Teachers of Speech held a dinner in the Mayflower Hotel in Washington, D. C., in the fall of 1940. Sir Wilmott Lewis, Washington correspondent of *The London Times,* addressed the gathering. He told of the heroic sacrifices of the women of England in the war effort, and as he got deeper into his story he was overcome with emotion. He had to turn his back upon the audience until he regained his composure. At that pause there was not a dry eye in the audience of several hundred people. Sir Wilmott did not make his pause for effect. Yet it was very effective, simply because it gave the audience time to reciprocate his own pure, genuine feeling. We cite this example here to show that when emotion is gripping, we must give the audience time to feel its pull. Try reading one of Elizabeth Barrett Browning's *Sonnets from the Portuguese:* to communicate the poet's emotions to your listeners, you must yourself take time to feel them.

Remember: "When you are in a hurry, skip everything but the pauses!"

2. Change of Pace

Variety! Ah, there's the word. In giving so much attention to the pause, the student is likely to think that his reading will become slow and monotonous. Not at all. Just as in playing baseball or basketball, a change of pace helps a team win; so in reading, change of pace helps to whet the appetite of the listener. The lullaby lulls because of its sameness. The reader who never spits out a phrase, one word cascading over another; who never dawdles over this word, nor fondles and caresses that word, loses an opportunity to hold attention through change of pace. Listen to records of Walter Hampden's readings. He does not speak slowly, stolidly, in a ponderous fashion. He hurls his words at you, and then gives you time to reflect upon them. By judiciously using the pause, along with change of pace, he rivets your attention upon his words. In reading the line from the parable of the Prodigal Son: "He ran and fell on his neck and . . . kissed him," the initial rapid pace echoing the running feet is slowed down until, with the pause before the word "kissed" and the great tenderness with which that word is spoken, Walter Hampden conveys the deep emotions of a father greeting a son "who was dead, and is alive again; was lost, and is found."

Analyze the passage you are going to read for its *verbs*. See what you can do with the verbs of action. In "The Highwayman," by Alfred Noyes, note the difference of pace suggested by the repetition of *riding, riding, riding,* from that natural to the words *marching, marching, marching*. Surely one marches more slowly than one rides.

John Mason Brown's appraisal of the Lunts in his review of *O Mistress Mine,* contains some interesting observations about their handling of *pace:*

> They know how to hold a sentence back, and then send it scurrying suddenly to its conclusion. They never miss the meaningful or explosive word, and never overstress it. . . . They are shrewd judges of what to underscore and what to throw away. They realize that the very act of seeming to throw a phrase or word away is in itself a form of emphasis. They are no less adroit in altering the tempo of their separate scenes than they are in changing the pace of their single sentences. What is more, their watches are always synchronized.[5]

C. *Variety in Volume and Force*

Still another means of breaking monotony is by variation in volume (the amount of sound), and force (the application of the sound). We can illustrate this point quite adequately by taking a few well-known poems as examples. In a sound reading of Whitman's "The Open Road," the voice is firm, particularly on such words as "healthy," "free," and "wherever I choose." The force is sustained, stressed—there is more than normal vocal pressure. When we read "Who doth ambition shun," et cetera, the touch, the "attack," at the beginnings of syllables is brisk, staccato, but is a lighter application of force than that used for "The Open Road." In "Tears, idle tears," the inherent sadness of the mood governs the voice in a muted, measured application of force. The voice is quieter here, it has less volume than in the other selec-

[5] *The Saturday Review of Literature,* February 16, 1946.

tions. It is muffled, as the tones of a bell are muffled when it is struck by a hammer wrapped in felt.

Stress is the application of force to the different parts of a sound or syllable. A change of the location of force from one part of a sound, syllable, or word to another will change the sentiment or meaning. How important stress is in attracting attention is seen in Edward R. Murrow's war identification *This // Is London* and now in peace *This // Is the News*. Murrow's employment of stress is no accident. Ida Lou Anderson, Murrow's speech teacher, suggested that he put more emphasis on the "This." Students of stress have found the following six variations useful in understanding its importance.

1. *Radical.* If a direct question is asked, and the simple answer "No" is given with radical stress, it implies an ordinary answer unmarked by sentiment. This is a basic stress.

2. *Final.* When the force has been put on the final part of the syllable, sound, or word, the impression of determination or impatience is given. Recite the following line and discover what happens when you put the stress on the third *Din* and on the word *been*. (Be sure to rhyme these two words.)

> It was Din! Din! Din!
> You 'eathen, where the mischief have you been?

3. *Compound.* This stress implies irony or sarcasm. The sentence "Brutus is an honorable man" with a compound stress on the word *honorable* implies that he was not quite so honorable. Put the compound stress on *ow's* and *soul* and you will see the effect of this stress.

> Then it's Tommy this, an' Tommy that, an' Tommy, ow's yer soul?

4. *Median.* The force is placed chiefly upon the middle part of the sound, making a swell of the voice which varies according to the intensity required. It suggests pathos, sorrow, reverence. Say the following line with this use in mind:

> O Romeo, Romeo! Wherefore art thou Romeo?

5. *Thorough.* The force continues about the same throughout the sound. This is the appropriate stress for command, triumph, shouting, warning, apostrophe, lofty appeal, all of which embody

the idea of calling. The opening lines of Carl Sandburg's "Chicago" call for this stress:

Hog butcher for the world

6. *Intermittent.* As the designation suggests, the force is placed upon periodic parts of the sound. The force is recurrent. Physical agitation is suggested. King Lear upon the heath might use this stress.

VII. Bodily Action

So far in this chapter we have been concentrating on the vocal method to be acquired for oral interpretation. But we say now, and we shall reiterate again and again: The thing is not done by voice alone! The whole body is in it. Watch people broadcasting on the radio when no visible audience is present in the studio. See them double up their fists to help their vocal emphasis, see their faces glow with enthusiasm, and hear the vocal reflection of that glow in their voices. We use the term *empathy* to describe these muscular responses, this co-ordination of body and voice. We respond *empathically* as we, the spectators, help our player carry the ball across the goal line. Our muscles tense as, in the darkness of the movie theater, we try to frustrate the villain's dastardly deed! We sway to the rhythm of music. Social inhibitions enter into many of these situations, in which case our empathy may be only an inner response; but it is there just the same. All this is perfectly normal and spontaneous, and so it should be when we come to read aloud. The poker face, the inert hands and body have no place in speaking and reading. Nothing could be more incongruous than to have an animated voice with an expressionless face behind it; or to have the voice express joy or sorrow and the face express—absolutely nothing—a blank, a deadpan. Get before a mirror and wrinkle the forehead; raise and lower the brow; wriggle the nose; work the lips; bring the hands into the picture, not necessarily in formal gestures, but as part of the emphatic response. The eye is quicker than the ear. The gestures, the expressions are the frame in which the picture is set. Charles Dickens gives us a powerful bit of testimony as to the effectiveness of bodily action. James T. Fields in writing about Dickens tells us:

He liked to talk about the audiences that came to hear him read, and he gave the palm to his Parisian one, saying it was the quickest to catch his meaning. Although he said there were many always present in his room in Paris who did not fully understand English, yet the French eye is so quick to detect expression that it never failed instantly to understand what he meant by a look or an act. "Thus, for instance," he said, "when I was impersonating Steerforth in 'David Copperfield,' and gave that peculiar grip of the hand to Emily's lover, the French audience burst into cheers and rounds of applause." [6]

Words can not do the work alone. The reader must be alive physically. He must suit the action to the word. Gay MacLaren, an excellent reader of Chautauqua days, gives us a vivid picture of the author of *Ben Hur* failing to respond to the scene he was trying to depict.

One of their first speakers was General Lew Wallace, reading from his own book, *Ben Hur*. Vast crowds poured in to hear the distinguished author and it was a gala day for Chautauqua. "But he could not be heard by the eager throng," said George Vincent in relating the incident. "He treated his own work with profound apathy. I thought when he got to the chariot race he would speed up and raise a dust, but he never got his horses out of a walk." [7]

Pantomimes are excellent practice. Try the following, with or without some speech:

1. As a returned soldier, walk along Main Street greeting friends.
2. Bring in an armful of wood for the fireplace, drop some, open the door, etc.
3. Make a grandiloquent campaign speech in pantomime; gesture, pound the desk, stomp, etc.
4. Pantomime a phone conversation, long-distance, perhaps.
5. Be a cheerleader at a football game.
6. Be an orchestra director.
7. Reread the poem, "Chicago," by Carl Sandburg, page 369. Grip the floor with your feet, straighten up, feel tall.

---

[6] James T. Fields, *Yesterdays with Authors* (Boston: James R. Osgood and Company, 1872), p. 240.

[7] Gay MacLaren, *Morally We Roll Along* (Boston: Little, Brown and Company, 1938), p. 77. Copyright, 1938, by Gay MacLaren Backman.

8. Read these heroic lines from "Invictus," p. 350. Hold the head erect, feeling the courage and pride of the lines:

I am the Master of my fate,
 I am the Captain of my soul.

VIII. Interpreting Emotions

One of the problems that the interpreter faces is that of sensing the particular emotion the author is trying to portray and to stir up, arouse, communicate that emotion to the audience. The inartistic handling of emotion by the "elocutionist" of the past century jarred the sensibilities of the judicious and helped to hurry him into disfavor. Here are some questions that should be answered by the interpreter as he faces the problem of interpreting emotions: (1) What emotion is present in the selection? (2) Did the author intend for the listener to participate in the emotion? (3) Did the author intend for the listener to contemplate the emotion? (4) Should the oral reader do the responding for the listener? (5) Would it be better for the oral reader to suggest or imitate? No hard and fast answers can be given to these questions. Circumstances alter answers. Much will depend upon the oral reader, upon the selection, and upon the audience, but it is a good thing to ponder them.

For example, try reading Robert Browning's "Evelyn Hope" and snivel throughout the selection and see how ridiculous such a performance can be, how it can ruin a great poem. Or read Robert Frost's "Home Burial" and weep and wail and tear your hair over the part of the wife. Do you see what happens? Another experiment would be to read "Boots" by Kipling and imagine that you are the soldier going lunatic and express loudly appropriate emotions. Still another illustration might be Robert Frost's "Out, Out——". Let yourself go on this slice of life and see what happens.

All of which reminds one of the anecdote Bliss Perry tells of his teacher of elocution, Professor J. W. Churchill. "Once when I was reading to him an assigned passage from Hamlet he stopped me. 'Do you really understand the difference between suggestion and imitation, in interpreting character? Have you read Lessing?' I said that I knew Lessing's plays, but nothing else. 'Well, you must read his Laocoön—here is my copy—and then read the

Hamburgische Dramaturgie.'"[8] One also remembers the story about Demosthenes and Aeschines, the two antagonists in the "Oration on the Crown." When Aeschines finished speaking, his listeners were awed by his speaking ability, but when Demosthenes concluded, the crowd cried out, "Come, let us fight Philip."

In other words, does the reader want the audience to contemplate or participate? Shall the reader vocally diagram the lines that have been written for him with such restraint as to let the author speak through his lines? If the author has been skillful at his craft, will not the listener on hearing the lines react the way the author intended? Will the reader in any way interfere with the entering into the emotion by the audience?

IX. Summary

We have been discussing technique, the most effective way of conveying, through speech, ideas, moods, and emotions to an audience. We can see that our voices must be adequate, our bodies responsive. We know that we must watch the following: grouping of words, distinctness, communication, variety, rhythm, and bodily action. But attention to such matters need not betray us into artificiality and insincerity. It is just common sense to read to be understood, to express to the fullest what is in the material we read. An extreme example, perhaps, would be the radio announcer, reiterating with supreme conviction for the hundredth time that FLOATO soap is best for the complexion, that GLISTEN toothpaste makes the teeth sparkle, or that SMOOTHE tobacco doesn't bite the tongue. It is the announcer's business to make his commercial sound forceful, fresh, spontaneous, and convincing. That is what he is paid for; that is the way he earns his living. No doubt technique enters into his vocal method, but what of it? It is his job and he does it to the best of his ability. The average reader does not have so extreme a task to perform, but he, too, will find it to his advantage to use the instruments at his disposal, his voice and body, in as effective a way as possible.

---

[8] Bliss Perry, *And Gladly Teach* (Boston: Houghton Mifflin, 1935), p. 76. See also W. M. Parrish, "Interpreting Emotions in Poetry," *Southern Speech Journal,* XIX, 205.

X. Projects for Chapter VII

1. Bring to class and read one of the following narrative poems:
   - (a) John Keats .... "The Eve of St. Agnes"
   - (b) William Wordsworth ..... "Michael"
   - (c) Walter de la Mare .... "The Listeners"
   - (d) William Morris .... "The Haystack in the Floods"
   - (e) Anonymous .... "Sir Patrick Spens"
   - (f) John Keats .... "La Belle Dame Sans Merci"
   - (g) Anonymous .... "Edward"
   - (h) T. S. Eliot .... "The Journey of the Magi"

2. Bring to class and read one of the following poems of characterization:
   - (a) George Meredith .... "Juggling Jerry"
   - (b) Alfred Lord Tennyson .... "Ulysses"
   - (c) Robert Browning .... "The Bishop Orders His Tomb in St. Praxed's Church"
   - (d) H. D. .... "Phaedra"
   - (e) T. S. Eliot .... "Portrait of a Lady"
   - (f) Gerard Manley Hopkins .. "Felix Randal"
   - (g) Edwin Arlington Robinson.. "Flammonde"
   - (h) Kenneth Fearing .... "Portrait"

3. Bring to class and read one of the following poems of feeling and emotion:
   - (a) Stephen Spender .... "I Think Continually of Those Who Were Truly Great"
   - (b) Percy Bysshe Shelley ..... "Ode to the West Wind"
   - (c) John Keats .... "Ode to a Nightingale"
   - (d) John Donne .... "The Funeral"
   - (e) John Donne .... "A Valediction: Forbidding Mourning"
   - (f) Andrew Marvell .... "To His Coy Mistress"
   - (g) John Crowe Ransom ...... "Here Lies a Lady of Beauty and High Degree"
   - (h) Gerard Manley Hopkins ... "The Windhover"

4. Bring to class and read one of the following descriptive poems:
   - (a) Gerard Manly Hopkins ... "Pied Beauty"
   - (b) John Keats .... "To Autumn"
   - (c) Robert Frost .... "After Apple Picking"
   - (d) Elinor Wylie .... "Velvet Shoes"
   - (e) William Butler Yeats ..... "The Wild Swans at Coole"

(f) Stephen Spender. . . . . "The Express"
(g) Marianne Moore. . . . . "Peter"
(h) Stephen Spender. . . . . "Landscape Near an Aerodrome"

5. Bring to class and read one of the following religious and philosophical poems:

(a) Alfred Lord Tennyson . . . . "Crossing the Bar"
(b) Matthew Arnold . . . . "Dover Beach"
(c) William Wordsworth . . . . . "Ode: Intimations of Immortality from Recollections of Early Childhood"
(d) Francis Thompson. . . . . "The Kingdom of God"
(e) William Blake. . . . . "The Tiger"
(f) William Butler Yeats . . . . . "Sailing to Byzantium"
(g) T. S. Eliot. . . . . "The Waste Land"
(h) Marianne Moore. . . . . "Poetry"

For most of these poems consult Fred B. Millett, *Reading Poetry* (New York: Harper, 1950).

p 171
Ch 8:

Reading
Narrative
Prose

CHAPTER VIII

Reading Narrative Prose

I. THE STORYTELLING IMPULSE

II. TYPE OF STORY
   A. Character
   B. Plot
   C. Setting

III. UNIFIED EFFECT

IV. THE READER AND THE AUDIENCE

V. SHARING THE STORY

VI. SUMMARY

VII. PROJECTS FOR CHAPTER VIII

I. THE STORYTELLING IMPULSE [1]

The storytelling impulse is as old as the race. One can scarcely imagine a time when man did not indulge in telling tall stories of his experiences, real or imaginary. Ancient literature is filled with fables, myths, stories of gods and goddesses and of the heroic exploits of supermen. Homer, or the group of shadowy bards time has deprived of separate identity, was a storyteller, and the stories he told were written down to become great classics of literature, the *Iliad* and the *Odyssey*. Before men learned how to read, the material of these primitive stories was circulated by word of mouth, and the stories grew and developed as they were told and re-told. In medieval times great cycles of narratives evolved about the persons of King Arthur and his knights of the Round Table, about Lancelot and Elaine, Queen Guinevere, Galahad, Tristram and Iseult, and all the rest of that magic company. Similarly, a whole host of tales was told of Robin Hood, the good outlaw, and his companions, Friar Tuck and Little John, and their adventures in Sherwood Forest. Such cycles of stories may have been centuries in developing before they were actually written down.

[1] Read John Masefield, "The Joy of Story Telling," *The Atlantic*, March, 1951.

Today we have Hemingway, Bromfield, Caldwell, Faulkner, Farrell, Steinbeck, Dos Passos, Ring Lardner, Sinclair Lewis, and a host of others telling us stories. What pleasure we have had as we read such short stories as *The Boy Penrod,* by Booth Tarkington; *The Chink and the Child,* by Thomas Burke; *The Doll's House,* by Katherine Mansfield; *P & O,* by Somerset Maugham; *The End of Candia,* by Gabriele D'Annunzio; *The Cloak,* by Nikolai Gogol; *A Dark-Brown Dog,* by Stephen Crane; *Quality,* by John Galsworthy; *Mateo Falcone,* by Prosper Mérimée. Storytellers all! [2]

We have all felt the thrill of enjoyment that comes with the discovery of a new story, a good yarn. It is something of that thrill of enjoyment that we must communicate to our listeners when we read the yarn to them.

You may remember the long-winded enumeration of types of drama by old Polonius, in Act II, Scene 2, of *Hamlet:* "tragedy, comedy, history, pastoral, pastoral-comical, historical-pastoral, tragical-historical, tragical-comical-historical-pastoral." One might easily make a similar list of types of stories: fairy tales, fables, myths, legends, stories of historical events, sociological and psychological stories, local-color tales, parables, fantasies, allegories, detective stories. How celebrated narratives of these types stand out in our memories! The parable of the good Samaritan; the mental studies, such as Stevenson's *Markheim,* Hawthorne's *Great Stone Face,* and Poe's *Telltale Heart;* local-color tales, such as Bret Harte's *The Outcasts of Poker Flat* and O. Henry's series, *The Four Million;* tales of history, usually with plenty of imagination added: Stephen Vincent Benét's *The Devil and Daniel Webster* and Edward Everett Hale's *The Man Without a Country.* A whole chapter might be devoted to the enumeration of celebrated "thrillers" and detective stories. Sherlock Holmes certainly set a vogue, and he has had many descendants. It is well to know a list of such types of stories as these.

---

[2] Three collections of stories we have found useful are: Oscar James Campbell, Jr. and Richard Ashley Rice, *A Book of Narratives* (New York: D. C. Heath, 1917); Brander Matthews, *The Short Story* (New York: American Book Company, 1907); E. Lucia Turnbull, *The Teacher's Omnibus of Stories to Tell* (London: Oxford, 1936). For a list of stories suitable for the classroom, see Eva Richardson, "Stories for the Classroom—a Bibliography," *Quarterly Journal of Speech Education,* VIII, 8.

II. Type of Story

In preparing to read a story to a group, it is helpful to identify the story as one of character, of plot, or of setting. Let us take up each one of these types in turn, and ask some questions that will help us to analyze a particular example in order to read it more intelligently.[3]

A. *Character*

Suppose you have chosen a story of *character* to read, a story such as *Hair Cut,* by Ring Lardner; *The Piece of String,* by Maupassant; *The Substitute,* by Coppée; *Uncle Jim and Uncle Billy,* by Bret Harte; *A Cosmopolite in a Café* and the *Romance of a Busy Broker,* by O. Henry; *Only a Subaltern* and *Namgay Doola,* by Rudyard Kipling; *Brooksmith,* by Henry James; *Once More,* by John Galsworthy. First of all, ask yourself questions like these:

Where does the author find his characters? How does he manage to make them clear to the reader? Do you know any real people like them? Do you know people like those Sinclair Lewis writes about? Is a particular character taken from life, from indirect experience, or from the imagination?

What is the writer's attitude toward his characters? Does he gaze upon them with admiration? Does he dissect them, as an anatomist dissects a laboratory specimen? Or does he take a friendly interest in them? Does the author reveal himself in his characters? Does his work have moral perspective, and do his characters exhibit it? Do they have the pulse of life beating in them?

How does the author delineate his characters? Do the characters explain each other? Does the author narrate their actions? Does he tell you what they are thinking? What one trait does each character show that dominates his other traits? Do the characters struggle toward perfection, or is there deterioration of character?

Do the characters represent certain classes of society? In the story *I'm a Fool!,* by Sherwood Anderson,[4] note how the author indicates class distinctions. Do the characters represent profes-

---

[3] Two books on analysis that might prove useful to the student are: Bliss Perry, *A Study of Prose Fiction* (Boston: Houghton, Mifflin, 1902), and Thomas H. Uzzell, *Narrative Technique* (New York: Harcourt, Brace, 1923).

[4] See p. 393.

sional traits? Does the author substitute moral abstractions for life-like personalities, as John Bunyan does in *Pilgrim's Progress*? Or does the author give us caricature?

Does the author use the principle of contrast and comparison in introducing his characters? Does he classify his characters by their attitudes to certain facts?

B. *Plot* [5]

Plot means, as its etymology implies, a *weaving together*. How are the various interests represented by the characters made to harmonize or clash through external action, yet still remain part of the warp and the woof of the story? Is the plot one from life, one from the resources of the author's own inventiveness, or one that he has heard or read? Does the plot bear the marks of a careful and painstaking weaver, or is it the product of a natural story-teller? Does the author, to paraphrase Sir Walter Scott, "take the easiest path across country"?

The short short story represents plot in its simplest form. The plot of such a story may concern itself with nothing more than the progress of a single character, or with his development and experiences at different stages of his career. Usually, however, a plot concerns itself with two or more characters. The reader who chooses a story to read aloud is wise to select one with as few characters as possible, so that the listening audience can keep them straight. Radio serials do not confuse their audience with too many characters. The reader should take to heart Stevenson's advice in *A Humble Remonstrance* to the fiction writer:

> Let him (the fiction writer) choose a motive, whether of character or of passion; carefully construct his plot so that every incident is an illustration of the motive, and every property employed shall bear to it a near relation of congruity or contrast; avoid a sub-plot, unless, as sometimes in Shakespeare, the sub-plot be a reversion or complement of the main intrigue; . . . and allow neither himself in the narrative nor any character in the course of the dialogue, to utter one sentence that is not part and parcel of the business of the story. . . . And as the

[5] A valuable discussion of the "story of plot" as suitable material is found in Alma M. Bullowa's "The Reading-Telling Method in the Use of the Short Story in Teaching Spoken English," *The Quarterly Journal of Speech Education,* February, 1922. This article contains a list of stories suitable for reading.

root of the whole matter, let him bear in mind that his novel is not a transcript of life, to be judged by its exactitude; but a simplification of some side or point of life, to stand or fall by its significant simplicity.

In analyzing his story the reader should distinguish between incidents that *reveal* the true nature of the persons of the drama, and situations that *determine* character. Discover where the climax of the story comes, so that you yourself know when you reach it.

C. *Setting*

Is the story one of mood, or setting; of atmosphere, or milieu? If so, is the re-creation of the atmosphere based upon the author's observation, upon his reading, or upon his imagination? Is the setting historical? Does it have local color? Do social ideas or social institutions form its background? What effect does the setting have on the characters?[6]

In *The Merry Men,* by Stevenson, the main character of the story is the sea about the Isle of Aros, off the west coast of Ireland. The sea's desolate melancholy is produced by its storms, rocks, reefs, and shipwrecks. The influence of this milieu is so powerful that an old ex-sailor living on the island is driven by superstitious melancholy into a morbid fear of the sea, which ends in his rushing into the swirling surf to drown. *The Lagoon,* by Joseph Conrad, to be found in his *Tales of Unrest,* shows the influence of the Malay country on two lovers. In his story *Prisoner of the Sand,* Antoine de Saint Exupéry[7] writes of two men trapped in the desert, and the effect it has upon them. Edgar Allan Poe's *Fall of the House of Usher,* Edna Ferber's *The Gay Old Dog,* Chauncey Thomas's *The Snow Story,* all have, as their central device, the exposition of the power of *atmosphere* in motivating the action of the story.

III. Unified Effect

We must keep always in mind the reading situation. It is im-

[6] The student might enjoy reading what a novelist has to say about the influence of the milieu upon his characters. See Bruce Lancaster, "The Insides of a Novel," *The Atlantic,* February, 1946.

[7] Belle Baker and Robert N. Linscott, *Bedside Book of Famous French Stories* (New York: Random House, 1945).

possible for the audience to pay attention all the time. The single reader, when he is comfortably nestled in his chair before the fire, can go back and re-read a page if he happens to doze; but the listener in the audience whose mind wanders (as it surely will) must catch the thread of the story again as best he may. The reader, therefore, must select a story with a single, unified effect. When he gets through, all must know what the point of it was. This necessity of leaving a single, unified effect with the audience has been expressed by Edgar Allan Poe in another connection, but the application can be made here:

> A skillful literary artist has constructed a tale. If wise, he has not fashioned his thoughts to accommodate his incidents; but having conceived, with deliberate care, a certain unique or single effect to be wrought out, he then invents such incidents—he then combines such events as may best aid him in establishing this preconceived effect. If his very initial sentence tends not to the outbringing of this effect, then he has failed in his first step. In the whole composition there should be no word written of which the tendency, direct or indirect, is not to the one pre-established design. As by such means, with such care and skill, a picture is at length painted which leaves in the mind of him who contemplates it with a kindred art a *sense of the fullest satisfaction.*

In this connection do not overlook the possibility of the short short story appearing in *The Atlantic, Harper's, Saturday Evening Post* and other current magazines. These stories are very well written. They say much about life in a small compass. They are condensed, simple, and illustrate the classic unities of single place, single time, and single mood. Because it is so brief, the short-short plunges right into the problem without preliminaries. The first paragraph usually states the chief character's dilemma, and states it in terms of action. Characterization generally begins immediately, but there is little actual description. Most of the characteristics of the persons of the story are revealed in the course of weaving and unravelling the plot. Because of its brevity, the short-short makes excellent classroom material.

IV. The Reader and the Audience

The oral reader and the public speaker have much in common when their relation to the audience is considered. Each must ask himself: "What common, unifying bond unites my audience?

What age group will be present? What can I do for this audience?" If the audience does not get something out of the experience, it loses interest. The oral reader must consider all these factors in choosing the story he is to read; and others as well. Will the story help the audience escape for a while from the world of reality? Will it entertain the audience? Will it inspire them? Will you set old truths in new lights as you read? Will your story warm the hearts of your listeners and move them to noble earnestness? Will you entertain your audience with wholesome jokes and excite them to honest laughter? Are there tears in the story? Are there passages that will bring a lump into the throat?

Let us remember that an audience likes to laugh. "Read us something funny," the youngsters say to their teachers and, somehow, that desire remains with us in spite of the passage of the years. Something of Mark Twain's, Irvin S. Cobb's, Clarence Day's, or Robert Fontaine's is always a safe bet. Current magazines feature humorous stories.

And audiences also love to weep! Hear the sniffles at a sad movie; how chagrined we are when the lights go on and catch us dabbing at our eyes! Just so the tragic stories of the late war, as related by Ernie Pyle or Quentin Reynolds, move us in spite of our social inhibitions.

But perhaps the best material of all is a combination of humor and pathos, a swaying back and forth from laughter to tears and from tears to laughter. That is the open sesame to the hearts of really human folk. That combination accounts largely for the success of an author like Charles Dickens, who wields the key to our hearts as he makes us laugh and cry over David Copperfield and Dora and Agnes, over Oliver Twist and Tiny Tim. It is in this blending of humor and pathos that the average listener finds the most enjoyable entertainment. And it is in wielding this power of drawing laughter or tears from an audience that the reader finds his greatest satisfaction.

V. Sharing the Story

You must get the feeling of *sharing* the story with your listeners. Go to the platform in this state of mind: "I have a good story I'm sure you will like. I want to share it with you." Get the highest degree of communication and directness of which you are capable.

The listeners are to participate, to enjoy the story with you. They are not to be mere on-lookers. If you are reading from the book, don't let the book be a wall between you and the audience. You should lift the ideas out of the printed page, re-create them, vitalize them, convey them to your listeners. Have the story practically memorized so that you can look up frequently and use the eyes effectively.

Your diction must be clear. Enunciate easily but distinctly, clearly but without exaggeration, and make it simple for the audience to understand you. Progress smoothly from idea to idea, make it easy for your audience to follow the unravelling of the plot. If there is dialogue, you will face the problem of impersonation, about which much was said in the chapter on the "Provinces of the Reader, the Actor, and the Speaker." Nowhere do we need a more genuinely speaking-reading conversational method than in the reading of the narrative containing dialogue. Nowhere is there greater need of the variety in vocal method that we have stressed throughout this book. Monotony in speech pattern here would be just about fatal. We re-emphasize that the degree to which you carry your impersonation of the characters of the story depends upon (1) your native gift for mimicry, and (2) your freedom from book or manuscript. Most important of all, however, is your ability to share the story with your listeners.

We call attention to the following practice selections in the Anthology: *The Grapes of Wrath, Told by the Schoolmaster, I'm a Fool, A Service of Love.*[8] The reader will readily perceive that so far as oral readability is concerned, the prose of some writers is better than that of others. A marked rhythm is a great assistance to the reader; not a regular beat, like that created by poetic meter, and yet a decided swing. Note the rhythm of this passage from Steinbeck:

> Tom grinned affectionately at him. "Ain't he a heller?" he said. And Granpa's mouth was so full that he couldn't even sputter, but his mean little eyes smiled, and he nodded his head violently.

[8] The student will find W. Somerset Maugham's *Introduction to Modern English and American Literature* (Philadelphia: The Blakiston Company, 1943) an inexpensive collection of good materials. Other sources not to be overlooked are *The Reader's Digest, Omnibook, Coronet, The Atlantic,* and *Harper's.* See Appendix XI.

Granma said proudly, "A wicketer, cussin'er man never lived. He's going to hell on a poker, praise Gawd! Wants to drive the truck!" she said spitefully. "Well, he ain't goin' ta."

Look for the rhythms. Practice them and let them help you convey the story.

VI. Summary

Choose the story you are going to read with the utmost care. First of all, be sure that you have enjoyed it yourself. A story, however, that interests you may not have interest for the particular group before whom you are going to read, so study your audience to determine its tastes. Watch the time limit—be sure you can get your story comfortably within it. If you have to cut, do it skillfully; prepare your summaries with care, so that your audience can follow you without difficulty. Practice reading the story many, many times so that you know where the affecting parts are. Do not be overcome with the emotion yourself. Remember, "when most impressed, be self-possessed." Be careful to make the dialogue an integral part of the story; it should be subservient to the story as a whole. By means of change of pace, keep interest focused on the elements of suspense in the story. Keep alive the sense of expectancy by your voice and body movements. Try to make your hearers lose themselves in the story; make them forget their surroundings.

VII. Projects for Chapter VIII

1. Here are 20 of the best short stories in the Bible. Assign one to each member of the class:

(a) Joseph. Gen. 37–48.
(b) Balaam and Balak. Num. 22–24.
(c) The Capture of Jericho. Josh. 6.
(d) The Wars of Gideon. Judg. 6–8.
(e) Jepthah's Daughter. Judg. 11.
(f) Samson. Judg. 14–16.
(g) Ruth. The entire book.
(h) David and Goliath. I Sam. 17.
(i) David and Jonathan. I Sam. 18–20.
(j) Elijah and the Prophets of Baal. I Kings 18.

(k) NABOTH'S VINEYARD. I Kings 21.
(l) THE ASCENSION OF ELIJAH. II Kings 2.
(m) ESTHER. The entire book.
(n) THE THREE HEBREW CHILDREN. Dan. 3.
(o) DANIEL IN THE LION'S DEN. Dan. 6.
(p) JONAH. The entire book.
(q) THE GOOD SAMARITAN. Luke 10:25–37.
(r) THE PRODIGAL SON. Luke 16:11–32.
(s) THE HEALING OF THE LAME MAN AT BETHESDA. John 5:1–9.
(t) THE SHIPWRECK OF SAINT PAUL. Acts 27.

2. Get a copy of John Steinbeck's *Grapes of Wrath* and read one of the episodes to the class.

3. Prepare and present an episode from Morton Thompson's *Not as a Stranger* to the class.

4. Prepare a reading of Ring Lardner's *Hair Cut* to the class.

5. Assign each member of the class one of the following short stories for class presentation:

(a) Edgar Allan Poe, "Ligeia"
(b) Nathaniel Hawthorne, "Dr. Heidegger's Experiment"
(c) Francis Bret Harte, "The Outcasts of Poker Flat"
(d) Prosper Mérimée, "Taking the Redoubt"
(e) Thomas Bailey Aldrich, "Marjorie Daw"
(f) Henry Cuyler Bunner, "The Love Letters of Smith"
(g) Alphonse Daudet, "The Last Class"
(h) Henry James, "The Lesson of the Master"
(i) Frank Richard Stockton, "The Lady or the Tiger?"
(j) Guy de Maupassant, "The Necklace"
(k) Mary E. Wilkins Freeman, "The Revolt of Mother"
(l) Anatole France, "The Procurator of Judea"
(m) Thomas Hardy, "The Three Strangers"
(n) Rudyard Kipling, "The Man Who Would Be King"
(o) O. Henry, "A Municipal Report"
(p) Katherine Mansfield, "The Fly"
(q) Ernest Hemingway, "Fifty Grand"
(r) Katharine Brush, "Night Club"
(s) Frank O'Connor, "Guests of the Nation"

CHAPTER IX

The Reader's Relationships

I. RELATION TO THE AUTHOR
- A. Value and Use of Biographical Material
- B. Relevancy
- C. Abuses of Biographical Approach
  1. Use of Make-Up
  2. Effacing One's Own Personality

II. RELATION TO THE SELECTION
- A. The Reader's Convictions
- B. The Reader's Appreciation
- C. The Reader's Listening to the Selection
- D. Choosing Responsive Materials

III. RELATION TO THE AUDIENCE
- A. The Captive Audience
- B. The Voluntary Audience
- C. The Listening Audience

IV. RELATION TO THE OCCASION

V. SUMMARY

VI. PROJECTS FOR CHAPTER IX

I. RELATION TO THE AUTHOR

A. *Value and Use of Biographical Material* [1]

What shall be our stand in the controversy over the value and use of biographical material? Shall we say, as some do: "We don't care who wrote this; we don't care who or what he was; we have the poem (or story, or play), that's all that is important." Or shall we use data about the life of the author, and about the circumstances under which he wrote, to enlarge further our understanding, to intensify our creative processes, to make our reading richer and more expressive? Certainly, the latter is the more intelligent and reasonable process.

To be sure, the historical attitude can be overdone. In some classes in English literature, the required study of biography and

[1] See Holbrook Jackson, *The Reading of Books* (New York: Scribner's, 1947), chap. iv, "Interaction of Author and Reader."

of critical matter about a work of literature is so extensive that the work itself is neglected. It may not be necessary or even wise to drag in all the scandal about an author that present-day research may reveal. Yet to glory in ignorance of literary history is surely an unwholesome vanity for people of intelligence to indulge. Whenever biographical facts can be of assistance, and this is usually the case, let us by all means use them to the fullest. One understands the novelist Thomas Wolfe better after reading the interview that his mother, Julia Elizabeth Wolfe, gave to a New York University English class. One discovers that Tom's mother was "the tireless fountain of folktale, reminiscence, and anecdote that fed the literary stream of her son." [2] The letters of Keats are valuable in understanding "Endymion" and some of the earlier contemporaneous pieces and they are necessary to an understanding of his character, intellect, and genius.[3] And what background the oral reader of William Faulkner gets from reading *The Tangled Fire of William Faulkner* (1954) by William Van O'Connor. The influence of Sherwood Anderson and of T. S. Eliot is brought out. Of course, this takes time.

What light is thrown upon Edna St. Vincent Millay's work when we learn that she was very active in dramatics at Vassar! What insight we gain into the works of Theodore Dreiser when we realize that he fed on Herbert Spencer's shallow philosophy and on the amorphous novels of Balzac! Carl Sandburg's illumination of industrial America derived its brilliance from his experiences as harvest hand, dishwasher, porter in a barber shop, and truck handler.[4] John Masefield's poetry lay nascent in his mind while he spent his formative years as an able seaman, with an episode as barkeeper's assistant in Greenwich Village. Current dictionaries of biography, book reviews, the *Reader's Guide to Periodical Literature,* may all be helpful in creating for us the background for our performances.

---

[2] See Ruth Davis, "Look Homeward, Angel," *The Saturday Review of Literature,* January 5, 1946.

[3] See Maurice Buxton Forman, ed., *The Letters of John Keats* (New York: Oxford, 1952).

[4] The student might enjoy reading Lois Joan Sander's "The Writings of Carl Sandburg: An Appraisal of Their Value to the Public Reader," M.A. Thesis, University of Wisconsin, 1950, abstracted in *Speech Monographs,* XVIII, 209.

B. *Relevancy*

Biographical and historical background may be of even more immediate interest and value to the oral reader. Often it is directly germane to the content, as in the case of readings from Wordsworth; or from Robert Louis Stevenson, with his optimistic philosophy of life in spite of many years' battle against tuberculosis; from Zona Gale, with her accurate pictures of small-town life, as in *Miss Lulu Bett;* or from Elizabeth Barrett Browning, expressing her love for her husband in her sonnets. The additional interest and inspiration gained from such study will intensify the meaning of the selection and the reader's comprehension of it; and will be reflected in superior oral expression.

C. *Abuses of Biographical Approach*

1. Use of Make-up

A great deal has been written on the subject of the reader's relation to the author of the selection he reads. Some even go to extremes, and say that the reader should be a trickster, should try to deceive the audience into believing that they are in the presence of the author. This view, however, seems to be due to a confusion of the function of oral reading with that of the drama. Many G.I.'s saw the production of *The Barretts of Wimpole Street,* a play concerning Elizabeth Barrett and her lover, Robert Browning, which Katherine Cornell and her company put on for them overseas. No doubt Brian Aherne had studied all the available portraits of Robert Browning, and with the aid of costume, wig, make-up, and false side-burns, contrived to make himself look as much like him as possible. Similarly, Katherine Cornell, in the rôle of Elizabeth Barrett, tried to resemble the Victorian daguerreotypes of the poetess. But these were actors and actresses in a play; even so, it is very doubtful that they would refer to their work as "trickery" or deceit. Rather, it is the Aristotelian *mimesis,* or *imitation* of life. But, in any case, the *reader* of a poem by Robert Browning or Elizabeth Barrett Browning should not use the methods of the theater. Let Hollywood struggle with the problem of making its actors look like the people they impersonate. *Mission to Moscow,* for instance, was loaded with replicas of such big-wigs as Joseph E. Davies, Winston Churchill, and

Joseph Stalin. Jimmy Doolittle, as portrayed by Spencer Tracy, popped up in *Thirty Seconds Over Tokyo,* and Burgess Meredith, with a white and wooly hair-do, represents the late, beloved Ernie Pyle in *The Story of G.I. Joe.*

2. Effacing One's Own Personality

Apparently, another way of stating this strained conception of the relation between reader and author—that of the one as the *impersonator* of the other—is to say that the reader should "efface his own personality." This point of view is extremely fallacious. It tends to make the whole process of oral reading highly artificial. Although it is true that we should ascertain beforehand all we can about the author of a selection and the particular circumstances under which it was written, yet when we come before the audience, we are ourselves and no one else. We read words written by another, but they are strained through the medium of our own personality. The selection becomes, in a very real sense, our own. One should not reason: "I am reading a poem by Wordsworth; therefore, I must cease to be myself, I must be Wordsworth."

And why, in any event, should one *try* to efface one's own personality? In the first place, it can't be done. And in the second place, why should one do it if one could? It is not done even in the realm of acting. There have been many great *Hamlets* in the history of the theater. But theatrical history describes "Garrick's *Hamlet,*" "Forrest's *Hamlet,*" "Edwin Booth's *Hamlet,*" "John Barrymore's *Hamlet.*" Many of us have seen, in our own generation, the great Shakespearean rôles as they were played by Henry Irving, Richard Mansfield, Johnston Forbes-Robertson, Robert Mantell, E. H. Sothern, Walter Hampden, and Maurice Evans. And now our conceptions of these characters from the plays are colored unmistakably by our vivid memories of Irving and the rest. Did *they* efface their personalities? Of course not! Instead, their very individual personalities shone through their interpretations of their rôles. To efface one's personality would be a stunt. One might black one's face and dress so that friends would not recognize one. But that would be a feat, not art.

Even over the radio the average voice reveals very plainly the personality back of it. Did anyone ever mistake the "My friends" of Franklin Delano Roosevelt? Note how you detect instantly the voice of a friend over the phone. Not even in voice alone can one efface one's personality.

It is a moot question whether, in reading a selection by an author whom one happens to have heard reading his own works, one should attempt to imitate the latter's delivery. The answer seems to be that it just can't be done! We have heard numerous unsuccessful attempts to imitate Robert Frost's reading of his poems. The truth is that there is only one Robert Frost, only one Edith Sitwell. There was only one Vachel Lindsay and only one Edna St. Vincent Millay. Let us get all the inspiration we can from hearing contemporary writers read their own works, but let us not attempt mimicry. If asked for their opinion on the subject, many writers would probably say: "I wrote the poem (or short story, or essay), but it is yours now. Make the most of it." As a matter of fact, there are many oral readers of contemporary prose and poetry who can read it much more effectively than can the writers themselves. This is perfectly natural, since the latter may have had no training whatever in oral reading; may, indeed, have abominable voices.

II. Relation to the Selection

A. *The Reader's Convictions*

What is to be said in this section has to do almost entirely with radio and TV commercials and little or nothing to do with literature *per se*. Here are a number of questions that lead to the heart of the controversy: Should one read patent medicine advertisements, even though one's own background and education makes him want to rebel? Should the announcer on one program extol the merits of one product and then in the next program make extravagant claims for a rival product? In other words, is there any justification for the announcer being just a mouthpiece? Does the oral reader in such situations need to protect his own integrity? What happens to the identity of the announcer? Or doesn't he have any? Must the announcer assume any responsibility for what he reads? Is the radio employee only an instrument as the microphone is? Do announcers whom we respect refuse to plug products whose merit is suspect? Does the announcer have as much responsibility for saying what he thinks is the truth as does the preacher? Is it dangerous for one's own feeling of well being to evade responsibility? These questions, like most ethical questions, can not be answered categorically. Each one will have to answer in his own way, but the questions should be asked and answered.

In a similar, but not parallel, situation the radio industry, as far as the playing of records is concerned, is taking steps to protect the disc jockey from a vicious system. Norman Nadel writing in *The Columbus Citizen* (September 9, 1952) praises the attempt to help the individual maintain his honesty.

> A radio station in Chattanooga, Tenn., finally has taken positive action against bad practices indulged in by disc jockeys. The management of WMFS in that city has put out a primer for deejays, and backs up its suggestions with the word that any platter-spinner who doesn't conform will seek his livelihood elsewhere.
>
> Principal objection is to the acceptance of gifts—the "payola," as it is called—from people in the music racket to the jockeys for spinning their discs. These favors, according to Variety, range from a cigaret lighter to the down payment on a new car.
>
> Also, the record-player is to steer clear of free commercials for the disc factories, and should not mention firm names, be they Victor, Columbia, Decca or whatever. He is not employed as a critic, and will keep opinions of his records to himself. He is to introduce the records briefly and factually.
>
> If this were to spread over the nation, it would be a real blessing for radio and television listeners.

Should not the announcer be given the same protection as the disc jockey is in this instance? That is, he is not for sale. If the reader of commercials says he is caught in the system, should not the system be changed? And if the system can not be changed, should not the announcer for the sake of his own self-respect seek other employment?

B. *The Reader's Appreciation*

It is not enough to understand a selection. The student reader must appreciate, have a liking for, what is read. If there is not already an appreciation of the selection, the student must take the time to build this appreciation up to the point where he is enthusiastic about it and wants to share it with the audience. Allys Dwyer Vergara in her doctoral dissertation (Columbia University, 1946) found that the chief barriers to a reader's effectiveness were in this area:

> The case studies suggested not only traits which helped in the interpretation of poetry but also traits which formed barriers. Such hindrances found in particular cases were: lack of general experience; unassimilated education; inferior intellect; limited vocabulary; restricted reading interests; prejudices; conceit; want of assurance; overabundance of emotion; sameness of emotion; and unimaginativeness.

This is a comprehensive check list for the would-be reader. The student must constantly keep pushing back the frontiers of his interest. When students are criticized for lack of creativeness, they respond with, "I was not interested in it." We must watch that we do not develop a negative attitude toward anything that is new and different. It is unbelievable but true that our mass culture tends to make us all appreciate the same things. Only the remnant will take the time and trouble to hear the person who has not achieved a reputation through the mass media of television, radio, and movies.

Sometimes reading about the author or his contemporaries or getting acquainted with the intellectual and emotional climate in which the piece was written will engender enthusiasm. See your instructor. Talk over the selection with him. He will be glad that you show signs of development.

Remember that audiences are quick to detect the note of pleasure, enthusiasm, delight that creeps into a reader's voice when he is eager to share what he has found. And, of course, the audience is just as quick to detect the lack of enthusiasm, the boredom that the uninspired reader labors under. Don't be a wet blanket.

C. *The Reader's Listening to the Selection*

If it is possible the student should use tape recordings of his voice. When you play these back, have your instructor or some interested individual listen with you. Listen for one thing at each play-back. You might listen first to your *rate*. Make notes on the speed of your delivery. As a part of this study pay attention to your pauses. Do you ever slow down deliberately for emphasis?

After you have studied your sense of time, take up some other phase of reading such as *melody*. How about the ups and downs in your voice production? Does your voice stay pretty much on the same pitch? Is it monotonous? Is there as much change as you might wish? Does the *quality* of your voice change at all? Do you get variety through change in quality? Then listen for *force*. Do you put more behind your voice in order to bring out the meaning? Do you seem to have resources of *power?*

Now it is one thing to read into a machine which is recording your voice and another to talk or read to others. Can you listen to yourself as you speak or read and make judgments? Can you set up a monitor which serves to check on your performance? We, who type, know that the monitor within us tells us when we hit the wrong key. So the monitor can be taught to keep us mentally alert to quality, pitch, time, and force when we read and speak to others to secure variety.

D. *Choosing Responsive Materials*

Readers need to find materials that will offer the audience the utmost pleasure of reacting. What will secure a response from the audience? The too familiar may permit the mind to go wandering, and yet Ruth Draper always sprinkled her programs with sketches she had used before. What kind of an audience would be attracted to the reading of *Don Juan in Hell* by the quartet of readers Charles Laughton, Charles Boyer, Agnes Moorehead, and Sir Cedric Hardwicke? [5] Certainly previous acquaintance with these actors on the screen and television would stimulate attendance. An interest in Bernard Shaw might help draw the audience. The novelty of the performance might be a drawing card. Also, and we must not forget this, there is a desire for uplift in the American audience, a wish for culture that motivates attendance. We must not play down to audiences but play up to their highest aims and ideals.

Charles Laughton has said that he experimented seven years with audiences in army cantonments to discover the right kind of materials for his solo performances. Note in the following program

[5] See Agnes Moorehead, "Staging Don Juan in Hell," *Western Speech,* May, 1954, p. 163.

the excellence of the numbers. The selections have substance and would delight individuals of taste and refinement throughout the English-speaking world. This is one of the evenings he gave and in this order:

Several limericks
Fables by Aesop and Thurber
"To His Coy Mistress"
Selection from Thomas Wolfe on Trains
Selection from *Pickwick Papers* on Christmas
The Chorus from *Henry V*
Act I, Sc. ii and Act III, Sc. i from *A Midsummer-Night's Dream*
Daniel 3: "Three Hebrew Children in the Fiery Furnace"
Psalm 139
Jammes's "The Little Prostitute"
Lincoln's "Gettysburg Address"

Here is variety, the old and the new, the religious and the patriotic, the poetic and the dramatic.

It will be noticed in the Laughton program that there is not much poetry included. If you are going to read a program of poetry, you would be interested in the conclusions of Moiree Compere's doctoral dissertation (Michigan State College, 1952) on audience response, or lack or it, to poetry: that students neither liked nor disliked poetry—they just ignored it; that they were indifferent to it because they had never been brought face to face with the implications of poetry for their own lives; that students like poetry that expresses values felt in their own lives; that it is not so much the method of presenting poetry that matters as it is the skill of the interpreter using the method; that students are impatient of monotony of any type and want poetry presented not only on the pleasure principle but as a challenge to their understanding.

III. Relation to the Audience

A. *The Captive Audience*

The classroom reader is in double trouble when he has to read to his fellow students who are there more or less under compulsion to attend. The chances are, too, that the selections the student must read were given to him by the instructor. With these two strikes against him the reader must work twice as hard to capture the interest of this classroom audience. However, this attempt to read under such unfavorable conditions is good training. The conscientious student will double his efforts to project his materials into the interests of his captive listeners. It is a tribute to the good sportsmanship of most classes in interpretation that they listen as readily as they do. And yet, it is also true that most literature chosen for interpretation texts has a wide appeal and with diligence the reader can make it interesting. And it must also be said for the captive audience that there is a high degree of interest in learning. If the reader will study his selection to emphasize those parts which are of especial interest to his class room audience, he may find success in holding attention.

Have you analyzed your captive audience? What is their age? What are their chief interests? What has been their direct and indirect experience? Are there men and women or only one or the other? Realize what you are up against when you have to read a selection you did not choose to an audience that did not come especially to hear you or the selection. Is it not a worthy ambition and a challenge to stretch the ability to appreciate, to capture the interest of your audience in what is considered good literature? You may not be able to do this without a great deal of effort, but as a college student it is your responsibility and it is worth while.

B. *The Voluntary Audience*

When a reader is faced with people who come of their own accord to listen, he has a vastly different problem than when he is in the artificial situation of facing a captive audience. In the first place the reader can choose those selections he thinks will attract and hold an audience. All the techniques he has learned in the analysis of an audience will be of service. And also he will have an audience that has come willingly to sit and listen. The audience is already well motivated. The reader can exercise all his ingenuity in devising a program based on variety—the familiar and the novel, the realistic and the imaginative, the emotional and the logical, the concrete and the abstract, the specific and the general.

Think with what eagerness audiences fill lecture halls to hear

Charles Laughton, Agnes Moorehead, Cornelia Otis Skinner, Ruth Draper, Basil Rathbone, and others who read in solo performances. All the factors of interestingness combine to make these attractions enjoyable—familiar faces, a well known actor, a novel manner of presentation, an active audience participation.

If the reader has perfect freedom in his choice of selection, he has only himself to blame if his diagnosis of the audience and occasion has been mistaken. Unlike the speaker who can watch his audience for signs of interest and change his theme and development as he proceeds, the reader is stuck with his selection to the (bitter) end. Any reader on radio or television faces the constant threat of a refusal to listen. Of course captive audiences also refuse to listen but they do it more subtly.

What sort of an audience will you draw? Children? Adults? Adults and children? What will they have read? Are they used to listening? Have they been trained to use their imaginations? Can you predict anything definite about the interests of the people who will be there to listen?

C. *The Listening Audience*

Peter Vierick, the poet and historian of Mount Holyoke College, in giving a public lecture which he was reading, paused after his first five minutes to go back and recapitulate his main points so as to put the late-comers in his audience in the train of thought he was developing. He knew that these people would be uneasy until they caught the thread of his argument.

A responsibility rests upon the reader to see to it that listening is made as easy as possible for the audience. The manuscript must not be a barrier between the reader and the audience.

The trained reader can feel the listening audience. Developing an awareness of and a responsiveness to the audience is one of the benefits to be derived from a course in oral interpretation. One of the sweetest experiences on earth is the feeling that the reader and the audience are doing something together, that they are fused in a common project. Why is it that moving picture stars leave off making movies to go back to the stage at a much smaller income? Is it not to recapture this sense of the audience?

Barbara Higdon in her article on "John Neihardt and His Oral

Interpretation of Poetry" has told of the reader's concern with his listening audience.

John Neihardt's distinctive contribution to the field of interpretative theory is his attitude toward the audience. This philosophy evolved from the fear common to beginning interpreters, through a loss of self-consciousness in the desire to share, to an overwhelming love for his listener born of understanding. The expansion of consciousness that takes place in the creative experience brings an awareness of larger relations and has become for John Neihardt an habitual way of looking at the world. He regards his audience as individuals like himself with common experiences, problems, fears, and aspirations. They have come to hear poetry and to receive the renewal of spirit that it can bring. As the interpreter he is the instrument through which the poetry will find expression. Waiting to take the platform, he concentrates on his desire to give his audience the thing they have come to receive. This concentration takes the form of an unspoken prayer that the experience may be meaningful for his listeners. His self-consciousness dwindles, and as he surveys his audience he feels an outsurge of affection toward those in front of him. As a result of the release of this love the power of his personality is increased. It manifests itself in his voice that is compassionate and understanding and in his facial expression that is warm and affectionate. His body, inclined slightly toward the audience, and his eyes, disclosing a poise born of inward peace, reveal his magnetism. Although he actually looks only at those directly in front of him and does not turn his head from side to side, his listeners on the edges of the group feel encompassed by the gaze. His loss of self-consciousness in love for the audience brings him insight into the response of his listeners. Aware of the powerful love that envelops them, they relax their sense of strangeness and fuse their individual egos into a group desire, the quest for lofty feeling. In his early interpretative experience Neihardt could sense this moment of fusion that occurred after a period of restlessness. Having fully developed the attitude of love toward his audience, he is aware of the relaxation that now comes as soon as he begins to read.[6]

IV. Relation to the Occasion

Often one can strike fire with an audience by cooperating with the mood of the occasion. At this point in reading to an audience, one has to be very sensitive. National holidays may be a clue to

[6] *The Southern Speech Journal,* December, 1952, p. 97.

the type of materials that should be read. If the reader can capitalize upon a prevailing mood or attitude the reader may ride the wave of interest. For example, Christmas time or Lincoln's birthday or Memorial Day give the reader a clue as to the type of materials that will fit into the mood of the audience.

Does the occasion call for a number of short selections or one long one? What limitations are imposed by the time limit?

An audience of students in a classroom differs from any other audience. The mind set of the student differs from the mind set of the individual who wants only to be entertained. The age of the classroom student has much to do, too, with what he is interested in.

Youngsters gathered on a public playground on a hot summer day for the story hour present problems that would be different from the story hour in a public library.

Reading before a woman's club on a cozy winter afternoon before an open hearth would be different in its possibilities and demands than reading before ladies' night of the combined service clubs.

V. Summary

Important, then, as we may consider historical background material and the reader's relation to the author, to the selection, to the audience, and to the occasion, we must conclude that literature is not a static thing. We cannot blot out one hundred fifty years of recorded history when we read Wordsworth's Sonnet written in 1807. Literature is a fluid thing, changing every day, and with every reader. When teachers try to make it a thing of one time and one meaning only, they are very apt to kill its quick spirit. Great literature should and can be read partly in the light of our own times, and in terms of our own lives.[7]

VI. Projects for Chapter IX

1. Find an essay by one of the following and come to class prepared to digest it and read excerpts from it.

---

[7] The student who is interested in pursuing this subject further would delight in Opal Frazier Cole, "Scholarship and Milton: A Study in the Method of the Oral Interpreter," Unpublished M.A. Thesis, University of Oklahoma, 1953.

(a) Chesterton
(b) John Ruskin
(c) Edmund Burke
(d) DeQuincey
(e) Cardinal Newman
(f) E. B. White
(g) Gilbert Highet
(h) Robert M. Hutchins
(i) John Dewey
(j) Bernard DeVoto

2. Bring to class one of the current newspaper columnists and read excerpts from the column to the class. Look for work by Walter Lippmann, Dorothy Thompson, George Sokolsky, Holmes Alexander, John O'Donnell, Ed Sullivan, et cetera.

3. Give a book review of one of the following texts on interpretation:

(a) Charlotte Lee, *Oral Interpretation* (Boston: Houghton Mifflin Company, 1952)
(b) C. C. Cunningham, *Making Words Come Alive* (Dubuque, Iowa: Wm. C. Brown Company, 1951)
(c) Moiree Compere, *Living Literature for Oral Interpretation* (New York: Appleton-Century-Crofts, Inc., 1949)
(d) Wayland Maxfield Parrish, *Reading Aloud* (New York: The Ronald Press Company, 1953), 3rd ed.
(e) Sara Lowrey and Gertrude E. Johnson, *Interpretative Reading* (New York: Appleton-Century-Crofts, Inc., 1953), rev. ed.
(f) Charles H. Woolbert and Severina E. Nelson, *The Art of Interpretative Speech* (New York: Appleton-Century-Crofts, Inc., 1945), 3rd ed.

4. Select one of the Shakespearean readings listed in the appendix and present it to the class.

5. Select a reading from one of the humorists, Peter DeVries, Robert Benchley, or James Thurber, and present it to the class.

6. Find something suitable to read to the class from the current magazines: *The New Yorker, The Atlantic, Harper's Magazine, The Reader's Digest.*

CHAPTER X

The Public Recital

I. Miscellaneous Recitals
- A. Length
- B. Unity

II. Recitals of Plays, Novels, and Stories
- A. Criteria Governing Choice
  1. Interesting Plot
  2. Worth Doing
  3. Laughter and Tears
  4. Characters as Human Beings
  5. Number of Characters
  6. Personal Limitations
- B. Problem of Cutting
  1. Length
  2. Order of Events
  3. Transitions
- C. Differentiating the Characters
- D. The Mechanics of the Recital
- E. Introductory Material
  1. Getting Acquainted
  2. Characters
  3. Descriptions
  4. Setting
  5. Historical Introduction

III. The Dramatic Monologue
- A. Characteristics
- B. The Listener
- C. Study Needed
- D. Robert Browning

IV. Summary

V. Projects for Chapter X

I. Miscellaneous Recitals

A. *Length*

An interesting program for an oral reading recital, and one exhibiting impressive diversity (narrative prose, poetry, scenes from plays), might easily be made up from the selections presented in this volume, or from many other readily available sources. Especially helpful are the inexpensive anthologies of various types, selections from the writings of numerous authors, that have appeared in recent years.[1] Such recitals, ranging from twenty min-

[1] Several anthologies of poetry have been edited by Louis Untermeyer and published by Harcourt, Brace and Company. Excellent collections of prose, poetry, and plays are: Hollister, R. D. T., *Literature for Oral Interpretation* (Ann Arbor, Mich.: G. Wahr, 1929) and Farma, W. J., *Prose, Poetry, and Drama for Oral Interpretation* (New York: Harper, 1936). Collections of short stories and plays without number are also readily available. See Appendix II.

utes to an hour and a half in length, are quite suitable for women's clubs, church organizations, parent-teacher groups, luncheon clubs, and similar audiences. One hour is perhaps the safest maximum length for a miscellaneous recital, lest someone say, with Polonius, "This is too long."

B. *Unity*

Some thread of unity should run through such a recital—it should not be just a conglomeration, a hodgepodge of unrelated readings. The unity might be that of source, the selections having been chosen from the works of a single writer, with a bit of biography as introduction or running commentary. Or the program might have unity of theme: one dominant philosophy of life as expressed by a series of writers; a succession of commentaries on love, friendship, death, nature, religion, or any other topic of universal interest. Still another device is to ring the changes on one particular dialect: Negro, Irish, Scotch, Italian, German, et cetera. This last is particularly rewarding, since it is a rare audience that does not respond to humor. "Read us something funny" is not only the plea of childhood; it is in the minds of us all, this cry for relief from the tedium and pain of everyday life. That fact does not countenance trash, nor does it necessarily intend to promote the all-humorous program; there is much excellent literature of the lighter, cheerful kind, not designedly "funny," which may be used to leaven more serious presentations.

II. Recitals of Plays, Novels, and Stories

As students of some experience in reading, you are now ready to make your own choice of material for recitals of a more formal and solid type, namely, the presentation of a play or a novel. After all, miscellaneous recitals are never quite as satisfying, for they lack the "something" that calls forth true artistry. Let us then discuss the recital (often called the lecture recital, because of the insertion of data about the author, explanatory matter, et cetera) of a play, a novel, or a series of short stories.

A. *Criteria Governing Choice*

1. Interesting Plot

The play or novel you select for presentation should have an interesting plot. It should tell a story that carries the listeners along with it. The story should *move,* and the motivation should be sprightly and brisk. Deliver us from dullness! Long and tedious descriptions in a novel, heavy dialogue in a play, these are fatal. One saving grace is the fact that often one must cut a work extensively, in order to confine it within the narrow bounds of a recital; in this way, otherwise dull material can be redeemed, its action speeded up. But the element of suspense must be there inherently; the story must rise steadily to a high point of interest, to a climax, and then move quickly to the close. The great classical dramas, the best plays of our own times (and certainly the best for recital purposes) begin low, rise higher, reach a peak, then terminate quickly. Note how, in *Hamlet,* the interest rises by successive waves right up to the duel between the Prince and Laertes, then rapidly dies away; how, in *The Merchant of Venice,* we are carried forward on a mounting swell of tension to the point at which Shylock, knife in hand, advances toward Antonio—only to be dramatically stopped by Portia, whereupon the play concludes in the moonlight and happiness of the last act. Your play or story, then, should be well motivated.

2. Worth Doing

Again, what you read should be worth the time and effort you put into it. To work up an effective recital is no small job. Many hours of hard labor are needed to produce a smooth, polished performance. Let us, then, choose something worthy of presentation to an audience. One should avoid, for example, light farces, which are merely for amusement of a silly and frivolous nature.

3. Laughter and Tears

In the history of the theater, the so-called long-run plays, the plays that have proved most popular with the greatest number of audiences, have been a combination of the serious and the humorous, a mixture of laughter and tears, like *Rip Van Winkle,* which the great actor Joseph Jefferson kept before the American public for forty years; and the play that has had the longest run of all, *Uncle Tom's Cabin.* By this observation, we do not wish to discourage the use of the great tragedies (even in those, of course, the playwrights were usually careful to break the unbearable tension with bits of comic relief, such as the drunken porter in *Macbeth* and the foppish Osric in *Hamlet*), but merely to suggest the dramatic formula that has always been the open sesame to the minds and hearts of the American people.

4. Characters as Human Beings

The characters in the play or novel you choose should be human. They should have warmth of life; they should be convincing as real human beings, they should be capable of transformation into flesh and blood in the imagination of the audience. Ideally, their personalities should be individual and well defined, so that definite impersonation is possible. Since the reader, unlike the actor, may have to undertake several rôles in the play or novel, it will assist him in portraying, and his audience in understanding, the various characters if he can definitely differentiate among them by voice and action. Referring again to *The Merchant of Venice,* we see how ideal the play is from that standpoint. In it we have Shylock, slow and dignified in action, tense, firm, deep-voiced; Antonio, slow-speaking, gentle; Bassanio, a lively young man, rather rapid of speech; Gratiano, a happy-go-lucky, jolly fellow, "on his toes," speaking rapidly with great variety in pitch; and Portia "of many parts," gentle and lovely in some scenes; soft-spoken, light, and gay in others; dignified and firm in the court scene. And there are plays of every era that have characters ideally suited for recital purposes.

5. Number of Characters

Obviously, a small number of characters is preferable. Too many make the problems of impersonation more difficult and add to the danger of confusion in the mind of the audience. Many readers prefer the dominant-character type of drama, in which one person is supreme and all the other people and all the events revolve around the central figure. If this central character is distinctly set off from the others as, for example, by marked eccentricity, the task of the reader is greatly simplified.

6. Personal Limitations

Last but not least, in choosing the play or story he wishes to present, the reader must take into consideration his own limitations as to voice, stature, and personality. A small woman with a soprano voice had best not choose a play in which the chief rôle is that of a big, burly fellow with a raucous, bass voice. And a big, burly fellow with a deep, bass voice had better avoid *Penrod,* or a play in which the central character is a sweet and dainty lass with a high-pitched and lovely voice.

B. *Problem of Cutting*

1. Length

Having chosen the play or novel or group of short stories, the reader must next undertake the task of cutting it to a reasonable length. This is a big job. The full-length play, as produced on the stage, occupies from two to three hours; the Shakespearean play takes even longer. Obviously that is too much for one person to undertake, without the aid of other actors, scenery, lighting, and all the trappings of the stage. Consequently, if the recital is to last not longer than an hour to an hour and a half, the play must be cut to one-half or two-thirds of its original length, allowing time for the introduction and for the narration of omitted portions. The novel requires even more drastic slashing. Let us say that three hundred pages is its average length. Of this, one would have time to read only about thirty pages, or less. In consequence, two hundred and seventy pages must be eliminated. One must become hardened to sacrificing delightful material; one must slash right and left; whole scenes, entire chapters and acts must be dropped, as well as hundreds of single lines and pages. Often sub-plots may be omitted entirely, minor characters dropped, and just the story of the principals carried through. Such an arrangement might serve in the case of *The Taming of the Shrew*. The sub-plot concerning Bianca and her lovers (delightful though it is) may be omitted, and the chief plot dealing with Katherine and Petruchio featured. In a contemporary play, *The Barretts of Wimpole Street,* the story of Robert Browning and Elizabeth Barrett is practically all that one would have time to retain. Put your watch in front of you and get an idea of the approximate number of minutes required to read an average page. This will give you a basis for estimating the number of pages you can use. Then begin cutting the principal scene, the climax, the scene you positively *must* include. Time this shortened version, cut it further, re-time, cut some more! Then round it out and give it proportion by the addition of a limited amount of material from less important passages. In a novel lengthy descriptions may be reduced to a minimum. This process may seem like ruthless slaughter, but it is grim necessity, a matter of expediency. Too lengthy a recital, even if well given, may fatigue an audience and ruin the impression that might have been made, had more extensive cutting been done.

2. Order of Events

Often material can be shortened by a rearrangement of the order of events. In a play recital, it is questionable whether there should be any mention of the mechanical divisions of act and scene. The very words *act* and *scene* bring too vividly to the minds of listeners all the paraphernalia of the stage. It puts the audience into a "theater" state of mind and prepares them to receive a stage, rather than a platform, presentation of the play. Mention of these divisions can often be avoided entirely, and the whole play presented as a connected story. Thus, in *The Taming of the Shrew,* we can telescope the scenes to effect an excellent tripartite arrangement: The Wooing, The Wedding, The Taming. But this is a matter that must be decided for each individual play.

3. Transitions

The omitted portions, the gaps left by cutting, must be bridged with concise sentences, and with few of those. In the case of the novel, this bridging may sometimes be accomplished in the author's own words by a skillful weaving together of scattered phrases. But little time should be spent in covering omitted material. Often beginning chapters or scenes, which deal with antecedent history, may be briefly narrated at a great saving of time.

When the reading is to be done "from the book," omitted pages may be clipped or tied together so as to facilitate ease in handling. Nothing is more embarrassing to an audience than to see a reader frantically fumble among the pages to locate his cutting. If the pages to be omitted are clipped together, the clips should be placed at the *bottom* of the page where they will not be visible to the audience. After a little practice, one can turn over the omitted portions from below in a thoroughly unobtrusive fashion. This may seem a minor point, but when the book is used in a recital, smoothness in handling the pages counts materially in the general impression made.

For an hour and a quarter recital of *The Merchant of Venice,* one might use the following scenes, allowing ten minutes extra for introductions, descriptions of characters, and narration of parts left out:

a. The "three thousand ducats" scene.
b. The "bait fish withal" scene.
c. Bassanio's choice of the right casket.
d. The court scene, to the exit of Shylock.
e. A few bits from the moonlight scene.

Thus, only five out of the existent twenty scenes could be used in the time allotted, and several of these would have to be cut materially. The importance of skillful transitions and summaries is obvious.

C. *Differentiating the Characters* [2]

Usually, in portraying a number of characters, just a bit of differentiation is sufficient to keep the rôles separate and distinct: a little change in vocal method—a bit higher pitch, a bit lower, more variety in pitch, less variety, a slower rate of speaking, a faster rate, more force, less force, more abruptness, more smoothness—

[2] As collateral reading for this section, the student might enjoy reading "Characterization," Chapter VIII of Clayton Hamilton's *So You're Writing a Play* (Boston: Little, Brown, 1935).

there are endless ways of changing the voice to indicate a change of speaker. Similarly, there are many ways to individualize the movements of the body in order to identify the particular character speaking or spoken of at any one moment: by slight changes of posture—more erect, less erect, head up, head nodding, eyebrows up, eyebrows down, mouth firm, mouth relaxed; or by a variety of mannerisms, such as ways of holding the hand, playing with an imaginary watch chain or with imaginary eyeglasses, a slant of the head—again the possibilities are limitless. Now, our bearing here should be just as spontaneous as in the reading of poetry. If we respond to these characters and abandon ourselves to the characterizations, what happens to the voice and body (with a little encouragement, perhaps) will be quite automatic and natural.

Let us illustrate this point by considering three characters from a very delightful play by Sir James Barrie, entitled *The Will* (see p. 413). In the opening scene, we are introduced to three persons. The first is Mr. Devizes, Senior. He is described as a middle-aged, prosperous, business lawyer. This very description gives us our cue to the impersonation. There is an air of importance about Mr. Devizes. We grow a size larger, we feel prosperous, we stand foursquare. As we read his lines, our voices are brisk and firm.

Next we meet Robert Devizes, the son. Robert is a "gay young chap, just graduated from Oxford." The seriousness of life has not yet impressed itself upon him. In the change-over from the rôle of Mr. Devizes to that of Robert, the reader's voice assumes greater variety in pitch, a lighter touch, a hint of gaiety. Also, his manner changes; he substitutes for the heavy efficiency of Mr. Devizes the sprightly "on the toes" posture of Robert.

The third character is a middle-aged clerk by the name of Surtees. Barrie wishes the audience to see from the beginning that Surtees is laboring under impending disaster: a dreadful fate is hanging over him, and he *knows it*. At once, if the reader responds to the author's depiction of this character, there comes a muscular tension, a striving for control, a "holding oneself in," that will be reflected in a falsely quiet voice with great strain back of it. We see, then, how these three characters may be differentiated, and kept definite and distinct in the mind of the reader and in that of his audience.

As we said in the preceding chapter, the problem of how far one can go in suggesting the voice and personality of a particular character is one on which the experts have ever been at loggerheads. One can simply repeat the advice not to overstep the bounds of sweet reasonableness. If one might be permitted a generalization, it is that more students underdo than overdo the thing. They read the lines of Shylock in exactly the same way as they read those of Antonio, Portia, Bassanio, and Gratiano! The other extreme is to enter unmistakably into the realm of acting. This, too, is to be avoided. For many it is harder to tone down exaggeration than to heighten weak expression. For example, we have seen the following exhibitions by readers who should have known better: marching about the platform while giving a poem in which the marching of soldiers was described; trundling a chair across the platform as if it were a wheelbarrow; trotting (actually!) on the line "the horses trotted homeward." Certainly, such violations of all that is artistic and in good taste should be condemned. When it comes to the indication of such bits of action as drinking from a glass, eating, writing, kneeling, falling, et cetera, one can only lay down a general rule: do not go so far in your impersonation as the actor would. *Suggest* rather than act.

D. *The Mechanics of the Recital*

Certain rather well-defined techniques in the art of oral interpretation have become generally recognized among readers. When there are two characters to be portrayed, a useful convention represents the one as speaking toward the right, the other toward the left; the corners of the room furnishing about the correct angles, and a slight movement of the reader's head to left or right acting as a sufficient indication of a change of speaker. The reader has a certain poetic license here: he need not turn to the degree necessary to simulate the actual physical presence of another person or persons on the platform; instead, he can talk out over the audience. If there are three or more characters to be represented, a consistent angle of speech should be maintained for each, so as to assist the audience to keep the *dramatis personae* distinct in their minds. In a reading of *The Will,* spoken of above, Mr.

Devizes might be made to speak down right; Robert, toward the left; and Surtees, down center.

E. *Introductory Material*

1. Getting Acquainted

What shall we say to the audience before we begin our reading? Again there is a wide variety of opinion. We believe the best practice is to get acquainted with your audience before beginning the actual recital. A few sentences about the author, his philosophy, his career, other works he has written—things of that sort are interesting, and serve to stimulate the listener's interest in the particular selection to follow.

2. Characters

What shall be said about the characters of the play or story to follow? Inasmuch as the reader has to free them from the confines of the printed page and bring them to life all by himself, without the aid of other actors, special costumes, make-up, or scenery, and since he does not carry his impersonations as far as the actor does, it may be well for him to tell the audience something about the characters he intends to introduce to them. When shall this be done? Some readers discuss all the characters in the story at the beginning of the recital; others discuss each character prior to his first entrance on the scene. The former method has the advantage of allowing the reader fully to prepare the way, and then to give all his attention to the lines of the play or novel. Once he begins the recital proper, he can remain "in character" to the close. The disadvantage lies in the danger that the audience may forget what has been said about characters who do not appear immediately, before they come upon the scene.

3. Descriptions

These descriptions, whenever given, should be quite brief. A concise sentence or two presenting the chief traits, if possible arousing a mental image, of an individual is all that is necessary.

The more vividly this can be done, the better. Sometimes the author has pictured his characters so aptly in introductory passages that his own words serve best. J. M. Barrie, G. B. Shaw, Maxwell Anderson, and many others are adept at this sort of thing. But if one must rely upon one's own resources, a goodly stock of adjectives in one's vocabulary is very helpful. Suppose your character is a typical sea captain of the old school. The use of a few adjectives such as *red-faced, bulky, gruff-voice* will at once give a sufficient impression of the type.

4. Setting

The setting, or scene, needs no such minute description by the reader as is often given in the book. The audience does not need to know that there is a sofa down left, two chairs at the right, and a table in the back center; that the window at the left has lace curtains; and that the wall boasts a Van Gogh. Occasionally, of course, such details are important to the plot itself; but usually the creation of the general impression of a "richly furnished room," for example, will suffice. Outdoor scenes call for the same technique.

5. Historical Introduction

If your novel or play has a historical setting, a few minutes of discussion beforehand may be needed to adjust the audience's perspective. We live very much in the present. Our imaginations have to be coaxed to carry us back through time to the days of Valley Forge, or to those of the Civil War or of Queen Elizabeth.

Make the transition from introductory material to the opening lines of play or story easily and unobtrusively. Avoid too obvious a break. Do not say: "I have completed my discussion of the characters. I will now begin the play." Change from direct address to oblique impersonation in the least noticeable fashion. Let us illustrate this advice with a proposed introduction for Shakespeare's *Taming of the Shrew*. After speaking of the play as one of the lightest and gayest of Shakespeare's comedies, trusting that such discussion may induce the audience to receive the play in the spirit of fun (audiences are often so dreadfully serious!), one might lead into the story like this:

In the city of Padua there dwelt an old gentleman by the name of Baptista, a wealthy merchant and a man of high social standing in the community. Now Baptista has two daughters, Katherina, the elder, and Bianca, the younger. Bianca is very pretty and has a multitude of suitors; all the eligible young bachelors in the prominent families of Padua flock to her father's house. But Katherina, the elder daughter, has no suitors, for Katherina is the shrew, renowned throughout the city for her scolding tongue and fierce temper. In spite of her father's wealth, the young fellows are afraid to court her. They know they would probably get their ears boxed for their pains if they tried. Now this situation in his family troubles old Baptista exceedingly. He feels it his duty to get both his daughters married to fine young men; but, lo and behold, one is a shrew and no one will have anything to do with her. In this perplexity the old gentleman hits upon a clever scheme. He lays down the law that no one is to marry Bianca until Katherina has a husband. Now, you recognize the shrewdness of Baptista in this plan: he feels that the young fellows who want Bianca will rush out and find a husband for her sister, to get her out of the way. When his edict is made public, proclaiming that Bianca is to be locked up from all suitors until Katherina is married off, a howl of protest goes up. One day we find two of Bianca's prospective suitors, Hortensio, a fine young chap, and Gremio, an old dangling bachelor of sixty or more, complaining to Baptista. But the old gentleman stops their protests, saying:

"Gentlemen, importune me no farther,
For how I firmly am resolved you know;
That is not to bestow my youngest daughter
Before I have a husband for the elder."

Thus we are launched into the play itself in an unobtrusive manner.

You have now studied enough of the technique and theory of oral reading, and have had sufficient practice in it, to enable you to present rather extensive complete recitals. If you can secure opportunities to do so outside the classroom, all the better. Following is material that may be used in whole or in part. And in the appendix are suggestions for plays and novels that lend themselves well to recital adaptation.

III. The Dramatic Monologue

A. *Characteristics*

Let us close this chapter with a discussion of a particular type of literature known as the *dramatic monologue*. The monologue may be in either prose or verse; perhaps the most distinguished examples of the type are poems. As the name implies, the monologue represents one individual speaking. In its highest form, the speaker reveals his inmost thought, his very soul, upon some matter of vital import to him. A reformer, far ahead of his time, reveals his thoughts as he passes to his execution at the hands of the very people who, a few months before, had hailed him as a prophet. A duke, about to remarry, evaluates his first wife. An old soldier relives one of war's episodes. An old man expresses his philosophy of life.[3]

B. *The Listener*

In some dramatic monologues it is easy to imagine a second presence—a listener, whose character may be well delineated by the answers the speaker gives to apparent questions put to him. In others, the speaker indulges in soliloquy, talks to himself; in still others, he speaks to all the world. But it is never to be supposed that he is "making a speech" to a listener. In the finer monologues the situation is too intensely subjective, it entails too much "thinking inward," too much self-revelation, for it to be regarded as a mere extension of public speaking.

C. *Study Needed*

Nowhere is more intensive silent study needed than in preparing to read the dramatic monologue aloud. It is necessary to steep oneself in the character of the speaker, no matter how foreign to one's own nature that character may be. All the inspiration that observation, past reading, and imagination can furnish may be needed to breathe life into the figure. If the person represented as speaking is a villain, it is the reader's business to make his

[3] The references are to the celebrated monologues by Robert Browning: 1. "The Patriot," 2. "My Last Duchess," 3. "Incident of the French Camp," 4. "Rabbi Ben Ezra."

speech sound villainous. If his words deal with fine spiritual values, the reader must rise to the occasion. Often, in presenting a dramatic monologue, the reader comes perilously close to the realm of the actor.

D. *Robert Browning*

Robert Browning is the author to whom we are indebted for the most complete development of the dramatic monologue in poetic form. He has given us a great gallery of portraits—of good men and of bad, who reveal themselves as they speak. In the anthology we present a few of these portraits. Study them silently; grasp the character disclosed in each poem; imagine his face, his appearance, above all, his voice and manner. Let your conception of the man stamp itself upon your reading. Do not make a speech to the audience. A quiet, intense method is what is desired; a very reflective approach. Take your time! Don't rattle the monologue off. Be deliberate. Think each idea through.

IV. Summary

We suggest, then, that your recital run not over an hour in length, that it have unity and coherence, that the material for presentation be chosen carefully, with your intended audience in mind. Working up such a recital is not an over-night undertaking. The task of choosing the material and cutting it to the proper length; of assembling and practicing the material thus chosen, should be spread over several weeks. Once prepared—and well prepared—you have at hand a form of entertainment that can be used over and over again.

V. Projects for Chapter X

1. Present an hour long recital of *Caponsacchi* by Arthur Goodrich and Rose A. Palmer (New York: Appleton-Century-Crofts, 1933). If this play is not available see R. D. T. Hollister, *Literature for Oral Interpretation* (Ann Arbor: George Wahr, 1940) for lecture-recital materials for *The Ring and the Book* by Robert Browning.
2. Work up a lecture-recital of *A Christmas Carol* by Charles Dickens.

3. Choose one of the great biographies, such as Phillips Brooks, Edward A. Bok, Booker T. Washington, Wendell Phillips, and give a 20 minute lecture-recital on a great character.

4. Present a 20 minute lecture-recital from a one-act play.

5. Present a 30 minute lecture-recital from a Pulitzer Prize Play.

CHAPTER XI

Choral Reading

I. Values
   A. Dramatic Effects
   B. Improved Speech
   C. Social Understanding
II. The Conductor
III. The Choir
IV. Materials
   A. Reading in Unison
   B. Solo and Chorus
   C. Antiphonal Reading
V. Selections
   A. A Negro Sermon: Simon Legree
   B. Jesse James
VI. Summary
VII. Projects for Chapter XI

I. Values

A. *Dramatic Effects*

In his play *Abraham Lincoln,* John Drinkwater employs the device, familiar to us from the use of the Chorus in Greek drama, of advancing his ideas by means of "Chroniclers," who recite singly and in unison.[1] Communal reading is capable of creating unusual dramatic effects, and when it is well done there are few audiences who do not like it. Edgar Allan Poe declared that when he was looking around for the most universal device to employ as the structural unit of his poem "The Raven," he chose the refrain. For the refrain is, of course, of communal origin. Who among us has not sat around a campfire and chanted a refrain as some narrator recited a ballad or sang a song? The refrain is indigenous to group recitation, and is therefore particularly impressive when given choral treatment. Verse choirs speaking in refrain, antiphonally, or in unison produce dramatic effects obtainable in no other way. (Advertisers on radio and television use choral reading with dramatic effect.) Shakespeare, of course, used the refrain in *Macbeth.* The play opens to reveal the three witches, who speak first singly and then in unison:

[1] These passages might well be mimeographed and used in class for exercises.

First Witch. When shall we three meet again
In thunder, lightning, or in rain?
Second Witch. When the hurlyburly's done,
When the battle's lost and won.
Third Witch. That will be ere the set of sun.
First Witch. Where the place?
Second Witch. Upon the heath.
Third Witch. There to meet with Macbeth.
First Witch. I come Graymalkin!
Second Witch. Paddock calls.
Third Witch. Anon.
All. Fair is foul, and foul is fair:
Hover through the fog and filthy air.

Exeunt.

B. *Improved Speech*

For successful choral reading, mumbling and inhibited speech in an individual have to give way before the demands of a group speaking together with sufficient clarity to be fully intelligible to an audience. Whistling *s* sounds must be tamed down so as to blend with the total *s* of the group. Each word must be accurately and distinctly spoken: *accept,* for example, must not be indistinguishable from *except.* In being trained to take part in a choral group, students learn how to breathe correctly, how to phrase, how to place the voice. They begin to feel a sense of rhythm. Through imitation they gain resonance, range, and flexibility of tone, and perfect timing. Students *energize* one another.

As the first step in training such a group, the teacher may well have them learn some short poem, rich in consonants, which they then recite at the beginning or end of each class period. Timid voices become stronger as they blend with others. Self-confidence in vocal production is gained.

C. *Social Understanding*

One blessing that all students have in common, whatever their individual differences, is their mother tongue. They may divide into sororities and fraternities, into religous sects and political cliques, but they do all speak—after a fashion—the same language. The teacher of speech performs a social function in utilizing this link to band students together in some form of activity. Here all social distinctions are sublimated. Man is a social animal; he likes to be with his fellow men. He likes to eat with others, and where fraternity spirit is strong, the song-fests around the dinner table are of great joy to the participants. The church through the ages has used communal reading, in unison and in response. The recitation of prayers together has a beneficial effect upon the worshippers. Language is the repository of the culture of a race, and when individuals share in a community-speaking project, they share in that culture. Who does not feel a thrill along his spine when he repeats the *Salute to the Flag* with thousands of his fellow citizens!

II. The Conductor

The conductor of a choral group must have all the characteristics of the leader of any group. People must like him. He must draw others to him through his courtesy, his fairness, and his concern for their welfare. The conductor must get to know every one of the students in the group by his first name. There must be absolute trust between the choir and the leader. This means, of course, that the leader must be an effective reader. He must know his business.

Group loyalty—and nothing can be accomplished if this does not exist—is largely a result of stimulation by the leader. The leader must know in advance what effects he wants, and although in rehearsal different approaches are discussed and experimented with, thus avoiding slavish imitation, it is up to the conductor to decide finally how a particular selection should be recited. He must be sensitive to word values, and to all the possibilities of the voice, such as sound effects, tone production, tone coloring, melody, and cadence.

The conductor should have a good audience sense. He must know what audiences like. In building his program, he must employ unity, coherence, emphasis, contrast, humor, balance, and good taste, so that the audience goes away refreshed in spirit.

Of these factors, good taste is particularly important. The conductor must have it in abundance. There should be no desire to show off. In fact, the best leader is the one who is least noticeable in the finished performance. And if some arrangement can be effected for the public appearance whereby the leader is not seen at all, so much the better. The audience does not like to be distracted when it is listening to the spoken word. They want to see who is speaking and catch the full import of his words; a leader merely gets in the way. Situations differ, and each leader will have to work out the most effective procedure for himself. Sometimes he can stand in the wings; sometimes below the platform, so as to be as unobtrusive as possible.

In conducting, the leader may use both hands; one to direct phrasing and rhythm, the other to regulate timing. But after weeks of working together, the group should find the slightest suggestion of movement sufficient.

Sometimes one of the experienced members of the group may act as its leader. Or the group may be trained to regulate its own timing; a silent count to four, for example, may be used to obtain unison on the opening syllable. Other groups bow their heads in a formal gesture, and when they have raised them until their eyes meet, begin their performance. And as groups work together, they discover many different ways and means of beginning that are ingenious and highly effective.

III. The Choir

Of how many voices should the choir consist? It is difficult to obtain the effects of group work with less than eight. And in so small a group each member must be an advanced student. At the other extreme, a group as large as fifty can be handled without too much difficulty; but perhaps the ideal group is about fifteen strong.

At first the group should be as compact as possible, for harmonious feeling and speaking. There should be only the slightest division between light and dark voices. This means that those whose speaking voices are tenor or soprano in pitch should be grouped together; as likewise those whose speaking voices are contralto and bass.

An elevated, semicircular, and compact set of steps rising to an apex is a helpful stage setting for the choral performance. By its use voices can get out to the audience, and all the performers can be seen; no one is lost in the crowd. If a poem to be given is for solo voice and chorus, the soloist can stand at the apex.[2]

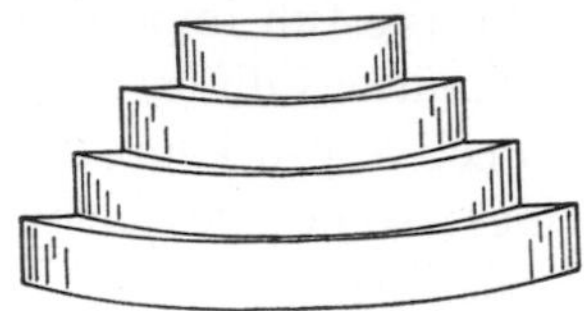

The following grouping of voices can be used consistently for choral work on concert- or lecture-hall platform:

Generally speaking, light voices are used for appeal or question; dark voices, for response or answer.

IV. Materials

Because communal speaking has been used in the theatre for dramatic effects and in churches for religious response, the conductor of a choral group has to fight the tendency to use only very serious materials. And yet the verse choir is capable of doing beautiful work with nonsense verse. Arthur Guiterman's *Lyric Laughter* [3] and Samuel Hoffenstein's *Poems in Praise of Practically Nothing*,[4] to mention but two sources, are teeming with suggestions. Usually, in choral performances, the audience is ready to go home after it has heard but one number; this because the chorus chose, unwisely, as its opening selection material of the deadly serious variety and intoned it with funereal solemnity.

[2] For other arrangements, see Cécile de Banke, *The Art of Choral Speaking* (Boston: Baker's Plays, 1937), chap. vi.

[3] Arthur Guiterman, *Lyric Laughter* (New York: Dutton, 1939).

[4] Samuel Hoffenstein, *Poems in Praise of Practically Nothing* (New York: Garden City Publishing Company, 1941).

Dullness, singing the words, and heavy labored utterance can kill a program.

The principle of universality, whether in humorous or in serious selections, should govern their choice. The lyric, which is essentially personal, is difficult for a chorus to give. Poems of this type, which demand deep introspection, are obviously unsuitable for communal enjoyment.

There should be *sweep* to the material chosen, racial rather than personal. The audience must be able to meet quickly, and match, the emotion of the author; that emotion, therefore, must be objective rather than subjective. There must be a social element in the poetry chosen for group performance. The Psalms are the product of a social situation and are therefore eminently suitable. Ballads, the great odes, passages of narrative in long lines, the great elegies, sea chanties, marching ditties, likewise came to fruition in the experience of the group, and are consequently adapted to choral performance.[5]

There must be, in the selection chosen, a predominating value that gives it unity. It must possess, in addition, values of melody, rhythm, a prevailing emotion, strongly contrasted moods. It will do well to contain vivid word pictures that help hold attention. Thought and feeling must move to a climax.

A group may, after working together for a considerable length of time, use an almost infinite number of combinations in its delivery. There may be solos with chorus work, a chorus speaking in unison, a chorus divided into two or more parts for antiphonal work, delivery of a line by each individual member with the chorus joining in at the close. Let us consider three of the arrangements which a beginning choir can use with profit.

---

[5] The teacher will find these books valuable for selections that have been carefully marked for group reading:

Helen Gertrude Hicks, *The Reading Chorus* (New York: Noble and Noble, 1939).

Marjorie Gullan, *Choral Speaking* (London: Methuen & Co., 1931).

Agnes Curran Hamm, *Choral Speaking* (Milwaukee, Wis.: Tower Press, 1941).

Elizabeth Keppie, *The Teaching of Choric Speech* (Boston: The Expression Company, 1931).

A book of ballads which may prove useful is Arthur Quiller-Couch, *The Oxford Book of Ballads* (London: Oxford, 1910).

A. *Reading in Unison*

In reading in unison, the group and leader must decide after much experimentation where the pauses are and how long these should be. They must decide where the rising and falling inflections come. These should be marked on the individual copies of the script for each reader to memorize. Each reader should try to blend his voice into that of the group so that it does not stand out. All voices should sound like the tone of one instrument. The climax of the selection should be decided upon, so that all help to produce it.

A poem that lends itself to unison reading is "Richard Cory," [6] by Edwin Arlington Robinson:

Whenever Richard Cory went down town
We people on the pavement looked at him:
He was a gentleman from sole to crown,
Clean favoured, and imperially slim.

And he was always quietly arrayed,
And he was always human when he talked;
But still he fluttered pulses when he said,
"Good morning," and he glittered when he walked.

And he was rich—yes, richer than a king—
And admirably schooled in every grace:
In fine, we thought that he was everything
To make us wish that we were in his place.

So on we worked, and waited for the light,
And went without the meat, and cursed the bread;
And Richard Cory, one calm summer night,
Went home and put a bullet through his head.

B. *Solo and Chorus*

Ballads are well suited to this type of choral work. *The Oxford Book of Ballads,* chosen and edited by Sir Arthur Quiller-Couch, is a rich source of material. And on pages 218 to 221 of the present book you will find a number of ballads, among them William Rose Benét's *Jesse James,* which, if they are given effective per-

[6] From *The Children of the Night,* by Edwin Arlington Robinson. By permission of Charles Scribner's Sons, publishers.

formance, are sure to please an audience. Keep in mind the total rhythm, pace, and mood of the ballad as you read the solo parts. The refrain will catch and reflect these from the soloist.

C. *Antiphonal Reading*

We are familiar with this type of group reading in church services. And Biblical poetry depends upon the intoning of the priest and the response of the congregation for its form. A selection the verse choir will find it easy to begin with is the *Beatitudes*. We might combine solo and antiphonal work in this selection:

The Sermon on the Mount

MATTHEW 5

SOLO: And seeing the multitudes, he went up into a mountain; and when he was set, his disciples came unto him:
And he opened his mouth, and taught them, saying,
L.V.: [7] Blessed are the poor in spirit:
D.V.: For theirs is the kingdom of heaven.

L.V.: Blessed are they that mourn:
D.V.: For they shall be comforted.

L.V.: Blessed are the meek:
D.V.: For they shall inherit the earth.

L.V.: Blessed are they which do hunger and thirst after righteousness:
D.V.: For they shall be filled.

L.V.: Blessed are the merciful:
D.V.: For they shall obtain mercy.

L.V.: Blessed are the pure in heart:
D.V.: For they shall see God.

L.V.: Blessed are the peacemakers:
D.V.: For they shall be called the children of God.

L.V.: Blessed are they which are persecuted for righteousness' sake:
D.V.: For theirs is the kingdom of heaven.

L.V.: Blessed are ye, when men shall revile you, and persecute you,

[7] L.V. (Light voices): D.V. (Dark voices).

and shall say all manner of evil against you falsely, for my sake.

D.V.: Rejoice, and be exceeding glad: for great is your reward in heaven: for so persecuted they the prophets which were before you.

V. Selections

A.

A Negro Sermon: Simon Legree [8]

VACHEL LINDSAY

FIRST READER. Legree's big house was white and green.
His cotton-fields were the best to be seen.
He had strong horses and opulent cattle,
And bloodhounds bold, with chains that would rattle.
His garret was full of curious things:
Books of magic, bags of gold,
And rabbits' feet on long twine strings,
CHORUS. But he went down to the Devil.

SECOND READER. Legree, he sported a brass-buttoned coat,
A snake-skin necktie, a blood-red shirt.
Legree, he had a beard like a goat,
And a thick hairy neck, and eyes like dirt.
His puffed-out cheeks were fish-belly white,
He had great long teeth, and an appetite.
He ate raw meat, 'most every meal,
And rolled his eyes till the cat would squeal.
His fist was an enormous size
To mash poor niggers that told him lies:
He was surely a witch-man in disguise.
CHORUS. But he went down to the Devil.

THIRD READER. He wore hip-boots, and would wade all day
To capture his slaves that had fled away.
But he went down to the Devil.
He beat poor Uncle Tom to death
Who prayed for Legree with his last breath.

---

[8] From *Collected Poems* by Vachel Lindsay. By permission of The Macmillan Company, publishers.

Then Uncle Tom to Eva flew,
To the high sanctoriums bright and new;
And Simon Legree stared up beneath,
And cracked his heels, and ground his teeth:

CHORUS. And went down to the Devil.

FOURTH READER. He crossed the yard in the storm and gloom;
He went into his grand front room.
He said, "I killed him, and I don't care."
He kicked a hound, he gave a swear;
He tightened his belt, he took a lamp,
Went down cellar to the webs and damp.
There in the middle of the moldy floor
He heaved up a slab; he found a door—

CHORUS. And went down to the Devil.

FIFTH READER. His lamp blew out, but his eyes burned bright.
Simon Legree stepped down all night—

CHORUS. Down, down to the Devil.

SIXTH READER. Simon Legree he reached the place,
He saw one half of the human race,
He saw the Devil on a wide green throne
Gnawing the meat from a big ham-bone,
And he said to Mister Devil:
"I see that you have much to eat—
A red ham-bone is surely sweet.
I see that you have lion's feet;
I see your frame is fat and fine,
I see you drink your poison wine—
Blood and burning turpentine."

SEVENTH READER. And the Devil said to Simon Legree:
"I like your style, so wicked and free.
Come sit and share my throne with me,
And let us bark and revel."
And there they sit and gnash their teeth,
And each one wears a hop-vine wreath.
They are matching pennies and shooting craps,
They are playing poker and taking naps.
And old Legree is fat and fine:
He eats the fire, he drinks the wine—
Blood and burning turpentine—

CHORUS. Down, down with the Devil;
Down, down with the Devil;
Down, down, with the Devil.

B.

Jesse James [9]

WILLIAM ROSE BENÉT

SOLO. Jesse James was a two-gun man,
CHORUS. (Roll on, Missouri!)
SOLO. Strong-arm chief of an outlaw clan.
CHORUS. (From Kansas to Illinois!)
SOLO. He twirled an old Colt forty-five;
CHORUS. (Roll on, Missouri!)
SOLO. They never took Jesse James alive.
CHORUS. (Roll, Missouri, roll!)

SOLO. Jesse James was King of the Wes';
CHORUS. (Cataracts in the Missouri!)
SOLO. He'd a di'mon' heart in his lef' breas';
CHORUS. (Brown Missouri rolls!)
SOLO. He'd a fire in his heart no hurt could stifle;
CHORUS. (Thunder, Missouri!)
SOLO. Lion eyes an' a Winchester rifle.
CHORUS. (Missouri, roll down!)

SOLO. Jesse James rode a pinto hawse;
Come at night to a water-cawse;
Tetched with the rowel that pinto's flank;
She sprung the torrent from bank to bank.

SOLO. Jesse rode through a sleepin' town;
Looked the moonlit street both up an' down;
Crack-crack-crack, the street ran flames
An' a great voice cried, "I'm Jesse James!"

SOLO. Hawse an' afoot they're after Jess!
CHORUS. (Roll on, Missouri!)
SOLO. Spurrin' an' spurrin'—but he's gone Wes'.
CHORUS. (Brown Missouri rolls!)
SOLO. He was ten foot tall when he stood in his boots;

---

[9] Reprinted by permission of Dodd, Mead & Company.

CHORUS. (Lightnin' like the Missouri!)
SOLO. More'n a match fer sich galoots.
CHORUS. (Roll, Missouri, roll!)

SOLO. Jesse James rode outa the sage;
Roun' the rocks come the swayin' stage;
Straddlin' the road a giant stan's
An' a great voice bellers, "Throw up yer han's!"

SOLO. Jesse raked in the di'mon' rings,
The big gold watches an' the yuther things;
Jesse divvied 'em then an' thar
With a cryin' child had lost her mar.

SOLO. They're creepin'; they're crawlin', they're stalkin' Jess;
CHORUS. (Roll on, Missouri!)
SOLO. They's a rumor he's gone much further Wes';
CHORUS. (Roll, Missouri, roll!)
SOLO. They's word of a cayuse hitched to the bars
CHORUS. (Ruddy clouds on Missouri!)
SOLO. Of a golden sunset that busts into stars.
CHORUS. (Missouri, roll down!)

SOLO. Jesse James rode hell fer leather;
He was a hawse an' a man together;
In a cave in a mountain high up in air
He lived with a rattlesnake, a wolf, an' a bear.

SOLO. Jesse's heart was as sof' as a woman;
Fer guts an' stren'th he was sooper-human;
He could put six shots through a woodpecker's eye
And take in one swaller a gallon o' rye.

SOLO. They sought him here an' they sought him there,
CHORUS. (Roll on, Missouri!)
SOLO. But he strides by night through the ways of the air;
CHORUS. (Brown Missouri rolls!)
SOLO. They say he was took an' they say he is dead,
CHORUS. (Thunder, Missouri!)
SOLO. But he ain't—he's a sunset overhead!
CHORUS. (Missouri down to the sea!)

SOLO. Jesse James was a Hercules.
When he went through the woods he tore up the trees.

When he went on the plains he smoked the groun'.
And the hull lan' shuddered fer miles aroun'.

SOLO. Jesse James wore a red bandanner
That waved on the breeze like the Star Spangled Banner;
In seven states he cut up dadoes.
He's gone with the buffler an' the desperadoes.

SOLO. Yes, Jesse James was a two-gun man
CHORUS. (Roll on, Missouri!)
SOLO. The same as when this song began;
CHORUS. (From Kansas to Illinois!)
SOLO. An' when you see a sunset bust into flames
CHORUS. (Lightnin' like the Missouri!)
SOLO. Or a thunderstorm blaze—that's Jesse James!
CHORUS. (Hear that Missouri roll!) [10]

VI. Summary

The acquisition of good speech habits is, we know, largely an imitative process. In a choral group the student whose speech is poor has an opportunity to imitate better models. Idiosyncrasies of speech are dropped, and the student tends to correct his diction in order that it may blend with the acceptable norm. Moreover, the expressiveness of the average voice is enhanced as it struggles to adumbrate, in the symbols of speech, emotions which are common to the whole human race. An enrichment of personality takes place; this is one of the valuable by-products of speech training. An understanding of word values, one that might otherwise escape him altogether, comes to the student as he voices, together with the group, the poet's consummate phrases. Cadence, rhythm, and tone are enriched beyond expectation as he learns to work with others to produce an artistic effect. As participant in a choral performance, he attains aesthetic heights that might be beyond his reach as an individual. For all these reasons, choric speech must be given high priority as a teaching device in a course in oral reading.[11]

---

[10] Experiment on these ballads with various individual, partial, and full choral effects.

[11] See Charlotte I. Lee, "Choric Reading and Kinetic Projection," *The Quarterly Journal of Speech,* XXVI, 545.

VII. Projects for Chapter XI

1. Mark your favorite ballad for solo and chorus voices.
2. Bring to class a list of five poems that lend themselves to choral reading. Be ready to discuss.
3. Mark your favorite psalm for solo and chorus voices.
4. Listen to radio and television broadcasts for choral treatment of advertisements. Discuss before the class.
5. Prepare a talk on the chorus in Greek drama. Illustrate.
6. Give a short talk on Marjorie Gullan and her work with choral reading.
7. Listen to radio and TV for examples of choral reading. Be able to talk about this in class with examples.

CHAPTER XII

Radio and Television Reading

I. You and Mass Media of Communication
II. Releasing the Author
III. Mike and Camera Fright
IV. Facing the Microphone
V. Facing the Camera
VI. You're on the Air
VII. Some Practical Suggestions
VIII. Use of Recordings
IX. Summary
X. Projects for Chapter XII

I. You and Mass Media of Communication

When educators state that they want college students to have a command of oral and written language, they mean a command of public as well as private means of communication. Today, this means radio and television. Whether one expects to go into these fields of mass communications as a professional or as an interested citizen, one should consider the problems of oral reading in these media. It has been suggested that oral reading is related to many of the facets of the field of speech, but to none is it more pertinent than to radio and television.

At the outset, it is fundamental for any person appearing on radio and TV to remember that you are asked to broadcast because you are you and no one else. Therefore, you must not try to be someone else, unless, of course, you are to act. But if you are to read or speak on either of these media, it is your peculiar style, your personality, your slant on things in general that is wanted. Do not be afraid of differences in opinion, differences that make you an individual, that set you apart from the crowd.

Nowhere does your general background count for more than in these media. The ability to ad lib when the prepared material fails to fill the time is invaluable. Talk to any studio manager and he will tell you that this ability is most uncommon. College professors will clam up and have nothing to say. College students usually will have nothing to say. They can not think of anything. Facility and versatility on the air are tested to the utmost. Such habits as reading the news magazines faithfully, reading a good newspaper every day, reading *Harper's, The Atlantic, Saturday Review,* and other current materials will help keep you abreast of what people are thinking and doing. This course can create habits and attitudes toward the world around you that will last life long. College students usually get so wrapped up in their college microcosm that they forget that the world macrocosm is daily going on its merry way without them.

II. Releasing the Author

In reviewing Maurice Evan's *Hamlet,* John Mason Brown makes this observation: "His voice is one of the finest musical instruments of our time. He does not so much read Shakespeare as release him." It is exactly this ability—the ability to *release the thought* of the author whose work is being read—that the reader before the microphone or camera must strive to acquire: *strive,* because it is no easy task. The ability must be earned. It takes a wide background and intelligence to figure out what the intent of the author was, and it takes skill to put that intent into symbols that will convey meaning to the listener and viewer. Behind the apparent ease and simplicity of Lowell Thomas's radio manner and Charles Laughton's television appearance is art gained through long years of study and performance. Lowell Thomas had earned a million dollars on the lecture platform with his famous account, "With Lawrence in Arabia," before he went on the air for *The Literary Digest*. Charles Laughton, with experience gained on the stage, on the public platform, on the radio, and on the screen was able to release the author before the cameras.[1] It is a mistake to think that all television programs demand a superabundance of overt action in order to hold attention. Think of the panel programs such as *Meet the Press, Keeping Posted, What's My Line?* Given a good script, an intelligent reader and good

[1] For an interesting account of Charles Laughton's performance on TV see Robert Lewis Shayon, *Saturday Review,* January 19, 1952.

camera work, interpretative reading will hold its own on TV. Artists like Jack Benny, Fred Allen, Groucho Marx, and Herb Shriner [2] for years have held radio audiences in the hollow of their hands through releasing the ideas in the script. This same skill is gradually being recognized in TV and experienced directors are demanding less and less overt action from people who know how to extract the meaning from a good script. It goes without saying that the script must have the power within it to hold attention. Charles Laughton, for example, has said that the average run of love poetry just would not hold an audience.[3] It takes a love poem like "To His Coy Mistress" to hold sustained attention. This poem, Laughton said, has movement, imagery, structure, variety, narrative, body. It is as if the camera were continually shifting its focus within the poem. Materials that handle the element of time and space so as to keep the sense of movement alive hold attention. Variations in spacial and temporal perception help hold the audience. Along with a good script in which the thought develops apace the skill of the speaker will help hold attention. This skill has its basis in "clear enunciation, correct pronunciation free from provincialisms, a well modulated, resonant voice, a capacity to read script as if it were extemporaneous, the power to interpret its contents, both intellectually and emotionally, an ability to edit copy when necessary, a knowledge of foreign language pronunciation and of music, a cultural background sufficient to keep ad-libbed remarks in good taste, and a dramatic instinct that senses what the public wants, or, in some instances, how much it will stand for." [4]

Releasing an author to only one or two listeners or viewers is a different problem from releasing him to a large audience. And if you have been trained to speak in public before a large audience, you will have to take the difference into account when you undertake radio and television reading. Arthur Godfrey has stated that his secret of success in these media is his intimate style.[5] One

---

[2] See *The Saturday Evening Post,* November 29, 1952, p. 25.

[3] Lionel Crocker, "Charles Laughton on Oral Reading," *The Central States Speech Journal,* III, 21.

[4] Alice Keith, *How to Speak and Write for Radio* (New York: Harper, 1944), p. xiii.

[5] See *Newsweek,* May 19, 1952.

reason why many radio and television programs now have a studio audience is to help the speakers get the necessary feeling of direct communication. The listener's interest is sustained for a longer period of time when he feels that he is seated with others in an audience; he is assisted by the concentration of the other listeners. This social pressure is, as if by magic, superimposed upon the listener in his living room. Ed Sullivan's technique of showing the home viewer the audience makes him feel a part of that audience.

In listening to the sets at home, however, the listener and viewer seldom plants himself before them and gives them his undivided attention. Often he carries on a partial conversation with members of his family, the phone rings, or other interruptions occur. The two-way response between speaker and audience is broken many times and the performer can do nothing about it.

III. Mike and Camera Fright

Remember that some nervousness is good for you as you undertake any speaking performance. Actors refer to this nervousness as the spark; it kindles the imagination. Edward R. Murrow has confessed, "I've never got over a slight sense of fright at the sight of a microphone." But we must not confuse this natural nervousness with the terror that seizes one at the thought of doing something new for the first time. The cure for this anxiety, which we all feel, is mere repetition of the dreaded act. The child crossing the road for the first time shrinks back and takes his mother's hand; but he soon learns that he can cross the road alone. And even if a latent fear still lurks in his mind, it is more friend than enemy; it protects him by keeping him alert. Fear is sometimes more of an asset than a liability.

Therefore be prepared for some nervousness as you face the unseen audience; don't be alarmed by it. Keep your mind on what you are going to say, and on one particular person out there listening. Prevent yourself from going into a panic. Don't think of anomalous millions, eagerly awaiting the sound of your voice. There are no faceless masses, no composite millions—only friendly individuals who want to hear what you have to say. If they were not friendly, they would not be listening. One of your listeners is probably leaning back in an easy chair; another, knitting by the fire.

Take care that you do not deliberately set the stage for a bad case of the jitters. Do not arrive at the studio long before you are to go on the air. Keep occupied doing something else. Keep your mind busy with other duties. Experienced actors arrive at the theatre only a few moments before they are to go on. They prepare their rôles thoroughly beforehand and then relax until it is time to appear. Only amateurs stand in the wings, thumbing their scripts and mumbling their lines to themselves before they go on. You merely show your amateurishness by reading and re-reading your script before you get the nod to begin. Act like a professional.

Do not ask too much of yourself. If you do not prepare, you deserve to fail. But even if, after thorough preparation, you still feel nervous, take it for granted that it is a natural reaction. A great many of the top-flight announcers admit that they too felt nervous when they first stepped before the mike or camera. Meet those expected qualms with nonchalance.

Use the same techniques in keeping your mind off yourself that you use when you are going to speak from the public platform. Mike and camera fright is self-consciousness, stimulated and exacerbated by the bizarre atmosphere of the studio. Do not let the new surroundings scare you. If you have a selection that is tried and true, one that has a strong pull to it, one that you have used on other occasions and you know how to release the author from the printed page, you have nothing to worry about. And there is always the comforting thought that you have the manuscript before you to see you through. Settle back and enjoy the experience.

IV. Facing the Microphone

When you go into the studio, the control-room engineer sets about finding the natural level of your voice. He will ask you to speak in your normal accents, and will then help you find the correct position to take up before the microphone. He does this with everyone, no matter how experienced, so do not be bothered by it. Take it in your stride. You will probably use the microphone that is "live" on one side only—the unidirectional type. (The other two types in common use are the bidirectional and the nondirectional, terms which are self-explanatory.) It is probable that you will sit at a table, at a distance of about eight or ten inches from the microphone. And if you seat yourself so as to talk directly into it, you will be in the best position for projecting your voice over the air. You will be speaking "on the beam." Now just be comfortable and relax. Unbutton the collar of your shirt and imagine that you are getting ready to talk to a friend across the table.

Let's take the clip off the manuscript and shuffle the pages loosely so they will slide easily over one another. Some readers drop each page to the floor as they finish reading it, in order to prevent any confusion with pages yet to come. Some use half sheets, to help the eye keep its place on the page. Whatever form the script takes, it is of the greatest importance that there be no rattle of paper to be picked up by the microphone; we want to appear to be *talking,* rather than reading. Another little point that makes for a smooth performance: try to clear your throat before you go on the air. Raymond Gram Swing has a device on his microphone to shut it off if he has to cough or clear his throat.

Here are some of the mistakes most of us make when we read over the air for the first time:

1. We read too fast.
2. We read above our normal pitch.
3. We are afraid to favor the lower tones of the voice, not realizing that we have power to carry these lower tones.
4. We read in a sing-song fashion.
5. We forget, and clear our throats after we are "on."
6. We let our voices slip back into our throats.
7. We smack our lips.
8. We use too much volume at the beginning, before we remember that it is the engineer's business to control the volume.
9. We talk to the side of the microphone.
10. We read to the manuscript instead of to the microphone.
11. We breathe too noticeably, because excitement has disturbed our normal breathing.

12. We give away the fact that we are *reading,* not talking in a natural conversational manner.

V. Facing the Camera

All the techniques the reader has learned in the use of his body to help project meaning will of course be useful in television, although they may have to be adapted. Gestures will be more intimate and less broad. Facial gesture that might not be noticeable in a large auditorium will be picked up by the camera. We remember how revealing the hands of Frank Costello were when he refused to have his face televised. How important lessons in posture and gesture are is emphasized by a recent study by Congressmen, who were getting ready for campaigning via television, of the techniques of appearing before the camera. And we are told that dignified members of Congress, like Sam Rayburn, finally consented, after much persuasion, to letting make-up be applied to their bald pates. We should cooperate in every way with those whose business it is to put on television programs. The following comment on Clare Booth Luce during a political campaign as she faced the camera is of interest:

> The most skilful use of the basic techniques of television was made by Clare Booth Luce. As she spoke of corruption or Chambers and Hiss or the war in Korea, film or maps or other visual material seemed to flow on to the screen and to flow out again to her, so that she really seemed to be looking at, or listening to, what she was showing us. She was herself not nearly as effective as she had been on radio, seeming more worried about her program than about her subject, being precise and angry without generating warmth; but her program was a technical masterpiece compared to most others.[6]

Technique can smother personality. Also distracting mannerisms can call attention to themselves and interfere with communication. Clothes that are unsuitable to strong lights should be discarded in favor of more photogenic materials. White shirts give way to colored ones. For the amateur it is interesting to study the clothing worn by successful artists on TV. These words from

---

[6] Gilbert Seldes, "TV and the Voter," *Saturday Review,* December 6, 1952, p. 19.

Worthington Miner on the dependence upon the visual arts in television are full of meaning: "Television is the most all-encompassing of all the varied forms of entertainment. It is somewhat doubtful, in fact, whether certain aspects of television should be classified as entertainment at all—whether they would not more aptly be described as educational, or instructive. . . . Television has the full scope of radio with additional emphasis upon those visual arts, which are the vital component of every production." [7]

The nature of the reading on television changes as inventions make the task easier and more effective. Following is a reply from the NBC Press Department concerning the reading on Arlene Francis's program "Home."

I presume your interest in the picture is to show your students just how the performers on "Home" deliver their lines.

I should like to make it clear that most of the regular members of the "Home" show ad-lib or deliver their lines from card notes, but in the case of commercials or other complicated segments involving specific facts, figures or situations, a "Telecue" is used. This is a gadget which is attached to the front of the camera just above the lens and is moved on rollers. In this manner the performers can read their lines directly from the "Telecue" and still look directly at the camera. It is controlled by an operator behind the scenes. When "Home" first went on the air written card cues were used but have since been abandoned.

VI. You're on the Air

In rehearsing the script, pace your delivery, marking your place in the margin as each minute elapses. This will help you to adjust your rate of speech so that you come out on time. Lowell Thomas [8] marks his script thus by minutes, up to the last three or four; then at 30-second intervals. Try it with your manuscript. If you find you exceed 130 to 140 words per minute, slow down.

Once you are on the air, your practice behind you, with a sound knowledge of your subject matter, speak with abandon. Speak with vitality, nerve, force, and dramatic power. We should not

[7] Worthington Miner, "Training for Television," *Quarterly Journal of Speech,* XXXVI, 1.

[8] See Lionel Crocker, "Lowell Thomas," *Quarterly Journal of Speech,* XXVIII, 27.

like to feel that our friends choose each word with the utmost circumspection when they talk to us. Your manuscript, of course, has been prepared with meticulous care; but never let that fact cripple the spontaneity of your delivery. When once you face your audience, via the microphone, let your speech go. Speak with that abandon of which Professor A. J. Latham has said: "It calls for that degree of the giving-up of self to the communication of experience that the experience and the purpose of the communication require. It is in harmony, not in discord, with ease, economy, and repose." [9] Listen with a critical ear to the radio speakers you most enjoy, and you will find that your enjoyment arises from this same controlled and restful ease. There is no slavish, disjointed reading of word for word; there is a smooth, onward movement of the phrase, the sentence, the whole speech to the climax.

Go over your script, marking it for ease in reading with studious care, when you are on the air. These signposts you erect will keep your sense of abandon within limits. Write notes to yourself on the script. Speaking of notes, you may be interested in this little story about a public speaker, which came out of the late war. As part of a government training course being given in Washington, a young major presented an hour-long lecture on abstruse military matters. He spoke fluently, pausing only occasionally to glance at a small slip of paper he had placed on the reading stand before him. At the conclusion of his lecture, he departed without taking the slip of paper with him, and one man in the audience went up and picked it up. He wanted to see how it was possible to boil such a long talk down to such a tiny page of notes. He found, however, that he was on the wrong track. The paper said simply, in large, well-spaced capitals:

SPEAK SLOWLY! DON'T TWIDDLE.

You too may have to adopt some such means of admonishing yourself. Professionals never hesitate to mark up their manuscripts.

Here, by way of illustration, is a marked script of Westbrook Van Voorhis's, announcer for "The March of Time on the Air."

[9] See A. J. Latham, "Abandon, A Characteristic of Perfected Speech," *Quarterly Journal of Speech,* XVI, 171.

You may recognize it, for it was used in an advertising campaign by *Time* magazine. Of course, you will gradually work out your own method of marking a script, but you may enjoy seeing how Mr. Van Voorhis did it.

The following letter was sent out by *Time* with the script, to explain its markings:

All of us have to make speeches sometime.

And so I thought you would like to see some professional speaking tricks that may come in handy the next time you have to give a talk or read a report to some group of your associates.

Attached is an actual example of how our famed "Time Marches *ON*" announcer marks up a script before he steps up to the microphone.

Van Voorhis does this ~~~~ under a word to remind himself that although he might be tempted to inflect it with unusual emphasis, he should give it only its natural weight in the sentence.

When he does this —— under a word it means hit the word hard. This ——— means not quite so hard, but do not slur. . . .

This / means a partial stop; this // means a complete stop; and this ||| means the end of the story.

The double underline means "slow down first and then give this word all you've got," and when Van puts quotes around a word it means he's probably had trouble with it in rehearsals, that it's an unusual word and he has to give it specially careful "orthoepic" handling.

Let's hope it won't be too long now before we hear him say, "I interrupt this program to announce that 'Hitler is "Ausgespielt"! ||| '"

And this is Mr. Van Voorhis's script with its markings:

VAN . . .

Endeavoring to keep up with world affairs is never an easy job. / Today, when there are so many tremendous events in the making, it is more difficult than ever before. // That is why Americans now have greater need than ever / for frank and forthright reporting of the news / —realistic reporting that cuts through the confusion to get at the facts. // As many an American believes today— //

MAN . . .

In those communiques we get from the front . . . they boil the news down to where you can hardly see it. And when you start reading those crystal gazers . . . why you just get more confused than ever.

VAN . . .

(*quick cue*)

Yes, as a result of cryptic communiques and hopeful crystal gazers, there is a special need today for TIME's kind of reporting. // Time Magazine's frank and forthright reporting is relentless in its presentation of the facts. / Pleasant or unpleasant, the facts are reported to Time's readers in Time's own analytical style, which helps them understand what is happening / and why. // Because of that, realistic Americans in all parts of the nation . . . (from the largest cities to the remotest crossroads) . . . have come to rely on Time. // In Time / they know they can get the facts they need to make their own plans . / . . the facts they need to take part in the public discussions through which the nation's plans are made. // To provide those facts through frank, forthright and realistic reporting / is the all-important wartime function of Time Magazine. | | |

(*music up*)

Another worth-while suggestion is to mark your script in such a way that you can judiciously cut it if you find that you are running over time. Conversely, experienced readers provide themselves with a "cushion" with which, if need be, they can pad out a script that falls short of the allotted time limit.

VII. Some Practical Suggestions

Read aloud every day before different length mirrors. Sometimes sit at a desk and face yourself in a mirror and try to look more at your image than you do at your script. At other times practice reading to a full length mirror as you stand in front of it. Pick up the evening newspaper and read the headlines, read the editorial page, read the comics.

Since ad libbing is such an important part of television reading, practice talking about what you have read, all the time looking yourself in the eye. Watch your general stance, your carriage, your natural appearance, and the use of your hands. Do not make too many gestures. Above all, do not move the hands directly into the mirror. This habit of gesturing toward the camera will put your hands out of focus and make them look larger.

As you come to the concluding words of your practice copy, note the expression on your face as you say the last word and then hold that expression for a count of five. Study TV programs and note how this is done. Note that the participants on such a program as "Meet the Press" have been coached in this technique. At first you will find it difficult to keep from looking just a bit self-conscious, or you will look away, or take on a slightly "blank" look during the brief moment after you have finished the copy and the time it takes to shut down or switch the camera. Do not spoil the effect of your message. Hold the expression. It is like the follow through in golf.

Be friendly and pleasant. This attitude can be developed. Practice a cordial manner on your daily rounds.

Be versatile. Read widely. Do not confine your interests. Try to talk about subjects introduced by your friends. If you do not know, look it up.

Develop your style of speaking. Do not be forced. Do not use unnatural tones. Know your own style.

Be perfectly familiar with the materials you have to read to prevent "fluffing."

Start training your memory so that you retain what you read. Try to repeat from memory as much as you can.

Project. Always imagine that you are talking to someone and someone is listening and reacting to what you are saying.

Remember that sound takes second place to the picture in TV.

VIII. Use of Recordings [10]

In most colleges and universities, the Department of Speech boasts a recording studio. Do not turn down this golden opportunity to record your voice. You can learn much from listening to your own reading. And if the record library possesses discs made by professional readers, listen to them, too, for the lessons they can give you. As you listen to a recording of your own, check your delivery for the following points:

Melody

1. Do you speak in a monotone?
2. Does your speech pattern resemble H. V. Kaltenborn's—i.e., are you guilty of the "preacher's cadence"? (See p. 235.)

[10] For a catalogue of recordings see Ted Cott, *A Treasury of the Spoken Word* (New York: Hermitage Press, 1949), p. 359.

3. Do you have two notes, and only two, to your voice?
4. Is the melody of your speech that of reading or that of talking?
5. Is the modulation meaningful?
6. Is the melody appropriate to the thought being expressed?
7. Is the melody *your* melody, does it express your personality?

Time

1. Do you change your pace as the thought or emotion changes?
2. Does material that demands a quickened pace get it?
3. Do you speak hurriedly and nervously—with nervous haste?
4. Do you use pauses to bring out the thought?
5. Do you speak spontaneously, as if you were ad-libbing?
6. Do you speak as if you were speaking *to* someone?
7. Do you put meaning into such transitional words as, "Well," "Oh," "Now," "Then," as one does in ordinary conversation?
8. With a stop watch, time the flow of words per minute.

Quality

1. Is your voice relaxed?
2. Does its quality reflect the mood of the material?
3. Is your voice breathy, guttural, squeaky, nasal?
4. Is your voice high and thin, without body?
5. Does your voice reflect your sincerity, the warmth of your personality?
6. Is its quality cultivated?
7. Is there enough resonance?
8. Is the diction satisfactory?
9. Is the quality conversational?
10. Is the quality pompous?
11. Is there an eagerness to communicate in the quality?
12. Is the voice free from whining?

Force

1. Does your voice have enough force to sound confident and convincing?
2. Does it sound authoritative?
3. Is your voice domineering?
4. Is it vigorous?
5. Does your voice sound like the voice of a sick man?
6. Is it quiet and restrained?
7. Does its force seem natural?

IX. Summary

Everything we have been trying to say in this chapter is either stated or suggested in the following words of the winner of the 1932 Gold Medal awarded by the American Academy of Arts and Letters for good diction on the air, Mr. David Ross. He lists what he considers to be the essential principles of good announcing:

1. A clear speaking voice.
2. An ability to enlist the voice in the service of good speech.
3. A knowledge of the tonal quality of words and their psychological effects beyond their dictionary meaning.
4. An announcer must first understand his continuity thoroughly before he can speak it intelligently.
5. He must understand the effect of understatement as well as emphasis.
6. He must never try to inflate by false accentuation what is essentially a simple, homey phrase to the proportions of grandeur. The phrase will die of pomposity.
7. He must remember that he is talking to live human beings who have loved, struggled, laughed, dreamed, despaired and hoped; therefore his work before the microphone must reflect his human experience so that his audience will recognize it as real.
8. He must bear in mind that the cheap wisecrack is as offensive as the direct insult.
9. An announcer must know when he knows not, and make it his business to find out.
10. If the announcer expects to be received into the homes of his hearers he must come with credentials of grace, sincerity and warm fellowship, and these may be found in his voice.

X. Projects for Chapter XII

1. Read and report on the profile of Edward R. Murrow appearing in *The New Yorker,* December 26, 1953, p. 28.
2. Read and report on two of the latest columns on radio and TV in *The Saturday Review.*
3. Send to one of the national hook-ups and ask for a script of your favorite radio commentator and prepare a reading for the class based on this script.
4. Listen to several television news broadcasters and make a list of the best features. Give a talk to the class on this. For example, what use is made of visual aids, of prompters, of action?

5. Read the following account by Philip Hamburger of an interview with Robert Frost and discuss the factors that made the interview successful.

Men of Faith[11]

Some months ago, in honor of Bertrand Russell's eightieth birthday, N.B.C. gave us the pleasure of a half hour in the great man's company, by means of a filmed interview with him at his home in England. To be in such a presence for thirty minutes was a remarkable experience, and I look back upon it with delight. Fortunately, the N.B.C. people must have been delighted with the endeavor, too, for late one Sunday afternoon a couple of weeks ago they came along with an interview of the same type, this time with Robert Frost. Like its predecessor, this program was quiet, unpretentious, informative, and exhilarating. We first caught a glimpse of Mr. Frost outside his farmhouse at Ripton, Vermont. He was approaching a horse with whom, obviously, he was on the best of terms. He next entered the house, and was greeted by Mr. Bela Kornitzer, a Hungarian writer, who was on hand to interview him. For twenty-seven minutes or so, Mr. Kornitzer kept himself discreetly in the background, asking a minimum of questions and in no way trying, in the accepted television-interviewing manner, to make himself more important than the subject. Mr. Frost was in a mellow mood. If granite could repose, one might say that his face was a study in reposed granite. He is now seventy-seven, and not the least bit ashamed of the wisdom he has picked up along the trail, and not ashamed, either, to discuss his thoughts and feelings about life.

He had a great many things to say. He talked of the virtue that, for him, counts the most—the courage to act on limited knowledge. "A general has to go into battle on limited knowledge, insufficient knowledge—insufficient," he said. "And someone has said that a poet ought to learn all that the other poets had ever said before he undertakes to say anything, so he'd avoid repetition, you know. But if he did that, he'd be fifty years old before he started." He talked of his father, a San Francisco newspaperman, who died when Frost was ten, and of the pride he took as a boy in watching his father swim out of sight in San Francisco Bay, "until he appeared again on a buoy somewhere out there in the evening." Under Mr. Kornitzer's gentle prodding, Mr. Frost, clasping and unclasping his large, weatherbeaten hands, told of having been a farmer, a newspaperman, a teacher—"I ought to say I got something out of being a teacher. I had to make things understood, and that put

[11] *The New Yorker,* December 13, 1952. By permission. Copyright 1952 The New Yorker Magazine, Inc.

me in the class of poets that wanted to be understood." He told of his debt to the British, who first published a collection of his poems. "They put me on my feet," he said. "I came home from there sort of a made poet, you know." He told, too, of his debt to his publisher here in America, and to the colleges that have put him on their faculties and left him alone to write as he pleased. Mr. Kornitzer suddenly threw a curve at him. "You are labelled by essayists and critics as nature poet, New England Yankee, symbolist, humanist, skeptic, and anti-Platonist, and as many other things. Which of these labels do you consider true?" Mr. Frost smiled. "I don't pick out any single one," he said. "I take them all, take them and put my arm around them." "Well," said Mr. Kornitzer, who was determined to put one across the plate, "what kind of poet do you consider yourself?" "Old as I am," said Mr. Frost, "I am not self-conscious enough to tell you. . . . I like to be called humanist, I guess, pretty well, though I'm not strictly a humanist. I guess I'm not a nature poet. I have only written two poems without a human being in them, only two."

Mr. Frost agreed to recite his "Stopping by Woods on a Snowy Evening" and proceeded to do so, in the slow, rich voice familiar to those who have heard him on the lecture platform. He recited the poem as though he loved it very much and was proud of it, and listening to this brief recitation by a man in control of himself and his work would alone have made the afternoon worth while. As soon as he had finished, Mr. Kornitzer said he had read somewhere that the poem was "a suicide poem," and asked, "Is this classification correct?" Mr. Frost stopped *that* one. "That's terrible—terrible, isn't it?" he said instantly. He talked awhile of the cruelty of nature ("The woods are killing each other anyway"), of the possibility of a happier world if poets were listened to more ("I'm satisfied with the division of the spoils. It's always been that way. Poetry hasn't had much of a say in the time of it. In Homer's time, the rhymes say, seven cities claimed Homer dead through which the living Homer begged his bread"), of promising young writers (". . . always some of them around. I know many of them—always half a dozen or so that are good bets, you know. You can't tell too far ahead. Some of them give it up, go into banking"). Toward the end of the half hour, Mr. Frost recited another poem, and said that he was less interested in political freedom than in the liberties he takes. "I am an internationalist in the same way as I am an interpersonalist," he said. "I don't care about spending much time with people who haven't a definite personality. I am that kind of an equalitarian. I like to mix with my equals, people who have as much personality as I have . . . but the great thing is taut boldness. . . . People . . . will tell you that freedom lies in being cautious." Here he violently shook his head. "Freedom lies in being bold."

CHAPTER XIII

The Reader Himself

I. The Overtones of the Voice
II. Originality
III. Taste
IV. Avoiding Self-Conceit
V. Your Speech Background
VI. Intellectual and Emotional Ownership
VII. Your Core of Belief
VIII. Personal Magnetism
IX. Summary
X. Projects for Chapter XIII

I. The Overtones of the Voice

When you come into a class in oral reading, you bring your baggage with you; and when you rise to speak, you prepare to reveal its contents to your audience. Your baggage consists of your mind, your emotions, and your character. The ear of the listener is quick to catch all the overtones of your voice as it tries to convey the meaning of the printed page. Whether you understand a particular allusion, whether you grasp the full meaning of a phrase, will be unmistakably revealed by the inflections of your voice. Consequently, the reader has to be more than a robot, converting the printed symbols into the appropriate sound waves. If you have ever heard a foreigner read English, a foreigner who was not fully aware of the implications and the overtones of the words he was reading, you have an extreme picture of what happens when the uninformed, the uneducated individual reads from the printed page—the person who does not fully appreciate what he is reading.

With Tennyson's "Ulysses," you can truly say that you are a part of all that you have met, and that all that you have met is a part of you. In consequence, your words glow with life or are pallid and colorless, accordingly as you yourself have been illuminated by the spectra of human experience.

The importance of being able to read a manuscript intelligently is illustrated in this picture of Arlene Francis on her NBC-TV "Home" show. Most of the regular members of the "Home" show ad-lib or deliver their lines from card notes, but in the case of commercials or other complicated segments involving specific facts, figures, or situations, a "Telecue" is used. This is a gadget which is attached to the front of the camera just above the lens and is moved on rollers. In this manner the performers can read their lines directly from the "Telecue" and still look directly at the camera. It is controlled by an operator behind the scenes.

Wide World Photo

Arthur Godfrey was one of the first to use the teleprompter. On one of his programs he stopped his show and explained how the device worked. In this picture you see Temporary Chairman Walter Hallanan of the Republican Convention watching the teleprompter which was used during the Republican Convention in July 1952. If you will watch television newsreporters and actors you can often detect them reading from the teleprompter which is out of range of the camera. These gadgets to aid the television reader are being constantly improved.

He cannot heal who has not suffered much,
For only sorrow sorrow understands.
They will not come for healing at our touch
Who have not seen the scars upon our hands.

If Shakespeare means nothing to you, if the Bible is only a word, if Robert Browning is a stranger to you, you will never pick up allusions to them with enthusiasm, as if meeting with old friends.

Every bit of travel you have had, every place you have seen, every bit of first-hand experience of life you have acquired helps your words come to life. If you have visited Chicago, you will read Carl Sandburg's poem, "Chicago," with just a bit more appreciation than one who has never been there. As you read, recall your own impressions of the city. Smell the stockyards! Hear the babel of the railroad yards! See the prostitutes under the street lamps! If you have been to New England, you will read Robert Frost with more understanding. You will see with your own eyes the stonewalls and the birches of which the poet writes. You read *with* your experience, both direct and indirect. You read *to* the experience of the audience.

II. Originality

When you read you must give the audience your whole self. Thoreau expressed it this way: "Expression is the act of the whole man, that our speech may be vascular. The intellect is powerless to express thought without the aid of the heart and liver and of every member." The reader is always trying to find the realities of human experience, realities that lie below the surface of appearance and social convention, in the selections he reads, and striving to convey these realities to others. If he fails to seize upon them, his reading is likely to be, in the phrase of Barrett Wendell, "a diarrhoea of words and constipation of thought." Spontaneity and freedom of expression are to be sought in interpreting a passage, for where these two qualities are suppressed the reading is dead and lifeless.

How can you "give yourself" to a passage? The answer is by thorough assimilation of the passage with your own thoughts and emotions. In the following excerpt from the January, 1945, *Reader's Digest,* Warrant Officer George R. Tweed, U.S.N., gives us an idea of what "thorough assimilation" can mean. The article is called, "I Learned to Read on Guam":

I spent most of my two years and seven months on Jap-held Guam hiding in a kind of eagle's nest, a great crevice between two sheer rock cliffs overlooking the Pacific Ocean. Often as I crouched there the crackling of bushes told me that the fifty-man Jap patrol detailed to hunt me down was again beating the underbrush beneath my hideout.

Under such circumstances, pleasures were limited, but I found a few. Chief among them was reading two copies of *The Reader's Digest,* precious excess weight with which I could not bring myself to part, even in weeks of being pursued through treacherous, thorny, almost impenetrable bush.

By the sputtering light of a wick dipped in a sardine can filled with coconut oil, I suppose I read these magazines from cover to cover on an average of once every other week. Instead of rereading only my favorite articles, I always went straight through from page one to the end.

One article in the October 1940 issue seemed to be written expressly for me. It was called "You Become Someone—Alone." Mary Ellen Chase, the author, described the joy of taking a trip alone. One by one, as she counted the blessings of a solitary life, I made comparisons with my own state. During her long hours of solitude, Miss Chase said, she relived her life as a child, bringing up from the past persons and places which had helped form her personality. I discovered these same pleasures. Many a lonely supper of breadfruit was made more palatable by recalling hunting expeditions—the hours waiting in the woods, the coolness and quiet of certain forest spots, and the sudden excitement of startling from cover a coyote or a cougar. I reviewed all my boyhood, backyard horseshoes played with my father, and trips to the orchard for Oregon apples to be made into tart jellies by my mother and sister. I dug down into my memory and found dozens of friends whose names and faces I had not recalled for ten or even twenty years. Scenes from my early life came back to me as if I were watching slides flashed on the wall of the rock cliff.

Another article to which I returned with ever-renewed enjoyment was "My Most Unforgettable Character" by Stephen Vincent Benét. The "character" was his father, an Army ordnance colonel. The elder Benét reminded me of home. His comments on his son's actions were, like my father's, "often unexpected, sometimes drastic, but never uncomprehending." With each reading I became more endeared to the salty colonel and felt that I understood my own father better.

My two magazines were frequently splattered with blowing rain. As a result of putting them in the tropical sun to dry, the swollen pages gradually rotted and flaked off, so that every time I read them flecks of paper covered my dungarees like confetti. Perusing the ragged copies again and again, I realized how much I had missed in magazines before. In the States I read a story once and forgot it almost before I came to the ads in the back of the magazine. Now I saw that with only one exposure to an article a person fails to retain much of the information. Good writing, I decided, deserves deliberate reading.

This revelation, coming to me between days of agonized searching of the horizon for returning American ships and hours of fighting against despair of ever being rescued, taught me to read. Now, when my copy of the *Digest* arrives, I read it through once. A week later, I pick it up again and see how many articles I remember well enough to discuss. I find that surprisingly many escape me almost entirely. I then reread all which I have failed to make my own.

My second reading is more satisfying than the first. Since the general pattern is familiar, I concentrate upon details, illustrations that bring flesh, blood, and muscle to the skeleton. Almost miraculously, the ideas expressed become a part of my working knowledge, and the anecdotes remain with me to enliven future hours.

I have been a difficult pupil. I had to go through a world war and 31 months of solitude, every day of which my life was in danger, to learn how to read.

"Good writing deserves deliberate reading." Two actors can give widely different readings of the same rôle; the difference is due to the mold (the interpreter's past experience) in which the interpretation is cast. It is said that when George Arliss undertook a rôle in a play with a slum background, he lived for months in the dark corners of London's East End, making himself up for the part *from within,* as later he assumed its outer shreds and patches. Originality demands that we go from the inner to the outer. Nature herself unfolds; the oak tree grows from the acorn. Your interpretation must come from within you. What you *are* will determine *how* you read.

Students sometimes listen to records of John Barrymore's interpretation of *Hamlet* and then try to imitate his rendition. Such imitation can be constructive, if it is regarded merely as an exercise to improve one's own diction, or pace, or tonal range; a slavish attempt at exact reproduction, however, leads to a mechanical interpretation. Stephen Vincent Benét's reading of "The Ballad of William Sycamore"; Robert Frost's of "Mending Wall"; Archibald MacLeish's interpretation of Matthew Arnold's "Dover Beach"; and other recordings, may all be helpful as brilliant illustrations of the principles of oral interpretation, but the student should be aware of the dangers of slavish imitation. Nothing can take the place of deliberate reading, the process of finding the meaning and emotion of the selection for oneself.

III. Taste

Nothing about us is so revealing as our *taste*. As a reader you should strive to acquire catholicity of taste. But in improving your taste, you must beware lest you become a snob. Take as your model William Lyon Phelps, whose acquaintanceship with literature was equalled only by his knowledge of and liking for people. Although Professor Phelps taught courses in Tennyson and Browning, he counted Edgar Guest among his close acquaintances. He was at one and the same time a prominent Shakespearean scholar and a friend of Gene Tunney, the one-time heavyweight champion of the world. Interestingly enough it was Shakespeare who brought the two together. Professor Phelps had personal magnetism. People were drawn to him and he was drawn to them. Here is a secret of personal development.

People who live much with the printed page are likely to become separated from reality. The vigor and vitality of the market place are absent from their daily routine. False standards are easily set up in minds that occupy ivory towers exclusively. The taste of the man in the street comes to be frowned upon and yet it is often the man in the street to whom one must read. The reader does not know his audience. Perhaps, if we define improving one's taste to mean widening one's taste, we set up a standard worthier of attainment. For example, one, who is not a boxer himself, might conceivably learn to understand the fine points of boxing so that one could watch a boxing match and appreciate the finesse of a great boxer versus the slugging of an untrained fighter. And in our reading there can be degrees of enjoyment. Some things we will like more than others. This means that on our own we can say, "I like that" and we won't have to wait for someone to tell us what to like. This means that we can find at times articles in the current magazines and newspapers that strike us as particularly well done and enjoy them and know why we enjoy them. This means that we do not see life in fits and starts and only fractions of it, but that, in Matthew Arnold's words, it means that we see life steady and see it whole.

By developing our appreciation of the outside world we attempt to open out a way "whence the imprisoned splendor may escape."

> Truth is within ourselves; it takes no rise
> From outward things, whate'er you may believe:
> There is an inmost centre in us all,
> Where truth abides in fulness; and around,
> Wall upon wall, the gross flesh hems it in,
> This perfect, clear perception—which is truth;
> A baffling and perverting carnal mesh
> Blinds it, and makes all error: and 'to know'
> Rather consists in opening out a way
> Whence the imprisoned splendor may escape,
> Then in effecting entry for a light
> Supposed to be without.
>
> —BROWNING'S *Paracelsus.*

IV. AVOIDING SELF-CONCEIT

The reader must always keep himself in the background—there should be no place for conceit in his make-up. The selection must always come first. He must develop a freedom from self-consciousness. He need ask only one question: "How may I read most effectively for others?" The less he asks the question: "How may I read most creditably for myself?" the better.

In other words, the reader should be not an exhibitionist, but a conveyor of the truth, the real meaning of what he reads. As such, the more he fades into the background and lets the author speak, the better. Any mannerisms should be eliminated from his delivery. Any idiosyncrasy of dress or speech should be shunned. A few years ago we had in our classes a young lady with a pathological diction. We call it pathological because it seemed to us that she had adopted this British accent to cover up a feeling of inferiority. She had spent two years in England, and since then had carefully cultivated a broad *a* and the British habit of accenting the first syllable. We are sorry to say that we were not successful in helping this young lady to tear down this false façade masking her personality. When she went out to teach, she lost one position after another. Boys and girls made fun of her accent behind her back. Lack of respect led to lack of discipline.

The same simplicity and sincerity that mark your speech should find expression in your dress as well. An audience seizes upon every clue to detect what sort of person you are. Do you shine your shoes? Or are your unkempt shoes a pose? If you are a boy, do you tuck soiled cuffs back under your coat sleeves in defiance of custom? Do you wear frayed ties? Do you keep food spots off your clothing? If you are a girl, do you keep your hair combed? Are the seams in your stockings straight? Do you keep your skirts pressed, and are your sweaters immaculate? An audience knows that physical care proceeds from spiritual care. If there is inner disintegration, it will show up in outer neglect. Neatness is a manifestation of the workings of the mind. The audience looks for every sign to tell it what sort of person it has to deal with.

V. Your Speech Background

You are indeed fortunate if you have grown up in an environment where emphasis has been placed on the spoken word. In the complex and sometimes difficult process of learning to speak correctly, there is no substitute for good speech in the home. I have noticed that young men and women who have come from homes where there is respect for the power of the spoken word usually have an appreciation—and not only an appreciation but a mastery—of good speech, which is above average. Lowell Thomas is a good example of the advantage to a youngster of growing up with respect for good diction. If you have been denied such an advantage in your own home, you will have to make up for it by hard work. But let us quote Lowell Thomas's expression of gratitude for his early speech training:

> Nearly everything that I am as a public speaker I owe to my Dad. He was, and still is, a practicing physician and surgeon. As a young man he was a country school teacher, back in the days when debating was the great indoor sport. His father had been a school teacher, debater and speaker. His mother was a poet. And his grandfather on her side was a circuit rider and preacher who either had to be persuasive

or lose his scalp, because his listeners were Indians, back in the good old war-whoop and war-path days. When I was a youngster in a gold mining camp out West, my Dad decided to experiment with me. He had done just enough public speaking to become convinced that ability to hold an audience was much to be desired. That if you were an able public speaker you could make friends a hundred or a thousand at a time, instead of one or two at a time. I was twelve years old and he had been working on me for years. At that particular time we were going through the James Whitcomb Riley stage, memorizing dozens of the Hoosier poet's humorous verses, in dialect. One of my father's theories was that the way to knock monotony out of a speaker, make him put light and shade into his style, was to do things in dialect. If I used a nasal tone he would make me go over and over it until he eliminated that. Or, if the complex inflection of a line of dialect was not satisfactory he would keep me at it until I was more Hoosier than "Moonlight on the Wabash." My father kept everlastingly at it, year in and year out. Naturally this could not be kept a secret. And one result was that I was always asked to recite poems, or do something, at every church function and lodge entertainment in that mining camp. A Knights of Pythias supper or Royal Order of Moose celebration was never complete without my being on hand to tell the woes of "Ole Doc Siphers" or "The Raggety Man." [1]

VI. Intellectual and Emotional Ownership

This course in oral reading can enrich you, intellectually and emotionally. Already you are the possessor of many worth-while ideas gained in other courses. In this course we want you to realize the riches you already have and to stake out new claims. The more you know, the more you have read, the more you have travelled, and the more you realize the meaning of these experiences, the more the printed page will mean to you. Remember Spenser's words

It is the mind that maketh
Good or ill,
That maketh wretch or happy,
Rich or poor.

Death is merely a word upon the printed page, or an episode in a movie until it has struck deep into one's own household. Only

[1] Lowell Thomas, *How to Keep Mentally Fit* (New York: Howell, Soskin and Company, 1943), p. 222.

the sufferer from insomnia grasps the full import of Shakespeare's lines on sleep. The child of eight years who is taught the text, "He that is slow to anger is better than the mighty; and he that ruleth his spirit than he that taketh a city," can not possibly *own* this statement. Years later the text may become his, because he has bought it with dear experience.

But it is possible for you to have great experiences and to be unaware of the fact. You may be unprepared to appreciate what you see or feel, hear or taste. You may travel to the ends of the earth and come back as provincial as the day you left. On a student tour of the Holy Land, there were students who, when the ship docked at Jerusalem, sat all day in the hotel playing bridge. One who visits the Grand Canyon with some idea of the geology and geography of the region in mind will appreciate the experience far more than that college student the poverty of whose spirit echoed loudly in the comment: "Gee, this is a big hole"! Similarly, people who return from Niagara Falls and state laconically that they were "disappointed" reveal their lack of understanding.

In the same way, you may come in contact with great poetry and be unmoved by it. But before passing summary judgment, remember that it is really you who have been weighed and found wanting. The student who says with finality, "I don't see anything in that," of a Shakespearean sonnet merely reveals his own poverty; Shakespeare's riches are not diminished. They remain intact for future exploration. But no one can *give* us intellectual ownership. "By the sweat of thy brow shalt thou earn thy bread." And unless that effort is made, unless the impoverished mind is enriched, it is impossible to read with comprehension.

We read *with* our experience *to* the experience of the audience. The meaning of the symbols on the printed page must be transmitted to the audience through the medium of our own apprehension.

John Galsworthy gives us a vivid picture of how the artist stores up and uses experience:

> If one can imagine the Catacombs of Rome, or the old cellars under the Adelphi, stored to the brim with photographic films, one has perhaps some notion of what the human sub-conscious mind is like. Every minute, every second, indeed, of our existence, adds to recorded experience, stacked and piled ready to be drawn upon.

The lecturer, then, suspects that what we call our conscious or directive minds are normally only able to make a very limited and severely practical selective use of the treasures in our cellars, and that what we know as the creative gift in literature, or indeed in any art, is a more than normal power in certain people for dipping into the storehouse and fishing up the odds and ends of experience, together with a special aptitude for welding or grouping those odds and ends when they are fished up.[2]

To match those catacombs of experience that the author draws upon to write a particular work, the reader must draw upon his own storehouses to interpret it. He must weld or group his own experiences to correspond with those of the author. When, for example, we say that we have no interest in a particular selection, do we not mean that we have no experience to match that of its writer? The boy whose father is a real-estate broker, who has heard real estate discussed across the dining-room table all his life, is more interested in a chapter on rent in his text in economics than is a boy whose father is a preacher.

To be an effective reader, you need the inner capital of experience, the ownership of those emotions of which the authors whom you interpret write. Robert Frost has traced the source of a poem to its secret springs in the poet's own experience: "A poem is never a put-up job; it begins as a lump in the throat, a sense of wrong, a homesickness, a lovesickness." In the catacomb of your experience, is there a film that has been exposed to homesickness? Is there a film that records your reaction to a burning injustice? And have you, in your stored-up experience, a film with the imprint of desperate longing for a loved one?

Thy soul must overflow if thou
   Another's soul would reach.
It needs the overflow of heart
   To give the lips full speech.

Thought is deeper than all speech;
   Feeling deeper than all thought.
Souls to souls can never teach
   What unto themselves was taught.

[2] John Galsworthy, *The Creation of Character in Literature* (London: Oxford, 1931).

VII. Your Core of Belief

When you read, you read not only the *words* of the author, but his inner meaning; and you read not only with your own experience but with something else—with your fundamental belief. Your grasp, or lack of grasp, of the meaning of life is bound to show in your reading. Maxwell Anderson's declaration on this point is important to recall:

> And now I must give a definition of what seems to me morally sound. If an artist believes that there is good and that there is evil, and in his work favors what seems to him good, and expects ultimate victory for it, then he is morally sound. If he does not believe in the existence of good and evil, or if, believing in them, he asks, or even anticipates, the triumph of evil, he is morally unsound.[3]

Do you believe that your life counts toward the fulfillment of a purpose? Is it a framework awaiting a picture to frame? Does everything you do prepare you to fulfill the purpose of your life, a purpose which is eventually merged with the purpose of the universe? Does your life have a continuity with other lives? Do you agree with Robert Frost when he says, "Men work together whether they work together or apart"?

You are to be the channel through whom the author is to speak. *You* are to recreate what the author has said. If what has been said is of importance to the world, only a person with a sense of his own importance can read such material so that its significance is clear.

VIII. Personal Magnetism

An outgrowth of your personal belief will be personal magnetism. Just as a magnet sends out rays of influence, so all of us sent out invisible rays which attract other people to us. Some of us have developed this quality more than others. But it is possible for all of us to be more attractive if we try. The basic principle of personal magnetism is to be interested in other people. Do you remember the lines from "My Last Duchess,"

---

[3] *The Bases of Artistic Creation* (New Brunswick: Rutgers University Press, 1942).

She liked whate'er
She looked on, and her looks went everywhere.

The complete description of the Duchess is a good delineation of personal magnetism. Howard Thurman in writing of the personal magnetism of one of his professors put it this way, "George Cross, Professor of Systematic Theology, had a greater influence on my mind than any other person who ever lived. Everything about me was alive when I came into his presence. He was all stimulus and I was all response." Sir William Osler, M.D., had a personal magnetism that could not be interrupted by death. He still inspires the young physician.

Not only must the speaker have personal magnetism, but he must see to it that the conditions under which he speaks are favorable to the winning of the audience. The audience must not be seated too far from the speaker. All distractions must be minimized. Lights that are hard on the eyes must be eliminated. There must be no center aisle gaping before the reader. The audience must be right before the reader so that when he looks up the audience can see his eyes. Once Henry Ward Beecher was asked if he would rather speak before twelve people or three thousand and he said it made no difference if their elbows touched. There had to be the possibility of a circular response. When he built Plymouth Church in Brooklyn, he told the architect, "I want them to surround me, so that they will come up on every side, and behind me, so that I shall be in the centre of the crowd, and have the people surge all about me." And he goes on to say, "The result is, that there is not a better constructed hall in the world for the purposes of speaking and hearing than Plymouth Church. Charles Dickens, after giving one of his readings in it, sent me special word not to build any other hall for speaking; that Plymouth Church was perfect. It is perfect, because it was built on a principle,—the principle of social and personal magnetism, which emanates reciprocally from a speaker and from a close throng of hearers. This is perhaps the most important element of all the external conditions conducive to good and effective preaching." [4]

[4] *Yale Lectures on Preaching,* first series (New York: J. B. Ford and Company, 1872), p. 73.

IX. Summary

One cannot do better in attempting to summarize what has been said in this chapter than to quote from the article by Ralph B. Dennis,[5] late Dean of the School of Speech, Northwestern University, "One Imperative Plus":

> To interpret life one must know life—through many beautiful, happy, sad, painful, toilsome, light-hearted, heavy-hearted journeys into the land of experience; journeys made in the flesh, mayhap; mayhap in the spirit, in the imagination. But you must have been there. Out of this course comes a philosophy (simple and crude it may be—but it is) a vision of man and mankind. You may get this without reading a book, though that is a doubtful method. You may get it through books alone, again a doubtful method with lop-sided results. You may get it through both sources, books and life, the best way, I think. . . . What is the cultivated man? What is culture? There are many definitions. This is one. "The cultivated man is the one who has the most contacts—with music, art, literature, poetry, PEOPLE." And don't dare omit the people. We who live in or on college campuses, who have lost the ability to understand the common folk, who interpret art as we think other people ought to like it, who have been educated out of a taste for the simple things of life, who can't see God in the servant, the clerk, the postman, the day laborer, as well as in our educated equals, our social equals, our money equals,—if there be those of us like that, we have lost the imperative plus and have put down a minus sign in its stead.

X. Projects for Chapter XIII

1. Present a ten minute program of current poetry found in recent issues of *The Atlantic, Harper's Magazine, The Saturday Review,* and *The Saturday Evening Post.*
2. Give a ten minute report on a current best-selling biography. Read excerpts from the book aloud to the class.
3. Find a review of a good current movie in *The Saturday Review, Time,* or *Newsweek* and read it to the class.
4. Present a book report on some book in your special field of interest. If, for example, you are especially interested in medicine, review such a book as Hugh Cabot's *The Patient's Dilemma* or *Not as a Stranger* by Morton Thompson.
5. Build a ten minute program using poetry that deals with nature, such as Lew Sarett's "The Little Foxes."

---

[5] *The Quarterly Journal of Speech Education,* VIII, 218.

CHAPTER XIV

Listening to a Selection

I. Listening, a Skill

II. Developing an Attitude
- A. A Learning Situation
- B. Anticipatory Attitude

III. Fixing Attention
- A. Listen for Rhetorical Devices
- B. Listen to References to Your Experiences
- C. Make Associations
- D. Use Your Imagination
- E. Interpretative Listening

IV. Evaluation
- A. The Design
- B. The Medium
- C. Listenability
- D. The Critic

V. Retention

VI. Projects for Chapter XIV

I. Listening, a Skill

It was assumed that all one needed was intelligence and eyesight and one could read. But witness today the courses in remedial reading in college! We know that individuals can be trained to read better. The falsity of the assumption about reading is a comparable falsity to the assumption about listening. One needs more than intelligence and hearing acuity to listen efficiently. Just as one can be trained to read, so one can be trained to listen. It is to be hoped that a large part of your education in a class in oral interpretation will be in the development of your ability to listen. Appreciative listening to the spoken word is a rare phenomenon these mechanical days. Cities that have audiences trained to listen are marked for approbation by leading actresses of our time. It is no accident that Katharine Cornell and Helen Hayes open their plays in Columbus, Ohio. Here they find a listening public—individuals have been trained at the state university and at the colleges and universities that surround the capital to listen. Listening is creative. The audience must cooperate with the reader to create something that never existed before. A listening audience has an exhilarating effect upon the actor, the speaker, the reader. Note in the following the creative experience of Helen Hayes before a live audience.

> Before talking to her, I'd discussed her with the people she'd worked with during her Madelon Claudet and Arrowsmith days. I'd been told, "She always found the movies a tedious and difficult medium. They aren't done in continuity. They don't build. Her instincts are perfect for the stage. She's discovered the formula for portraying emotions to a live audience. She knows the technique to express them. But she is accustomed to wait for an audience reaction, and she found only blankness before a camera. Cameras don't sigh, weep, laugh. They don't send waves of emotion back across footlights which stimulate an actress." [1]

The actor on the legitimate stage is driven almost to distraction by an audience that has not been trained to listen. Skillful listeners are disturbed by those in the audience who are oblivious to the nuances of the human voice. Maurice Evans had to stop his *Richard II* at a matinee in one city and explain to his restless audience what he was trying to do. Audiences nurtured on canned sound in radio, movies, and television do not know how to listen to the unaided human voice. Popcorn crunching, seat hopping, necking, crying babies are all "enjoyed" along with the mechanical word, but are poor accompaniments for the shades of meaning, the nuances the face to face interpreter seeks to portray. Listening demands concentration and cooperation. The listener can not be passive if he is to get the most out of his experience in the study of oral interpretation of literature.

Instructors in such courses as economics and logic may induce an attitude of listening carefully by giving daily quizzes over what has been said in previous class hours. Such tests promote an *attitude* of receptivity, require constant *attention,* force review for *retention* of materials, and stimulate an *evaluation* of the ground covered. But instructors in oral reading do not usually resort to these methods of developing listening habits. And because there is no daily threat of a quiz over the selections that are read, the listener's attitude may become half-hearted. The listener in the oral reading class may indulge in daydreaming over his own concerns. And only when there is a group response, such as laughter,

---

[1] Pete Martin, "Helen Hayes Tries Hollywood Again," *The Saturday Evening Post,* August 30, 1952, p. 60.

does the daydreamer bestir himself to listen to what is going on. Listening in a class in oral reading is voluntary rather than compulsory. To set up self-imposed quizzes over what is listened to in class, therefore, becomes important for the student if he would get the most out of his experience. Let him ask himself these questions:

1. Am I assuming the proper *attitude?*
2. Am I directing my *attention?*
3. How do I *evaluate* the reading and the reader?
4. How do I *retain* the experience?

II. Developing an Attitude

A. *A Learning Situation*

As preparation for listening the listener needs to put himself in tune with what is being read. A class in oral interpretation can be an exciting adventure in the extension of one's knowledge. Let us suppose that in preparation all students read all selections for the day. Let us suppose further that background materials on the authors are read by all students. No two students will read exactly the same things in preparation, but all students will have some growing edges, some curiosity, to be satisfied during the class hour by the one who is doing the reading. Let us suppose that part of the program for the day is a selection by Judge Harold R. Medina. What do you know about him? How can you find out something about him? Well, *Who's Who in America* will give you a start. But Judge Medina came into public attention by the manner in which he conducted the trial against the Communists in New York City. How about going through the files of *The New York Times* and reading some of the daily accounts of the trial? You would also find magazines carrying stories about him during that time. And recently a book by Hawthorne Daniel has been written on him.

The point is that your pleasure in class will be enhanced if you have some background with which to appreciate what is being read. Professor G. M. Trevelyan in his Presidential Address before the English Association in November 1951 put this truth this way:

I do not mean that without knowledge of history the literature of the past may not be greatly enjoyed. But I do mean that even a little knowledge of history enhances the pleasure. And this for two reasons. First that some conception of the social and intellectual conditions of any period, like that of Chaucer, Shakespeare, the eighteenth century writers, or of Scott, Byron and Shelley, increases our understanding of much of their works. And, secondly, that apart from general understanding and sympathy, particular references are much more appreciated if the reader happens to know what they are about. Literature more than painting and music, is a matter of references, of play made with bits of knowledge common to the author and reader.

As preparation for listening we need to put ourselves in tune with what is being read. What period of history does the reading come from? What other things were happening at the time? What other persons were active? Who were friends of the author? If Woodrow Wilson's War Message of 1917 is being read, do you know enough history to fill in the background? Here was the presidential candidate who won on the slogan, "He kept us out of the war." What war? Do you know what the precipitating cause for his War Message was? In preparation for listening to this War Message, why not refresh your mind with the incidents leading up to the First World War by opening a history book?

Suppose the reading is from *The Liverpool Address* by Henry Ward Beecher. How did the speech happen to be given? Why was Henry Ward Beecher in England? You might find out that Henry Ward Beecher went to England in June, 1863, to propagandize in favor of the Northern cause, but found the British so hostile toward the North that he and his companion Henry Raymond, Editor of *The New York Times,* went to the continent to wait for a more favorable time. After Gettysburg and Vicksburg in early July, 1863, Henry Ward Beecher went back to England and prepared to speak. The first speech was in mid-October. There were five addresses in the campaign. The thoughtful people, the rulers, knew that the tide of the struggle was going in favor of the North, but the rank and file did not. The spinners in the mills thought the blockade of the Southern ports was starving their mills of cotton. Henry Ward Beecher took the position that what England needed was more customers and not more cotton. Freed Negroes would supply the new customers. Listening to *The Liverpool Address* becomes more pleasurable knowing this background.

Some students have become so interested in the selection in the Anthology from *Grapes of Wrath* by John Steinbeck that they have read the entire book. This is real education. After all, we have to educate ourselves.

B. *Anticipatory Attitude*

Let us suppose that the program for the day includes readings from the Bible, Shakespeare, Browning, Donne, Chaucer, and other classics. Let us suppose further that you have access to recordings by John Barrymore, John Gielgud, Maurice Evans, and other readers of some of these selections. If you will listen to the interpretation of these artists, it will help you to see the possibilities of the selections. We all know that unless we are hungry food does not taste good. We should adopt all the means within our power to stir our interest in the program for the day. Read over the selection yourself. How would you do it? In the class discussion that follows the program what will your contribution be? If thus you will build up within yourself an eagerness for the program of the day, you will be likely to look forward with interest. The musician who sits with the score in his hands and follows its performance is undoubtedly listening more intently and profitably than the individual who has not prepared for the performance. And he undoubtedly anticipated how the various parts would be played.

III. Fixing Attention

A. *Listen for Rhetorical Devices*

Attention to rhetorical details in a reading becomes a fascinating way in which to keep attention focused on a reading. Often students greet with incredulity the suggestion that artists have employed assonance, alliteration, rhythm. Such students believe that artists are born with these techniques and have not labored to acquire them. Yet, Thornton Wilder in his article "Toward an American Language" (*The Atlantic,* July, 1952) speaks admiringly as one craftsman of another in the field of letters. He is writing of the technique of Herman Melville in *Moby Dick.* By the way, this article would richly reward the curious student of oral interpretation.

The whale has been sighted—"a hump like a snowhill"—and the boats of the *Pequod* have started in pursuit.

"Like noiseless nautilus shells, their light prows sped through the sea; but only slowly they neared the foe."

Melville's emotion is gaining on him. The alliterations in *n* and *s* begin to introduce an incantatory tone which will presently be confirmed by constructions employing repetition; but the approach to a state of trance does not prevent his marking the rapidity of the boats with monosyllables and the dragging slowness—as felt by the whalers—by open vowels.

"As they neared him the ocean grew still more smooth; seemed drawing a carpet over its waves; seemed a noon-meadow, so serenely it spread. At length the breathless hunter came so nigh his seemingly unsuspecting prey, that his entire dazzling hump was distinctly visible, sliding along the sea as if an isolated thing, and continually set in a revolving ring of finest, fleecy, greenish foam. He saw the vast, involved, wrinkles of the slightly projecting head beyond. Before it, far out on the soft Turkish-rugged waters, went the glistening white shadow from his broad, milky forehead, a musical rippling playfully accompanying the shade; and behind, the blue waters interchangeably flowed over into the moving valley of his steady wake; and on either hand bright bubbles arose and danced by his side."

What use does the author make of sentence structure? Are they long or short or varied? Does he use sentence length to secure rhythm?

Are you familiar with all the words? Are there any new words or expressions? Does the author have the facility for coining phrases? Are there any combinations of words that strike you as unusual? In the poem "Richard Cory" by Edwin Arlington Robinson we have such phrases as "glittered when he walked" and "imperially slim." These phrases are now the property of Edwin Arlington Robinson just as much as musical phrases from "The Messiah" belong to Handel. Robert G. Ingersoll in his "The Liberty of Man, Woman and Child" speaks of "the countless hands of hate." When Eugene Debs in a speech uses the same phrase "hands of hate," we can be pretty sure that he has borrowed the phrase from Robert G. Ingersoll. Our language is enriched by phrases from the Bible and Shakespeare. In your listening can you recognize phrases as coming from the classics?

Figures of speech, especially the simile and metaphor, are worth noting as you listen. Does the figure employed strike you as felicitous? The following discussion of these two figures of speech by Robert Hillyer may make you more aware of their importance.

> Figurative language as a source of obscurity has not been so thoroughly considered, because the notions concerning it are so hazy. I believe that most young poets think that a metaphor is always "stronger" than a simile, and thus must always be preferred. But the gap between similes and metaphors is much greater than they seem aware of. A simile is really an expanding adjective. It does not bind the object to any one quality; it merely modifies it. Hence, it can be changed in an instant without confusion. We can, as Wordsworth noted, play with similes. Burns's Love in the first line of his lyric is like a red, red rose; in the third, she is like a melody. These qualifications are adjectival: she is rose-like, she is melody-like. There is no clash, for she can be like both. But a metaphor would identify her, at least for the space of one stanza, as either a rose or a melody; otherwise, we should notice the mixed metaphor. A simile is a suggestion, a metaphor matches the object quality by quality, and usually provides a picture appropriate in all its parts to the object. If I say a woman is a kangaroo, I transform her for an instant into the animal, pounce and pouch, with definiteness and, in this case, some spite. If I say she is like a kangaroo, I am good-naturedly pointing out one quality—that she is always on the go.[2]

To stimulate your attention, listen for the devices used by the author to organize his materials. What sort of organization is used? Does the form grow out of the materials? Is there a climax? Where does it occur? Does the author devote as much time to the development of one idea as he does to another? Does he use organization to secure emphasis?

Does the author use repetition? Does he use repetition to bind his materials together? Is there repetition of single words, phrases, whole sentences? Is there a refrain?

Does the author repeat the idea in different words? Do the parallel ideas echo the sense of each other? Are there internal summaries? Does the author stop and say, "Look, this is what I have been saying?" What sign post does the author use to tell you where he is in the development of his thoughts? Does the author vary his transitions?

---

[2] Robert Hillyer, "Modern Poetry vs. The Common Reader," *The Saturday Review,* March 24, 1945.

Anything you can do to stimulate your interest in the form of what is being read will help hold your attention. For example, what have you noticed about the form of such compositions as Sandburg's "Chicago"? If there is no end rhyme, is there internal rhyme? Is there repetition? Is there rhythm? Is there cataloguing?

Your attention may be kept from flagging if you keep seeking the reason for the composition. What is the point? Why did the author bother to compose this? Does he explicitly state the purpose? Is the purpose implied? Is the selection aimed at informing, moving to action, convincing, impressing, stimulating, entertaining, connoting, dramatizing? These are general purposes, but what is the specific purpose? Is there an attempt to make the audience aware of social inequalities? Of cruel treatment of children? The destiny of dictators, as in "Ozymandias," by Percy Bysshe Shelley? What is the purpose of the following poems: Edwin Markham's "The Man With the Hoe," William Wordsworth's "The World Is Too Much With Us," Matthew Arnold's "Dover Beach," Edna St. Vincent Millay's "Lament," Alfred Lord Tennyson's "Break, Break, Break," John Keats's "Ode on a Grecian Urn"?

B. *Listen to References to Your Experiences*

In previous generations the preacher could refer to the Bible and be sure that his congregation would know all the references. The symbol would be sufficient to evoke the response. The reading of the Bible in the family circle insured such a knowledge. Our ignorance of the Scriptures is lamentable. One major in English was invited to read the Scriptures from the pulpit and when he came to the word *Sadducees,* he pronounced it *sad duckies.* The poet in previous generations could make allusions to classical mythology and stir up the stories known to his readers. Do these references mean anything to you, *Icarus, Triton, Cerberus?* If you ran across them in a poem, would they go over your head? However, consider the plight of the preacher and the poet today. Consider how mass education by means of radio and television has cut down the time for reading.

The problem of connecting with the experience of the audience through a medium whether it be the spoken word, the written symbol, or the moving picture is vividly presented in the attempt to adapt *The Red Badge of Courage* by Stephen Crane to the screen.

(See *The New Yorker*, May 24, 31, June 7, 14, 21, 1952.) Those who knew the book eagerly awaited the transcription, but the bobby soxers, not knowing the superb prose of Stephen Crane, laughed at the tragic scenes so that the movie people decided to try to attract an audience that could appreciate what was being depicted. For one thing the movie was edited with narration. The fact that the movie was based on a classic of fiction was played up in the advertising. Moreover in releasing the movie for its premiere in New York City, an exclusive little theatre was chosen. All these steps indicate how important a listening audience is to the success of a performance.

Allusions, references to indirect and direct experiences, quotations, people you know, names of places are symbols by which the author tries to arouse your interest. You can make yourself an alert listener by being aware of the means the author is employing.

The author sometimes awakens our attention and holds it by showing uncanny insights into life, by making observations that are universal in their applications, by making you say, "That's true." How often we have run across truths expressed by philosophers, such as Ralph Waldo Emerson, and have said, "Why, I was thinking that just yesterday." When Robert Frost says that the hired man's despair is because he has "nothing to look backward to with pride, and nothing to look forward to with hope" (see p. 305), we know he is right because we all need pride and hope to live our daily lives. And when Robert Frost attempts to define home (see p. 308) in the following ways, we conclude that he has done some long thinking on the subject and has said something that is significant:

> Home is the place where, when you have to go there,
> They have to take you in.
>   I should have called it
> Something you somehow haven't to deserve.

In our listening, attention is sharpened when we hear truths uttered felicitously and memorably.

C. *Make Associations*

If the reading is from Robert Frost, set your mind working to bring up to the threshold of the conscious what you know about

Robert Frost. What other poems do you know? Which ones are your favorites? Where did you first make contact with Robert Frost? Have you ever heard Robert Frost read from his own works? Have you heard any of his recordings? In these ways you start thinking along with the reader. If you will think of your mind as a library catalogue file, and if you will file any new information along with the other cards you have on that topic, you will find that the process is attention-compelling and valuable.

When the reader gets into the selection can you start making what is read personal to yourself? Does this selection have any particular meaning for you? Does it remind you of anything? Is it like anything you have ever heard before? Have you had similar experiences?

Rosemary Clooney, the singer, said, on a television show, that she believed that a song's success depended on what it did to the audience. What memory did it stir? What new experience did it illumine? We must remember that all the reader can do for us is to stir up our own experience. The symbols used by the author and translated into living speech by the reader are attempts to rearrange our experience into a pattern which the author has deemed important. Do we recognize ourselves or our friends or acquaintances in what is read? Do we recognize deep, underlying experiences of life?

If you should hear the verse, "He hath shewed thee, O man, what is good; and what doth the Lord require of thee, but to do justly, and to love mercy, and to walk humbly with thy God?" (Micah 6:8), what would your reaction be? Could you write down the thoughts that arise? What is the difference between *justice* and *mercy?* Have you ever thought about it? If we listen to these words without an attempt to match them in our experience, we soon lose them. But if, for example, the word *mercy* stirs up within us Shakespeare's lines from *The Merchant of Venice,* we are helping to illumine the lines and make them ours.

> The quality of mercy is not strain'd
> It droppeth as the gentle rain from heaven
> Upon the place beneath. It is twice bless'd:
> It blesseth him that gives and him that takes.
> 'Tis mightiest in the mightiest: it becomes
> The throned monarch better than his crown;

His sceptre shows the force of temporal power,
The attribute to awe and majesty,
Wherein doth sit the dread and fear of kings;
But mercy is above this sceptred sway,
It is enthroned in the hearts of kings,
It is an attribute to God himself;
And earthly power doth then show likest God's
When mercy seasons justice.

D. *Use Your Imagination*

Students today brought up on pictures, and this is largely a visual age, what with *Life,* the movies, the comics, and TV, find difficulty in translating the unaided sound symbols into pictures. Our parents and grandparents brought up on only the radio had to use their imagination. Fred Allen, when questioned about TV, replied that this medium did not require the collaboration of the audience the way radio did. A few words from the announcer in radio were all that was necessary to set the scene. The voice gave the cues for the personality.

The ability to take an abstraction and fill it up with concretenesses helps to arouse and maintain attention. In Elizabeth Barrett Browning's (see p. 338) sonnet, "How Do I Love Thee?" the lines occur,

I love thee to the level of everyday's
Most quiet need, by sun and candlelight.

What does this mean—"level of everyday's most quiet need"? Well, I remember reading that whenever William Lyon Phelps left his home on a rainy day, his wife would call after him, "Willie, have you got your rubbers on?" You may think of other quiet needs of everyday living.

E. *Interpretative Listening*

We speak of interpretative reading but how about interpretative listening? Never can the listener get exactly what the speaker or reader intended. First of all, the author is limited by the language imperfections, then he is limited by the printing possibilities, then he is hampered by the equipment of the reader.

What finally gets to the listener may be far removed from what the author intended.

Even in the factual or cognitive realm it is possible to misunderstand the sounds. A classic example of this is the sentence:

The sun's rays meet.

However, the listener might interpret this as:

The sons raise meat.

Exactly the same sounds would have been uttered and an entirely different meaning would have been intended. However, the context of such sentences as these, the sentences that precede or follow, would help the listener get the intention of the reader.

On the other hand, the emotion of the listener might be quite different from that of the reader and thus color what is said. If a radio announcer, announcing the results of the Republican Convention of 1952 from Chicago, announced that Eisenhower had won on the first ballot, and if the announcer were an Eisenhower supporter, his emotion would be different from that of the listener if the listener happened to be a Taft supporter. Both the announcer and the listener would have the fact the same, but the emotional reaction would vary.

IV. Evaluation

A. *The Design*

In a public address the speaker will often at the outset give the outline of his remarks. This makes it easy for the audience to follow, but it may destroy audience curiosity as to what is coming next. In the reading you are studying, what plan is used?

How does the author handle the element of time? In *The Will* (see p. 413) by Sir James M. Barrie, we are told, "The only thing essential to the room, save the two men sitting in it, is a framed engraving on the wall of Queen Victoria, which dates sufficiently the opening scene, and will be changed presently to King Edward; afterwards to King George, to indicate the passing of time. No other alteration is called for."

Oliver Wendell Holmes, in "The Deacon's Masterpiece," begins with 1755, then comes to 1800, then to 1820, 1830, 1840, 1850, and finally 1855.

> First of November, 'Fifty-five
> The Parson was working his Sunday's text
> At half-past nine by the meet'n'-house clock.

How does the author handle the element of space? Sometimes a piece of literature will employ the technique which we often see in moving pictures, the far distance, the middle distance, the near distance, and the very near. You will recall westerns which show us a stage coach in the far distance, and then by degrees we are brought up to the occupants of the stage coach. Note in the following from "The Song of Songs" (see p. 335) how the author employs this technique:

> The voice of my beloved; behold, he cometh *leaping upon the mountains, skipping upon the hills.*
> My beloved is like a roe or a young hart; behold, he standeth *behind our wall,* he looketh forth *at the windows,* shewing himself *through the lattice.*
> My beloved spake, *and said unto me,* Rise up, my love, my fair one, *and come away.*[3]

These are the items used to indicate distance—mountains, hills, wall, windows, lattice, and finally, "my beloved spake."

B. *The Medium*

Does the author choose poetry or prose as his medium? Do you expect to get much factual material from poetry? Do you find yourself adopting a different attitude to a selection if it is to be in prose or in poetry? What does "The Death of the Hired Man" gain or lose by being expressed in poetry? Would *The Gettysburg Address* have achieved its purpose if it had been written in poetry? Would *Macbeth* and *Hamlet* have the same force as novels that they do as plays? Suppose that Ernest Hemingway had written *The Old Man and the Sea* as a long poem such as "The Ancient Mariner"?

We have many different forms of literature. It helps in listen-

[3] See Don Geiger, "A 'Dramatic' Approach to Interpretative Analysis," *The Quarterly Journal of Speech,* April 1952.

ing to identify the form, know something of its strengths and weaknesses, and reflect upon what is gained or sacrificed by the form. Is it a sonnet, lyric, dramatic monologue, ecalogue, heroic couplet? Is it a novel, short story, novelette? Is it a one act or a three act play? Is it an essay or a speech?

C. *Listenability*

This term is analogous to the term *readability*. Much study is now being given to making the written page readable. Should we not pay attention to making the spoken word listenable? As you listen to a selection ask yourself the question, "What is the reader doing to make himself and this selection more listenable?" Here are some fundamental questions:

1. How does the reader manage his voice?
   a. Does the reader project?
   b. How about the rate? Is it uniform? Does it vary to bring out the meaning?
   c. How about the force? Is it used to emphasize?
   d. How about quality? Does the quality change with meaning?
   e. Does the reader employ pitch changes to bring out meaning?
   f. Does the tone show confidence?
2. Is the reader's speech listenable?
   a. Does the way the reader utters the selection call attention to itself?
   b. Are there mispronunciations?
   c. Is the speech educated? Affected? Unnoticeable?
   d. Are the sounds clear cut or mushed?
   e. Is the speech regional?
3. Listen to the reader's grouping of words.
   a. Does the reader give you individual words or groups of words?
   b. Is the pause used effectively to bring out meaning? to emphasize?
   c. Does the reader use unusual groupings?
   d. Does the grouping indicate a knowledge of the cadence?
   e. Does the grouping show a grasp of the relationship of the main and the sub-ideas?
4. Does the reader promote listenability by use of his body?
   a. Do hand gestures help the meaning?
   b. Does the stance give the mood of the selection?

c. Do facial gestures, eyes, eyebrows, forehead, mouth help with projecting the meaning?
d. Does the reader use the larger muscle groups to suggest meaning? Shoulders, arms, legs?

D. *The Critic*

We can prod ourselves into listening profitably if we imagine ourselves as journalists who will have to evaluate what is being read. How would we size up the performance? What could we put down in black and white about what we see and hear before us? If we put ourselves into the frame of mind of formulating judgments on what is going on, we can keep from daydreaming.

On her 1952 appearance on the London stage, Ruth Draper was evaluated as follows by the drama critic of *The Times Weekly Review,* Thursday, May 29, 1952, p. 11 (Printer's Square). Note that the critic develops an interesting figure of speech to describe Miss Draper's performance:

> The least familiar study among the character sketches in Miss Draper's opening programme is that of a French actress. This gifted artist wears the emotion suited to the moment as becoming as though it were part and parcel of her inmost nature, and she discards it when a new moment presents a new need as lightly as she might drop a mask into the drawer of her wardrobe. She wears flattery for a ridiculously fat American patron, sympathetic understanding for a young French poet, anger for an impresario who has no use for the partner of her stage triumphs, a soothing calmness for the dismayed partner, fatigue for herself, and gaiety for the ambassadorial party which has arrived unexpectedly.

Suppose you were the one reading. Would you do it the way the present reader is executing the assignment?

Consider the technical details of the voice. How is it managed? Does the tempo suit the selection? Does the reader pause? Does the reader seem to be concerned with communicating with the audience by means of vocal inflection? Consider the technical details of posture and gesture. Does the reader seem to understand that communication is dependent upon the wise use of these techniques? Consider the reader's sense of values. Is there anything in the way the selection is read that would lead you to judge that the reader is this or that type of person? Would you care to know this individual better? Consider the reaction of the audience. Is the audience entering into the reading? Do you note signs of listlessness? Can you analyze this? On the other hand is the audience intensely interested? Can you figure this out?

By thus putting yourself into a critical frame of mind you help yourself become a better reader. You will teach yourself those things which, although you have heard them a thousand times, made no impression upon you. It is an axiom that the way to learn something is to try to teach it. By teaching yourself you learn the fundamentals of entering the minds of others by means of the read word.

To improve your ability to listen try the experiment of evaluating the teaching skill of one of your favorite professors. What techniques are used? Perhaps the teacher would be surprised if you should point these out to him, but sometime, somewhere, the teacher had to learn them in order to attract and hold attention. Contrast the experienced successful teacher with the inexperienced. Do the techniques show in the teaching of the inexperienced teacher? As you listen to your colleagues read in class are you aware of the techniques the reader is using? Is there a conscious striving to communicate?

V. Retention

Usually the program for the class hour is posted on the bulletin board. Fix this in mind. What selections are going to be read? A further step in preparation would be to read all the materials that are to be presented. This would aid in retaining them.

Before the class breaks up go over the program for the day. Which student gave which selection? This is the process of recall. After identifying the student and the selection try to recall what the central idea was. Did you have any associations with this selection before? Was it from a familiar author? Had you run across this author in some other class?

Practice recognition. If you find references to any of the materials that have been given in the oral reading class, make a note of them. As Pillsbury states, "Retention without recall is equally futile. Retention can be demonstrated only through recall. The knowledge that is stored in your brain at this moment gives no sign of its presence. You can be aware of what you know only by recalling it. Finally, if events when recalled were not recognized, recall would be valueless." [4]

A well-kept notebook can help to fix the materials of the class in mind. If you would spend fifteen minutes after each class hour reviewing what transpired during the class hour and making notes on it, you would find that your ability to listen would be quickened.

While the class is assembling, the teacher might ask one of the students to go before the class and give a résumé of what happened in the previous class hour. Who read? What did he read? What was the central idea of the reading? When we make a conscious effort to retain what is entering the mind, we listen more carefully.

VI. Projects for Chapter XIV

1. Evaluate the following suggestions on reading by Charles Laughton (*Time*, March 31, 1952).

HOW TO READ ALOUD AT HOME
(The Laughton System)

Don't Sit Down. You can read more easily and with less strain if your torso is erect. Put a bench or chair on a table and use it as a breast-high lectern. Lean on it all you want.

Speak Naturally. Your normal voice is your best reading voice—use it.

Don't Go Highbrow. Pick a book that you know and enjoy. Since it will be more fun for you, it will be more fun for your listeners.

Never Make It a Chore. Quit reading when you're tired or your attention begins to wander. If a story bores you, stop it and start another. There's no harm done if you skip a few evenings.

Let Your Listeners Alone. They can sew or knit or repair fishing tackle. Don't make them feel that listening is a duty.

When You Stop Reading, Start Talking. Mental stimulation is the goal. You've shared the reading, now share the ideas that come from it.

2. Pair off with another member of the class. Read to each other the next class assignment.

---

[4] Walter B. Pillsbury, *Essentials of Psychology* (New York: The Macmillan Co., 1911), p 189.

3. Read another treatment of listening in another book on speech and be prepared to discuss in class.

4. Bring one of your favorite psalms to class to read. Practice reading it several ways. Intone it. Chant it. Read it conversationally.

5. Bring to class the readings from *Life* (July 7, 1952) on "The Only Fabulous Country" by Charles Laughton. Have these well in mind. Make a program out of them.

6. After reading the Charles Laughton program, "The Only Fabulous Country," work out a similar program of your own from your favorite readings.

ANTHOLOGY

Wide World Photo

Paul Gregory had the idea for a drama quartette in an automobile when we were on the way to Canada for some readings. He saw four stars standing up like musicians in Soup and Fish and we thought of a lot of things to do but none of them would work until I remembered Don Juan in Hell, which I read to him and he fell for it and so did Charles Boyer, Agnes Moorhead and Cedric Hardwicke. . . . There are millions, nation wide, who have an appetite for the best stuff, who have not the facilities for a physically heavy show. Have you ever thought that almost all physically heavy shows are otherwise light? There are things that can be done in this form, old pieces and new. I am proud to say we have already been written for by a major writer.—*Charles Laughton,* New York Times Magazine, *March 23, 1952, p. 21.*

After I have written the sermon and meditated upon it as I do, I would not be at all surprised if I could preach from a brief outline, or maybe even without an outline, but for some reason I always feel better when I have the manuscript before me. It would not be fair to say that I read my sermon. I do not. Nor would it be fair to say that I memorize it. I presume my method would be a mixture of both. I frequently glance down at the manuscript in preaching, but I am not tied to it.—*Dr. Harold Cooke Phillips, Pastor of the First Baptist Church, Cleveland Heights, Ohio.*

PART I

Essays, Speeches, Reports

My Creed

DEAN ALFANGE

I do not choose to be a common man. It is my right to be uncommon—if I can. I seek opportunity—not security. I do not wish to be a kept citizen, humbled and dulled by having the state look after me. I want to take the calculated risk; to dream and to build, to fail and to succeed. I refuse to barter incentive for a dole. I prefer the challenges of life to the guaranteed existence; the thrill of fulfillment to the stale calm of utopia.

I will not trade freedom for beneficence nor my dignity for a handout. It is my heritage to think and to act for myself, enjoy the benefit of my creations, and to face the world boldly and say, this I have done. All this is what it means to be an American.

The Judgment of a Representative

EDMUND BURKE

Certainly, gentlemen, it ought to be the happiness and glory of a representative to live in the strictest union, the closest correspondence, and the most unreserved communication with his constituents. Their wishes ought to have great weight with him; their opinion high respect; their business unremitted attention. It is his duty to sacrifice his repose, his pleasures, his satisfactions, to theirs; and above all, ever, and in all cases, to prefer their interest to his own. But, his unbiased opinion, his mature judgment, his enlightened conscience, he ought not to sacrifice to you, to any man, or to any set of men living. These he does not derive from your pleasure; no, nor from the law and the constitution. They are a trust from Providence, for the abuse of which he is deeply answerable. Your representative owes you not his industry only, but his judgment; which he betrays, instead of serving you, if he sacrifices it to your opinion.

Dunkirk

WINSTON CHURCHILL

I have, myself, full confidence that if all do their duty, if nothing is neglected, and if the best arrangements are made, as they are being made, we shall prove ourselves once again able to defend our Island home, to ride out the storm of war, and to outlive the menace of tyranny, if necessary for years, if necessary alone. At any rate, that is what we are going to try to do. That is the resolve of His Majesty's Government—every man of them. That is the will of Parliament and the nation. The British Empire and the French Republic, linked together in their cause and in their need, will defend to the death their native soil, aiding each other like good comrades to the utmost of their strength. Even though large tracts of Europe and many old and famous States have fallen or may fall into the grip of the Gestapo and all the odious apparatus of Nazi rule, we shall not flag or fail. We shall go on to the end, we shall fight in France, we shall fight on the seas and oceans, we shall fight with growing confidence and growing strength in the air, we shall defend our Island, whatever the cost may be, we shall fight on the beaches, we shall fight on the landing grounds, we shall fight in the fields and in the streets, we shall fight in the hills; we shall never surrender, and even if, which I do not for a moment believe, this Island or a large part of it were subjugated and starving, then our Empire beyond the seas, armed and guarded by the British fleet, would carry on the struggle, until, in God's good time, the New World, with all its power and might, steps forth to the rescue and the liberation of the old.

Our Great Team [1]
Commander, the Symbol of Allied Victory

GENERAL DWIGHT D. EISENHOWER

Supreme Commander of the Allied Expeditionary Forces. Delivered at the Guildhall, London, England, June 12, 1945

The high sense of distinction I feel in receiving this great honor from the city of London is inescapably mingled with feelings of profound sadness. All of us must always regret that your great country and mine were ever faced with the tragic situation that compelled the appointment of an Allied Commander in Chief, the capacity in which I have just been so extravagantly commended.

[1] *Vital Speeches,* XI, No. 18.

Humility must always be the portion of any man who receives acclaim earned in the blood of his followers and the sacrifices of his friends.

Conceivably a commander may have been professionally superior. He may have given everything of his heart and mind to meet the spiritual and physical needs of his comrades. He may have written a chapter that will glow forever in the pages of military history.

Still, even such a man—if he existed—would sadly face the facts that his honors cannot hide in his memories the crosses marking the resting places of the dead. They cannot soothe the anguish of the widow or the orphan whose husband or father will not return.

The only attitude in which a commander may with satisfaction receive the tributes of his friends is in the humble acknowledgment that no matter how unworthy he may be his position is the symbol of great human forces that have labored arduously and successfully for a righteous cause. Unless he feels this symbolism and this rightness in what he has tried to do, then he is disregardful of courage, fortitude and devotion of the vast multitudes he has been honored to command. If all Allied men and women that have served with me in this war can only know that it is they whom this august body is really honoring today, then indeed I will be content.

This feeling of humility cannot erase, of course, my great pride in being tendered the freedom of London. I am not a native of this land. I come from the very heart of America. In the superficial aspects by which we ordinarily recognize family relationships, the town where I was born and the one where I was reared are far separated from this great city. Abilene, Kan., and Denison, Tex., would together equal in size possibly one five-hundredth of a part of great London.

By your standards those towns are young, without your aged traditions that carry the roots of London back into the uncertainties of unrecorded history. To those people I am proud to belong.

But I find myself today 5,000 miles from that countryside, the honored guest of a city whose name stands for grandeur and size throughout the world. Hardly would it seem possible for the London Council to have gone farther afield to find a man to honor with its priceless gift of token citizenship.

Yet kinship among nations is not determined in such measurements as proximity of size and age. Rather we should turn to those inner things—call them what you will—I mean those intangibles that are the real treasures free men possess.

To preserve his freedom of worship, his equality before law, his liberty to speak and act as he sees fit, subject only to provisions that he trespass not upon similar rights of others—a Londoner will fight. So will a citizen of Abilene.

When we consider these things, then the valley of the Thames draws closer to the farms of Kansas and the plains of Texas. To my mind it is clear that when two peoples will face the tragedies of war to defend the same spiritual values, the same treasured rights, then in the deepest sense those two are truly related. So even as I proclaim my undying Americanism, I am bold enough and exceedingly proud to claim the basis of kinship to you of London.

And what man who has followed the history of this war could fail to experience an inspiration from the example of this city?

When the British Empire stood—alone but unconquered, almost naked but unafraid—to defy the Hitler hordes, it was on this devoted city that the first terroristic blows were launched.

Five years and eight months of war, much of it on the actual battle-line, blitzes big and little, flying V-bombs—all of them you took in your stride. You worked, and from your needed efforts you would not be deterred. You carried on, and from your midst arose no cry for mercy, no wail of defeat. The Battle of Britain will take its place as another of your deathless traditions. And your faith and endurance have finally been rewarded.

You had been more than two years in war when Americans in numbers began swarming into your country. Most were mentally unprepared for the realities of war—especially as waged by the Nazis. Others believed that the tales of British sacrifice had been exaggerated. Still others failed to recognize the difficulties of the task ahead.

All such doubts, questions and complacencies could not endure a single casual tour through your scarred streets and avenues. With awe our men gazed upon the empty spaces where once had stood buildings erected by the toil and sweat of peaceful folk. Our eyes rounded as we saw your women, serving quietly and efficiently in almost every kind of war effort, even with flak batteries. We became accustomed to the warning sirens which seemed to compel from the native Londoner not even a single hurried step. Gradually we drew closer together until we became true partners in war.

In London my associates and I planned two great expeditions—that to invade the Mediterranean and later that to cross the Channel. London's hospitality to the Americans, her good-humored acceptance of the added inconvenience we brought, her example of fortitude and quiet confidence in the final outcome—all these helped to make the Supreme Headquarters of the two Allied expeditions the smooth-working organizations they became.

They were composed of chosen representatives of two proud and independent peoples, each noted for its initiative and for its satisfaction with its own customs, manners and methods. Many feared that those representatives could never combine together in an efficient fashion to solve the complex problems presented by modern war.

I hope you believe we proved the doubters wrong. And, moreover, I hold that we proved this point not only for war—we proved it can always be done by our two peoples, provided only that both show the same good-will, the same forbearance, the same objective attitude that the British and Americans so amply demonstrated in the nearly three years of bitter campaigning.

No man could alone have brought about this result. Had I possessed the military skill of a Marlborough, the wisdom of Solomon, the understanding of Lincoln, I still would have been helpless without the loyalty, vision and generosity of thousands upon thousands of British and Americans.

Some of them were my companions in the High Command. Many were enlisted men and junior officers carrying the fierce brunt of battle, and many others were back in the United States and here in Great Britain in London.

Moreover, back of us always stood our great national war leaders and their civil and military staffs that supported and encouraged us through every trial, every test. The whole was one great team. I know that on this special occasion 3,000,000 American men and women serving in the Allied Expeditionary Force would want me to pay a tribute of admiration, respect and affection to their British comrades of this war.

My most cherished hope is that after Japan joins the Nazis in utter defeat, neither my country nor yours need ever again summon its sons and daughters from their peaceful pursuits to face the tragedies of battle. But—a fact important for both of us to remember—neither London nor Abilene, sisters under the skin, will sell her birthright for physical safety, her liberty for mere existence.

No petty differences in the world of trade, traditions or national pride should ever blind us to our identities in priceless values.

If we keep our eyes on this guidepost, then no difficulties along our path of mutual cooperation can ever be insurmountable. Moreover, when this truth has permeated to the remotest hamlet and heart of all peoples, then indeed may we beat our swords into plowshares and all nations can enjoy the fruitfulness of the earth.

My Lord Mayor, I thank you once again for an honor to me and to the American forces that will remain one of the proudest in my memories.

Self-Reliance

RALPH WALDO EMERSON

To believe your own thought, to believe that what is true for you in your private heart, is true for all men,—that is genius. Speak your latent conviction and it shall be the universal sense; for always the inmost becomes the outmost,—and our first thought is rendered back to us by the trumpets of the Last Judgment. Familiar as the voice of the mind is to each, the highest merit we ascribe to Moses, Plato, and Milton, is that they set at naught books and traditions, and spoke not what men, but what *they* thought. A man should learn to detect and watch that gleam of light which flashes across his mind from within, more than the lustre of the firmament of bards and sages. Yet he dismisses without notice his thought, because it is his. In every work of genius we recognize our own rejected thoughts; they come back to us with a certain alienated majesty. Great works of art have no more affecting lesson for us than this. They teach us to abide by our spontaneous impression with good-humored inflexibility then most when the whole cry of voices is on the other side. Else, tomorrow a stranger will say with masterly good sense precisely what we have thought and felt all the time, and we shall be forced to take with shame our own opinion from another.

The Preparation of Citizens for Their Political Duties [1]

LEARNED HAND

Our nation is embarked upon a venture, as yet unproved; we have set our hopes upon a community in which men shall be given unchecked control of their own lives. That community is in peril; it is invaded from within, it is threatened from without; it faces a test which it may fail to pass. The choice is ours whether, when we hear the pipes of Pan, we shall stampede like a frightened flock, forgetting all those professions on which we have claimed to rest our polity. God knows, there is risk in refusing to act till the facts are all in; but is there not greater risk in abandoning the conditions of all rational inquiry? Risk for risk, for myself I had rather take my chance that some traitors will escape detection than spread abroad a spirit of general suspicion and distrust, which accepts rumor and gossip in place of undismayed and unintimidated inquiry. I believe that that community is already in process of

[1] *Vital Speeches,* XIX, No. 6.

dissolution where each man begins to eye his neighbor as a possible enemy, where non-conformity with the accepted creed, political as well as religious, is a mark of disaffection; where denunciation, without specification or backing, takes the place of evidence; where orthodoxy chokes freedom of dissent; where faith in the eventual supremacy of reason has become so timid that we dare not enter our convictions in the open lists to win or lose. Such fears as these are a solvent which can eat out the cement that binds the stones together; they may in the end subject us to a despotism as evil as any that we dread; and they can be allayed only in so far as we refuse to proceed on suspicion, and trust one another until we have tangible ground for misgiving. The mutual confidence on which all else depends can be maintained only by an open mind and a brave reliance upon free discussion. I do not say that these will suffice; who knows but we may be on a slope which leads down to aboriginal savagery. But of this I am sure: if we are to escape, we must not yield a foot upon demanding a fair field, and in honest race, to all ideas. "Blame not before thou hast examined; understand first and then rebuke. Answer not before thou hast heard; interrupt not in the midst of speech." Those words were written nearly 2,000 years ago; they came out of an experience already long, and refined in the fires of passion and conflict; they are the product of a wisdom, bought by ages of bitter trial; and by that wisdom alone shall we be saved, we, who boast ourselves to be the apostles of a faith in the eventual triumph of Wisdom. Listen also to these as ancient words that tell of the excellence of Wisdom. "There is in her a spirit quick of understanding, holy, alone in kind, manifold, subtile, freely moving, clear in utterance, unpolluted, distinct, unharmed, loving what is good, keen, unhindered, beneficent, loving toward man, steadfast, sure, free from care, all-powerful, all-surveying, and penetrating through all spirits that are quick of understanding, pure, most subtile. . . . And if a man longeth even for much experience, she knoweth the things of old, and divineth the things to come; she understandeth subtilities of speeches and interpretations of dark sayings; she forseeth signs and wonders, and the issues of reasons and times. I determined therefore to take her unto me to live with me, knowing that she is one who would give me good thoughts for counsel, and encourage me in cares and griefs. . . . For she knoweth all things and hath understanding thereof; and in my doings she shall guide me in the ways of soberness, and she shall guard me in her glory. And so shall my works be acceptable, and I shall judge the people righteously, and shall be worthy of my Father's throne."

On Reading Verse Aloud [1]

Most readers of poetry perform by ear, and depend on the free dramatization of meaning or mood to carry them along. Since few have a good natural ear, the results are generally embarrassing to the audience. Not even poets themselves can, as a rule, manage their own cadences properly. They chant, vociferate, mumble, and grunt. The inner ear may have accomplished wonders of subtlety, but the outer fails to observe them.

The first obstacles to be overcome are self-consciousness and the consequent instinct to interpret rather than present the work. One should aim to be the bow in the master's hand—not the master himself. Any poem worthy the name has enough intensity within itself to obviate the need for dramatization. The reader should deliver himself up to the poem as its instrument. "Make me thy lyre!" Since poetry should never be chanted, pitch should be flexible. The two extremes to be avoided are "elocution" and singsong.

For more concise and definite principles we must penetrate the inmost shrine of Rhythm where pulse those mysterious forces which move beneath the flow of English metre. Many prosodists have entered this shrine never again to emerge into the sweet light of the sun. Locked in mortal combat with each other, or lost in the gigantic mazes of Theory, they sacrifice both life and poetry.

First, we have the paradox of accent, or stress. English verse is indubitably based on a *theoretical* (but not an actual) pattern of recurrent accent. An iambic pentameter, we say, is a five-foot line, each foot containing an unaccented, followed by an accented, syllable. It would be difficult to find many such lines in the whole range of English poetry, for our verse is based on recurrent accent as an iceberg is based on the larger part that is submerged and invisible.

Much have / I trav / ell'd in / the realms / of gold.

Much and *trav* are full accents, but *much,* as I have already pointed out, is theoretically in the wrong half of the foot. *Realms* and *gold* are weaker accents. *In* can not be accented at all. Thus we have an iambic pentameter not with five, but with only two, primary accents. Why, then, is such a line permissible?

Because the *time rhythm* darts back and forth in everchanging units to give balance to the line as a whole. It shrinks where the accent is strong, and expands where the accent is weak. In the line quoted above,

[1] Reprinted with permission from Robert Hillyer, *First Principles of Verse* (Boston: The Writer, Inc., 1950), pp. 140–151.

in is not adequate to the metrical place it occupies. Therefore the time rhythm holds up the line with the long syllables *realms* and *gold,* which compensate for the missing stress. Thus we have a constant interplay between accent and time, between strength and length, which, in spite of irregularity in detail, brings every line to a metrical balance. Time rhythm is like the spider alert to repair every rent in the symmetry of the web. Accent rhythm is the web itself. With due apologies to Keats, let us rewrite his line, substituting short syllables for his long ones. "Much have I travell'd in the infinite." It drops to pieces (as poetry of the "infinite" generally does).

This time rhythm works through two equally important elements. The first is called *duration,* and depends on the length or shortness of an individual syllable. *It* is short; *slow* is long; and between these extremes lie innumerable variations of swiftness or length. Although long durations are generally dependent on long vowel sounds, in words like *strength,* wherein the consonants draw out the sound, we find not only a full accent, but a long duration as well. The second element in time rhythm is a silence, a *pause.* Pause corresponds to the "rest" in music. It is essential that the reader of poetry consider both duration and pause with rapt attention. They are the time rhythm, time smoothing out the irregularities of accent. They must be over-observed. Their differences must be brought out far more emphatically than in the reading of prose. Also, acceleration is just as important as retard. Short syllables must be staccato, or the long can not fulfill their contrasting function. For practice, take Housman's line:—

> The fleet foot X on the sill of shade.

It is as necessary to hurry over the quick syllables *on the* as to draw out the two equal longs, *fleet foot.* Note, in passing, that only the word *sill* receives a full accent. An even more striking example is Bridges's

> Ah X X soon X X X when Winter has all our vales opprest.

In this line the exceedingly long durations *ah* and *soon,* with their long attendant pauses, *are equal in time to the nine syllables which follow.* Only the first syllable of *Winter* and the second syllable of *opprest* receive a full accent. Yet in theory this is an iambic pentameter, scanned thus:—

> Ah soon / when Win / ter has all / our vales / opprest.

It is apparent how widely divergent are the underlying metres and the actual sounds of English verse.

At this point the reader is doubtless wondering what he should do about the accent rhythm. We have agreed that beneath the surge and thunder of the time rhythm a regular, though submerged, accentual pattern sustains the verse. Let us change our original figure and compare the accent to a skeleton, which, though unseen, holds the anatomy to its proper form and proportion. We can always scan metrical verse accentually even if we do not read it according to the scansion. Such a metrical chart might be compared to an X-ray picture of the bony structure beneath the flesh. Even such a line as Milton's

Hail ho / ly Light / off spring / of Heav'n / first-born.

will submit to the investigation. In Shakespere's

In sooth / I know / not why / I am / so sad

the bony contour is nearer the surface. Poets often delight in conjoining fat and lean lines for the sake of variety. For practical performance, the reader should disregard accent, provided that he read naturally so that the accents fall into their normal places as they would in lively conversation. Accent is the essence of the English tongue, and may be left to take care of itself. It is impossible not to accent where an accent truly belongs. More often words are falsely accented because of their metrical position. This fault should be avoided. It would be impossible not to accent these lines properly:—

X X Break X X Break X X Break X
on thy cold gray stones O Sea!

It is also very easy to overdo. Study the time units, the slow, the quick, the pause; then stress will assume its proper place. In the ordinary iambic pentameter, the average number of full stresses is not more than two.

Pitch presents a vaguer problem, because the raising or lowering of the voice varies with the individual. For example, a relative of mine used to start every sentence at the top of the scale, slide to the bottom about two thirds of the way through, and, at the end, slide half-way up again. A foreigner would have thought him in a perpetual state of questioning worry. For the most part, Americans do not avail themselves nearly enough of a changing pitch. They avoid it as an affectation and lose half the effectiveness of their native tongue in drone, drawl, and growl. Yet the American voice is, in general, far richer than the English. Leaving out Cockney,—and that super-Cockney, the "Oxford accent,"—we mistakenly accord superiority to the English *voice,* whereas actually the more flexible *pitch* gives the advantage. Pitch is to our tongue as hand-waving is to the French: its expressiveness, its emphasis, and its point. *Without sliding pitch the reading of verse can not be effective.* Yet I can not set any formula, or improvise a tune. I have noticed that, in moments of excitement, Americans lose their self-consciousness and sing out very well. Any good poem should arouse sufficient excitement to limber up the vocal chords. Away with constraint!

Enjambment (the overflow of one line into the next) is a problem which causes more confusion than pitch, yet has a clear solution. A large proportion of lines in English verse, especially in long poems and the drama, are locked together by their syntax: they "run over" into each other; they are "enjambed."

Thou by the Indian Ganges' side
Shouldst rubies find: I by the tide
Of Humber would complain. I would
Love you ten years before the Flood,
And you should, if you please, refuse
Till the conversion of the Jews.

In these lines of Marvell's, we note the sentence structures running through line after line, with no chance for a pause to indicate the end of a line. The same device is common in blank verse. More than two thirds of the lines in *Paradise Lost* are enjambed; and Shakespere, especially in his later plays, poured the lava of his thought over long series of boundary walls. The mishandling of Shakespere's enjambments is notorious.

There are two wrong ways of treating this device orally, and one right way. The poets themselves have so clearly pointed out the right way that I fail to understand how so many have missed it. The problem is this: a sentence leaps from line to line, ignoring metrical boundaries —how shall we preserve the integrity of the individual lines without placing pauses where they do not naturally occur? Or, on the other hand, preserve the normal syntax without melting the lines together into a formless mass? The old school of Shakesperean actors declaimed the speeches by the line and imparted a false rhetoric to the whole. The modern school follows the syntax merely and puts the poet to rout in favor of the dramatist.

But no such dilemma exists. All poets, consciously or instinctively, have indicated the method to be employed in reading enjambment. In enjambed passages, every line that runs over into the next is terminated by a syllable with a long vowel or with consonants that can be extended.

Here, then, is the rule: Draw out the last syllable of the first line; then, *without pause or change of pitch,* launch into the second line. Thus:—

→
Thou by the Indian Ganges' side
← →
Shouldst rubies find: I by the tide
← →
Of Humber would complain. I would
←
Love you ten years before the Flood,
→
And you should, if you please, refuse
←
Till the conversion of the Jews.

From what has been said so far, we may deduce the following principles for reading verse aloud:—

(1) Read out in a full but unstrained voice.

(2) Do not dramatize the poem.

(3) Do not chant it.

(4) Stress only the syllables that would be stressed in conversation; indeed, let the stress take care of itself.

(5) Read short syllables in a hurry and long ones at leisure.

(6) Observe all pauses extravagantly. Silence can never make a mistake.

(7) Vary the pitch eagerly.

(8) When lines overflow into each other, draw out the last syllable of the overflowing line, and, without pause or change of pitch, collide with the first syllable of the line that follows.

These eight principles would be valueless without the ninth, which governs them all. The ninth is, quite literally, the heart of the matter, for its steady pulse sends life through all the veins of English verse. My discovery of it was a happy accident. For years I had been vaguely conscious of swaying backward and forward in time to the verse I was reading. A poem of great syllabic irregularity, Walter de la Mare's "The Listeners," demanded an explanation of this weaving that evened out lines of very disproportionate length.

"Is there anybody there?" said the Traveler,
Knocking on the moonlit door.

Both the lines have three metrical feet, but the first line has twelve syllables, and the second, seven. Both of them divide into two equal time units; and these units are equal through the two lines and those that follow—in spite of the discrepancy in the number of syllables.

Is there anybody there | X X said the Traveler X
Knocking on the moon lit | door. X X

Continuing my experiment, I discovered the cardinal principle, the prime movement, of our verse. *All lines in English verse, more than one foot in length, divide into two equal time units. These units cut across feet, accent, syllables, and may even split a single word. More often than not, there is no pause between them.* Theoretically, then, the best way to read English verse is to a metronome. Practically, there are gradual accelerations and retards which change the general tempo, but never disorganize the equality of the two time units within the single line.

These two units are doubtless a survival from the prosody of our Anglo-Saxon ancestors. The Anglo-Saxon line broke into two equal time units, the only difference from our rhythm being that those units were always separated by a pause, whereas ours more frequently are not. It is not surprising that such a survival should prevail, for many more elements of our primitive verse remain than are generally recognized. There are lines in many modern poets, notably Meredith and Swinburne, which would fit Anglo-Saxon metrics perfectly.

The reason that this double metronomic rhythm does not become monotonous is that the number of syllables within the units constantly varies, along with the durations and the placing of the pauses.

The lone X couch X X | of his everlasting sleep.

In this line, three syllables balance against seven.

A good many consonants, such as *n, m, l,* and *ng,* have echoes which fill out a unit:—

Wake X for the sun | has scattered into flight.

Note how the two long syllables *Wake* and *flight* balance the two ends of the line.

When two similar consonants collide at the end of one word and the beginning of another, a pause is demanded to avoid running the two words together.

While she lies X |
Sleeping. X

As I have said, the units sometimes meet in the middle of a word, as in the first of these two lines:—

> Where in her Mediterran | ean mirror gazing
> Old Asia's dreamy face X | wrinkleth to a westward smile.

By way of final illustration, let us divide an entire poem into its time units. Fearful that my colleagues in the art might object if one of their productions were thus anatomized, I offer up a lyric of my own for vivisection. (Let no saucy reader substitute the word *autopsy.*)

Note well that, though I have had to divide each line to denote the two units, there should be no pause between them unless a pause is indicated.

Night Piece

There is always the sound | of falling water here,
By day, blended with | birdsong and windy leaves,
By night, the only sound, X | steady and clear
Through the darkness and half- | heard through sleepers' dreams.
Here in the mottled shadow | of glades, the deer
Unstartled, waits X | until the walker is near,
Then with a silent bound, | X without effort is gone,
While the sound of falling wa | ter goes on and on.

Those are not stars | reflected in the lake,
They are shadow of stars | that were there aeons ago;
When you walk by these waters | at night, you must forsake
All you have known of time; | X you are timeless, alone,
The mystery almost revealed | like the breath you take
In the summer dawn X | before the world is awake,
Or the last breath | X when the spirit beyond recalling
Goes forth to the sound | of water forever falling.

Swift as deer, X | half-thoughts in the summer mind
Flash with their hints of | happiness and are gone;
In the dark waters | X of ourselves we find
No stars but shadows | of stars which memory lost.
Dark are the waters | under the bridge we crossed,
And the sound of their falling | knows neither end nor start.
Frail are your stars, | X deep are your waters, mind;
And the sound of falling | water troubles my heart.

The Social Value of the College-Bred

WILLIAM JAMES

What the colleges—teaching humanities by examples which may be special, but which must be typical and pregnant—should at least try to give us, is a general sense of what, under various disguises, superiority has always signified and may still signify. The feeling for a good human job anywhere, the admiration of the really admirable, the disesteem of what is cheap and trashy and impermanent—this is what we call the critical sense, the sense for ideal values. It is the better part of what men know as wisdom. Some of us are wise in this way naturally and by genius; some of us never become so. But to have spent one's youth at college in contact with the choice and rare and precious, and yet still to be a blind prig or vulgarian, unable to scent out human excellence or to divine it amid its accidents, to know it only when ticketed and labeled and forced on us by others, this indeed should be accounted the very calamity and shipwreck of a higher education.

The sense for human superiority ought, then, to be considered our line, as boring subways is the engineer's line and the surgeon's is appendicitis. Our colleges ought to have lit up in us a lasting relish for the better kind of man, a loss of appetite for mediocrities, and a disgust for cheap jacks. We ought to smell, as it were, the difference of quality in men and their proposals when we enter the world of affairs about us. Expertness in this might well atone for some of our awkwardness at accounts, for some of our ignorance of dynamos. The best claim we can make for the higher education, the best single phrase in which we can tell what it ought to do for us, is, then, exactly what I said: it should enable us to know a good man when we see him.

Gettysburg Address

ABRAHAM LINCOLN

Fourscore and seven years ago our fathers brought forth upon this continent a new nation, conceived in liberty, and dedicated to the proposition that all men are created equal. Now we are engaged in a great civil war, testing whether that nation, or any nation so conceived and so dedicated, can long endure. We are met on a great battle-field of that war. We have come to dedicate a portion of that field as a final resting-place for those who here gave their lives that that nation might live. It is altogether fitting and proper that we should do this. But in a larger sense we cannot dedicate, we cannot consecrate, we cannot hallow this ground. The brave men, living and dead, who struggled here, have consecrated it far above our power to add or detract. The world will little note, nor long remember, what we say here, but it can never forget what they did here. It is for us, the living, rather to be dedicated here to the unfinished work which they who fought here have thus far sc nobly advanced. It is rather for us to be here dedicated to the great task remaining before us, that from these honored dead we take increased devotion to that cause for which they gave the last full measure of devotion; that we here highly resolve that these dead shall not have died in vain; that this nation, under God, shall have a new birth of freedom; and that government of the people, by the people, and for the people, shall not perish from the earth.

The Second Inaugural Address

ABRAHAM LINCOLN

FELLOW COUNTRYMEN: At this second appearing to take the oath of the presidential office, there is less occasion for an extended address than there was at the first. Then a statement, somewhat in detail, of a course to be pursued, seemed fitting and proper. Now, at the expiration of four years, during which public declarations have been constantly called forth on every point and phase of the great contest which still absorbs the attention and engrosses the energies of the nation, little that is new could be presented. The progress of our arms, upon which all else chiefly depends, is as well known to the public as to myself; and it is, I trust, reasonably satisfactory and encouraging to all. With high hope for the future, no prediction in regard to it is ventured.

On the occasion corresponding to this four years ago, all thoughts were anxiously directed to an impending civil war. All dreaded it—all sought to avert it. While the inaugural address was being delivered from this place, devoted altogether to saving the Union without war, insurgent agents were in the city seeking to destroy it without war—seeking to dissolve the Union, and divide effects, by negotiation. Both parties deprecated war; but one of them would make war rather than let the nation survive; and the other would accept war rather than let it perish. And the war came.

One-eighth of the whole population were colored slaves, not distributed generally over the Union, but localized in the Southern part of it. These slaves constituted a peculiar and powerful interest. All knew that this interest was, somehow, the cause of the war. To strengthen, perpetuate, and extend this interest was the object for which the insurgents would rend the Union, even by war; while the government claimed no right to do more than to restrict the territorial enlargement of it.

Neither party expected for the war the magnitude or the duration which it has already attained. Neither anticipated that the cause of the conflict might cease with, or even before, the conflict itself should cease. Each looked for an easier triumph, and a result less fundamental and astounding. Both read the same Bible, and pray to the same God; and each invokes His aid against the other. It may seem strange that any men should dare to ask a just God's assistance in wringing their bread from the sweat of other men's faces; but let us judge not, that we be not judged. The prayers of both could not be answered—that of neither has been answered fully.

The Almighty has his own purposes. "Woe unto the world because of offenses; for it must needs be that offenses come; but woe to that man by whom the offense cometh." If we shall suppose that American slavery is one of those offenses which, in the providence of God, must needs come, but which, having continued through his appointed time, he now wills to remove, and that he gives to both North and South this terrible war, as the woe due to those by whom the offense came, shall we discern therein any departure from those divine attributes which the believers in a living God always ascribe to him? Fondly do we hope—fervently do we pray—that this mighty scourge of war may speedily pass away. Yet, if God wills that it continue until all the wealth piled by the bondsman's two hundred and fifty years of unrequited toil shall be sunk, and until every drop of blood drawn with the lash shall be paid by another drawn with the sword, as was said three thousand years ago, so still it must be said, "The judgments of the Lord are true and righteous altogether."

With malice toward none; with charity for all; with firmness in the right, as God gives us to see the right, let us strive on to finish the work we are in; to bind up the nation's wounds; to care for him who shall have borne the battle, and for his widow, and his orphan—to do all which may achieve and cherish a just and lasting peace among ourselves, and with all nations.

Private Enterprise

ABRAHAM LINCOLN

Many independent men everywhere in these States, a few years back in their lives, were hired laborers. The prudent, penniless beginner in the world labors for wages awhile, saves a surplus with which to buy tools or land for himself, then labors on his own account another while, and at length hires another new beginner to help him. This is the just and generous and prosperous system which opens the way to all—gives hopes to all, and consequent energy and progress and improvement of condition to all. No men living are more worthy to be trusted than those who toil up from poverty—none less inclined to take or touch aught which they have not honestly earned. Let them beware of surrendering a political power which they already possess, and which, if surrendered, will surely be used to close the door of advancement against such as they, and to fix new disabilities and burdens upon them, till all of liberty shall be lost.

PART II

Narrative Prose

The Prodigal Son

LUKE 15:11–32

And he said, A certain man had two sons. And the younger of them said to his father, Father, give me the portion of goods that falleth to me. And he divided unto them his living. And not many days after the younger son gathered all together, and took his journey into a far country, and there wasted his substance with riotous living.

And when he had spent all, there arose a mighty famine in that land; and he began to be in want. And he went and joined himself to a citizen of that country; and he sent him into his fields to feed swine. And he would fain have filled his belly with the husks that the swine did eat: and no man gave unto him.

And when he came to himself, he said, How many hired servants of my father's have bread enough and to spare, and I perish with hunger! I will arise and go to my father, and will say unto him, Father, I have sinned against heaven, and before thee. And am no more worthy to be called thy son: make me as one of thy hired servants.

And he arose, and came to his father. But when he was yet a great way off, his father saw him, and had compassion, and ran, and fell on his neck, and kissed him.

And the son said unto him, Father, I have sinned against heaven, and in thy sight, and am no more worthy to be called thy son.

But the father said to his servants, Bring forth the best robe, and put it on him; and put a ring on his hand, and shoes on his feet: and bring hither the fatted calf, and kill it; and let us eat, and be merry: for this my son was dead, and is alive again; he was lost, and is found. And they began to be merry.

Now his elder son was in the field: and as he came and drew nigh to the house, he heard musick and dancing. And he called one of the servants, and asked what these things meant. And he said unto him, Thy brother is come; and thy father hath killed the fatted calf, because he hath received him safe and sound.

And he was angry, and would not go in: therefore came his father out, and intreated him. And he answering said to his father, Lo, these many years do I serve thee, neither transgressed I at any time thy commandment: and yet thou never gavest me a kid, that I might make merry with my friends: But as soon as this thy son was come, which had devoured thy living with harlots, thou hast killed for him the fatted calf.

And he said unto him, Son, thou art ever with me, and all that I have is thine. It was meet that we should make merry, and be glad: for this thy brother was dead, and is alive again; and was lost, and is found.

The Bombardment [1]

AMY LOWELL

Slowly, without force, the rain drops into the city. It stops a moment on the carved head of Saint John, then slides on again, slipping and trickling over his stone cloak. It splashes from the lead conduit of a gargoyle, and falls from it in turmoil on the stones in the Cathedral square. Where are the people, and why does the fretted steeple seep about in the sky? Boom! The sound swings against the rain. Boom, again! After it, only water rushing in the gutters, and the turmoil from the spout of the gargoyle. Silence. Ripples and mutters. Boom!

The room is damp, but warm. Little flashes swarm about from the firelight. The lustres of the chandeliers are bright, and clusters of rubies leap in the bohemian glasses on the *étagère*. Her hands are restless, but the white masses of her hair are quite still. Boom! Will it never cease to torture, this iteration! Boom! The vibration shatters a glass on the *étagère*. It lies there, formless and glowing, with all its crimson gleams shot out of patterns, spilled, flowing red, blood-red. A thin bell-note pricks through the silence. A door creaks. The old lady speaks: "Victor, clear away that broken glass." "Alas! Madam, the bohemian glass!" "Yes, Victor, one hundred years ago my father brought it—" Boom! The room shakes, the servitor quakes. Another goblet shivers and breaks. Boom!

It rustles at the window-pane, the smooth, streaming rain, and he is shut within its clash and murmur. Inside is his candle, his table, his ink, his pen, and his dreams. He is thinking, and the walls are pierced with beams of sunshine, slipping through young green. A fountain tosses itself up at the blue sky, and through the spattered water in the basin he

[1] Reprinted by permission of and arrangement with the publishers, Houghton Mifflin Company.

can see copper carp, lazily floating among cold leaves. A wind-harp in a cedar-tree grieves and whispers, and words blow in his brain, bubbled, iridescent, shooting up like flowers of fire, higher and higher. Boom! The flame-flowers snap on their slender stems. The fountain rears up in long broken spears of dishevelled water and flattens into the earth. Boom! And there is only the room, the table, the candle, and the sliding rain. Again, Boom!—Boom!—Boom! He stuffs his fingers into his ears. He sees corpses, and cries out in fright. Boom! It is night, and they are shelling the city! Boom! Boom!

A child wakes and is afraid, and weeps in the darkness. What has made the bed shake? "Mother, where are you? I am awake." "Hush, my darling, I am here." "But, Mother, something so queer happened, the room shook." Boom! "Oh. What is it? What is the matter?" Boom! "Where is Father? I am so afraid." Boom! The child sobs and shrieks. The house trembles and creaks. Boom!

Retorts, globes, tubes, and phials lie shattered. All his trials oozing across the floor. The life that was his choosing, lonely, urgent, goaded by a hope, all gone. A weary man in a ruined laboratory, that is his story. Boom! Gloom and ignorance, and the jig of drunken brutes.

Diseases like snakes crawling over the earth, leaving trails of slime. Wails from people burying their dead. Through the window, he can see the rocking steeple. A ball of fire falls on the lead of the roof, and the sky tears apart on a spike of flame. Up the spire, behind the lacings of stone, zigzagging in and out of the carved tracings, squirms the fire. It spouts like yellow wheat from the gargoyles, coils round the head of Saint John, and aureoles him in light. It leaps into the night and hisses against the rain. The Cathedral is a burning stain on the white, wet night.

Boom! The Cathedral is a torch, and the houses next to it begin to scorch. Boom! The bohemian glass on the *étagère* is no longer there. Boom! A stalk of flame sways against the red damask curtains. The old lady cannot walk. She watches the creeping stalk and counts. Boom!—Boom!—Boom!

The poet rushes into the street, and the rain wraps him in a sheet of silver. But it is threaded with gold and powdered with scarlet beads. The city burns. Quivering, spearing, thrusting, lapping, streaming, run the flames. Over roofs, and walls, and shops, and stalls. Smearing its gold on the sky, the fire dances, lances itself through the doors, and lisps and chuckles along the floors.

The child wakes again and screams at the yellow petalled flowers flickering at the window. The little red lips of flame creep along the ceiling beams.

The old man sits among his broken experiments and looks at the burning Cathedral. Now the streets are swarming with people. They seek shelter and crowd into the cellars. They shout and call, and over all, slowly and without force, the rain drops into the city. Boom! And the steeple crashes down among the people. Boom! Boom, again! The water rushes along the gutters. The fire roars and mutters. Boom!

The Death of Socrates

PLATO (427?–347)

When he had bathed, and his children had been brought to him,—he had two sons quite little, and one grown up,—and the women of his family were come, he spoke with them in Crito's presence, and gave them his last commands; then he sent the women and children away, and returned to us. By that time it was near the hour of sunset, for he had been a long while within. When he came back to us from the bath he sat down, but not much was said after that. Presently the servant of the eleven came and stood before him and said, "I know I shall not find you unreasonable like other men, Socrates. They are angry with me and curse me when I bid them drink the poison because the authorities make me do it. But I have found you all along the noblest and gentlest and best man that has ever come here; and now I am sure that you will not be angry with me, but with those who you know are to blame. And so farewell, and try to bear what must be as lightly as you can; you know why I have come." With that he turned away weeping, and went out.

Socrates looked up at him, and replied, "Farewell: I will do as you say." Then he turned to us and said, "How courteous the man is! And the whole time that I have been here, he has constantly come in to see me, and sometimes he has talked to me, and has been the best of men; and now, how generously he weeps for me! Come, Crito, let us obey him: let the poison be brought if it is ready; and if it is not ready, let it be prepared."

Crito replied: "Nay, Socrates, I think that the sun is still upon the hills, it has not set. Besides, I know that other men take the poison quite late, and eat and drink heartily, and even enjoy the company of their chosen friends, after the announcement has been made. So do not hurry; there is still time."

Socrates replied: "And those whom you speak of, Crito, naturally do so; for they think that they will be gainers by so doing. And I naturally shall not do so; for I think that I should gain nothing by drinking the poison a little later, but my own contempt for so greedily saving up a life which is already spent. So do not refuse to do as I say."

Then Crito made a sign to his slave who was standing by; and the slave went out, and after some delay returned with the man who was to give the poison, carrying it prepared in a cup. When Socrates saw him, he asked, "You understand these things, my good sir, what have I to do?"

"You have only to drink this," he replied, "and to walk about until your legs feel heavy, and then lie down; and it will act of itself." With that he handed the cup to Socrates, who took it quite cheerfully, Echecrates, without trembling, and without any change of colour or of feature, and looked up at the man with that fixed glance of his, and asked, "What say you to making a libation from this draught? May I, or not?" "We only prepare so much as we think sufficient, Socrates," he answered. "I understand," said Socrates. "But I suppose that I may, and must pray to the gods that my journey hence may be prosperous: that is my prayer; be it so." With these words he put the cup to his lips and drank the poison quite calmly and cheerfully. Till then most of us had been able to control our grief fairly well; but when we saw him drinking, and then the poison finished, we could do so no longer: my tears came fast in spite of myself, and I covered my face and wept for myself: it was not for him, but at my own misfortune in losing such a friend. Even before that Crito had been unable to restrain his tears, and had gone away; and Appolodorus, who had never once ceased weeping the whole time, burst into a loud cry, and made us one and all break down by his sobbing and grief, except only Socrates himself, "What are you doing, my friends?" he exclaimed. "I sent away the women chiefly in order that they might not offend in this way; for I have heard that a man should die in silence. So calm yourselves and bear up." When we heard that we were ashamed, and we ceased from weeping. But he walked about, until he said that his legs were getting heavy, and then he lay down on his back, as he was told. And the man who gave the poison began to examine his feet and legs, from time to time: then he pressed his foot hard, and asked if there was any feeling in it; and Socrates said, "No.": and then his legs, and so higher and higher, and showed us that he was cold and stiff. And Socrates felt himself, and said that when it came to his heart, he should be gone. He was already growing cold about the groin, when he uncovered his face, which had been covered, and spoke for the last time. "Crito," he said, "I owe a cock to Asclepius; do not forget to pay it." "It shall be done," replied Crito. "Is there anything else that you wish?" He made no answer to this question; but after a short interval there was a movement, and the man uncovered him, and his eyes were fixed. Then Crito closed his mouth and his eyes.

Such was the end, Echecrates, of our friend, a man, I think, who was the wisest and justest, and the best man that I have ever known.

Men Show Devotion to a Loved Officer [1]

ERNIE PYLE

AT THE FRONT LINES IN ITALY, January, 1944.—In this war I have known a lot of officers who were loved and respected by the soldiers under them. But never have I crossed the trail of any man as beloved as Capt. Henry T. Waskow, of Belton, Tex.

Capt. Waskow was a company commander in the 36th Division. He had led his company since long before it left the States. He was very young, only in his middle twenties, but he carried in him a sincerity and gentleness that made people want to be guided by him.

"After my own father, he came next," a sergeant told me.

"He always looked after us," a soldier said. "He'd go to bat for us every time."

"I've never known him to do anything unfair," another one said.

I was at the foot of the mule trail the night they brought Capt. Waskow down. The moon was nearly full, and you could see far up the trail, and even part way across the valley below. Soldiers made shadows as they walked.

Dead men had been coming down the mountain all evening, lashed onto the backs of mules. They came lying belly down across the wooden packsaddles, their heads hanging down on the left side of the mules, their stiffened legs sticking out awkwardly from the other side, bobbing up and down as the mules walked.

The Italian mule skinners were afraid to walk beside dead men, so Americans had to lead the mules down that night. Even the Americans were reluctant to unlash and lift off the bodies, when they got to the bottom, so an officer had to do it himself and ask others to help.

The first one came down early in the morning. They slid him down from the mule, and stood him on his feet for a moment while they got a new grip. In the half light he might have been merely a sick man standing there leaning on the others. Then they laid him on the ground in the shadow of the low stone wall alongside the road.

---

[1] Reprinted from *Brave Men* by permission of Henry Holt & Company, publishers.

I don't know who that first one was. You feel small in the presence of dead men, and you don't ask silly questions.

We left him there beside the road, that first one, and we all went back into the cowshed and sat on water cans or lay on the straw, waiting for the next batch of mules.

Somebody said the dead soldier had been dead for four days, and then nobody said anything more about it. We talked soldier talk for an hour or more; the dead men lay all alone, outside in the shadow of the wall.

Then a soldier came into the cowshed and said there were some more bodies outside. We went out into the road. Four mules stood there in the moonlight in the road where the trail came down off the mountain. The soldiers who led them stood there waiting.

"This one is Capt. Waskow," one of them said quietly.

Two men unlashed his body from the mule and lifted it off and laid it in the shadow beside the stone wall. Other men took the other bodies off. Finally, there were five lying end to end in a long row. You don't cover up dead men in the combat zones. They just lie there in the shadows until somebody else comes after them.

The unburdened mules moved off to their olive grove. The men in the road seemed reluctant to leave. They stood around, and gradually I could sense them moving, one by one, close to Capt. Waskow's body. Not so much to look, I think, as to say something in finality to him and to themselves. I stood close by and I could hear.

One soldier came and looked down, and he said out loud:

"God damn it!"

That's all he said, and then he walked away.

Another one came, and he said, "God damn it to hell anyway!" He looked down for a few moments and then turned and left.

Another man came. I think he was an officer. It was hard to tell officers from men in the dim light, for all were bearded and grimy. The man looked down into the dead captain's face and then spoke directly to him, as though he were alive:

"I'm sorry, old man."

Then a soldier came and stood beside the officer and bent over, and he, too, spoke to his dead captain, not in a whisper but awfully tenderly, and he said:

"I sure am sorry, sir."

Then the first man squatted down, and he reached down and took the dead hand, and he sat there for a full five minutes holding the dead hand in his own and looking intently into the dead face. And he never uttered a sound all the time he sat there.

Finally he put the hand down. He reached up and gently straightened the points of the captain's shirt collar, and then he sort of rearranged the tattered edges of the uniform around the wound, and then he got up and walked away down the road in the moonlight, all alone.

The rest of us went back into the cowshed, leaving the five dead men lying in a line end to end in the shadow of the low stone wall. We lay down on the straw in the cowshed, and pretty soon we were all asleep.

DR. KEITH'S LETTER TO HIS SON WILLIE FROM *The Caine Mutiny*[1]

HERMAN WOUK

Dear Willie:

By the time you read this letter, I think I will be dead. I'm sorry to startle you but I suppose there's no pleasant way to break such news. The trouble I've been having with my toe is due to a rather vicious disorder, malignant melanoma. The prognosis is one hundred per cent bad. I've known about my condition for a long time, and figured that I would probably die this summer. But the toe began to go a bit sooner. I suppose I should be in a hospital at this moment (two nights before you leave) but I hate to spoil your departure, and since there's no hope anyway, I've postponed it. I'm going to try to stall until I know you've left San Francisco. Your mother doesn't know anything yet. My guess is that I won't last more than three or four weeks, now.

I'm a little young to go, according to insurance tables, and I must say I don't feel ready, but I daresay that's because I've accomplished so little. I look back on my life, Willie, and there's not much there. Your mother has been a fine wife, and I have no regrets on that score. But I seem to have led such a thoroughly second-rate life—not only compared to my father, but in view of my own capabilities. I had quite a feeling for research. When I fell in love with your mother I thought I couldn't marry her without undertaking general practice in a high-income community. It was my plan to make a pile in ten or fifteen years of such work, and then return to research. I really think I might have done something in cancer. I had a theory—a notion, you might say—nothing I could have put on paper. It needed three years of systematic investigation. Nobody has touched it to this day. I've kept up with the literature. My name might have meant as much as my father's. But now there's no time even to outline the procedure. The worst of it is, I now

[1] New York: Doubleday and Company, 1951, pp. 59–62. Copyright 1951, by Herman Wouk, reprinted by permission of Doubleday & Company, Inc.

feel your mother would have stood by me and lived modestly if I'd really insisted.

But I've had a pleasant time, I can truly say that. I've loved reading and golf, and I've had all of that I wanted. The days have gone by all too fast.

I wish I might have met this girl of yours. It seems to me that she and the Navy, or both, are having quite a good effect on you. And believe me, Willie, that is by far the brightest thought I take with me into the hospital. I've let slide my relationship with you as I have so many other things, through plain sloth; particularly since your mother seemed anxious to take charge of you. It's too bad we had no more children. Just bad luck. Your mother had three miscarriages, which you may not know.

I'll tell you a curious thing. It seems to me that I have a higher opinion of you than your mother has. She regards you as a hopeless baby who will have to be coddled through life. But I am coming to believe that though you are pretty spoiled and soft at the surface, you are tough enough at the core. After all, I see, you have always done pretty much as you pleased with your mother, while giving her the sense of ruling you. I'm sure this was no plan on your part, but you've done it anyway.

You've never had a serious problem in your life, up to this Navy experience. I watched you in the forty-eights demerits business very closely. It had its comical side, but really it was a challenge. You rose to it in an encouraging way.

Perhaps because I know I'll never see you again I find myself sentimentalizing over you, Willie. It seems to me that you're very much like our whole country—young, naive, spoiled and softened by abundance and good luck, but with an interior hardness that comes from your sound stock. This country of ours consists of pioneers, after all, these new Poles and Italians and Jews as well as the older stock, people who had the gumption to get up and go and make themselves better lives in a new world. You're going to run into a lot of strange young men in the Navy, most of them pretty low by your standards, I daresay, but I'll bet—though I won't live to see it—that they are going to make the greatest Navy the world has ever seen. And I think you're going to make a good naval officer—after a while. After a great while, perhaps.

This is not criticism, Willie, God knows I am pretty soft myself. Perhaps I'm wrong. You may never make a naval officer at all. Perhaps we're going to lose the war. I just don't believe it. I think we're going to win, and I think you're going to come back with more honor than you believed possible.

I know you're disappointed at having been sent to a ship like the *Caine*. Now, having seen it, you're probably disgusted. Well, remember this, you've had your own way too long, and all your immaturity is due to that. You need some stone walls to batter yourself against. I strongly suspect you'll find plenty of them there on the *Caine*. I don't envy you the experience itself, but I do envy you the strengthening you're going to derive from it. Had I had one such experience in my younger years, I might not be dying a failure.

These are strong words, but I won't cross them out. They don't hurt too much and, furthermore, my hand isn't the one to cross them out any more. I'm finished now, but the last word on my life rests with you. If you turn out well, I can still claim some kind of success in the afterworld, if there is one.

About your singing versus comparative literature—you may have a different outlook when the war is over. Don't waste brain power over the far future. Concentrate on doing well now. Whatever assignment they give you on the *Caine,* remember that it's worthy of your best efforts. It's your way of fighting the war.

It's surprising, how little I have to say to you in these last words. I ought to fill up a dozen more sheets, and yet I feel you are pretty good at getting your way—and in other matters any words I might write would make little sense, without your own experience to fill the words with meaning. Remember this, if you can—there is nothing, nothing more precious than time. You probably feel you have a measureless supply of it, but you haven't. Wasted hours destroy your life just as surely at the beginning as at the end—only at the end it becomes more obvious. Use your time while you have it, Willie, in making something of yourself.

Religion. I'm afraid we haven't given you much, not having had much ourselves. But I think, after all, I will mail you a Bible before I go into the hospital. There is a lot of dry stuff in the Bible about Jewish wars and rituals that may put you off—but don't make the mistake of skipping the Old Testament. It's the core of all religion, I think, and there is a lot of everyday wisdom in it. You have to be able to recognize it. That takes time. Meantime get familiar with the words. You'll never regret it. I came to the Bible as I did to everything in life, too late.

About money matters. I'm leaving all my property to your mother. Uncle Lloyd is the executor. There is a ten-thousand dollar policy of which you're the beneficiary. If you want to get married, or go back to school, that should be enough to enable you to carry out your plans. Money is a very pleasant thing, Willie, and I think you can trade almost anything for it wisely except the work you really want to do. If you sell out your time for a comfortable life, and give up your natural work, I think you lose in the exchange. There remains an inner uneasiness that spoils the comforts.

Well, Willie, it's 3 A.M. by my old leather-covered desk clock. A waning moon is shining through the library window, and my fingers are stiff from writing. My toe is giving me the devil, too. Sleeping pills and bed for me. Thank God for the barbiturate.

Take care of your mother if she lives to be very old, and be kind to her if you come back from the war with enough strength to break away from her. She has many faults, but she's good, and she has loved you and me very truly.

(Willie began to sob. He read the last paragraphs through a blur of tears.)

Think of me and of what I might have been, Willie, at the times in your life when you come to crossroads. For my sake, for the sake of the father who took the wrong turns, take the right ones, and carry my blessing and my justification with you.

I stretch out my hand to you. We haven't kissed in many, many years. I liked to kiss you when you were a baby. You were a very sweet and good-natured child, with wonderful large eyes. God! Long ago.

Good-by, my son. Be a man.

Dad

PART III

Narrative Poetry

An Incident of the French Camp

ROBERT BROWNING

You know, we French stormed Ratisbon:
  A mile or so away,
On a little mound, Napoleon
  Stood on our storming-day;
With neck out-thrust, you fancy how,
  Legs wide, arms locked behind,
As if to balance the prone brow,
  Oppressive with its mind.

Just as perhaps he mused, "My plans
  That soar, to earth may fall,
Let once my army-leader Lannes
  Waver at yonder wall,"—
Out 'twixt the battery-smokes there flew
  A rider, bound on bound
Full-galloping; nor bridle drew
  Until he reached the mound.

Then off there flung in smiling joy,
  And held himself erect
By just his horse's mane, a boy:
  You hardly could suspect—
(So tight he kept his lips compressed,
  Scarce any blood came through)
You looked twice ere you saw his breast
  Was all but shot in two.

"Well," cried he, "Emperor, by God's grace
  We've got you Ratisbon!

The Marshal's in the market-place,
  And you'll be there anon
To see your flag-bird flap his vans
  Where I, to heart's desire,
Perched him!" The chief's eye flashed; his plans
  Soared up again like fire.

The chief's eye flashed; but presently
  Softened itself, as sheathes
A film the mother-eagle's eye
  When her bruised eaglet breathes;
"You're wounded!" "Nay," his soldier's pride
  Touched to the quick, he said:
"I'm killed, Sire!" And his chief beside,
  Smiling the boy fell dead.

Birches [1]

ROBERT FROST

When I see birches bend to left and right
Across the line of straighter darker trees,
I like to think some boy's been swinging them.
But swinging doesn't bend them down to stay.
Ice-storms do that. Often you must have seen them
Loaded with ice a sunny winter morning
After a rain. They click upon themselves
As the breeze rises, and turn many-colored
As the stir cracks and crazes their enamel.
Soon the sun's warmth makes them shed crystal shells
Shattering and avalanching on the snow-crust—
Such heaps of broken glass to sweep away
You'd think the inner dome of heaven had fallen.
They are dragged to the withered bracken by the load,
And they seem not to break; though once they are bowed
So low for long, they never right themselves:
You may see their trunks arching in the woods
Years afterwards, trailing their leaves on the ground,
Like girls on hands and knees that throw their hair
Before them over their heads to dry in the sun.

[1] This and the following two poems are reprinted from *The Collected Poems of Robert Frost* (New York: Henry Holt and Company). By permission of the publishers.

But I was going to say when Truth broke in
With all her matter-of-fact about the ice-storm
I should prefer to have some boy bend them
As he went out and in to fetch the cows—
Some boy too far from town to learn baseball,
Whose only play was what he found himself,
Summer or winter, and could play alone.
One by one he subdued his father's trees
By riding them down over and over again
Until he took the stiffness out of them,
And not one but hung limp, not one was left
For him to conquer. He learned all there was
To learn about not launching out too soon
And so not carrying the tree away
Clear to the ground. He always kept his poise
To the top branches, climbing carefully
With the same pains you use to fill a cup
Up to the brim, and even above the brim.
Then he flung outward, feet first, with a swish,
Kicking his way down through the air to the ground.

So was I once myself a swinger of birches;
And so I dream of going back to be.
It's when I'm weary of considerations,
And life is too much like a pathless wood
Where your face burns and tickles with the cobwebs
Broken across it, and one eye is weeping
From a twig's having lashed across it open.
I'd like to get away from earth awhile
And then come back to it and begin over.
May no fate willfully misunderstand me
And half grant what I wish and snatch me away
Not to return. Earth's the right place for love:
I don't know where it's likely to go better.
I'd like to go by climbing a birch tree,
And climb black branches up a snow-white trunk
Toward heaven, till the tree could bear no more,
But dipped its top and set me down again.
That would be good both going and coming back.
One could do worse than be a swinger of birches.

The Pasture

ROBERT FROST

I'm going out to clean the pasture spring;
I'll only stop to rake the leaves away
(And wait to watch the water clear, I may):
I shan't be gone long.—You come too.

I'm going out to fetch the little calf
That's standing by the mother. It's so young,
It totters when she licks it with her tongue.
I shan't be gone long.—You come too.

The Death of the Hired Man [1]

ROBERT FROST

Mary sat musing on the lamp-flame at the table
Waiting for Warren. When she heard his step,
She ran on tiptoe down the darkened passage
To meet him in the doorway with the news
And put him on his guard. "Silas is back."
She pushed him outward with her through the door
And shut it after her. "Be kind," she said.
She took the market things from Warren's arms
And set them on the porch, then drew him down
To sit beside her on the wooden steps.
"When was I ever anything but kind to him?
But I'll not have the fellow back," he said.
"I told him so last haying, didn't I?
'If he left then,' I said, 'that ended it.'
What good is he? Who else will harbor him
At his age for the little he can do?
What help he is there's no depending on.
Off he goes always when I need him most.
'He thinks he ought to earn a little pay,
Enough at least to buy tobacco with,
So he won't have to beg and be beholden.'
'All right,' I say, 'I can't afford to pay
Any fixed wages, though I wish I could.'

[1] For an analysis of this poem, see C. C. Cunningham, *Literature as a Fine Art* (New York: The Ronald Press Company, 1941), pp. 106 ff.

'Someone else can.' 'Then someone else will have to.'
I shouldn't mind his bettering himself
If that was what it was. You can be certain,
When he begins like that, there's someone at him
Trying to coax him off with pocket-money,—
In haying time, when any help is scarce.
In winter he comes back to us. I'm done."
"Sh! not so loud: he'll hear you," Mary said.
"I want him to: he'll have to soon or late."
"He's worn out. He's asleep beside the stove.
When I came up from Rowe's I found him here,
Huddled against the barn-door fast asleep,
A miserable sight, and frightening, too—
You needn't smile—I didn't recognize him—
I wasn't looking for him—and he's changed.
Wait till you see."
"Where did you say he'd been?"
"He didn't say. I dragged him to the house,
And gave him tea and tried to make him smoke.
I tried to make him talk about his travels,
Nothing would do: he just kept nodding off."
"What did he say? Did he say anything?"
"But little."
"Anything? Mary, confess
He said he'd come to ditch the meadow for me."
"Warren!"
"But did he? I just want to know."
"Of course he did. What would you have him say?
Surely you wouldn't grudge the poor old man
Some humble way to save his self-respect.
He added, if you really care to know,
He meant to clear the upper pasture, too.
That sounds like something you have heard before?
Warren, I wish you could have heard the way
He jumbled everything. I stopped to look
Two or three times—he made me feel so queer—
To see if he was talking in his sleep.
He ran on Harold Wilson—you remember—
The boy you had in haying four years since.
He's finished school, and teaching in his college.
Silas declares you'll have to get him back.
He says they two will make a team for work:
Between them they will lay this farm as smooth!

The way he mixed that in with other things.
He thinks young Wilson a likely lad, though daft
On education—you know how they fought
All through July under the blazing sun,
Silas up on the cart to build the load,
Harold along beside to pitch it on."
"Yes, I took care to keep well out of earshot."
"Well, those days trouble Silas like a dream.
You wouldn't think they would. How some things linger!
Harold's young college boy's assurance piqued him.
After so many years he still keeps finding
Good arguments he sees he might have used.
I sympathize. I know just how it feels
To think of the right thing to say too late.
Harold's associated in his mind with Latin.
He asked me what I thought of Harold's saying
He studied Latin like the violin
Because he liked it—that an argument!
He said he couldn't make the boy believe
He could find water with a hazel prong—
Which showed how much good school had ever done him.
He wanted to go over that. But most of all
He thinks if he could have another chance
To teach him how to build a load of hay—"
"I know, that's Silas' one accomplishment.
He bundles every forkful in its place,
And tags and numbers it for future reference,
So he can find and easily dislodge it
In the unloading. Silas does that well.
He takes it out in bunches like big birds' nests.
You never see him standing on the hay
He's trying to lift, straining to lift himself."
"He thinks if he could teach him that, he'd be
Some good perhaps to someone in the world.
He hates to see a boy the fool of books.
Poor Silas, so concerned for other folk.
And nothing to look backward to with pride,
And nothing to look forward to with hope,
So now and never any different."
Part of a moon was falling down the west,
Dragging the whole sky with it to the hills.
Its light poured softly in her lap. She saw
And spread her apron to it. She put out her hand

Among the harp-like morning-glory strings,
Taut with the dew from garden bed to eaves,
As if she played unheard the tenderness
That wrought on him beside her in the night.
"Warren," she said, "he has come home to die:
You needn't be afraid he'll leave you this time."
"Home," he mocked gently.
"Yes, what else but home?
It all depends on what you mean by home.
Of course he's nothing to us, any more
Than was the hound that came a stranger to us
Out of the woods, worn out upon the trail."
"Home is the place where, when you have to go there,
They have to take you in."
"I should have called it
Something you somehow haven't to deserve."
Warren leaned out and took a step or two,
Picked up a little stick, and brought it back
And broke it in his hand and tossed it by.
"Silas has better claim on us, you think,
Than on his brother? Thirteen little miles
As the road winds would bring him to his door.
Silas has walked that far no doubt today.
Why didn't he go there? His brother's rich,
A somebody—director in the bank."
"He never told us that."
"We know it though."
"I think his brother ought to help, of course.
I'll see to that if there is need. He ought of right
To take him in, and might be willing to—
He may be better than appearances.
But have some pity on Silas. Do you think
If he'd had any pride in claiming kin
Or anything he looked for from his brother,
He'd keep so still about him all this time?"
"I wonder what's between them."
"I can tell you.
Silas is what he is—we wouldn't mind him—
But just the kind that kinsfolk can't abide.
He never did a thing so very bad.
He don't know why he isn't quite as good
As anyone. He won't be made ashamed
To please his brother, worthless though he is."

"*I* can't think Si ever hurt anyone."
"No, but he hurt my heart the way he lay
And rolled his old head on that sharp-edged chair-back.
He wouldn't let me put him on the lounge.
You must go in and see what you can do.
I made the bed up for him there tonight.
You'll be surprised at him—how much he's broken.
His working days are done; I'm sure of it."
"I'd not be in a hurry to say that."
"I haven't been. Go, look, see for yourself.
But, Warren, please remember how it is:
He's come to help you ditch the meadow.
He has a plan. You mustn't laugh at him.
He may not speak of it, and then he may.
I'll sit and see if that small sailing cloud
Will hit or miss the moon."
It hit the moon.
Then there were three there, making a dim row,
The moon, the little silver cloud, and she.
Warren returned—too soon, it seemed to her,
Slipped to her side, caught up her hand and waited.
"Warren?" she questioned.
"Dead," was all he answered.

Gunga Din [1]

RUDYARD KIPLING

You may talk o' gin and beer
When you're quartered safe out 'ere,
An' you're sent to penny-fights an' Aldershot it;
But when it comes to slaughter
You will do your work on water,
An' you'll lick the bloomin' boots of 'im that's got it.
Now in Injia's sunny clime,
Where I used to spend my time
A-servin' of 'Er Majesty the Queen,
Of all them blackfaced crew
The finest man I knew
Was our regimental bhisti, Gunga Din.

[1] This and the following poem are reprinted from *Barrack Room Ballads,* by permission of Mrs. George Bambridge, copyright owner, and Doubleday & Company, Inc., American publishers.

It was "Din! Din! Din!
"You limpin' lump o' brick-dust, Gunga Din!
"Hi! Slippy hitherao!
"Water, get it! Panee lao
"You squidgy-nosed old idol, Gunga Din."

The uniform 'e wore
Was nothin' much before,
An' rather less than 'arf o' that be'ind,
For a piece o' twisty rag
An' a goatskin water-bag
Was all the field-equipment 'e could find.
When the sweatin' troop-train lay
In a sidin' through the day,
Where the 'eat would make your bloomin' eyebrows crawl,
We shouted "Harry By!
Till our throats were bricky-dry,
Then we wopped 'im 'cause 'e couldn't serve us all.
It was "Din! Din! Din!
"You 'eathen, where the mischief 'ave you been?
"You put some juldee in it
"Or I'll marrow you this minute
"If you don't fill up my helmet, Gunga Din!"

'E would dot an' carry one
Till the longest day was done;
An' 'e didn't seem to know the use o' fear.
If we charged or broke or cut,
You could bet your bloomin' nut,
'E'd be waitin' fifty paces right flank rear.
With 'is mussick on 'is back,
'E would skip with our attack,
An' watch us till the bugles made "Retire"
An' for all 'is dirty 'ide
'E was white, clear white, inside
When 'e went to tend the wounded under fire!
It was "Din! Din! Din!"
With the bullets kickin' dust-spots on the green.
When the cartridges ran out,
You could hear the front-ranks shout,
"Hi! ammunition-mules an' Gunga Din!"

I sha'n't forgit the night
When I dropped be'ind the fight
With a bullet where my belt-plate should 'a' been.
I was chokin' mad with thirst,
An' the man that spied me first
Was our good old grinnin', gruntin' Gunga Din.
'E lifted up my 'ead,
An' he plugged me where I bled,
An' 'e guv me 'arf-a-pint o' water—green.
It was crawlin' and it stunk,
But of all the drinks I've drunk,
I'm gratefullest to one from Gunga Din.
It was "Din! Din! Din!
" 'Ere's a beggar with a bullet through 'is spleen;
" 'E's chawin' up the ground,
"An' 'e's kickin' all around:
"For Gawd's sake git the water, Gunga Din!"

'E carried me away
To where a dooli lay,
An' a bullet come an' drilled the beggar clean.
'E put me safe inside,
An' just before 'e died,
"I 'ope you liked your drink," sez Gunga Din.
So I'll meet 'im later on
At the place where 'e is gone—
Where it's always double drill and no canteen.
'E'll be squattin' on the coals
Givin' drink to poor damned souls,
An' I'll get a swig in hell from Gunga Din!
Yes, Din! Din! Din!
You Lazarushian-leather Gunga Din!
Though I've belted you and flayed you,
By the livin' Gawd that made you,
You're a better man than I am, Gunga Din!

Tommy

RUDYARD KIPLING

I went into a public-'ouse to get a pint o' beer,
The publican 'e up an' sez, "We serve no red-coats here."
The girls be'ind the bar they laughed an' giggled fit to die,

I outs into the street again an' to myself sez I:
O it's Tommy this, an' Tommy that, an' "Tommy, go away";
But it's "Thank you, Mister Atkins," when the band begins to play—
The band begins to play, my boys, the band begins to play,
O it's "Thank you, Mister Atkins," when the band begins to play.

I went into a theatre as sober as could be,
They gave a drunk civilian room, but 'adn't none for me;
They sent me to the gallery or round the music-'alls,
But when it comes to fightin', Lord! they'll shove me in the stalls!
For it's Tommy this, an' Tommy that, an' "Tommy, wait outside";
But it's "Special train for Atkins" when the trooper's on the tide—
The troopship's on the tide, my boys, the troopship's on the tide,
O it's "Special train for Atkins" when the trooper's on the tide.

Yes, makin' mock o' uniforms that guard you while you sleep
Is cheaper than them uniforms, an' they're starvation cheap;
An' hustlin' drunken soldiers when they're goin' large a bit
Is five times better business than paradin' in full kit.
Then it's Tommy this, an' Tommy that, an' "Tommy, ow's yer soul?"
But it's "Thin red line of 'eroes" when the drums begin to roll—
The drums begin to roll, my boys, the drums begin to roll,
O it's "Thin red line of 'eroes" when the drums begin to roll.

We aren't no thin red 'eroes, nor we aren't no blackguards too,
But single men in barricks, most remarkable like you;
An' if sometimes our conduct isn't all your fancy paints,
Why, single men in barricks don't grow into plaster saints;
While it's Tommy this, an' Tommy that, an' "Tommy, fall be'ind,"
But it's "Please to walk in front, sir," when there's trouble in the wind—
There's trouble in the wind, my boys, there's trouble in the wind,
O it's "Please to walk in front, sir," when there's trouble in the wind.

You talk o' better food for us, an' schools, an' fires, an' all:
We'll wait for extry rations if you treat us rational.
Don't mess about the cook-room slops, but prove it to our face
The Widow's uniform is not the soldier-man's disgrace.
For it's Tommy this, an' Tommy that, an' "Chuck him out, the brute!"
But it's "Saviour of 'is country" when the guns begin to shoot;

An' it's Tommy this, an' Tommy that, an' anything you please;
An' Tommy ain't a bloomin' fool—you bet that Tommy sees!

John Brown [1]

VACHEL LINDSAY

READER I. I've been to Palestine. (*Steps forward*)
CHORUS. What did you see in Palestine?
READER I. I saw the ark of Noah—
It was made of pitch and pine.
I saw old Father Noah
Asleep beneath his vine
I saw Shem, Ham and Japhet
Standing in a line.
I saw the tower of Babel
In the gorgeous sunrise shine—
By a weeping willow tree
Beside the Dead Sea. (*Steps back*)

READER II. I've been to Palestine. (*Steps forward*)
CHORUS. What did you see in Palestine?
READER II. I saw abominations
And Gadarene swine.
I saw the sinful Canaanites
Upon the shewbread dine,
And spoil the temple vessels
And drink the temple wine.
I saw Lot's wife, a pillar of salt
Standing in the brine—
By a weeping willow tree
Beside the Dead Sea. (*Steps back*)

READER III. I've been to Palestine. (*Steps forward*)
CHORUS. What did you see in Palestine?
READER III. Cedars on Mount Lebanon,
Gold in Ophir's mine.
And a wicked generation
Seeking for a sign.
And Baal's howling worshippers
Their god with leaves entwine.

[1] This and the following two selections are from *Collected Poems of Vachel Lindsay*. Reprinted by permission of The Macmillan Company, publishers.

And . . .
I saw the war-horse ramping
And shake his forelock fine—
By a weeping willow tree
Beside the Dead Sea. (*Steps back*)

READER IV. I've been to Palestine. (*Steps forward*)
CHORUS. What did you see in Palestine?
READER IV. Old John Brown.
CHORUS. Old John Brown.
READER IV. I saw his gracious wife
Dressed in a homespun gown.
I saw his seven sons
Before his feet bow down.
And he marched with his seven sons,
His wagons and goods and guns,
To his campfire by the sea,
By the waves of Galilee. (*Steps back*)

READER V. I've been to Palestine. (*Steps forward*)
CHORUS. What did you see in Palestine?
READER V. I saw the harp and psalt'ry
Played for Old John Brown.
I heard the ram's horn blow,
Blow for Old John Brown.
I saw the Bulls of Bashan—
They cheered for Old John Brown.
I saw the big Behemoth—
He cheered for Old John Brown.
I saw the big Leviathan—
He cheered for Old John Brown.
I saw the Angel Gabriel
Great power to him assign.
I saw him fight the Canaanites
And set God's Israel free.
I saw him when the war was done
In his rustic chair recline—
By his campfire by the sea
By the waves of Galilee. (*Steps back*)

READER VI. I've been to Palestine. (*Steps forward*)
CHORUS. What did you see in Palestine?

READER VI. Old John Brown.
CHORUS. Old John Brown.
READER VI. And there he sits
To judge the world.
His hunting-dogs
At his feet are curled.
His eyes half-closed,
But John Brown sees
The ends of the earth,
The Day of Doom.
And his shot-gun lies
Across his knees—
CHORUS. (*slowly*) Old John Brown,
(*retard*) Old John Brown.

The Congo

PART I

VACHEL LINDSAY

Fat black bucks in a wine-barrel room,
Barrel-house kings, with feet unstable,
Sagged and reeled and pounded on the table, *A deep rolling bass.*
Pounded on the table,
Beat an empty barrel with the handle of a broom,
Hard as they were able,
Boom, boom, BOOM,
With a silk umbrella and the handle of a broom,
Boomlay, boomlay, boomlay, BOOM.

THEN I had religion, THEN I had a vision.
I could not turn from their revel in derision.
THEN I SAW THE CONGO, CREEPING THROUGH THE BLACK, *More deliberate.*
CUTTING THROUGH THE JUNGLE WITH A GOLDEN TRACK. *Solemnly chanted.*

Then along that riverbank
A thousand miles
Tattooed cannibals danced in files;
Then I heard the boom of the blood-lust song
And a thigh-bone beating on a tin-pan gong.

And "Blood" screamed the whistles and the fifes of the warriors,
"Blood" screamed the skull-faced, lean witch-doctors,
"Whirl ye the deadly voo-doo rattle,
Harry the uplands,
Steal all the cattle,
Rattle-rattle, rattle-rattle,
Bing!
Boomlay, boomlay, boomlay, Boom,"
A roaring, epic, rag-time tune
From the mouth of the Congo
To the Mountains of the Moon.
Death is an Elephant,
Torch-eyed and horrible,
Foam-flanked and terrible.
Boom, steal the pygmies,
Boom, kill the Arabs,
Boom, kill the white men,
Hoo, Hoo, Hoo.
Listen to the yell of Leopold's ghost
Burning in Hell for his hand-maimed host.
Hear how the demons chuckle and yell.
Cutting his hands off, down in Hell.
Listen to the creepy proclamation,
Blown through the lairs of the forest-nation,
Blown past the white-ants' hill of clay,
Blown past the marsh where the butterflies play:—
"Be careful what you do,
Or Mumbo-Jumbo, God of the Congo,
And all of the other
Gods of the Congo,
Mumbo-Jumbo will hoo-doo you,
Mumbo-Jumbo will hoo-doo you,
Mumbo-Jumbo will hoo-doo you."

A rapidly piling climax of speed and racket.

With a philosophic pause.

Shrilly and with a heavily accented meter.

Like the wind in the chimney.

All the o *sounds very golden. Heavy accents very heavy. Light accents very light. Last line whispered.*

General William Booth Enters into Heaven

VACHEL LINDSAY

I

Booth led boldly with his big bass drum—
(Are you washed in the blood of the Lamb?)
The Saints smiled gravely and they said: "He's come."

(Are you washed in the blood of the Lamb?)
Walking lepers followed, rank on rank,
Lurching bravos from the ditches dank,
Drabs from the alleyways and drug fiends pale—
Minds still passion-ridden, soul-powers frail:—
Vermin-eaten saints with moldy breath,
Unwashed legions with the ways of Death—
(Are you washed in the blood of the Lamb?)

Every slum had sent its half-a-score
The round world over. (Booth had groaned for more.)
Every banner that the wide world flies
Bloomed with glory and transcendent dyes.
Big-voiced lasses made their banjos bang,
Tranced, fanatical, they shrieked and sang:—
"Are you washed in the blood of the Lamb?"

Hallelujah! It was queer to see
Bull-necked convicts with that land make free.
Loons with trumpets blowed a blare, blare, blare
On, on upward thro' the golden air!
(Are you washed in the blood of the Lamb?)

II

Booth died blind and still by faith he trod,
Eyes still dazzled by the ways of God.
Booth led boldly, and he looked the chief,
Eagle countenance in sharp relief,
Beard a-flying, air of high command
Unabated in that holy land.

Jesus came from out the court-house door,
Stretched his hands above the passing poor.
Booth saw not, but led his queer ones there
Round and round the mighty court-house square.
Yet in an instant all that blear review
Marched on spotless, clad in raiment new.
The lame were straightened, withered limbs uncurled
And blind eyes opened on a new, sweet world.

Drabs and vixens in a flash made whole!
Gone was the weasel-head, the snout, the jowl!
Sages and sibyls now, and athletes clean,
Rulers of empires, and of forests green!

The hosts were sandaled, and their wings were fire!
(Are you washed in the blood of the Lamb?)
But their noise played havoc with the angel-choir.
(Are you washed in the blood of the Lamb?)
Oh, shout Salvation! It was good to see
Kings and Princes by the Lamb set free.
The banjos rattled and the tambourines
Jing-jing-jingled in the hands of Queens.

And when Booth halted by the curb for prayer
He saw his Master thro' the flag-filled air.
Christ came gently with a robe and crown
For Booth the soldier, while the throng knelt down.
He saw King Jesus. They were face to face,
And he knelt a-weeping in that holy place.
Are you washed in the blood of the Lamb?

Frailty, Thy Name is a Misnomer[1]

OGDEN NASH

Once there was a couple named Mr. and Mrs. Pepperloaf and they were simply devoted,
Because each other was upon what they doted,
And in Mrs. Pepperloaf's eyes Mr. Pepperloaf could never err.
And he admitted only one flaw in her,
But it was a flaw that took many virtues to assuage,
Consisting in always asking him the date while she was reading the paper with the date clearly printed on every page,
And whenever he called her attention to this least admirable of her traits
She would retort that he didn't trust the paper's weather forecasts so then why should she trust its dates.
For eleven years his patience held
But finally he rebelled.
It was on the evening of Friday the seventh that she looked up from her paper and asked him the date,
And he replied firmly that she would find it at the top of the page so she looked at the top of the page and that was that, and presently they sat down to supper and ate,

[1] Reprinted from *Good Intentions* (Boston: Little, Brown and Company, 1942), by permission of the publishers.

And they were miserable because they had never disagreed and this
    contretemps was a beginner for them,
And at nine his employer's wife called up to ask where were they, she
    and eleven guests were waiting dinner for them,
And Mr. Pepperloaf asked Mrs. Pepperloaf how she could have so
    misreckoned,
And she said she knew that they had been invited out on the seventh
    but, according to the newspaper he had instructed her to consult,
    tonight was only the second,
And he picked up the paper and it was last week's not today's,
And she said certainly, she had just been reading over some recipes for
    different delicious soufflés,
And now she found the first flaw in him because she had obeyed his
    order to look for the date in the paper, hadn't she, so his irritation
    was uncalled for and unseasonable.
Women would rather be right than reasonable.

Miniver Cheevy [1]

EDWIN ARLINGTON ROBINSON

Miniver Cheevy, child of scorn,
    Grew lean while he assailed the seasons;
He wept that he was ever born,
    And he had reasons.

Miniver loved the days of old
    When swords were bright and steeds were prancing;
The vision of a warrior bold
    Would set him dancing.

Miniver sighed for what was not,
    And dreamed, and rested from his labors;
He dreamed of Thebes and Camelot,
    And Priam's neighbors.

Miniver mourned the ripe renown
    That made so many a name so fragrant;
He mourned Romance, now on the town,
    And Art, a vagrant.

[1] From *The Town Down the River,* by E. A. Robinson. Reprinted by permission of Charles Scribner's Sons, publishers.

Miniver loved the Medici,
  Albeit he had never seen one;
He would have sinned incessantly
  Could he have been one.

Miniver cursed the commonplace
  And eyed a khaki suit with loathing;
He missed the medieval grace
  Of iron clothing.

Miniver scorned the gold he sought,
  But sore annoyed was he without it;
Miniver thought, and thought and thought,
  And thought about it.

Miniver Cheevy, born too late,
  Scratched his head and kept on thinking;
Miniver coughed, and called it fate,
  And kept on drinking.

Marmion

SIR WALTER SCOTT

O, young Lochinvar is come out of the west,
Through all the wide Border his steed was the best;
And save his good broadsword he weapons had none,
He rode all unarm'd, and he rode all alone.
So faithful in love, and so dauntless in war,
There never was knight like the young Lochinvar.

'I long woo'd your daughter, my suit you denied;—
Love swells like the Solway, but ebbs like its tide—
And now am I come, with this lost love of mine,
To lead but one measure, drink one cup of wine.
There are maidens in Scotland more lovely by far,
That would gladly be bride to the young Lochinvar.'

The bride kiss'd the goblet: the knight took it up,
He quaff'd off the wine, and he threw down the cup.
She look'd down to blush, and she look'd up to sigh,
With a smile on her lips and a tear in her eye.

He took her soft hand, ere her mother could bar,—
'Now tread we a measure!' said young Lochinvar.

So stately his form, and so lovely her face,
That never a hall such a galliard did grace;
While her mother did fret, and her father did fume,
And the bridegroom stood dangling his bonnet and plume;
And the bride-maidens whisper'd, 'Twere better by far,
To have match'd our fair cousin with young Lochinvar.'

One touch to her hand, and one word in her ear,
When they reach'd the hall-door, and the charger stood near;
So light to the croupe the fair lady he swung,
So light to the saddle before her he sprung!
'She is won! we are gone, over bank, bush, and scaur;
They'll have fleet steeds that follow,' quoth young Lochinvar.

The Shooting of Dan McGrew [1]

ROBERT W. SERVICE

A bunch of the boys were whooping it up in the Malamute saloon;
The kid that handles the music-box was hitting a jagtime tune.
Back of the bar, in a solo game, sat Dangerous Dan McGrew,
And watching his luck was his light-o'-love, the lady that's known as Lou.

When out of the night, which was fifty below, and into the din and the glare,
There stumbled a miner fresh from the creeks, dog-dirty and loaded for bear.
He looked like a man with a foot in the grave and scarcely the strength of a louse,
Yet he tilted a poke of dust on the bar, and he called for drinks for the house.
There was none could place the stranger's face, though we searched ourselves for a clue;
But we drank his health, and the last to drink was Dangerous Dan McGrew.

[1] This and the following poem are reprinted from *The Spell of the Yukon,* by Robert W. Service. Copyright, 1907, by Dodd, Mead & Company, Inc.

There's men that somehow just grip your eyes, and hold them hard
like a spell;
And such was he, and he looked to me like a man who had lived in hell;
With a face most hair, and the dreary stare of a dog whose day is done,
As he watered the green stuff in his glass, and the drops fell one by one.
Then I got to figgering who he was, and wondering what he'd do,
And I turned my head—and there watching him was the lady that's
known as Lou.

His eyes went rubbering round the room, and he seemed in a kind of a
daze,
Till at last that old piano fell in the way of his wandering gaze.
The ragtime kid was having a drink; there was no one else on the stool,
So the stranger stumbles across the room, and flops down there like a
fool.
In a buckskin shirt that was glazed with dirt he sat, and I saw him
sway;
Then he clutched the keys with his talon hands—my God! but that
man could play.

Were you ever out in the Great Alone, when the moon was awful clear,
And the icy mountains hemmed you in with a silence you most could
hear;
With only the howl of a timber wolf, and you camped there in the cold,
A half-dead thing in a stark, dead world, clean mad for the muck called
gold;
While high overhead, green, yellow and red, the North Lights swept in
bars?—
Then you've a hunch what the music meant . . . hunger and night and
the stars.

And hunger not of the belly kind, that's banished with bacon and
beans,
But the gnawing hunger of lonely men for a home and all that it means;
For a fireside far from the cares that are, four walls and a roof above;
But oh, so cramful of cosy joy, and crowned with a woman's love—
A woman dearer than all the world, and true as Heaven is true—
(God! how ghastly she looks through her rouge, the lady that's known
as Lou!)

Then on a sudden the music changed, so soft that you scarce could
hear;

But you felt that your life had been looted clean of all that it once held
dear;
That someone had stolen the woman you loved, that her love was a
devil's lie,
That your guts were gone, and the best for you was to crawl away and
die.
'Twas the crowning cry of a heart's despair, and it thrilled you through
and through.
"I guess I'll make it a spread misere," said Dangerous Dan McGrew.

The music almost died away . . . then it burst like a pent-up flood;
And it seemed to say, "Repay, repay," and my eyes were blind with
blood.
The thought came back of an ancient wrong, and it stung like a frozen
lash,
And the lust awoke to kill, to kill . . . then the music stopped with a
crash,
And the stranger turned and his eyes they burned in a most peculiar
way.
In a buckskin shirt that was glazed with dirt he sat, and I saw him
sway.

Then his lips went in in a kind of grin, and he spoke, and his voice
was calm,
And "Boys," says he, "you don't know me, and none of you care a
damn;
But I want to state, and my words are straight, and I'll bet my poke
they're true,
That one of you is a hound of hell . . . and that one is Dan McGrew."

Then I ducked my head, and the lights went out, and two guns blazed
in the dark,
And a woman screamed, and the lights went up, and two men lay stiff
and stark.
Pitched on his head, and pumped full of lead, was Dangerous Dan
McGrew,
While the man from the creeks lay clutched to the breast of the lady
that's known as Lou.

These are the simple facts of the case, and I guess I ought to know.
They say that the stranger was crazed with "hootch," and I'm not
denying it's so.

I'm not so wise as the lawyer guys, but strictly between us two,
The woman that kissed him and—pinched his poke—was the lady that's known as Lou.

The Cremation of Sam McGee

ROBERT W. SERVICE

There are strange things done in the midnight sun
By the men who moil for gold;
The Arctic trails have their secret tales
That would make your blood run cold;
The Northern Lights have seen queer sights,
But the queerest they ever did see
Was that night on the marge of Lake Lebarge
I cremated Sam McGee.

Now Sam McGee was from Tennessee, where the cotton blooms and blows.
Why he left his home in the South to roam 'round the Pole, God only knows.
He was always cold, but the land of gold seemed to hold him like a spell;
Though he'd often say in his homely way that "he'd sooner live in hell."

On a Christmas day we were mushing our way over the Dawson trail.
Talk of your cold! through the parka's fold it stabbed like a driven nail.
If our eyes we'd close, then the lashes froze till sometimes we couldn't see;
It wasn't much fun, but the only one to whimper was Sam McGee.

And that very night, as we lay packed tight in our robes beneath the snow,
And the dogs were fed, and the stars o'er head were dancing heel and toe,
He turned to me, and "Cap," says he, "I'll cash in this trip, I guess;
And if I do, I'm asking that you won't refuse my last request."

Well, he seemed so low that I couldn't say no; then he says with a sort of moan;

"It's the cursed cold, and it's got right hold till I'm chilled clean through to the bone.
Yet 'tain't being dead—it's my awful dread of the icy grave that pains;
So I want you to swear that, foul or fair, you'll cremate my last remains."

A pal's last need is a thing to heed, so I swore I would not fail;
And so we started on at the streak of dawn; but God! he looked ghastly pale.
He crouched on the sleigh, and he raved all day of his home in Tennessee;
And before nightfall a corpse was all that was left of Sam McGee.

There wasn't a breath in that land of death, and I hurried, horror-driven,
With a corpse half-hid that I couldn't get rid, because of a promise given;
It was lashed to the sleigh, and it seemed to say: "You may tax your brawn and brains.
But you promised true, and it's up to you to cremate these last remains."

Now a promise made is a debt unpaid, and the trail has its own stern code.
In the days to come, though my lips were dumb, in my heart how I cursed that load.
In the long, long night, by the lone firelight, while the huskies, round in a ring,
Howled out their woes to the homeless snows—O God! how I loathed the thing.

And every day that quiet clay seemed to heavy and heavier grow;
And on I went, though the dogs were spent and the grub was getting low;
The trail was bad, and I felt half mad, but I swore I would not give in;
And I'd often sing to the hateful thing, and it harkened with a grin.

Till I came to the marge of Lake Lebarge, and a derelict there lay;
It was jammed in the ice, but I saw in a trice it was called the "Alice May."
And I looked at it, and I thought a bit, and I looked at my frozen chum;
Then "Here," said I, with a sudden cry, "is my cre-ma-to-re-um."

Some planks I tore from the cabin floor, and I lit the boiler fire;
Some coal I found that was lying around, and I heaped the fuel higher;
The flames just soared, and the furnace roared—such a blaze you seldom see;
And I burrowed a hole in the glowing coal, and I stuffed in Sam McGee.

Then I made a hike for I didn't like to hear him sizzle so;
And the heavens scowled, and the huskies howled, and the wind began to blow.
It was icy cold, but the hot sweat rolled down my cheeks, and I don't know why;
And the greasy smoke in an inky cloak went streaking down the sky.

I do not know how long in the snow I wrestled with grisly fear;
But the stars came out and they danced about ere again I ventured near;
I was sick with dread, but I bravely said: "I'll just take a peep inside.
I guess he's cooked, and it's time I looked"; . . . then the door I opened wide.

And there sat Sam, looking cool and calm, in the heart of the furnace roar;
And he wore a smile you could see a mile, and he said: "Please close that door.
It's fine in here, but I greatly fear you'll let in the cold and storm—
Since I left Plumtree down in Tennessee, it's the first time I've been warm."

There are strange things done in the midnight sun
By the men who moil for gold;
The Arctic trails have their secret tales
That would make your blood run cold;
The Northern Lights have seen queer sights,
But the queerest they ever did see
Was that night on the marge of Lake Lebarge
I cremated Sam McGee.

The Fool's Prayer [1]

EDWARD ROWLAND SILL

The royal feast was done; the King
  Sought some new sport to banish care,
And so to his jester cried: "Sir Fool,
  Kneel now, and make for us a prayer!"

The jester doffed his cap and bells,
  And stood the mocking court before;
They could not see the bitter smile
  Behind the painted grin he wore.

He bowed his head, and bent his knee
  Upon the monarch's silken stool;
His pleading voice arose: "O Lord,
  Be merciful to me, a fool!

"No pity, Lord, could change the heart
  From red with wrong to white as wool;
The rod must heal the sin; but, Lord,
  Be merciful to me, a fool!

"'Tis not by guilt the onward sweep
  Of truth and right, O Lord, we stay;
'Tis by our follies that so long
  We hold the earth from heaven away.

"These clumsy feet, still in the mire,
  Go crushing blossoms without end;
These hard, well-meaning hands we thrust
  Among the heartstrings of a friend.

"The ill-timed truth we might have kept—
  Who knows how sharp it pierced and stung?
The word we had no sense to say—
  Who knows how grandly it had rung?

"Our faults no tenderness should ask,
  The chastening stripes must cleanse them all;

[1] From *Poems,* by permission of Houghton Mifflin Company, publishers.

But for our blunders—oh, in shame
  Before the eyes of heaven we fall.

"Earth bears no balsam for mistakes;
  Men crown the knave and scourge the tool
That did his will; but Thou, O Lord,
  Be merciful to me, a fool!"

The room was hushed; in silence rose
  The king, and sought his gardens cool,
And walked apart, and murmured low,
  "Be merciful to me, a fool!"

The Wound-Dresser[1]

WALT WHITMAN

1

An old man bending I come among new faces,
(Arous'd and angry, I'd thought to beat the alarum, and urge relentless war,
But soon my fingers fail'd me, my face droop'd and I resign'd myself,
To sit by the wounded and soothe them, or silently watch the dead);

2

Bearing the bandages, water and sponge,
Straight and swift to my wounded I go,
Where they lie on the ground after the battle brought in,
Where their priceless blood reddens the grass the ground,
Or to the rows of the hospital tent, or under the roof'd hospital,
To the long rows of cots up and down each side I return,
To each and all one after another I draw near, not one do I miss,
An attendant follows holding a tray, he carries a refuse pail,
Soon to be fill'd with clotted rags and blood, emptied, and fill'd again.
I onward go, I stop,
With hinged knees and steady hand to dress wounds,
I am firm with each, the pangs are sharp yet unavoidable,
One turns to me his appealing eyes—poor boy! I never knew you,
Yet I think I could not refuse this moment to die for you, if that would save you.

---

[1] From *Leaves of Grass* (Philadelphia: David McKay Company, 1900). By permission.

3

On, on I go, (open doors of time! open hospital doors!)
The crush'd head I dress, (poor crazed hand tear not the bandage away,)
The neck of the cavalry-man with the bullet through and through I examine,
Hard the breathing rattles, quite glazed already the eye, yet life struggles hard,
(Come sweet death! be persuaded O beautiful death!
In mercy come quickly.)
From the stump of the arm, the amputated hand,
I undo the clotted lint, remove the slough, wash off the matter and blood,
Back on his pillow the soldier bends with curv'd neck and side-falling head,
His eyes are closed, his face is pale, he dares not look on the bloody stump,
And has not yet look'd on it.
I dress a wound in the side, deep, deep,
But a day or two more, for see the frame all wasted and sinking,
And the yellow-blue countenance see.
I dress the perforated shoulder, the foot with the bullet-wound,
Cleanse the one with a gnawing and putrid gangrene, so sickening, so offensive,
While the attendant stands behind aside me holding the tray and pail.
I am faithful, I do not give out,
The fractur'd thigh, the knee, the wound in the abdomen,
These and more I dress with impassive hand (yet deep in my breast a fire, a burning flame).

4

Thus in silence in dreams' projections,
Returning, resuming, I thread my way through the hospitals,
The hurt and wounded I pacify with soothing hand,
I sit by the restless all the dark night, some are so young,
Some suffer so much, I recall the experience sweet and sad,
(Many a soldier's loving arms about this neck have cross'd and rested,
Many a soldier's kiss dwells on these bearded lips.)

PART IV

Lyrical Poetry

Bread and Music [1]

CONRAD AIKEN

Music I heard with you was more than music,
And bread I broke with you was more than bread;
Now that I am without you, all is desolate;
All that was once so beautiful is dead.

Your hands once touched this table and this silver,
And I have seen your fingers hold this glass.
These things do not remember you, beloved,
And yet your touch upon them will not pass.

For it was in my heart you moved among them,
And blessed them with your hands and with your eyes;
And in my heart they will remember always,—
They knew you once, O beautiful and wise.

Dover Beach

MATTHEW ARNOLD

The sea is calm to-night,
The tide is full, the moon lies fair
Upon the straits;—on the French coast the light
Gleams and is gone; the cliffs of England stand
Glimmering and vast, out in the tranquil bay.
Come to the window, sweet is the night-air!
Only, from the long line of spray
Where the sea meets the moon-blanch'd land,

[1] From *Selected Poems,* by Conrad Aiken. Reprinted by permission of Charles Scribner's Sons, publishers.

Listen! you hear the grating roar
Of pebbles which the waves draw back, and fling,
At their return, up the high strand,
Begin, and cease, and then again begin,
With tremulous cadence slow, and bring
The eternal note of sadness in.
Sophocles long ago
Heard it on the Aegean, and it brought
Into his mind the turbid ebb and flow
Of human misery; we
Find also in the sound a thought,
Hearing it by this distant northern sea.

The Sea of Faith
Was once, too, at the full, and round earth's shore
Lay like the folds of a bright girdle furl'd.
But now I only hear
Its melancholy, long, withdrawing roar,
Retreating, to the breath
Of the night-wind, down the vast edges drear
And naked shingles of the world.

Ah, love, let us be true
To one another! for the world, which seems
To lie before us like a land of dreams,
So various, so beautiful, so new,
Hath really neither joy, nor love, nor light,
Nor certitude, nor peace, nor help for pain;
And we are here as on a darkling plain
Swept with confused alarms of struggle and flight,
Where ignorant armies clash by night.

As I Walked Out One Evening [1]

W. H. AUDEN

As I walked out one evening,
  Walking down Bristol Street,
The crowds upon the pavement
  Were fields of harvest wheat.

[1] Reprinted by permission of Random House, Inc.

And down by the brimming river
  I heard a lover sing
Under an arch of the railway:
  "Love has no ending.

I'll love you, dear, I'll love you
  Till China and Africa meet
And the river jumps over the mountain
  And the salmon sing in the street.

I'll love you till the ocean
  Is folded and hung up to dry
And the seven stars go squawking
  Like geese about the sky.

The years shall run like rabbits
  For in my arms I hold
The Flower of the Ages
  And the first love of the world."

But all the clocks in the city
  Began to whirr and chime;
"O let not Time deceive you,
  You cannot conquer Time.

In the burrows of the Nightmare
  Where Justice naked is,
Time watches from the shadow
  And coughs when you would kiss.

In headaches and in worry
  Vaguely life leaks away,
And Time will have his fancy
  To-morrow or to-day.

Into many a green valley
  Drifts the appalling snow;
Time breaks the threaded dances
  And the diver's brilliant bow.

O plunge your hands in water,
  Plunge them in up to the wrist;

Stare, stare in the basin
  And wonder what you've missed.

The glacier knocks in the cupboard,
  The desert sighs in the bed,
And the crack in the tea-cup opens
  A lane to the land of the dead.

Where the beggars raffle the banknotes
  And the Giant is enchanting to Jack,
And the Lily-white Boy is a Roarer
  And Jill goes down on her back.

O look, look in the mirror,
  O look in your distress;
Life remains a blessing
  Although you cannot bless.

O stand, stand at the window
  As the tears scald and start:
You shall love your crooked neighbour
  With your crooked heart."

It was late, late in the evening,
  The lovers they were gone;
The clocks had ceased their chiming
  And the deep river ran on.

Psalm XXIII

The Lord is my shepherd; I shall not want.
He maketh me to lie down in green pastures; he leadeth me beside the still waters.
He restoreth my soul: he leadeth me in the paths of righteousness for his name's sake.
Yea, though I walk through the valley of the shadow of death, I will fear no evil—for thou art with me; thy rod and thy staff they comfort me.
Thou preparest a table before me in the presence of mine enemies: thou anointest my head with oil; my cup runneth over.
Surely goodness and mercy shall follow me all the days of my life: and I will dwell in the house of the Lord for ever.

Psalm CVII [1]

i

They wandered in the wilderness in a solitary way;
They found no city to dwell in.
Hungry and thirsty,
Their souls fainted in them.
  Then they cried unto the Lord in their trouble,
  And he delivered them out of their distresses.
He led them forth by a straight way,
That they might go to a city of habitation.
  Oh that men would praise the Lord for his goodness,
  And for his wonderful works to the children of men!
For he satisfieth the longing soul,
And filleth the hungry soul with goodness.

ii

Such as sit in darkness, and in the shadow of death,
Being bound in affliction and iron;
Because they rebelled against the words of God,
And contemned the counsel of the most High:
Therefore he brought down their heart with labour;
They fell down, and there was none to help.
  Then they cried unto the Lord in their trouble,
  And he saved them out of their distresses.
He brought them out of darkness and the shadow of death,
And brake their bands in sunder.
  Oh that men would praise the Lord for his goodness,
  And for his wonderful works to the children of men!
For he hath broken the gates of brass,
And cut the bars of iron in sunder.

iii

Fools because of their transgression,
And because of their iniquities, are afflicted,
Their soul abhorreth all manner of meat;
And they draw near unto death's door.
  Then they cry unto the Lord in their trouble,
  And he saveth them out of their distresses.
He sendeth his word and healeth them
And delivereth them from their destructions.
  Oh that men would praise the Lord for his goodness,

[1] Arranged by Sir Arthur Quiller-Couch.

  And for his wonderful works to the children of men!
And let them offer the sacrifices of thanksgiving,
And declare his works with singing!

iv

They that go down to the sea in ships,
That do business in great waters;
These see the works of the Lord,
And his wonders in the deep.
For he commandeth, and raiseth the stormy wind,
Which lifteth up the waves thereof.
They mount up to the heaven,
They go down again to the depths;
Their soul melteth away because of trouble.
They reel to and fro,
And stagger like a drunken man,
And are at their wits' end.
  Then they cry unto the Lord in their trouble,
  And he bringeth them out of their distresses.
He maketh the storm a calm
So that the waves thereof are still.
Then are they glad because they be quiet;
So he bringeth them unto the haven where they would be.
  Oh that men would praise the Lord for his goodness,
  And for his wonderful works to the children of men!
Let them exalt him also in the assembly of the people,
And praise him in the seat of the elders!

FROM *The Song of Songs*

I am the rose of Sharon and the lily of the valleys.

As the lily among thorns, so is my love among the daughters.

As the apple tree among the trees of the wood, so is my beloved among the sons. I sat down under his shadow with great delight, and his fruit was sweet to my taste.

He brought me to the banqueting house, and his banner over me was love.

Stay me with flagons, comfort me with apples; for I am sick of love.

His left hand is under my head, and his right hand doth embrace me.

I charge you, O ye daughters of Jerusalem, by the roes, and by the hinds of the field, that ye stir not up, nor awake my love, till he please.

The voice of my beloved; behold, he cometh leaping upon the mountains, skipping upon the hills.

My beloved is like a roe or a young hart: behold, he standeth behind our wall, he looketh forth at the windows, shewing himself through the lattice.

My beloved spake, and said unto me. Rise up, my love, my fair one, and come away.

The flowers appear on the earth; the time of the singing of birds is come, and the voice of the turtle is heard in our land;

The fig tree putteth forth her green figs, and the vines with the tender grape give a good smell. Arise, my love, my fair one, and come away.

O my dove, that art in the clefts of the rock, in the secret places of the stairs, let me see thy countenance, let me hear thy voice; for sweet is thy voice, and thy countenance is comely.

Take us the foxes, the little foxes, that spoil the vines: for our vines have tender grapes.

My beloved is mine, and I am his; he feedeth among the lilies.

Until the day break, and the shadows flee away, turn, my beloved, and be thou like a roe or a young hart upon the mountains of Bether.

The Tiger

WILLIAM BLAKE

Tiger! Tiger! burning bright
In the forests of the night,
What immortal hand or eye
Could frame thy fearful symmetry?

In what distant deeps or skies
Burnt the fire of thine eyes?
On what wings dare he aspire?
What the hand dare seize the fire?

And what shoulder, and what art,
Could twist the sinews of thy heart?
And when thy heart began to beat,
What dread hands? and what dread feet?

What the hammer? what the chain?
In what furnace was thy brain?

What the anvil? what dread grasp
Dare its deadly terrors clasp?

When the stars threw down their spears,
And water'd heaven with their tears,
Did He smile His work to see?
Did He who made the Lamb make thee?

Tiger! Tiger! burning bright
In the forests of the night,
What immortal hand or eye,
Dare frame thy fearful symmetry?

The Soldier [1]

RUPERT BROOKE

If I should die, think only this of me;
  That there's some corner of a foreign field
That is forever England. There shall be
  In that rich earth a richer dust concealed;
A dust whom England bore, shaped, made aware,
  Gave, once, her flowers to love, her ways to roam,
A body of England's breathing English air,
  Washed by the rivers, blest by suns of home.

And think, this heart, all evil shed away,
  A pulse in the eternal mind, no less
    Gives somewhere back the thoughts by England given;
Her sights and sounds; dreams happy as her day;
  And laughter, learnt of friends; and gentleness,
    In hearts at peace, under an English heaven.

Sonnets from the Portuguese

ELIZABETH BARRETT BROWNING

XIV

If thou must love me, let it be for nought
Except for love's sake only. Do not say
"I love her for her smile—her look—her way

[1] From *The Collected Poems of Rupert Brooke.* Copyright, 1915, by Dodd, Mead & Company, Inc.

Of speaking gently,—for a trick of thought
That falls in well with mine, and certes brought
A sense of pleasant ease on such a day"—
For these things in themselves, Belovèd, may
Be changed, or change for thee,—and love, so wrought,
May be unwrought so. Neither love me for
Thine own dear pity's wiping my cheeks dry,—
A creature might forget to weep, who bore
Thy comfort long, and lose thy love thereby!
But love me for love's sake, that evermore
Thou mayst love on, through love's eternity.

XLIII

How do I love thee? Let me count the ways.
I love thee to the depth and breadth and height
My soul can reach, when feeling out of sight
For the ends of Being and ideal Grace.
I love thee to the level of every day's
Most quiet need, by sun and candle-light.
I love thee freely, as men strive for Right;
I love thee purely, as they turn from Praise.
I love thee with the passion put to use
In my old griefs, and with my childhood's faith.
I love thee with a love I seemed to lose
With my lost saints,—I love thee with the breath,
Smiles, tears, of all my life!—and, if God choose,
I shall but love thee better after death.

Home Thoughts from Abroad

ROBERT BROWNING

I

Oh, to be in England
Now that April's there,
And whoever wakes in England
Sees, some morning, unaware,
That the lowest boughs and the brushwood sheaf
Round the elm-tree bole are in tiny leaf,
While the chaffinch sings on the orchard bough
In England—now!

II

And after April, when May follows,
And the whitethroat builds, and all the swallows!
Hark, where my blossomed pear-tree in the hedge
Leans to the field and scatters on the clover
Blossoms and dewdrops—at the bent spray's edge—
That's the wise thrush; he sings each song twice over,
Lest you should think he never could recapture
The first fine careless rapture!
And though the fields look rough with hoary dew,
All will be gay when noontide wakes anew
The buttercups, the little children's dower
—Far brighter than this gaudy melon-flower!

Parting at Morning

ROBERT BROWNING

Round the cape of a sudden came the sea,
And the sun looked over the mountain's rim;
And straight was a path of gold for him,
And the need of a world of men for me.

Prospice

ROBERT BROWNING

Fear death?—to feel the fog in my throat,
  The mist in my face,
When the snows begin, and the blasts denote
  I am nearing the place,
The power of the night, the press of the storm,
  The post of the foe;
Where he stands, the Arch Fear in a visible form,
  Yet the strong man must go:
For the journey is done and the summit attained,
  And the barriers fall,
Though a battle's to fight ere the guerdon be gained,
  The reward of it all.
I was ever a fighter, so—one fight more,
  The best and the last!
I would hate that death bandaged my eyes, and forebore,
  And bade me creep past.

No! let me taste the whole of it, fare like my peers
  The heroes of old,
Bear the brunt, in a minute pay glad life's arrears
  Of pain, darkness and cold.
For sudden the worst turns the best to the brave,
  The black minute's at end,
And the elements' rage, the fiend voices that rave,
  Shall dwindle, shall blend,
Shall change, shall become first a peace out of pain,
  Then a light, then thy breast,
O thou soul of my soul! I shall clasp thee again,
  And with God be the rest!

To a Waterfowl

WILLIAM CULLEN BRYANT

  Whither, midst falling dew,
While glow the heavens with the last steps of day,
Far, through their rosy depths, dost thou pursue
  Thy solitary way?

  Vainly the fowler's eye
Might mark thy distant flight to do thee wrong,
As, darkly painted on the crimson sky,
  Thy figure floats along.

  Seekest thou the plashy brink
Of weedy lake, or marge of river wide,
Or where the rocking billows rise and sink
  On the chafed ocean side?

  There is a Power whose care
Teaches thy way along the pathless coast,
Thy desert, and illimitable air,
  Lone wandering, but not lost.

  All day thy wings have fanned
At that far height, the cold, thin atmosphere,
Yet stoop not, weary, to the welcome land,
  Though the dark night is near.

Thou'rt gone, the abyss of heaven
Hath swallowed up thy form; yet on my heart
Deeply has sunk the lesson thou hast given,
And shall not soon depart.

He, who from zone to zone,
Guides through the boundless sky thy certain flight,
In the long way that I must tread alone,
Will lead my steps aright.

Honest Poverty

ROBERT BURNS

Is there for honest poverty
That hings his head, an' a' that?
The coward slave, we pass him by—
We dare be poor for a' that!
For a' that, an' a' that,
Our toil obscure, an' a' that,
The rank is but the guinea's stamp,
The man's the gowd for a' that.

What though on hamely fare we dine,
Wear hoddin grey, an' a' that?
Gie fools their silks, and knaves their wine—
A man's a man for a' that.
For a' that, an' a' that,
Their tinsel show, an' a' that,
The honest man, tho' e'er sae poor,
Is king o' men for a' that.

Ye see yon birkie ca'd "a lord,"
Wha struts, an' stares, an' a' that?
Tho' hundreds worship at his word,
He's but a coof for a' that.
For a' that, an' a' that,
His ribband, star, an' a' that,
The man o' independent mind,
He looks an' laughs at a' that.

A prince can make a belted knight,
A marquis, duke, an' a' that!

But an honest man's aboon his might—
  Guid faith, he mauna fa' that!
For a' that, an' a' that,
  Their dignities, an' a' that,
The pith o' sense an' pride of worth
  Are higher rank than a' that.

Then let us pray that come it may
  (As come it will for a' that)
That sense and worth o'er a' the earth
  Shall bear the gree an' a' that!
For a' that, an' a' that,
  It's comin' yet for a' that,
That man to man the world o'er
  Shall brothers be for a' that.

To Thomas Moore

LORD BYRON

I

My boat is on the shore,
  And my bark is on the sea;
But, before I go, Tom Moore,
  Here's a double health to thee!

II

Here's a sigh to those who love me,
  And a smile to those who hate;
And, whatever sky's above me,
  Here's a heart for every fate.

III

Though the ocean roar around me,
  Yet it still shall bear me on;
Though a desert should surround me,
  It hath springs that may be won.

IV

Were't the last drop in the well,
  As I gasp'd upon the brink,

Ere my fainting spirit fell,
  'Tis to thee that I would drink.

V

With that water, as this wine,
  The libation I would pour
Should be—with peace to thine and mine,
  And a health to thee, Tom Moore.

Deserted[1]

MADISON CAWEIN

The old house leans upon a tree
  Like some old man upon a staff;
The night wind in its ancient porch
  Sounds like a hollow laugh.

The heaven is wrapped in flying clouds
  As grandeur cloaks itself in gray;
The starlight flitting in and out,
  Glints like a lanthorn ray.

The dark is full of whispers. Now
  A fox-hound howls; and through the night,
Like some old ghost from out its grave,
  The moon comes, misty white.

The Man Hunt

MADISON CAWEIN

The woods stretch wild to the mountain side,
And the brush is deep where a man may hide.

They have brought the bloodhounds up again
To the roadside rock where they found the slain.

They have brought the bloodhounds up, and they
Have taken the trail to the mountain way.

[1] This and the following two poems are taken from *The Vale of Tempe,* by Madison Cawein, published and copyrighted by E. P. Dutton & Co., Inc., New York.

Three times they circled the trail and crossed,
And thrice they found it and thrice they lost.

Now straight through the pines and the underbrush
They follow the scent through the forest's hush.

And their deep-mouthed bay is a pulse of fear
In the heart of the wood that the man must hear.

The man who crouches among the trees
From the stern-faced men that follow these.

A huddle of rocks that the ooze has mossed—
And the trail of the hunted again is lost.

An upturned pebble; a bit of ground
A heel has trampled—the trail is found.

And the woods re-echo the bloodhounds' bay
As again they take to the mountain way.

A rock; a ribbon of road; a ledge,
With a pine-tree clutching its crumbling edge.

A pine, that the lightning long since clave,
Whose huge roots hollow a ragged cave.

A shout; a curse; and a face aghast,
And the human quarry is laired at last.

The human quarry, with clay-clogged hair
And eyes of terror, who waits them there;

That glares and crouches and rising then
Hurls clods and curses at dogs and men.

Until the blow of a gun-butt lays
Him stunned and bleeding upon his face.

A rope, a prayer, and an oak-tree near,
And a score of hands to swing him clear.

A grim, black thing for the setting sun
And the moon and the stars to look upon.

Snow

MADISON CAWEIN

The moon, like a round device
On a shadowy shield of war,
Hangs white in a heaven of ice
With a solitary star.

The wind has sunk to a sigh,
And the waters are stern with frost;
And gray, in the eastern sky,
The last snow-cloud is lost.

White fields, that are winter-starved,
Black woods, that are winter-fraught,
Cold, harsh as a face death-carved
With the iron of some black thought.

I Never Saw a Moor [1]

EMILY DICKINSON

I never saw a moor,
I never saw the sea;
Yet know I how the heather looks,
And what a wave must be.

I never spoke with God,
Nor visited in Heaven;
Yet certain am I of the spot
As if the chart were given.

[1] From *The Poems of Emily Dickinson,* edited by Martha Dickinson Bianchi and Alfred Leete Hampson. Reprinted by permission of Little, Brown & Company.

The Hollow Men [1]

A Penny for the Old Guy

T. S. ELIOT

I

We are the hollow men
We are the stuffed men
Leaning together
Headpiece filled with straw. Alas!
Our dried voices, when
We whisper together
Are quiet and meaningless
As wind in dry grass
Or rats' feet over broken glass
In our dry cellar

Shape without form, shade without colour,
Paralysed force, gesture without motion;

Those who have crossed
With direct eyes, to death's other Kingdom
Remember us—if at all—not as lost
Violent souls, but only
As the hollow men,
The stuffed men.

II

Eyes I dare not meet in dreams
In death's dream kingdom

These do not appear:
There, the eyes are
Sunlight on a broken column
There, is a tree swinging
And voices are
In the wind's singing
More distant and more solemn
Than a fading star.

---

[1] From *Collected Poems of T. S. Eliot.* By permission of Harcourt, Brace & Company, Inc.

Let me be no nearer
In death's dream kingdom
Let me also wear
Such deliberate disguises
Rat's skin, crowskin, crossed staves
In a field
Behaving as the wind behaves
No nearer—

Not that final meeting
In the twilight kingdom

III

This is the dead land
This is cactus land
Here the stony images
Are raised, here they receive
The supplication of a dead man's hand
Under the twinkle of a fading star.

Is it like this
In death's other kingdom
Waking alone
At the hour when we are
Trembling with tenderness
Lips that would kiss
Form prayers to broken stone.

IV

The eyes are not here
There are no eyes here
In this valley of dying stars
In this hollow valley
This broken jaw of our lost kingdoms

In this last of meeting places
We grope together
And avoid speech
Gathered on this beach of the tumid river

Sightless, unless
The eyes reappear

As the perpetual star
Multifoliate rose
Of death's twilight kingdom
The hope only
Of empty men.

V

Here we go round the prickly pear
Prickly pear prickly pear
Here we go round the prickly pear
At five o'clock in the morning.

Between the idea
And the reality
Between the motion
And the act
Falls the Shadow
For Thine is the Kingdom

Between the conception
And the creation
Between the emotion
And the response
Falls the Shadow
Life is very long

Between the desire
And the spasm
Between the potency
And the existence
Between the essence
And the descent
Falls the Shadow
For Thine is the Kingdom

For Thine is
Life is
For Thine is the

This is the way the world ends
This is the way the world ends
This is the way the world ends
Not with a bang but a whimper.

Days

RALPH WALDO EMERSON

Daughters of Time, the hypocritic Days,
Muffled and dumb like barefoot dervishes,
And marching single in an endless file,
Bring diadems and fagots in their hands.
To each they offer gifts after his will,
Bread, kingdoms, stars, and sky that holds them all.
I, in my pleached garden, watched the pomp,
Forgot my morning wishes, hastily
Took a few herbs and apples, and the Day
Turned and departed silent. I, too late,
Under her solemn fillet saw the scorn.

The Storyteller [1]

FRANCES FROST

She had a voice like music and like storm,
And when she talked, the very poles grew warm,
The Equator dangled icicles, the seas
Were gentle spray upon a child's bare knees.

She had a voice like magic. When she talked,
Parrots sang madrigals, and phantoms walked,
Wallpaper moved with peasant girls and kings,
And carrousels had a hundred golden rings.

A pool became a wishing well, a star
Fell smack down in the middle of a war,
Rainbows wandered upside-down through rains,
And foot-loose trees went riding off on trains.

The alphabet ran backward, and a horse
Went tail first, head behind, as matter of course;
Kittens scrubbed mother cats behind their ears,
And every child wept crystal-candy tears.

She had a voice like wonder, and the land
Lay cupped in miniature within her hand,

[1] Reprinted by permission of the author.

Ships sailed in meadows, hillsides went afloat,
And the world was delicious fable in her throat!

Stopping by Woods on a Snowy Evening [1]

ROBERT FROST

Whose woods these are I think I know.
His house is in the village though;
He will not see me stopping here
To watch his woods fill up with snow.

My little horse must think it queer
To stop without a farmhouse near
Between the woods and frozen lake
The darkest evening of the year.

He gives his harness bells a shake
To ask if there is some mistake.
The only other sound's the sweep
Of easy wind and downy flake.

The woods are lovely, dark and deep,
But I have promises to keep,
And miles to go before I sleep,
And miles to go before I sleep.

Invictus

WILLIAM ERNEST HENLEY

Out of the night that covers me,
  Black as the Pit from pole to pole,
I thank whatever gods may be
  For my unconquerable soul.

In the fell clutch of circumstance
  I have not winced nor cried aloud.
Under the bludgeonings of chance
  My head is bloody, but unbowed.

---

[1] From *The Collected Poems of Robert Frost* (New York: Henry Holt and Company). By permission.

Beyond this place of wrath and tears
  Looms but the horror of the shade,
And yet the menace of the years
  Finds, and shall find me, unafraid.

It matters not how strait the gate,
  How charged with punishments the scroll,
I am the master of my fate;
  I am the captain of my soul.

To the Virgins to Make Much of Time

ROBERT HERRICK

Gather ye rosebuds while ye may,
  Old Time is still a-flying;
And this same flower that smiles today,
  To-morrow will be dying.

The glorious lamp of heaven, the sun,
  The higher he's a-getting,
The sooner will his race be run,
  And nearer he's to setting.

That age is best which is the first,
  When youth and blood are warmer;
But being spent, the worse and worst
  Times still succeed the former.

Then be not coy, but use your time,
  And while ye may, go marry;
For, having lost but once your prime,
  You may forever tarry.

I Remember, I Remember

THOMAS HOOD

I remember, I remember
The house where I was born,
The little window where the sun
Came peeping in at morn;
He never came a wink too soon,

Nor brought too long a day;
But now, I often wish the night
Had borne my breath away.

I remember, I remember
The roses red and white,
The violets, and the lily-cups,
Those flowers made of light!
The lilacs where the robin built,
And where my brother set
The laburnum on his birthday,—
The tree is living yet!

When I Was One-and-Twenty [1]

A. E. HOUSMAN

When I was one-and-twenty
  I heard a wise man say,
"Give crowns and pounds and guineas
  But not your heart away;
Give pearls away and rubies
  But keep your fancy free."
But I was one-and-twenty,
  No use to talk to me.

When I was one-and-twenty
  I heard him say again,
"The heart out of the bosom
  Was never given in vain;
'Tis paid with sighs a-plenty
  And scld for endless rue."
And I am two-and-twenty,
  And oh, 'tis true, 'tis true.

---

1 From *A Shropshire Lad,* by A. E. Housman (New York: Henry Holt and Company). By permission.

The Excesses of God[1]

ROBINSON JEFFERS

Is it not by his high superfluousness we know
Our God? For to equal a need
Is natural, animal, mineral: but to fling
Rainbows over the rain
And beauty above the moon, and secret rainbows
On the domes of deep sea-shells,
And make the necessary embrace of breeding
Beautiful also as fire,
Not even the weeds to multiply without blossom
Nor the birds without music:
There is the great humaneness at the heart of things,
The extravagant kindness, the fountain
Humanity can understand, and would flow likewise
If power and desire were perch-mates.

Song to Celia

BEN JONSON

Drink to me only with thine eyes,
  And I will pledge with mine;
Or leave a kiss but in the cup,
  And I'll not look for wine.
The thirst that from the soul doth rise
  Doth ask a drink divine;
But might I of Jove's nectar sup,
  I would not change for thine.

I sent thee late a rosy wreath,
  Not so much honoring thee
As giving it a hope, that there
  It could not withered be,
But thou thereon didst only breathe,
  And sent'st it back to me;
Since when it grows, and smells, I swear,
  Not of itself, but thee.

[1] From *Be Angry at the Sun* (New York: Random House, 1941). By permission.

FROM *Endymion*

A Thing of Beauty Is a Joy Forever

JOHN KEATS

A thing of beauty is a joy forever:
Its loveliness increases: it will never
Pass into nothingness; but still will keep
A bower quiet for us, and a sleep
Full of sweet dreams, and health, and quiet breathing.
Therefore, on every morrow, are we wreathing
A flowery band to bind us to the earth,
Spite of despondence, of the inhuman dearth
Of noble natures, of the gloomy days,
Of all the unhealthy and o'er-darkened ways
Made for our searching: yes, in spite of all,
Some shape of beauty moves away the pall
From our dark spirits. Such the sun, the moon,
Trees old, and young, sprouting a shady boon
For simple sheep; and such are daffodils
With the green world they live in; and clear rills
That for themselves a cooling covert make
'Gainst the hot season; the mid forest brake,
Rich with a sprinkling of fair musk-rose blooms:
And such too is the grandeur of the dooms
We have imagined for the mighty dead;
All lovely tales that we have heard or read:
An endless fountain of immortal drink,
Pour unto us from the heaven's brink.
Nor do we merely feel these essences
For one short hour; no, even as the trees
That whisper round a temple become soon
Dear as the temple's self, so does the moon,
The passion poesy, glories infinite,
Haunt us till they become a cheering light
Unto our souls, and bound to us so fast,
That, whether there be shine, or gloom o'ercast,
They always must be with us, or we die.

When I Have Fears that I May Cease To Be

JOHN KEATS

When I have fears that I may cease to be
  Before my pen has glean'd my teeming brain,
Before high-pilèd books, in charact'ry,
  Hold like rich garners the full ripen'd grain;
When I behold, upon the night's starr'd face,
  Huge cloudy symbols of a high romance,
And think that I may never live to trace
  Their shadows, with the magic hand of chance;
And when I feel, fair creature of an hour!
  That I shall never look upon thee more,
Never have relish in the faery power
  Of unreflecting love!—then on the shore
Of the wide world I stand alone, and think
  Till Love and Fame to nothingness do sink.

Young and Old

CHARLES KINGSLEY

When all the world is young, lad,
  And all the trees are green;
And every goose a swan, lad,
  And every lass a queen;
Then hey for boot and horse, lad,
  And round the world away;
Young blood must have its course, lad,
  And every dog his day.

When all the world is old, lad,
  And all the trees are brown;
And all the sport is stale, lad,
  And all the wheels run down:
Creep home, and take your place there,
  The spent and maimed among:
God grant you find one face there,
  You loved when all was young.

The Old Familiar Faces

CHARLES LAMB

I have had playmates, I have had companions,
In my days of childhood, in my joyful school-days—
All, all are gone, the old familiar faces.

I have been laughing, I have been carousing,
Drinking late, sitting late, with my bosom cronies—
All, all are gone, the old familiar faces.

I loved a Love once, fairest among women:
Closed are her doors on me, I must not see her—
All, all are gone, the old familiar faces.

I have a friend, a kinder friend has no man:
Like an ingrate, I left my friend abruptly;
Left him, to muse on the old familiar faces.

Ghost-like I paced round the haunts of my childhood,
Earth seem'd a desert I was bound to traverse,
Seeking to find the old familiar faces.

Friend of my bosom, thou more than a brother,
Why wert not thou born in my father's dwelling?
So might we talk of the old familiar faces—

How some they have died, and some they have left me,
And some are taken from me; all are departed—
All, all are gone, the old familiar faces.

A Ballad of Trees and the Master

SIDNEY LANIER

Into the woods my Master went,
Clean forspent, forspent.
Into the woods my Master came,
Forspent with love and shame.
But the olives they were not blind to Him,
The little gray leaves were kind to Him:

The thorn tree had a mind to Him
When into the woods he came.

Out of the woods my Master went,
And he was well content.
Out of the woods my Master came,
Content with death and shame.
When Death and Shame would woo Him last:
'Twas on a tree they slew Him—last
When out of the woods he came.

The Spires of Oxford[1]

WINIFRED M. LETTS

I saw the spires of Oxford
As I was passing by,
The gray spires of Oxford
Against the pearl-gray sky.
My heart was with the Oxford men
Who went abroad to die.

The years go fast in Oxford,
The golden years and gay,
The hoary Colleges look down
On careless boys at play.
But when the bugles sounded war
They put their games away.

They left the peaceful river,
The cricket-field, the quad,
The shaven lawns of Oxford,
To seek a bloody sod—
They gave their merry youth away
For country and for God.

God rest you happy gentlemen,
Who laid your good lives down,
Who took the khaki and the gun
Instead of cap and gown.

---

[1] Taken from *The Spires of Oxford and Other Poems* by Winifred M. Letts, published and copyrighted by E. P. Dutton & Co., Inc., New York.

God bring you to a fairer place
Than even Oxford town.

The Rainy Day

HENRY WADSWORTH LONGFELLOW

The day is cold, and dark, and dreary;
It rains, and the wind is never weary;
The vine still clings to the mouldering wall,
But at every gust the dead leaves fall,
And the day is dark and dreary.

My life is cold, and dark, and dreary;
It rains, and the wind is never weary;
My thoughts still cling to the mouldering Past,
But the hopes of youth fall thick in the blast,
And the days are dark and dreary.

Be still sad heart! and cease repining;
Behind the clouds is the sun still shining;
Thy fate is the common fate of all,
Into each life some rain must fall,
Some days must be dark and dreary.

A Lady [1]

AMY LOWELL

You are beautiful and faded,
Like an old opera tune
Played upon a harpsichord;
Or like the sun-flooded silks
Of an eighteenth-century boudoir.
In your eyes
Smolder the fallen roses of outlived minutes,
And the perfume of your soul
Is vague and suffusing,
With the pungence of sealed spice-jars.
Your half-tones delight me,

[1] Reprinted from *Sword Blades and Poppy Seeds,* by Amy Lowell, by permission of the publishers, Houghton Mifflin Company.

And I grow mad with gazing
At your blent colors.

My vigor is a new-minted penny,
Which I cast at your feet.
Gather it up from the dust
That its sparkle may amuse you.

The Fountain

JAMES RUSSELL LOWELL

Into the sunshine,
  Full of the light,
Leaping and flashing
  From morn till night!

Into the moonlight,
  Whiter than snow,
Waving so flower-like
  When the winds blow!

Into the starlight
  Rushing in spray,
Happy at midnight,
  Happy by day;

Ever in motion,
  Blithesome and cheery,
Still climbing heavenward
  Never aweary;—

Glad of all weathers;
  Still seeming best,
Upward or downward,
  Motion thy rest;—

Full of a nature
  Nothing can tame,
Changed every moment
  Ever the same;—

Ceaseless aspiring
  Ceaseless content,

Darkness or sunshine
  Thy element;—

Glorious fountain!
  Let my heart be
Fresh, changeful, constant,
  Upward, like thee!

Lincoln, the Man of the People[1]

EDWIN MARKHAM

When the Norn Mother saw the Whirlwind Hour
Greatening and darkening as it hurried on,
She left the Heaven of Heroes and came down
To make a man to meet the mortal need.
She took the tried clay of the common road—
Clay warm yet with the genial heat of earth,
Dasht through it all a strain of prophecy;
Tempered the heap with thrill of human tears;
Then mixt a laughter with the serious stuff.
Into the shape she breathed a flame to light
That tender, tragic, ever-changing face;
And laid on him a sense of the Mystic Powers,
Moving—all husht—behind the mortal veil.
Here was a man to hold against the world,
A man to match the mountains and the sea.

The color of the ground was in him, the red earth;
The smack and tang of elemental things;
The rectitude and patience of the cliff;
The good-will of the rain that loves all leaves;
The friendly welcome of the wayside well;
The courage of the bird that dares the sea;
The gladness of the wind that shakes the corn;
The pity of the snow that hides all scars;
The secrecy of streams that make their way
Under the mountain to the rifted rock;
The tolerance and equity of light
That gives as freely to the shrinking flower
As to the great oak flaring to the wind—

[1] Reprinted by permission.

To the grave's low hill as to the Matterhorn
That shoulders out the sky. Sprung from the West,
He drank the valorous youth of a new world.
The strength of virgin forests braced his mind,
The hush of spacious prairies stilled his soul.
His words were oaks in acorns; and his thoughts
Were roots that firmly gript the granite truth.

And so he came—
Up from the log cabin to the Capitol,
One fire was on his spirit, one resolve—
To send the keen ax to the root of wrong,
Clearing a free way for the feet of God,
The eyes of conscience testing every stroke,
To make his deed the measure of a man.
He built the rail-pile as he built the State,
Pouring his splendid strength through every blow:
The grip that swung the ax in Illinois
Was on the pen that set a people free.

So came the Captain with the mighty heart;
And when the judgment thunders split the house,
Wrenching the rafters from their ancient rest,
He held the ridgepole up, and spiked again
The rafters of the Home. He held his place—
Held the long purpose like a growing tree—
Held on through blame and faltered not at praise.
And when he fell in whirlwind, he went down
As when a lordly cedar, green with boughs,
Goes down with a great shout upon the hills,
And leaves a lonesome place against the sky.

God's World [1]

EDNA ST. VINCENT MILLAY

O world, I cannot hold thee close enough!
  Thy winds, thy wide gray skies!
  Thy mists that roll and rise!
Thy woods, this autumn day, that ache and sag
And all but cry with color! That gaunt crag

[1] Copyright, 1913, 1941, by Edna St. Vincent Millay. From *Renascence and Other Poems,* published by Harper & Bros.

To crush! To lift the lean of that black bluff!
World, World, I cannot get thee close enough!

Long have I known a glory in it all,
  But never knew I this;
  Here such a passion is
As stretcheth me apart. Lord, I do fear
Thou'st made the world too beautiful this year.
My soul is all but out of me,—let fall
No burning leaf; prithee, let no bird call.

Lament [1]

EDNA ST. VINCENT MILLAY

Listen, Children:
Your father is dead
From his old coats
I'll make you little jackets;
I'll make you little trousers
From his old pants.
There'll be in his pockets
Things he used to put there,
Keys and pennies
Covered with tobacco;
Dan shall have the pennies
To save in his bank;
Anne shall have the keys
To make a pretty noise with.
Life must go on,
And the dead be forgotten;
Life must go on,
Though good men die;
Anne, eat your breakfast;
Dan, take your medicine;
Life must go on;
I forget just why.

[1] Copyright, 1921, 1949, by Edna St. Vincent Millay. From *Second April,* published by Harper & Bros.

When I Consider How My Light Is Spent

JOHN MILTON

When I consider how my light is spent,
  E're half my days, in this dark world and wide,
  And that one talent which is death to hide,
Lodg'd with me useless, though my soul more bent
To serve therewith my Maker, and present
  My true account, lest he returning chide;
  Doth God exact day-labour, light deny'd,
I fondly ask. But patience to prevent
That murmur, soon replies, God doth not need
  Either man's work or his own gifts; who best
  Bear his mild yoke, they serve him best, his state
Is kingly. Thousands at his bidding speed
  And post o'er land and ocean without rest:
  They also serve who only stand and wait.

FROM *L'Allegro*

JOHN MILTON

Haste thee, Nymph, and bring with thee
Jest and youthful Jollity,
Quips, and Cranks, and wanton Wiles,
Nods, and Becks, and wreathèd Smiles,
Such as hang on Hebe's cheek,
And love to live in dimple sleek;
Sport that wrinkled Care derides,
And Laughter holding both his sides.
Come, and trip it as ye go,
On the light fantastic toe;
And in thy right hand lead with thee
The mountain Nymph, sweet Liberty.

In Distrust of Merits [1]

MARIANNE MOORE

Strengthened to live, strengthened to die for
  medals and positioned victories?

[1] From *Collected Poems* by Marianne Moore. Reprinted by permission of the Macmillan Company, publishers.

They're fighting, fighting, fighting the blind
man who thinks he sees,—
who cannot see that the enslaver is
enslaved; the hater, harmed. O shining O
firm star, O tumultuous
ocean lashed till small things go
as they will, the mountainous
wave makes us who look, know

depth. Lost at sea before they fought! O
star of David, star of Bethlehem,
O black imperial lion
of the Lord—emblem
of a risen world—be joined at last, be
joined. There is hate's crown beneath which all is
death; there's love's without which none
is king; the blessed deeds bless
the halo. As contagion
of sickness makes sickness,

contagion of trust can make trust. They're
fighting in deserts and caves, one by
one, in battalions and squadrons;
they're fighting that I
may yet recover from the disease, *my*
self; some have it lightly, some will die. "Man's
wolf to man?" And we devour
ourselves? The enemy could not
have made a greater breach in our
defenses. One pilot-

ing a blind man can escape him, but
Job disheartened by false comfort knew,
that nothing is so defeating
as a blind man who
can see. O alive who are dead, who are
proud not to see, O small dust of the earth
that walks so arrogantly,
trust begets power and faith is
an affectionate thing. We
vow, we make this promise

to the fighting—it's a promise—"We'll
  never hate black, white, red, yellow, Jew,
Gentile, Untouchable." We are
  not competent to
make our vows. With set jaw they are fighting,
fighting, fighting,—some we love whom we know,
    some we love but know not—that
      hearts may feel and not be numb.
    It cures me; or am I what
      I can't believe in? Some

in snow, some on crags, some in quicksands,
  little by little, much by much, they
are fighting fighting fighting that where
  there was death there may
be life. "When a man is prey to anger,
he is moved by outside things; when he holds
    his ground in patience patience
      patience, that is action or
    beauty," the soldier's defense
      and hardest armor for

the fight. The world's an orphans' home. Shall
  we never have peace without sorrow?
without pleas of the dying for
  help that won't come? O
quiet form upon the dust, I cannot
look and yet I must. If these great patient
    dyings—all these agonies
      and woundbearings and blood shed—
    can teach us how to live, these
      dyings were not wasted.

Hate-hardened heart, O heart of iron,
  iron is iron till it is rust.
There never was a war that was
  not inward; I must
fight till I have conquered in myself what
causes war, but I would not believe it.
    I inwardly did nothing.
      O Iscariotlike crime!
    Beauty is everlasting
      and dust is for a time.

Oft, in the Stilly Night

THOMAS MOORE

Oft, in the stilly night,
Ere Slumber's chain has bound me,
Fond Memory brings the light
Of other days around me;
The smiles, the tears,
Of boyhood's years,
The words of love then spoken;
The eyes that shone,
Now dimm'd and gone,
The cheerful hearts now broken!
Thus, in the stilly night,
Ere Slumber's chain has bound me,
Sad Memory brings the light
Of other days around me.
When I remember all
The friends, so link'd together,
I've seen around me fall,
Like leaves in wintry weather;
I feel like one
Who treads alone
Some banquet-hall deserted,
Whose lights are fled,
Whose garlands dead,
And all but he departed!
Thus, in the stilly night,
Ere Slumber's chain has bound me,
Sad Memory brings the light
Of other days around me.

To a Post-office Inkwell [1]

CHRISTOPHER MORLEY

How many humbled hearts have dipped
In you, and scrawled their manuscript!
Have shared their secrets, told their cares,
Their curious and quaint affairs!

---

[1] From *Poems,* copyright, 1919, by Christopher Morley, published by J. B. Lippincott Company.

Your pool of ink, your scratchy pen,
Have moved the lives of unborn men,
And watched young people, breathing hard,
Put Heaven on a postal card.

Annabel Lee

EDGAR ALLAN POE

It was many and many a year ago,
  In a kingdom by the sea,
That a maiden there lived whom you may know
  By the name of Annabel Lee.
And this maiden she lived with no other thought
  Than to love and be loved by me.

I was a child and she was a child
  In this kingdom by the sea:
But we loved with a love that was more than love—
  I and my Annabel Lee;
With a love that the wingèd seraphs of heaven
  Coveted her and me.

And this was the reason that, long ago,
  In this kingdom by the sea,
A wind blew out of a cloud, chilling
  My beautiful Annabel Lee
So that her high-born kinsman came
  And bore her away from me,
To shut her up in a sepulchre,
  In this kingdom by the sea.

The angels, not half so happy in heaven
  Went envying her and me—
Yes! that was the reason (as all men know,
  In this kingdom by the sea)
That the wind came out of the cloud by night,
  Chilling and killing my Annabel Lee.

But our love it was stronger by far than the love
  Of those who were older than we—
  Of many far wiser than we—

And neither the angels in heaven above,
  Nor the demons down under the sea,
Can ever dissever my soul from the soul
  Of the beautiful Annabel Lee.

For the moon never beams without bringing me dreams
  Of the beautiful Annabel Lee;
And the stars never rise, but I feel the bright eyes
  Of the beautiful Annabel Lee;
And so, all the night-tide, I lie down by the side
Of my darling—my darling—my life and my bride,
  In the sepulchre there by the sea,
  In her tomb by the sounding sea.

FROM *An Essay on Man*

ALEXANDER POPE

Heav'n from all creatures hides the book of Fate,
All but the page prescribed, their present state;
From brutes what men, from men what spirits know;
Or who could suffer Being here below?
The lamb thy riot dooms to bleed today,
Had he thy Reason would he skip and play?
Pleas'd to the last he crops the flowery food,
And licks the hand just rais'd to shed his blood.
O blindness to the future! kindly giv'n,
That each may fill the circle mark'd by Heav'n;
Who sees with equal eye, as God of all,
A hero perish or a sparrow fall,
Atoms or systems into ruin hurl'd,
And now a bubble burst, and now a world.
Hope humbly then; with trembling pinions soar;
Wait the great teacher Death, and God adore.
What future bliss He gives not thee to know,
But gives that hope to be thy blessing now.
Hope springs eternal in the human breast:
Man never is, but always to be, blest.
The soul, uneasy and confin'd from home,
Rests and expatiates in a life to come.

Calvary [1]

EDWIN ARLINGTON ROBINSON

Friendless and faint, with martyred steps and slow,
Faint for the flesh, but for the spirit free,
Stung by the mob that came to see the show,
The Master toiled along to Calvary;
We gibed him, as he went, with houndish glee,
Till his dimmed eyes for us did overflow;
We cursed his vengeless hands thrice wretchedly—
And this was nineteen hundred years ago.

But after nineteen hundred years the shame
Still clings, and we have not made good the loss
That outraged faith had entered in his name.
Ah, when shall come love's courage to be strong!
Tell me, O Lord—tell me, O Lord, how long
Are we to keep Christ writhing on the cross!

Chicago [2]

CARL SANDBURG

Hog Butcher for the World,
Tool Maker, Stacker of Wheat,
Player with Railroads and the Nation's Freight Handler;
Stormy, husky, brawling,
City of the Big Shoulders:
They tell me you are wicked and I believe them, for I have seen your painted women under the gas lamps luring the farm boys.
And they tell me you are crooked and I answer: Yes, it is true I have seen the gunman kill and go free to kill again.
And they tell me you are brutal and my reply is: On the faces of women and children I have seen the marks of wanton hunger.
And having answered so I turn once more to those who sneer at this my city, and I give them back the sneer and say to them:
Come and show me another city with lifted head singing so proud to be alive and coarse and strong and cunning.

---

[1] From *Children of the Night,* by Edwin Arlington Robinson, by permission of the publishers, Charles Scribner's Sons.

[2] From *Chicago Poems,* by Carl Sandburg (New York: Henry Holt and Company). By permission.

Flinging magnetic curses amid the toil of piling job on job, here is a tall bold slugger set vivid against the little soft cities;
Fierce as a dog with tongue lapping for action, cunning as a savage pitted against the wilderness,
    Bareheaded,
    Shoveling,
    Wrecking,
    Planning,
    Building, breaking, rebuilding.
Under the smoke, dust all over his mouth, laughing with white teeth,
Under the terrible burden of destiny laughing as a young man laughs,
Laughing even as an ignorant fighter laughs who has never lost a battle,
Bragging and laughing that under his wrist is the pulse, and under his ribs the heart of the people,
    Laughing!
Laughing the stormy, husky, brawling laughter of Youth, half-naked, sweating, proud to be Hog Butcher, Tool Maker, Stacker of Wheat, Player with Railroads and Freight Handler to the Nation.

Grass [1]

CARL SANDBURG

Pile the bodies high at Austerlitz and Waterloo.
Shovel them under and let me work—
    I am the grass; I cover all.

And pile them high at Gettysburg
And pile them high at Ypres and Verdun.
Shovel them under and let me work.
Two years, ten years, and passengers ask the conductor:
    What place is this?
    Where are we now?

    I am the grass.
    Let me work.

---

[1] From *The Cornhuskers,* by Carl Sandburg (New York: Henry Holt and Company). By permission.

The Lay of the Last Minstrel

SIR WALTER SCOTT

Breathes there the man with soul so dead,
Who never to himself hath said,
  This is my own, my native land!
Whose heart hath ne'er within him burn'd,
As home his footsteps he hath turn'd,
  From wandering on a foreign strand!
If such there breathe, go, mark him well;
For him no Minstrel raptures swell;
High though his titles, proud his name,
Boundless his wealth as wish can claim;
Despite those titles, power, and pelf,
The wretch, concentred all in self,
Living, shall forfeit fair renown,
And, doubly dying, shall go down
To the vile dust, from whence he sprung,
Unwept, unhonour'd, and unsung.

FROM THE *Sonnets*

WILLIAM SHAKESPEARE

XV

When I consider every thing that grows
Holds in perfection but a little moment,
That this huge stage presenteth nought but shows
Whereon the stars in secret influence comment;
When I perceive that men as plants increase,
Cheered and check'd e'en by the self-same sky,
Vaunt in their youthful sap, at height decrease,
And wear their brave state out of memory;
Then the conceit of this inconstant stay
Sets you most rich in youth before my sight,
Where wasteful Time debateth with Decay,
To change your day of youth to sullied night;
  And, all in war with Time for love of you,
  As he takes from you, I engraft you new.

XVIII

Shall I compare thee to a Summer's day?
Thou art more lovely and more temperate:
Rough winds do shake the darling buds of May,
And summer's lease hath all too short a date:
Sometime too hot the eye of heaven shines,
And often is his gold complexion dimm'd;
And every fair from fair sometime declines,
By chance, or nature's changing course untrimmed;
But thy eternal Summer shall not fade,
Nor lose possession of that fair thou ow'st,
Nor shall Death brag thou wander'st in his shade,
When in eternal lines to time thou grow'st;
  So long as men can breathe, or eyes can see,
  So long lives this, and this gives life to thee.

XXIX

When in disgrace with fortune and men's eyes
I all alone beweep my outcast state,
And trouble deaf heaven with my bootless cries,
And look upon myself, and curse my fate,
Wishing me like to one more rich in hope,
Featur'd like him, like him with friends possess'd,
Desiring this man's art, and that man's scope,
With what I most enjoy contented least;
Yet in these thoughts myself almost despising,
Haply I think on thee,—and then my state,
Like to the lark at break of day arising
From sullen earth, sings hymns at Heaven's gate;
  For thy sweet love remember'd such wealth brings
  That then I scorn to change my state with Kings.

XXX

When to the Sessions of sweet silent thought
I summon up remembrance of things past,
I sigh the lack of many a thing I sought,
And with old woes new wail my dear time's waste:
Then can I drown an eye, unus'd to flow,
For precious friends hid in death's dateless night,
And weep afresh love's long since cancell'd woe,
And moan the expense of many a vanish'd sight:
Then can I grieve at grievances foregone,

And heavily from woe to woe tell o'er
The sad account of fore-bemoanèd moan,
Which I new pay as if not paid before.
  But if the while I think on thee, dear friend,
  All losses are restor'd and sorrows end.

LXXI

No longer mourn for me when I am dead
Then you shall hear the surly sullen bell
Give warning to the world that I am fled
From this vile world, with vilest worms to dwell:
Nay, if you read this line, remember not
The hand that writ it; for I love you so,
That I in your sweet thoughts would be forgot,
If thinking on me then should make you woe.
O! if, —I say, you look upon this verse,
When I perhaps compounded am with clay,
Do not so much as my poor name rehearse,
But let your love even with my life decay;
  Lest the wise world should look into your moan,
  And mock you with me after I am gone.

LXXIII

That time of year thou mayst in me behold
When yellow leaves, or none, or few, do hang
Upon those boughs which shake against the cold,
Bare ruin'd choirs, where late the sweet birds sang.
In me thou see'st the twilight of such day
As after sunset fadeth in the west;
Which by and by black night doth take away,
Death's second self, that seals up all in rest.
In me thou see'st the glowing of such fire,
That on the ashes of his youth doth lie,
As the death-bed whereon it must expire
Consum'd with that which it was nourish'd by.
  This thou perceiv'st, which makes thy love more strong,
  To love that well which thou must leave ere long.

CIV

To me, fair friend, you never can be old,
For as you were when first your eye I ey'd,
Such seems your beauty still. Three winters cold

Have from the forests shook three summers' pride,
Three beauteous springs to yellow autumn turn'd
In process of the seasons have I seen,
Three April perfumes in three hot Junes burn'd,
Since first I saw you fresh, which yet are green.
Ah! yet doth beauty, like a dial-hand,
Steal from his figure, and no pace perceiv'd;
So your sweet hue, which methinks still doth stand,
Hath motion, and mine eye may be deceiv'd:
For fear of which, hear this, thou age unbred:
Ere you were born was beauty's summer dead.

To a Skylark

PERCY BYSSHE SHELLEY

Hail to thee, Blithe Sprit!
Bird thou never wert,
That from Heaven, or near it,
Pourest thy full heart
In profuse strains of unpremeditated art.

Higher still and higher
From the earth thou springest
Like a cloud of fire;
The blue deep thou wingest,
And singing still dost soar, and soaring ever singest.

In the golden lightning
Of the sunken sun,
O'er which clouds are bright'ning,
Thou dost float and run;
Like an unbodied joy whose race is just begun.

The pale purple even
Melts around thy flight;
Like a star of Heaven,
In the broad daylight
Thou art unseen, but yet I hear thy shrill delight.

What thou art we know not;
What is most like thee?

From rainbow clouds there flow not
  Drops so bright to see
As from thy presence showers a rain of melody.

Like a Poet hidden
  In the light of thought,
Singing hymns unbidden,
  Till the world is wrought
To sympathy with hopes and fears it heeded not:

Like a glow-worm golden
  In a dell of dew,
Scattering unbeholden
  Its aërial hue
Among the flowers and grass, which screen it from the view:

Teach us, Sprite or Bird,
  What sweet thoughts are thine:
I have never heard
  Praise of love or wine
That panted forth a flood of rapture so divine.

We look before and after,
  And pine for what is not:
Our sincerest laughter
  With some pain is fraught;
Our sweetest songs are those that tell of saddest thought.

Yet if we could scorn
  Hate, and pride, and fear;
If we were things born
  Not to shed a tear,
I know not how thy joy we ever should come near.

Better than all measures
  Of delightful sound,
Better than all treasures
  That in books are found,
Thy skill to poet were, thou scorner of the ground!

Teach me half the gladness
  That thy brain must know,

Such harmonious madness
From my lips would flow
The world should listen then—as I am listening now.

In Railway Halls [1]

STEPHEN SPENDER

In railway halls, on pavements near the traffic,
They beg, their eyes made big by empty staring
And only measuring Time, like the blank clock.

No, I shall weave no tracery of pen-ornament
To make them birds upon my singing-tree:
Time merely drives these lives which do not live
As tides push rotten stuff along the shore.

—There is no consolation, no, none
In the curving beauty of that line
Traced on our graphs through history, where the oppressor
Starves and deprives the poor.

Paint here no draped despairs, no saddening clouds
Where the soul rests, proclaims eternity.
But let the wrong cry out as raw as wounds
This Time forgets and never heals, far less transcends.

What Word for Spring? [2]

SYLVIA STALLINGS

What word for spring, O men of the aircraft carriers?
What April word for the pilots, hunters and harriers,
At the falling hour, for the kiss of ship with the foam?
Four days' leave, O seaman; days to stand
In the wheat-bright, the beloved land;
Time to remember ploughing and turn home.
(For great blue plumes of lilac sway in the wind;
Round narcissus and deep-belled hyacinths blow
All over Carolina and a low

[1] Reprinted by permission of Random House, Inc.
[2] Reprinted by permission of the author and of *Harper's Magazine*.

Moon wakes the mockingbird, a slow, blind
Moon at the full, heavy and high.)
Sailor, four days of furlough in the spring: O take my
Life with you on the voyage over and unwind
The wealth of hours that so lightly lie
Stretching endlessly before me and behind.
When fog folds the convoy in its sheets and rain drips
All night upon the loaded ships,
Then wear my fortunate eye and see how the gold-
Flounced sycamore rakes at the sky.
Remember too wild pink azalea and the cold
Creeks between the corn-planted river-bottom lands.
Take also my heart into your hands,
Since it is made of earth and flower and tree,
And having these you cannot but have me.

Peter Quince at the Clavier [1]

WALLACE STEVENS

I

Just as my fingers on these keys
Make music, so the self-same sounds
On my spirit make a music too.

Music is feeling then, not sound;
And thus it is that what I feel,
Here in this room, desiring you,
Thinking of your blue-shadowed silk,
Is music. It is like the strain
Waked in the elders by Susanna:

Of a green evening, clear and warm,
She bathed in her still garden, while
The red-eyed elders, watching, felt

The basses of their being throb
In witching chords, and their thin blood
Pulse pizzicati of Hosanna.

II

In the green water, clear and warm,
Susanna lay.

---

[1] Reprinted from *The Collected Poems of Wallace Stevens,* by permission of Alfred A. Knopf, Inc. Copyright 1923, 1931, 1954 by Wallace Stevens.

She searched
The touch of springs,
And found
Concealed imaginings.
She sighed
For so much melody.

Upon the bank she stood
In the cool
Of spent emotions.
She felt, among the leaves,
The dew
Of old devotions.

She walked upon the grass,
Still quavering.
The winds were like her maids,
On timid feet,
Fetching her woven scarves,
Yet wavering.

A breath upon her hand
Muted the night.
She turned—
A cymbal crashed,
And roaring horns.

III

Soon, with a noise like tambourines,
Came her attendant Byzantines.

They wondered why Susanna cried
Against the elders by her side:

And as they whispered, the refrain
Was like a willow swept by rain.

Anon their lamps' uplifted flame
Revealed Susanna and her shame.

And then the simpering Byzantines,
Fled, with a noise like Tambourines.

IV

Beauty is momentary in the mind—
The fitful tracing of a portal;
But in the flesh it is immortal.

The body dies; the body's beauty lives.
So evenings die, in their green going,
A wave, interminably flowing.
So gardens die, their meek breath scenting
The cowl of Winter, done repenting.
So maidens die to the auroral
Celebration of a maiden's choral.

Susanna's music touched the bawdy strings
Of those white elders; but, escaping,
Left only Death's ironic scraping.
Now in its immortality, it plays
On the clear viol of her memory,
And makes a constant sacrament of praise.

The House Beautiful [1]

ROBERT LOUIS STEVENSON

A naked house, a naked moor,
A shivering pool before the door,
A garden bare of flowers and fruit,
And poplars at the garden foot,—
Such is the place that I live in,
Bleak without and bare within.
Yet shall yon ragged moor receive
The incomparable pomp of eve,
And the cold glories of the dawn
Behind your shivering trees be drawn;
And when the wind from place to place
Doth the unmoored cloud-galleons chase,
Your garden gleam and bloom again,
With leaping sun, with dancing rain.
Here shall the wizard moon ascend
The heavens, in the crimson end

[1] From *Collected Poems of Robert Louis Stevenson,* published by Charles Scribner's Sons.

Of day's declining splendor; here
The army of the stars appear.
The neighbor hollows dry or wet,
Spring shall with tender flowers beset;
And oft the morning muser see
Larks rising from the roomy lea,
And every fairy wheel and thread
Of cobweb dew-bediamonded.
When daisies go, shall winter time
Silver the simple grass with rime,
Autumnal frosts enchant the pool
And make the cart-ruts beautiful
And when snow-bright the moor expands,
How shall your children clap their hands!
To make this earth, our hermitage,
A cheerful and a pleasant page,
God's bright and intricate device
Of days and seasons doth suffice.

The Constant Lover

SIR JOHN SUCKLING

Out upon it, I have loved
  Three whole days together!
And am like to love three more,
  If it prove fair weather.

Time shall moult away his wings
  Ere he shall discover
In the whole wide world again
  Such a constant lover.

But the spite on't is, no praise
  Is due at all to me:
Love with me had made no stays,
  Had it any been but she.

Had it any been but she,
  And that very face,
There had been at least ere this
  A dozen dozen in her place.

Barter [1]

SARA TEASDALE

Life has loveliness to sell—
  All beautiful and splendid things,
Blue waves whitened on a cliff,
  Soaring fire that sways and sings,
And children's faces looking up
Holding wonder like a cup.

Life has loveliness to sell—
  Music like a curve of gold,
Scent of pine trees in the rain,
  Eyes that love you, arms that hold,
And for your spirit's still delight,
Holy thoughts that star the night.

Spend all you have for loveliness,
  Buy it and never count the cost,
For one white singing hour of peace
  Count many a year of strife well lost,
And for a breath of ecstasy
Give all you have been or could be.

Break, Break, Break

ALFRED LORD TENNYSON

Break, break, break,
  On thy cold gray stones, O Sea!
And I would that my tongue could utter
  The thoughts that arise in me.

O well for the fisherman's boy,
  That he shouts with his sister at play!
O well for the sailor lad,
  That he sings in his boat on the bay!

And the stately ships go on
  To their haven under the hill;

[1] From *The Collected Poems of Sara Teasdale.* By permission of The Macmillan Company, publishers.

But O for the touch of a vanish'd hand,
And the sound of a voice that is still!

Break, break, break,
At the foot of thy crags, O Sea!
But the tender grace of a day that is dead
Will never come back to me.

Flower in the Crannied Wall

ALFRED LORD TENNYSON

Flower in the crannied wall,
I pluck you out of the crannies,
I hold you here, root and all, in my hand,
Little flower—but if I could understand
What you are, root and all, and all in all,
I should know what God and man is.

Ulysses

ALFRED LORD TENNYSON

It little profits that an idle king,
By this still hearth, among these barren crags,
Matched with an agèd wife, I mete and dole
Unequal laws unto a savage race,
That hoard, and sleep, and feed, and know not me.
I cannot rest from travel: I will drink
Life to the lees. All times I have enjoyed
Greatly, have suffered greatly, both with those
That loved me, and alone; on shore, and when
Through scudding drifts the rainy Hyades
Vexed the dim sea. I am become a name;
For always roaming with a hungry heart
Much have I seen and known—cities of men
And manners, climates, councils, governments,
Myself not least, but honored of them all;
And drunk delight of battle with my peers,
Far on the ringing plains of windy Troy.
I am a part of all that I have met;
Yet all experience is an arch wherethrough
Gleams that untraveled world, whose margin fades
Forever and forever when I move.

How dull it is to pause, to make an end,
To rust unburnished, not to shine in use!
As though to breathe were life! Life piled on life
Were all too little, and of one to me
Little remains: but every hour is saved
From that eternal silence, something more,
A bringer of new things; and vile it were
For some three suns to store and hoard myself,
And this gray spirit yearning in desire
To follow knowledge like a sinking star,
Beyond the utmost bound of human thought.

Crossing the Bar

ALFRED LORD TENNYSON

Sunset and evening star
  And one clear call for me!
And may there be no moaning of the bar
  When I put out to sea.

But such a tide as moving seems asleep,
  Too full for sound and foam
When that which drew from out the boundless deep
  Turns again home.

Twilight and evening bell
  And after that the dark;
And may there be no sadness of farewell
  When I embark;

For though from out our bourne of Time and Place
  The flood may bear me far,
I hope to see my Pilot face to face
  When I have crossed the bar.

FROM *In Memoriam A. H. H.*

ALFRED LORD TENNYSON

Strong Son of God, immortal Love,
  Whom we, that have not seen thy face,
  By faith, and faith alone, embrace,
Believing where we cannot prove;

Thine are these orbs of light and shade;
  Thou madest Life in man and brute;
  Thou madest Death; and lo, thy foot
Is on the skull which thou hast made.

Thou wilt not leave us in the dust:
  Thou madest man, he knows not why,
  He thinks he was not made to die;
And thou hast made him: thou art just.

Thou seemest human and divine,
  The highest, holiest manhood, thou:
  Our wills are ours, we know not how;
Our wills are ours, to make them thine.

Our little systems have their day;
  They have their day and cease to be:
  They are but broken lights of thee,
And thou, O Lord, art more than they.

We have but faith: we cannot know;
  For knowledge is of things we see;
  And yet we trust it comes from thee,
A beam in darkness: let it grow.

Let knowledge grow from more to more,
  But more of reverence in us dwell;
  That mind and soul, according well,
May make one music as before,

But vaster. We are fools and slight;
  We mock thee when we do not fear:
  But help thy foolish ones to bear;
Help thy vain worlds to bear thy light.

Forgive what seem'd my sin in me,
  What seem'd my worth since I began;
  For merit lives from man to man,
And not from man, O Lord, to thee.

Forgive my grief for one removed,
  Thy creature, whom I found so fair.

I trust he lives in thee, and there
I find him worthier to be loved.

Forgive these wild and wandering cries,
Confusions of a wasted youth;
Forgive them where they fail in truth,
And in thy wisdom make me wise.

Of Old Sat Freedom on the Heights

ALFRED LORD TENNYSON

Of old sat Freedom on the heights,
The thunders breaking at her feet:
Above her shook the starry lights:
She heard the torrents meet.

There in her place she did rejoice,
Self-gather'd in her prophet-mind,
But fragments of her mighty voice
Came rolling on the wind.

Then stept she down thro' town and field
To mingle with the human race,
And part by part to men reveal'd
The fullness of her face—

Grave mother of majestic works,
From her isle-altar gazing down,
Who, God-like, grasps the triple forks,
And, King-like, wears the crown:

Her open eyes desire the truth.
The wisdom of a thousand years
Is in them. May perpetual youth
Keep dry their light from tears;

That her fair form may stand and shine,
Make bright our days and light our dreams,
Turning to scorn with lips divine
The falsehood of extremes!

The Eagle

ALFRED LORD TENNYSON

He clasps the crag with crookèd hands;
Close to the sun in lonely lands,
Ring'd with the azure world, he stands.

The wrinkled sea beneath him crawls;
He watches from his mountain walls,
And like a thunderbolt he falls.

Moonlight [1]

JOHN V. A. WEAVER

Say—listen—
If you could only take a bath in moonlight!

Hey! Can't you just see yourself
Take a runnin' dive
Inta a pool o' glowin' blue,
Feel it glidin' over you
All aroun' and inta you—
Grab a star—huh?—
Use it for soap;
Beat it up to bubbles
And white sparklin' foam—
Roll and wash—

Gee!

I just like to bet
You could wash your soul clean
In moonlight!

---

[1] Reprinted from *In American,* by John V. A. Weaver, by permission of Alfred A. Knopf, Inc. Copyright, 1926, by Alfred A. Knopf, Inc.

Vocalism [1]

WALT WHITMAN

I

Vocalism, measure, concentration, determination, and the divine power to speak words;
Are you full-lung'd and limber-lipp'd from long trial? from vigorous practice? from physique?
Do you move in these broad lands as broad as they?
Come duly to the divine power to speak words?
For only at last after many years, after chastity, friendship, procreation, prudence, and nakedness,
After treading ground and breasting river and lake,
After loosen'd throat, after absorbing eras, temperaments, races, after knowledge, freedom, crimes,
After complete faith, after clarifyings, elevations, and removing obstructions,
After these and more, it is just possible there comes to a man, a woman, the divine power to speak words;
Then toward that man or that woman swiftly hasten all—none refuse, all attend,
Armies, ships, antiquities, libraries, paintings, machines, cities, hate, despair, amity, pain, theft, murder, aspiration, form in close ranks.
They debouch as they are wanted to march obediently through the mouth of that man or that woman.

II

O what is it in me that makes me tremble so at voices?
Surely whoever speaks to me in the right voice him or her I shall follow,
As the water follows the moon, silently, with fluid steps, anywhere around the globe.
All waits for the right voices;
Where is the practised and perfect organ? where is the developed soul?
For I see every word utter'd thence has deeper, sweeter, new sounds, impossible on less terms.
I see brains and lips closed, tympans and temples unstruck,
Until that comes which has the quality to strike and to unclose,
Until that comes which has the quality to bring forth what lies slumbering forever ready in all words.

---

[1] This and the following four poems are taken from *Leaves of Grass* (Philadelphia: David McKay Company, 1900). By permission.

O Captain! My Captain

WALT WHITMAN

O Captain! my Captain! our fearful trip is done,
The ship has weather'd every rack, the prize we sought is won,
The port is near, the bells I hear, the people all exulting,
While follow eyes the steady keel, the vessel grim and daring;
        But O heart! heart! heart!
          O the bleeding drops of red,
            Where on the deck my Captain lies,
              Fallen cold and dead.

O Captain! my Captain! rise up and hear the bells;
Rise up—for you the flag is flung—for you the bugle trills,
For you bouquets and ribbon'd wreaths—for you the shores a-crowding,
For you they call, the swaying mass, their eager faces turning;
        Here Captain! dear father!
          This arm beneath your head!
            It is some dream that on the deck,
              You've fallen cold and dead.

My Captain does not answer, his lips are pale and still,
My father does not feel my arm, he has no pulse nor will,
The ship is anchor'd safe and sound, its voyage closed and done,
From fearful trip the victor ship comes in with object won;
        Exult O shores, and ring O bells!
          But I with mournful tread,
            Walk the deck my Captain lies,
              Fallen cold and dead.

Beat! Beat! Drums!

WALT WHITMAN

Beat! beat! drums!—blow! bugles! blow!
Through the windows—through the doors—burst like a ruthless force,
Into the solemn church, and scatter the congregation,
Into the school where the scholar is studying;
Leave not the bridegroom quiet—no happiness must he have now with
    his bride,
Nor the peaceful farmer any peace, plowing his field or gathering his
    grain,
So fierce you whirr and pound you drums—so shrill you bugles blow.

Beat! beat! drums!—blow! bugles! blow!
Over the traffic of cities—over the rumble of wheels in the streets;
Are beds prepared for sleepers at night in the houses? no sleepers must sleep in those beds,
No bargainers' bargains by day—no brokers or speculators—would they continue?
Would the talkers be talking? would the singer attempt to sing?
Would the lawyer rise in the court to state his case before the judge?
Then rattle quicker, heavier drums—you bugles wilder blow.

Beat! beat! drums!—blow! bugles! blow!
Make no parley—stop for no expostulation,
Mind not the timid—mind not the weeper or prayer,
Mind not the old man beseeching the young man,
Let not the child's voice be heard, nor the mother's entreaties,
Make even the trestles to shake the dead where they lie awaiting the hearses,
So strong you thump, O terrible drums—so loud you bugles blow.

For You, O Democracy

WALT WHITMAN

Come, I will make the continent indissoluble,
I will make the most splendid race the sun ever shone upon,
I will make divine magnetic lands,
With the love of comrades,
With the life-long love of comrades.

I will plant companionship thick as trees along the rivers of America, and along the shores of the great lakes, and all over the prairies,
I will make inseparable cities with their arms about each other's necks,
By the love of comrades,
By the manly love of comrades.
For you these from me, O Democracy, to serve you *ma femme!*
For you, for you I am trilling these songs.

I Hear America Singing

WALT WHITMAN

I hear America singing, the varied carols I hear,
Those mechanics, each one singing his as it should be blithe and strong,

The carpenter singing his as he measures his plank or beam,
The mason singing his as he makes ready for work, or leaves off work,
The boatman singing what belongs to him in his boat, the deckhand singing on the steamboat deck,
The shoemaker singing as he sits on his bench, the hatter singing as he stands,
The wood-cutter's song, the playboy's on his way in the morning, or at noon intermission or at sundown,
The delicious singing of the mother, or of the young wife at work, or of the girl sewing or washing,
Each singing what belongs to him or her and to none else,
The day what belongs to the day—at night the party of young fellows, robust, friendly,
Singing with open mouths their strong melodious songs.

Dear Lord and Father of Mankind

JOHN GREENLEAF WHITTIER

Dear Lord and Father of mankind,
Forgive our feverish ways;
Reclothe us in our rightful mind;
In purer lives Thy service find,
In deeper reverence, praise.

In simple trust like theirs who heard,
Beside the Syrian sea,
The gracious calling of the Lord,
Let us, like them, without a word,
Rise up and follow Thee.

O Sabbath rest by Galilee!
O calm of hills above!
Where Jesus knelt to share with Thee
The silence of eternity,
Interpreted by love.

Drop Thy still dews of quietness,
Till all our strivings cease;
Take from our souls the strain and stress,
And let our ordered lives confess
The beauty of Thy peace.

Breathe through the heats of our desire
Thy coolness and Thy balm;
Let sense be dumb, let flesh retire;
Speak through the earthquake, wind, and fire,
O still small voice of calm!

Composed upon Westminster Bridge

SEPTEMBER 3, 1802

WILLIAM WORDSWORTH

Earth has not anything to show more fair:
Dull would he be of soul who could pass by
A sight so touching in its majesty:
This City now doth, like a garment, wear
The beauty of the morning; silent, bare,
Ships, towers, domes, theatres, and temples lie
Open unto the fields, and to the sky;
All bright and glittering in the smokeless air.
Never did sun more beautifully steep
In his first splendour, valley, rock, or hill;
Ne'er saw I, never felt, a calm so deep!
The river glideth at his own sweet will:
Dear God! the very houses seem asleep;
And all that mighty heart is lying still!

It is a Beauteous Evening, Calm and Free

WILLIAM WORDSWORTH

It is a beauteous evening, calm and free,
The holy time is quiet as a Nun
Breathless with adoration; the broad sun
Is sinking down in its tranquillity;
The gentleness of heaven broods o'er the Sea:
Listen! the mighty Being is awake
And doth with his eternal motion make
A sound like thunder—everlastingly.
Dear Child! dear Girl! that walkest with me here,
If thou appear untouched by solemn thought,
Thy nature is not therefore less divine:
Thou liest in Abraham's bosom all the year;

And worshipp'st at the Temple's inner shrine,
God being with thee when we know it not.

London, 1802

WILLIAM WORDSWORTH

Milton! thou shouldst be living at this hour:
England hath need of thee: she is a fen
Of stagnant waters: altar, sword, and pen,
Fireside, the heroic wealth of hall and bower,
Have forfeited their ancient English dower
Of inward happiness. We are selfish men;
Oh! raise us up, return to us again;
And give us manners, virtue, freedom, power!
Thy soul was like a Star, and dwelt apart;
Thou hadst a voice whose sound was like the sea:
Pure as the naked heavens, majestic, free,
So didst thou travel on life's common way,
In cheerful godliness; and yet thy heart
The lowliest duties on herself did lay.

Golden Bough[1]

ELINOR WYLIE

These lovely groves of fountain-trees that shake
  A burning spray against autumnal cool,
Descend again in molten drops to make
  The rutted path a river and a pool.

They rise in silence, fall in quietude,
  Lie still as looking-glass to every sense;
Only their lion-color in the wood
  Roars to miraculous heat and turbulence.

[1] Reprinted from *The Collected Poems of Elinor Wylie,* by permission of Alfred A. Knopf, Inc. Copyright, 1932, by Alfred A. Knopf, Inc.

PART V

Stories with Dialogue

I'm a Fool[1]

SHERWOOD ANDERSON

It was a hard jolt for me, one of the bitterest I ever had to face. And it came about through my own foolishness, too. Even yet sometimes, when I think of it, I want to cry or swear or kick myself. Perhaps, even now, after all this time, there will be a kind of satisfaction in making myself look cheap by telling of it.

It began at three o'clock one October afternoon as I sat in the grand-stand at the fall trotting-and-pacing meet at Sandusky, Ohio.

To tell the truth, I felt a little foolish that I should be sitting in the grand-stand at all. During the summer before I had left my home town with Harry Whitehead and, with a nigger named Burt, had taken a job as swipe with one of the two horses Harry was campaigning through the fall race-meets that year. Mother cried and my sister Mildred, who wanted to get a job as a school-teacher in our town that fall, stormed and scolded about the house all during the week before I left. They both thought it something disgraceful that one of our family should take a place as a swipe with race-horses. I've an idea Mildred thought my taking the place would stand in the way of her getting the job she'd been working so long for.

But after all I had to work, and there was no other work to be got. A big lumbering fellow of nineteen couldn't just hang around the house and I had got too big to mow people's lawns and sell newspapers. Little chaps who could get next to people's sympathies by their sizes were always getting jobs away from me. There was one fellow who kept saying to every one who wanted a lawn mowed or a cistern cleaned, that he was saving money to work his way through college, and I used to lay awake nights thinking up ways to injure him without being found out. I kept thinking of wagons running over him and bricks falling on his head as he walked down the street. But never mind him.

---

[1] Copyright, 1927, by Eleanor Anderson. Reprinted by her permission.

I got the place with Harry and I liked Burt fine. We got along splendid together. He was a big nigger with a lazy sprawling body and soft, kind eyes, and when it came to a fight he could hit like Jack Johnson. He had Bucephalus, a big black pacing stallion that could do 2.09 or 2.10, if he had to, and I had a little gelding named Doctor Fritz that never lost a race all fall when Harry wanted him to win.

We set out from home late in July in a box car with the two horses, and after that, until late November, we kept moving along to the race-meets and the fairs. It was a peachy time for me, I'll say that. Sometimes now I think that boys who are raised regular in houses, and never have a fine nigger like Burt for best friend, and go to high schools and college, and never steal anything, or get drunk a little, or learn to swear from fellows who know how, or come walking up in front of a grand-stand in their shirt sleeves and with dirty horsy pants on when the races are going on and the grand-stand is full of people all dressed up— What's the use of talking about it? Such fellows don't know nothing at all. They've never had no opportunity.

But I did. Burt taught me how to rub down a horse and put the bandages on after a race and steam a horse out and a lot of valuable things for any man to know. He could wrap a bandage on a horse's leg so smooth that if it had been the same color you would think it was his skin, and I guess he'd have been a big driver, too, and got to the top like Murphy and Walter Cox and the others if he hadn't been black.

Gee whizz! it was fun. You got to a county seat town, maybe say on a Saturday or Sunday, and the fair began the next Tuesday and lasted until Friday afternoon. Doctor Fritz would be, say in the 2.25 trot on Tuesday afternoon, and on Thursday afternoon Bucephalus would knock 'em cold in the 'free-for-all' pace. It left you a lot of time to hang around and listen to horse talk, and see Burt knock some yap cold that got too gay, and you'd find out about horses and men and pick up a lot of stuff you could use all the rest of your life, if you had some sense and salted down what you heard and felt and saw.

And then at the end of the week when the race-meet was over, and Harry had run home to tend up to his livery-stable business, you and Burt hitched the two horses to carts and drove slow and steady across country, to the place for the next meeting, so as to not overheat the horses, etc. etc., you know.

Gee whizz! Gosh a'mighty! the nice hickory-nut and beech-nut and oaks and other kinds of trees along the roads, all brown and red, and the good smells, and Burt singing a song that was called *Deep River,* and the country girls at the windows of houses and everything. You can stick your colleges up your nose for all me. I guess I know where I got my education.

Why, one of those little burgs of towns you come to on the way, say now on a Saturday afternoon, and Burt says, "Let's lay up here." And you did.

And you took the horses to a livery stable and fed them, and you got your good clothes out of a box and put them on.

And the town was full of farmers gaping, because they could see you were race-horse people, and the kids maybe never see a nigger before and was afraid and run away when the two of us walked down their main street.

And that was before prohibition and all that foolishness, and so you went into a saloon, the two of you, and all the yaps come and stood around, and there was always someone pretended he was horsy and knew things and spoke up and began asking questions, and all you did was to lie and lie all you could about what horses you had, and I said I owned them, and then some fellow said 'Will you have a drink of whisky?' and Burt knocked his eye out the way he could say, offhand like, 'Oh well, all right, I'm agreeable to a little nip. I'll split a quart with you.' Gee whizz!

But that isn't what I want to tell my story about. We got home late in November and I promised mother I'd quit the race-horses for good. There's a lot of things you've got to promise a mother because she don't know any better.

And so, there not being any work in our town any more than when I left there to go to the races, I went on to Sandusky and got a pretty good place taking care of horses for a man who owned a teaming and delivery and storage and coal and real-estate business there. It was a pretty good place with good eats, and a day off each week, and sleeping on a cot in a big barn, and mostly just shoveling in hay and oats to a lot of big good-enough skates of horses, that couldn't have trotted a race with a toad. I wasn't dissatisfied and I could send money home.

And then, as I started to tell you, the fall races come to Sandusky and I got the day off and I went. I left the job at noon and had on my good clothes and my new brown derby hat, I'd just bought the Saturday before, and a stand-up collar.

First of all I went down town and walked about with the dudes. I've always thought to myself, 'Put up a good front,' and so I did it. I had forty dollars in my pocket, and so I went into the West House, a big hotel, and walked up to the cigar-stand. 'Give me three twenty-five-cent cigars,' I said. There was a lot of horsemen and strangers and dressed-up people from other towns standing around in the lobby and in the bar, and I mingled amongst them. In the bar there was a fellow with a cane and a Windsor tie on, that it made me sick to look at him. I like a man to be a man and dress up, but not to go put on that kind of airs. So I pushed him aside, kind of rough, and had me a drink of whisky. And then he looked at me, as though he thought maybe he'd get gay, but he changed his mind and didn't say anything. And then I had another drink of whisky, just to show him something, and went out and had a hack out to the races, all to myself, and when I got there I bought myself the best seat I could get up in the grandstand, but didn't go in for any of these boxes. That's putting on too many airs.

And so there I was, sitting up in the grand-stand as gay as you please and looking down on the swipes coming out with their horses, and with their dirty horsy pants on and the horse blankets swung over their shoulders, same as I had been doing all the year before. I liked one thing about the same as the other, sitting up there and feeling grand and being down there and looking up at the yaps and feeling grander and more important, too. One thing's about as good as another, if you take it just right. I've often said that.

Well, right in front of me, in the grand-stand that day, there was a fellow with a couple of girls and they was about my age. The young fellow was a nice guy all right. He was the kind maybe that goes to college and then comes to be a lawyer or maybe a newspaper editor or something like that, but he wasn't struck on himself. There are some of that kind are all right and he was one of the ones.

He had his sister with him and another girl and the sister looked around over his shoulder, accidental at first, not intending to start anything—she wasn't the kind—and her eyes and mine happened to meet.

You know how it is. Gee, she was a peach! She had on a soft dress, kind of a blue stuff and it looked carelessly made, but was well sewed and made and everything. I knew that much. I blushed when she looked right at me and so did she. She was the nicest girl I've ever seen in my life. She wasn't struck on herself and she could talk proper grammar without being like a school-teacher or something like that. What I mean is, she was O.K. I think maybe her father was well-to-do, but not rich to make her chesty because she was his daughter, as some are. Maybe he owned a drugstore or a dry-goods store in their home town, or something like that. She never told me and I never asked.

My own people are all O.K., too, when you come to that. My grandfather was Welsh and over in the old country, in Wales he was— But never mind that.

The first heat of the first race come off and the young fellow sitting there with the two girls left them and went down to make a bet. I knew what he was up to, but he didn't talk big and noisy and let every one around know he was a sport, as some do. He wasn't that kind. Well, he come back and I heard him tell the two girls what horse he'd bet on, and when the heat was trotted they all half got their feet and acted in the excited, sweaty way people do when they've got money down on a race, and the horse they bet on is up there pretty close at the end, and they think maybe he'll come on with a rush, but he never does because he hasn't got the old juice in him, come right down to it.

And then, pretty soon, the horses came out for the 2.18 pace and there was a horse in it I knew. He was a horse Bob French had in his string, but Bob didn't own him. He was a horse owned by a Mr. Mathers down at Marietta, Ohio.

This Mr. Mathers had a lot of money and owned some coal mines or something, and he had a swell place out in the country, and he was struck on race-horses, but was a Presbyterian or something, and I think more than likely his wife was one, too, maybe a stiffer one than himself, and the story round the Ohio race-tracks was that when one of his horses got ready to go to the races he turned him over to Bob French and pretended to his wife he was sold.

So Bob had the horses and he did pretty much as he pleased and you can't blame Bob, at least, I never did. Sometimes he was out to win and sometimes he wasn't. I never cared much about that when I was swiping a horse. What I did want to know was that my horse had the speed and could go out in front, if you wanted him to.

And, as I'm telling you, there was Bob in this race with one of Mr. Mathers's horses, which was named 'About Ben Ahem' or something like that, and was fast as a streak. He was a gelding and had a mark of 2.21, but could step in .08 or .09.

Because when Burt and I were out, as I've told you, the year before, there was a nigger, Burt knew, worked for Mr. Mathers and we went out there one day when we didn't have no race on at the Marietta Fair and our boss Harry was gone home.

And so every one was gone to the fair but just this one nigger and he took us all through Mr. Mathers's swell house and he and Burt tapped a bottle of wine Mr. Mathers had hid in his bedroom, back in a closet, without his wife knowing, and he showed us this Ahem horse. Burt was always struck on being a driver but didn't have much chance to get to the top, being a nigger, and he and the other nigger gulped that whole bottle of wine and Burt got a little lit up.

So the nigger let Burt take this About Ben Ahem and step him a mile in a track Mr. Mathers had all to himself, right there on the farm. And Mr. Mathers had one child, a daughter, kinda sick and not very good looking, and she came home and we had to hustle and get About Ben Ahem stuck back in the barn.

I'm only telling you to get everything straight. At Sandusky, that afternoon I was at the fair, this young fellow with the two girls was fussed, being with the girls and losing his bet. You know how a fellow is that way. One of them was his girl and the other his sister. I had figured that out.

'Gee whizz!' I says to myself, 'I'm going to give him the dope.'

He was mighty nice when I touched him on the shoulder. He and the girls were nice to me right from the start and clear to the end. I'm not blaming them.

And so he leaned back and I give him the dope on About Ben Ahem. 'Don't bet a cent on this first heat because he'll go like an oxen hitched to a plough, but the first heat is over go right down and lay on your pile.' That's what I told him.

Well, I never saw a fellow treat any one sweller. There was a fat man sitting beside the little girl, that had looked at me twice by this time, and I at her, and both blushing, and what did he do but have the nerve to turn back and ask the fat man to get up and change places with me so I could sit with his crowd.

Gee whizz, craps a'mighty! There I was. What a chump I was to go and get gay up there in the West House bar, and just because that dude was standing there with a cane and that kind of a necktie on, to go and get all balled up and drink that whisky, just to show off.

Of course she would know, me sitting right beside her and letting her smell of my breath. I could have kicked myself right down out of that grand-stand and all around that race-track and made a faster record than most of the skates of horses they had there that year.

Because that girl wasn't any mutt of a girl. What wouldn't I have given right then for a stick of chewing-gum to chew, or a lozenger, or some licorice, or most anything. I was glad I had those twenty-five-cent cigars in my pocket and right away I give that fellow one and lit one myself. Then that fat man got up and we changed places and there I was, plunked right down beside her.

They introduced themselves and the fellow's best girl, he had with him, was named Miss Elinor Woodbury, and her father was a manufacturer of barrels from a place called Tiffin, Ohio. And the fellow himself was named Wilbur Wessen and his sister was Miss Lucy Wessen.

I suppose it was their having such swell names got me off my trolley. A fellow, just because he has been a swipe with a race-horse, and works taking care of horses for a man in the teaming, delivery, and storage business, isn't any better or worse than any one else. I've often thought that, and said it, too.

But you know how a fellow is. There's something in that kind of nice clothes, and the kind of nice eyes she had, and the way she had looked at me, awhile before, over her brother's shoulder, and me looking at her, and both of us blushing.

I couldn't show her up for a boob, could I?

I made a fool of myself, that's what I did. I said my name was Walter Mathers from Marietta, Ohio, and then I told all three of them the smashingest lie you ever heard. What I said was that my father owned the horse About Ben Ahem and that he had let him out to this Bob French for racing purposes, because our family was proud and had never gone into racing that way, in our own name, I mean. Then I had got started and they were all leaning over and listening, and Miss Lucy Wessen's eyes were shining, and I went the whole hog.

I told about our place down at Marietta, and about the big stables and the grand brick house we had on a hill, up above the Ohio River, but I knew enough not to do it in no bragging way. What I did was to start things and then let them drag the rest out of me. I acted just as reluctant to tell as I could. Our family hasn't got any barrel factory, and, since I've known us, we've always been pretty poor, but not asking anything of any one at that, and my grandfather, over in Wales— But never mind that.

We sat there talking like we had known each other for years and years, and I went and told them that my father had been expecting maybe this Bob French wasn't on the square, and had sent me up to Sandusky on the sly to find out what I could.

And I bluffed it through I had found out all about the 2.18 pace, in which About Ben Ahem was to start.

I said he would lose the first heat by pacing like a lame cow and then he would come back and skin 'em alive after that. And to back up what I said I took thirty dollars out of my pocket and handed it to Mr. Wilbur Wessen and asked him would he mind, after the first heat, to go down and place it on About Ben Ahem for whatever odds he could get. What I said was that I didn't want Bob French to see me and none of the swipes.

Sure enough the first heat come off and About Ben Ahem went off his stride, up the back stretch, and looked like a wooden horse or a sick one, and come in to be last. Then this Wilbur Wessen went down to the betting-place under the grand-stand and there I was with the two girls, and when that Miss Woodbury was looking the other way once, Lucy Wessen kinda, with her shoulder you know, kinda touched me. Not just tucking down, I don't mean. You know how a woman can do. They get close, but not getting gay either. You know what they do. Gee whizz!

And then they give me a jolt. What they had done, when I didn't know was to get together and they had decided Wilbur Wessen would bet fifty dollars, and the two girls had gone and put in ten dollars each, of their own money, too. I was sick then, but I was sicker later.

About the gelding, About Ben Ahem, and their winning their money, I wasn't worried a lot about that. It come out O.K. Ahem stepped the next three heats like a bushel of spoiled eggs going to market before they could be found out, and Wilbur Wessen had got nine to two for the money. There was something else eating at me.

Because Wilbur come back, after he had bet the money, and after that he spent most of his time talking to that Miss Woodbury, and Lucy Wessen and I was left alone together like on a desert island. Gee, if I'd only been on the square, or if there had been any way of getting myself on the square. There ain't any Walter Mathers, like I said to her and them, and there hasn't ever been one, but if there was I bet I'd go to Marietta, Ohio, and shoot him to-morrow.

There I was, big boob that I am. Pretty soon the race was over, and Wilbur had gone down and collected our money, and we had a hack down-town, and he stood us a swell supper at the West House, and a bottle of champagne beside.

And I was with that girl and she wasn't saying much, and I wasn't saying much either. One thing I know. She wasn't struck on me because of the lie about my father being rich and all that. There's a way you know. . . . Craps a'mighty! There's a kind of girl, you see just once in your life, and if you don't get busy and make hay, then you're gone for good and all, and might as well go jump off a bridge. They give you a look from inside of them somewhere, and it ain't no vamping, and what it means is—you want that girl to be your wife, and you want nice things around her like flowers and swell clothes, and you want her to have the kids you're going to have, and you want good music played and no ragtime. Gee whizz!

There's a place over near Sandusky, across a kind of bay, and it's called Cedar Point. And after we had supper we went over to it in a launch, all by ourselves. Wilbur and Miss Lucy and that Miss Woodbury had to catch a ten o'clock train back to Tiffin, Ohio, because when you're out with girls like that, you can't get careless and miss any trains and stay out all night, like you can with some kinds of Janes.

And Wilbur blowed himself to the launch, and it cost him fifteen cold plunks, but I wouldn't never have knew if I hadn't listened. He wasn't no tinhorn kind of a sport.

Over at the Cedar Point place, we didn't stay around where there was a gang of common kind of cattle at all.

There was big dance-halls and dining-places for yaps, and there was a beach you could walk along and get where it was dark, and we went there.

She didn't talk hardly at all and neither did I, and I was thinking how glad I was my mother was all right, and always made us kids learn to eat with a fork at table, and not swill soup, and not be noisy and rough like a gang you see around a race-track that way.

Then Wilbur and his girl went away up the beach and Lucy and I sat down in a dark place, where there was some roots of old trees the water had washed up, and after that the time, till we had to go back in the launch and they had to catch their trains, wasn't nothing at all. It went like winking your eye.

Here's how it was. The place we were sitting in was dark, like I said, and there was the roots from that old stump sticking up like arms, and there was a watery smell, and the night was like—as if you could put your hand out and feel it—so warm and soft and dark and sweet like an orange.

I 'most cried and I 'most swore and I 'most jumped up and danced, I was so mad and happy and sad.

When Wilbur come back from being alone with his girl, and she saw him coming, Lucy she says, 'We got to go to the train now,' and she was 'most crying, too, but she never knew nothing I knew, and she couldn't be so all busted up. And then, before Wilbur and Miss Woodbury got up to where we was, she put her face up and kissed me quick and put her head up against me and she was all quivering and—Gee whizz!

Sometimes I hope I have cancer and die. I guess you know what I mean. We went in the launch across the bay to the train like that, and it was dark, too. She whispered and said it was like she and I could get out of the boat and walk on the water, and it sounded foolish, but I knew what she meant.

And then quick we were right at the depot, and there was a big gang of yaps, the kind that goes to the fairs, and crowded and milling around like cattle, and how could I tell her? 'It won't be long because you'll write and I'll write to you.' That's all she said.

I got a chance like a hay-barn afire. A swell chance I got.

And maybe she would write me, down at Marietta that way, and the letter would come back, and stamped on the front of it by the U.S.A., 'There ain't any such guy,' or something like that, whatever they stamp on a letter that way.

And me trying to pass myself off for a big bug and a swell—to her, as decent a little body as God ever made. Craps a'mighty—a swell chance I got!

And then the train come in, and she got on it, and Wilbur Wessen he come and shook hands with me, and that Miss Woodbury was nice, too, and bowed to me, and I at her, and the train went and I busted out and cried like a kid.

Gee, I could have run after that train and made Dan Patch look like a freight train after a wreck, but, socks a'mighty, what was the use? Did you ever see such a fool?

I'll bet you what—if I had an arm broke right now or a train had run over my foot—I wouldn't go to no doctor at all. I'd go sit down and let her hurt and hurt—that's what I'd do.

I'll bet you what—if I hadn't a drunk that booze I'd a never been such a boob as to go tell such a lie—that couldn't never be made straight to a lady like her.

I wish I had that fellow right here that had on a Windsor tie and carried a cane. I'd smash him for fair. Gosh darn his eyes. He's a big fool—that's what he is.

And if I'm not another you just go find me one and I'll quit working and be a bum and give him my job. I don't care nothing for working, and earning money, and saving it for no such boob as myself.

Told by the Schoolmaster [1]

JOHN GALSWORTHY

We all remember still, I suppose, the singular beauty of the summer when the war broke out. I was then schoolmaster in a village on the Thames. Nearly 50, with a game shoulder and extremely deficient sight, there was no question of my fitness for military service, and this, as with many other sensitive people, induced in me, I suppose, a mood abnormally receptive. The perfect weather, that glowing countryside, with corn harvest just beginning, the quiet nights trembling with moonlight and shadow, and, in it all, this great horror launched and growing.

One of those evenings toward the end of August, I left my house and walked up toward the Downs. It was perhaps half past nine when I passed two of my former scholars, a boy and a girl, standing silently at the edge of an old gravel pit. They looked up and gave me a good evening.

I remember thinking that Joe Beckett and Betty Roofe were absurdly young to be sweethearting. They could hardly be 16 yet, for they had only left school last year. Betty Roofe—an interesting child, alert, self-contained—was the daughter of the village laundress, and I used to think too good for washing clothes, but she was already at it and as things went in that village would probably go on doing it till she mar-

[1] Reprinted by permission of Charles Scribner's Sons, publishers.

ried. Joe Beckett was working on Carver's farm down there below me, and the gravel pit was about halfway between their homes. A good boy, Joe, freckled, reddish in the hair, and with blue eyes that looked at you very straight.

I was still standing there when he came on his way to Carver's and I look back to that next moment with as much regret as to any in my life.

He held out his hand. "Good-bye, sir, in case I don't see you again. I'm joinin' up."

"Joining up? But, my dear boy, you're two years under age, at least."

"I'm 16 this month, but I bet I can make out to be 18. They ain't particular, I'm told."

What a crime was war! From this hushed, moonlit peace, boys were hurrying off to that business of man-made death as if there were not Nature's deaths galore to fight against. And we—could only admire them for it! I have never ceased to curse the sentiment which stopped me from informing the recruiting authorities of that boy's real age.

Crossing back over the crest of the hill toward home, I came on the child Betty, at the edge of the gravel pit where I had left her. Her voice was even enough, but she was quivering all over. "He's so headstrong, Joe! He just gets things into his head. I don't see that he has any call to go, and—leave me."

I couldn't help a smile. She saw it, and said suddenly:

"Yes, I'm young, and so's Joe; but he's my boy, for all that!"

And then, startled at such expansiveness, she tossed her head and ran off among the trees.

So Joe went, and we knew him no more for a whole year. And Betty continued with her mother, washing for the village.

In September, 1915, I was standing one afternoon in the village schoolroom and thinking, as usual, of the war and its lingering deadlock. Under the lime trees on the far side of the street I could see a soldier standing with a girl. Suddenly he crossed over to the school, and there in the doorway was young Joe Beckett.

"I thought I'd like to see you. Just got our marching orders. Off to France tomorrow, been havin' my leave."

I felt the catch at my throat that we all felt when youngsters whom we knew were going out for the first time.

"I've got something to tell you, sir. Betty and I were spliced last week." He went to the door, and whistled. In came Betty, dressed in dark blue, very neat and self-contained. "Show him your lines, Betty, and your ring."

The girl held out the official slip, and from it I read that a registrar had married them under right names and wrong ages. Then she slipped a glove off, and held up her left hand—there was the magic hoop! Well! The folly was committed—no use in crabbing it!

"What time is it, sir?" Joe asked me suddenly.

"Five o'clock."

"I must run. My kit's at the station. Could I leave her here, sir?"

I nodded, and walked into the little room beyond. When I came back she was sitting where she used to sit in school, bowed over her arms spread out on the inky desk. Her dark bobbed hair was all I could see, and the quivering jerky movement of her young shoulders. Joe had gone! Well! That was the normal state of Europe, then! I went back into the little room to give her time, but when I returned once more, she, too, had gone.

The second winter passed, more muddy, more bloody even than the first, and less shot through with hopes of an ending. Betty showed me three or four of Joe's letters, simple screeds with a phrase here and there of half-smothered feeling, and signed always: "Your loving hubby, Joe." Her marriage was accepted in the village. Child marriage was quite common then. In April it began to be obvious that their union was to be "blessed," as they call it.

One day early in May I was passing Mrs. Roofe's, and stopped to ask after Betty.

"Nearin' her time. I've written to Joe. Happen he'll get leave."

"I think that was a mistake, Mrs. Roofe. I would have waited till it was over."

"Maybe you're right, sir, but Betty's that fidgety about him not knowin'. She dreadful young, you know, t'ave a child."

"Everything goes fast these days, Mrs. Roofe."

I was sitting over my Pensions work one evening a month later, when someone knocked at my door, and who should be standing there but Joe Beckett! "Why! Joe! Got leave?"

"Ah! I had to come and see her. I haven't been there yet—didn't dare. I haven't had any sleep for nights, thinking of her—such a kid, she is!"

"Does she know you're coming?"

"No, haven't said nothing."

He was only just in time, for two days later Betty had a boy-child. Joe came to me, the same evening, after dark, very excited.

"She's a wonder," he said, "but if I'd known, I'd never ha' done it, sir, I never would. You can't tell what you're doing till it's too late, it seems."

Strange saying from that young father, till afterwards it was made too clear!

Betty recovered quickly and was out within three weeks. Joe seemed to have long leave, for he was still about, but I had little talk with him, for, though always friendly, he seemed shy of me, and as to talking of the war—not a word!

It was no business of mine to have my doubts, but I had been having them long before that very dreadful night when, just as I was going to bed, something rattled on my window, and going down, I found Betty outside, distracted.

"Oh, sir, come quick! They've 'rested Joe. I was afraid there was some mistake about his leave—it was so long. I thought he'd get into trouble over it, so I asked the constable, and now they've come and 'rested him for deserting. Oh! What have I done?"

Outside the Roofes' cottage, Joe was standing between a corporal's guard, and Betty flung herself into his arms. Inside, I could hear Mrs. Roofe expostulating with the corporal, and the baby crying.

I spoke to Joe. He answered quietly in her arms: "I asked for leave, but they wouldn't give it. I had to come. I couldn't stick it, knowing how it was with her."

"Where was your regiment?"

"In the line."

"Good God!"

Just then the corporal came out. "I was his schoolmaster, corporal," I said. "The poor chap joined up when he was just 16—he's still under age, you see—and now he's got this child wife and a new-born baby!"

The corporal nodded. "I know, sir. Cruel work, but I've got to take him. He'll have to go back to France."

"What does it mean?"

"Deserting in face of the enemy. Bad business! Can you get that girl away, sir?"

But Joe himself undid the grip of her arms, and held her from him; bending, he kissed her hair and face; then, with a groan, he literally pushed her into my arms and marched straight off between the guard.

All the rest of that night, after Mrs. Roofe had got Betty back into the cottage, I sat up writing in duplicate the facts about Joe Beckett. I sent one copy to his regimental headquarters, the other to the chaplain of his regiment in France. I sent fresh copies two days later with duplicates of his birth certificate to make quite sure. It was all I could do. Then came a fortnight of waiting for news. Betty was still distracted. The thought that, through her anxiety, she herself had delivered him into their hands nearly sent her off her head. Probably her baby alone kept her from insanity or suicide. And all that time the battle of the Somme raged, and hundreds of thousands of women in England and

France and Germany were in daily terror for their menfolk. Yet none, I think, could have had quite the feeling of that child.

And then one day I did get news—a letter from the chaplain, and seeing what it was, I stuck it in my pocket and sneaked down to the river—literally afraid to open it till I was alone. Crouched up there, with my back to a haystack, I took it out with trembling fingers.

"Dear Sir: The boy Joe Beckett was shot today at dawn. I am distressed at having to tell you and the poor child, his wife. War is a cruel thing, indeed!"

I had known it. Poor Joe! Poor Betty! Poor, poor Betty! I read on:

"I did all I could; the facts you sent were put before the Court Martial and the point of his age considered. But all leave had been stopped; his request had been definitely refused; the regiment was actually in the line, with fighting going on, and the situation extremely critical in that sector. Private considerations count for nothing in such circumstances—the rule is adamant. Perhaps it has to be, I cannot say. But I have been greatly distressed by the whole thing, and the Court itself was much moved. The poor boy seemed dazed; he wouldn't talk, didn't seem to take in anything; indeed, they tell me that all he said after the verdict, certainly all I heard him say, was: 'My poor wife! My poor wife!' over and over again. He stood up well at the end."

He stood up well at the end! I can see him yet, poor impulsive Joe. Desertion, but not cowardice, by the Lord! No one who looked into those straight blue eyes could believe that. But they bandaged them, I suppose. Well! A bullet in a billet more or less, what was it in the wholesale slaughter? As a raindrop on a willow tree drips into the river and away to sea—so that boy, like a million others, dripped to dust. A little ironical though, that his own side should shoot him who wouldn't be legal food for powder for another month! A little ironical, perhaps, that he had left this son, legacy to such an implacable world!

A Service of Love [1]

O. HENRY

Joe Larrabee came out of the post-oak flats of the Middle West pulsing with a genius for pictorial art. At six he drew a picture of the town pump with a prominent citizen passing it by,—hastily. At twenty he left for New York with a flowing necktie and a capital tied up somewhat closer.

---

[1] From *The Four Million,* by O. Henry, copyright, 1906, by Doubleday, Doran & Company, Inc.

Delia Caruthers did things in six octaves so promisingly in a pine-tree village in the South that her relatives chipped in enough for her to go North and "finish." They could not see her f—, but that is our story.

Joe and Delia met in a studio where a number of art and music students had gathered to discuss chiaroscuro, Wagner, Chopin, Rembrandt's works, and wall paper. Joe and Delia became enamoured one of the other, or each of the other, as you please, and in a short time were married.

Mr. and Mrs. Larrabee began housekeeping in a flat. And they were happy; for they had their Art, and they had each other. Joe was painting in the class of the great Magister—you know his fame. His fees are high; his lessons are light. Delia was studying under Rosenstock—you know his repute as a disturber of the piano keys.

They were mighty happy as long as their money lasted. Their aims were very clear and defined. Joe was to become capable very soon of turning out pictures that old gentlemen with thin side-whiskers and thick pocketbooks would sandbag one another for the privilege of buying. Delia was to become familiar and then contemptuous with Music, so that when she saw the orchestra seats and boxes unsold she could have sore throat and lobster in a private dining-room and refuse to go on the stage.

But after a while, Art lagged. Money was lacking to pay Mr. Magister and Herr Rosenstock their prices. When one loves one's Art, no service seems too hard. So, Delia said she must give music lessons to keep the chafing dish bubbling.

For two or three days she went out canvassing for pupils. One evening she came home elated.

"Joe, dear," she said, gleefully, "I've a pupil. And oh, the loveliest people. General—General A. B. Pinckney's daughter—on Seventy-first street. Such a splendid house, Joe. I never saw anything like it before.

"My pupil is his daughter, Clementina. I dearly love her already. She's a delicate thing—dresses always in white; and the sweetest, simplest manners. Only eighteen years old. I'm to give three lessons a week; and, just think, Joe, 5 dollars a lesson. I don't mind it a bit; for when I get two or three more pupils I can resume my lessons with Herr Rosenstock. Now, smooth out that wrinkle between your brows, dear, and let's have a nice supper."

"That's all right for you, Dele," said Joe, attacking a can of peas with a carving knife and a hatchet, "but how about me? Do you think I'm going to let you hustle for wages while I philander in the regions of high art? Not by the bones of Benvenuto Cellini! I can sell papers or lay cobblestones, and bring in a dollar or two."

Delia came and hung about his neck.

"Joe, dear, you are silly. You must keep on at your studies. It is not as if I had quit my music and gone to work at something else. While I teach, I learn. I am always with my music. You mustn't think of leaving Mr. Magister."

"All right," said Joe, reaching for the blue scalloped vegetable dish. "But I hate for you to be giving lessons. It isn't Art. But you're a trump and a dear to do it."

"When one loves one's Art, no service seems too hard," said Delia.

During all of the next week the Larrabees had an early breakfast. Joe was enthusiastic about some morning-effect sketches he was doing in Central Park, and Delia packed him off breakfasted, coddled, praised and kissed at 7 o'clock. Art is an engaging mistress. It was most times 7 o'clock when he returned in the evening.

At the end of the week Delia, sweetly proud but languid, triumphantly tossed three five-dollar bills on the 8x10 (inches) center table of the 8x10 (feet) flat parlor.

"Sometimes," she said, a little wearily, "Clementina tries me. I'm afraid she doesn't practice enough, and I have to tell her the same things so often."

And then Joe, with the air of a Monte Cristo, drew forth a ten, a five, a two and a one—all legal tender notes—and laid them beside Delia's earnings.

"Sold that watercolor of the obelisk to a man from Peoria," he announced overwhelmingly.

"Don't joke with me," said Delia—"not from Peoria."

"All the way. I wish you could see him, Dele. Fat man with a woolen muffler and a quill toothpick. He ordered another—an oil sketch of the Lackawanna freight depot—to take back with him. Music lessons! Oh, I guess Art is still in it."

"I'm so glad you've kept on," said Delia heartily. "You're bound to win, dear. Thirty-three dollars. We never had so much to spend before. We'll have oysters to-night."

On the next Saturday evening Joe reached home first. He spread his $18 on the parlor table and washed what seemed to be a great deal of dark paint from his hands.

Half an hour later Delia arrived, her right hand tied up in a shapeless bundle of wraps and bandages.

"How is this?" asked Joe after the usual greeting. Delia laughed, but not very joyously.

"Clementina," she explained, "insisted upon a Welsh rabbit after her lesson. The General was there. You should have seen him run for the chafing dish, Joe, just as if there wasn't a servant in the house. I know Clementina isn't in good health. She is so nervous. In serving the rabbit she spilled a great lot of it, boiling hot, over my hand and wrist. It hurt awfully, Joe. And the dear girl was so sorry. But Gen. Pinckney!—Joe, that old man nearly went distracted. He rushed downstairs and sent somebody—they said the furnace man or somebody in the basement—out to a drug store for some oil and things to bind it with. It doesn't hurt so much now. Oh, Joe, did you sell another sketch?"

"Did I? Just ask the man from Peoria. He got his depot today, and he isn't sure but he thinks he wants another parkscape and a view on the Hudson. What time this afternoon did you burn your hand, Dele?"

"Five o'clock, I think. You ought to have seen Gen. Pinckney, Joe,—"

"Sit down here a moment, Dele," said Joe. He drew her to the couch, sat beside her and put his arm across her shoulders.

"What have you been doing for the last two weeks, Dele?" he asked.

She braved it for a moment or two with an eye full of love and stubbornness, and murmured a phrase or two vaguely of Gen. Pinckney; but at length down went her head and out came the truth and tears.

"I couldn't get any pupils," she confessed. "And I couldn't bear to have you give up your lessons; and I got a place ironing shirts in that big Twenty-fourth street laundry. And I think I did very well to make up both General Pinckney and Clementina, don't you, Joe? And when a girl in the laundry set down a hot iron on my hand, this afternoon, I was all the way home making up that story about the Welsh rabbit. You're not angry, are you, Joe? And if I hadn't got the work you mightn't have sold your sketches to that man from Peoria."

"He wasn't from Peoria," said Joe slowly.

"Well, it doesn't matter where he was from. How clever you are, Joe—and— Kiss me, Joe—and what made you suspect that I wasn't giving music lessons to Clementina?"

"I didn't, until tonight. And I wouldn't have then, only I sent up this cotton waste and oil from the engine-room this afternoon for the girl upstairs who had her hand burned with a smoothing iron. I've been firing the engine in that laundry for the last two weeks."

"And then you didn't—"

"My purchaser from Peoria," said Joe, "and Gen. Pinckney are both creations of the same art—but you wouldn't call it either painting or music."

And then they both laughed, and Joe began:

"When one loves one's Art no service seems—"

But Delia stopped him with her hand to his lips.

"No," she said—"just— When one loves."

FROM *The Grapes of Wrath* [1]
WE'LL HAVE A GRACE

JOHN STEINBECK

"Jus' like I said, they ain't a gonna keep no Joad in jail. I says, 'Tommy'll come a-bustin' outa that jail like a bull through a corral fence,' an' you done it. Get outa my way, I'm hungry." He crowded past, sat down, loaded his plate with pork and two big biscuits and poured the thick gravy over the whole mess, and before the others could get in, Grampa's mouth was full.

Tom grinned affectionately at him. "Ain't he a heller?" he said. And Grampa's mouth was so full that he couldn't even splutter, but his mean little eyes smiled, and he nodded his head violently.

Granma said proudly, "A wicketer, cussin'er man never lived. He's going to hell on a poker, praise Gawd! Wants to drive the truck!" she said spitefully, "Well, he ain't goin' ta."

Grampa choked, and a mouthful of paste sprayed into his lap, and he coughed weakly.

Granma smiled up at Tom. "Messy, ain't he?" she observed brightly.

Noah stood on the step, and he faced Tom, and his wide-set eyes seemed to look around him. His face had little expression. Tom said, "How ya, Noah?"

"Fine," said Noah. "How a' you?" That was all, but it was a comfortable thing.

Ma waved the flies away from the bowl of gravy, "We ain't got room to set down," she said. "Jus' get yaself a plate an' set down wherever ya can. Out in the yard or someplace."

Suddenly Tom said, "Hey! Where's the preacher? He was right here. Where'd he go?"

Pa said, "I see him, but he's gone."

And Granma raised a shrill voice, "Preacher? You got a preacher? Go git him. We'll have a grace." She pointed at Grampa. "Too late for him—he's et. Go git the preacher."

Tom stepped out on the porch. "Hey, Jim! Jim Casy!" he called. He walked out in the yard. "Oh, Casy!" The preacher emerged from under the tank, sat up, and then stood up and moved toward the house. Tom asked, "What was you doin', hidin'?"

"Well, no. But a fella shouldn' butt his head in where a fambly got fambly stuff. I was jus' settin' a-thinkin'."

---

[1] Copyright, 1939, by John Steinbeck. By permission of The Viking Press, Inc., New York.

"Come on in an' eat," said Tom. "Granma wants a grace."

"But I ain't a preacher no more," Casy protested.

"Aw, come on. Giv'er a grace. Don't do you no harm, an' she likes 'em." They walked into the kitchen together.

Ma said quietly, "You're welcome."

And Pa said, "You're welcome. Have some breakfast."

"Grace fust," Granma clamored. "Grace fust."

Grampa focused his eyes fiercely until he recognized Casy. "Oh, that preacher," he said. "Oh, he's all right. I always liked him since I seen him—" He winked so lecherously that Granma thought he had spoken and retorted, "Shut up, you sinful ol' goat."

Casy ran his fingers through his hair nervously. "I got to tell you, I ain't a preacher no more. If me jus' bein' glad to be here an' bein' thankful for people that's kind and generous, if that's enough—why, I'll say that kinda grace. But I ain't a preacher no more."

"Say her," said Granma. "An' get in a word about us goin' to California." The preacher bowed his head, and the others bowed their heads. Ma folded her hands over her stomach and bowed her head. Granma bowed so low that her nose was nearly in her plate of biscuit and gravy. Tom, leaning against the wall, a plate in his hand, bowed stiffly, and Grampa bowed his head sidewise, so that he could keep one mean and merry eye on the preacher. And on the preacher's face there was a look not of prayer, but of thought; and in his tone not supplication, but conjecture.

"I been thinkin'," he said. "I been in the hills, thinkin', almost you might say like Jesus went into the wilderness to think His way out of a mess of troubles."

"Pu-raise Gawd!" Granma said, and the preacher glanced over at her in surprise.

"Seems like Jesus got all messed up with troubles, and He couldn't figure nothin' out, an' He got to feelin' what the hell good is it all, an' what's the use fightin' an' figurin'. Got tired, got good an' tired, an' His sperit all wore out. Jus' about come to the conclusion, the hell with it. An' so He went off into the wilderness."

"A—men," Granma bleated. So many years she had timed her responses to the pauses. And it was so many years since she had listened to or wondered at the words used.

"I ain't sayin' I'm like Jesus," the preacher went on. "But I got tired like Him, an' I got mixed up like Him, an' I went into the wilderness like Him, without no campin' stuff. Nighttime I'd lay on my back an' look up at the stars; morning I'd set an' watch the sun come up; midday I'd look out from a hill at the rollin' dry country; evenin' I'd foller the sun down. Sometimes I'd pray like I always done. On'y I couldn' figure what I was prayin' to or for. There was the hills, an' there was me, an' we wasn't separate no more. We was one thing. An' that one thing was holy."

"Hallelujah," said Granma, and she rocked a little, back and forth, trying to catch hold of an ecstasy.

"An' I got thinkin', on'y it wasn't thinkin', it was deeper down than thinkin'. I got thinkin' how we was holy when we was one thing, an' mankin' was holy when it was one thing. An' it on'y got unholy when one mis'able little fella got the bit in his teeth and run off his own way, kickin' an' draggin' an' fightin'. Fella like that bust the holiness. But when they're all workin' together, not one fella for another fella, but one fella kinda harnessed to the whole shebang—that's right, that's holy. An' then I got thinkin' I don't even know what I mean by holy." He paused, but the bowed heads stayed down, for they had been trained like dogs to rise at the "amen" signal. "I can't say no grace like I use' ta say. I'm glad of the holiness of breakfast. I'm glad there's life here. That's all." The heads stayed down. The preacher looked around. "I've got your breakfast cold," he said; and then he remembered. "Amen," he said, and all the heads rose up.

"A—men," said Granma, and she fell to her breakfast, and broke down the soggy biscuits with her hard old toothless gums. Tom ate quickly, and Pa crammed his mouth. There was no talk until the food was gone, the coffee drunk; only the crunch of chewed food and the slup of coffee cooled in transit to the tongue. Ma watched the preacher as he ate, and her eyes were questioning, probing, and understanding. She watched him as though he were suddenly a spirit, not human any more, a voice out of the ground.

PART VI

Plays

The Will[1]

SIR JAMES M. BARRIE

The scene is any lawyer's office.

It may be, and no doubt will be, the minute reproduction of some actual office, with all the characteristic appurtenances thereof, every blot of ink in its proper place; but for the purpose in hand any bare room would do just as well. The only thing essential to the room, save the two men sitting in it, is a framed engraving on the wall of Queen Victoria, which dates sufficiently the opening scene, and will be changed presently to King Edward; afterwards to King George, to indicate the passing of time. No other alteration is called for. Doubtless different furniture came in, and the tiling of the fire-place was renewed, and at last someone discovered that the flowers in the window-box were dead, but all that is as immaterial to the action as the new blue-bottles; the succession of monarchs will convey allegorically the one thing necessary, that time is passing, but that the office of Devizes, Devizes, and Devizes *goes on.*

The two men are DEVIZES SENIOR *and* JUNIOR. SENIOR, *who is middle-aged, succeeded to a good thing years ago, and as the curtain rises we see him bent over his table making it a better thing. It is pleasant to think that before he speaks he adds another thirteen and fourpence, say, to the fortune of the firm.*

JUNIOR *is quite a gay dog, twenty-three, and we catch him skilfully balancing an office ruler on his nose. He is recently from Oxford—*

If you show him in Hyde Park, lawk, how they will stare,
Tho' a very smart figure in Bloomsbury Square.

Perhaps JUNIOR *is a smarter figure in the office (among the clerks) than he was at Oxford, but this is one of the few things about him that his shrewd father does not know.*

[1] Reprinted by permission of Charles Scribner's Sons, publishers.

There moves to them by the only door into the room a middle-aged clerk called SURTEES, *who is perhaps worth looking at, though his manner is that of one who has long ceased to think of himself as of any importance to either God or man. Look at him again, however (which few would do), and you may guess that he has lately had a shock—touched a living wire—and is a little dazed by it. He brings a card to* MR. DEVIZES, SENIOR, *who looks at it and shakes his head.*

MR. DEVIZES. 'Mr. Philip Ross.' Don't know him.

SURTEES (*who has an expressionless voice*). He says he wrote you two days ago, sir, explaining his business.

MR. DEVIZES. I have had no letter from a Philip Ross.

ROBERT. Nor I. (*He is more interested in his feat with the ruler than in a possible client, but* SURTEES *looks at him oddly.*)

MR. DEVIZES. Surtees looks as if he thought you had. (ROBERT *obliges by reflecting in the light of* SURTEES'S *countenance.*)

ROBERT. Ah, you think it may have been that one, Surty?

MR. DEVIZES (*sharply*). What one?

ROBERT. It was the day before yesterday. You were out, father, and Surtees brought me in some letters. His mouth was wide open. (*Thoughtfully.*) I suppose that was why I did it.

MR. DEVIZES. What did you do?

ROBERT. I must have suddenly recalled a game we used to play at Oxford. You try to fling cards one by one into a hat. It requires great skill. So I cast one of the letters at Surtees's open mouth, and it missed him and went into the fire. It may have been Philip Ross's letter.

MR. DEVIZES (*wrinkling his brows*). Too bad, Robert.

ROBERT (*blandly*). Yes, you see I am out of practice.

SURTEES. He seemed a very nervous person, sir, and quite young. Not a gentleman of much consequence.

ROBERT (*airily*). Why not tell him to write again?

MR. DEVIZES. Not fair.

SURTEES. But she—

ROBERT. She? Who?

SURTEES. There is a young lady with him, sir. She is crying.

ROBERT. Pretty?

SURTEES. I should say she is pretty, sir, in a quite inoffensive way.

ROBERT (*for his own gratification*). Ha!

MR. DEVIZES. Well, when I ring show them in.

ROBERT (*with roguish finger*). And let this be a lesson to you, Surty, not to go about your business with your mouth open. (SURTEES *tries to smile as requested, but with poor success.*) Nothing the matter, Surty? You seem to have lost your sense of humour.

SURTEES (*humbly enough*). I'm afraid I have, sir. I never had very much, Mr. Robert. (*He goes quietly. There has been a suppressed emotion about him that makes the incident poignant.*)

ROBERT. Anything wrong with Surtees, father?

MR. DEVIZES. Never mind him. I am very angry with you, Robert.

ROBERT (*like one conceding a point in a debating society*). And justly.

MR. DEVIZES (*frowning*). All we can do is to tell this Mr. Ross that we have not read his letter.

ROBERT (*bringing his knowledge of the world to bear*). Is that necessary?

MR. DEVIZES. We must admit that we don't know what he has come about.

ROBERT (*tolerant of his father's limitations*). But don't we?

MR. DEVIZES. Do you?

ROBERT. I rather think I can put two and two together.

MR. DEVIZES. Clever boy! Well, I shall leave them to you.

ROBERT. Right.

MR. DEVIZES. Your first case, Robert.

ROBERT (*undismayed*). It will be as good as a play to you to sit there and watch me discovering before they have been two minutes in the room what is the naughty thing that brings them here.

MR. DEVIZES (*drily*). I am always ready to take a lesson from the new generation. But of course we old fogies could do that also.

ROBERT. How?

MR. DEVIZES. By asking them.

ROBERT. Pooh. What did I go to Oxford for?

MR. DEVIZES. God knows. Are you ready?

ROBERT. Quite.

(MR. DEVIZES *rings.*)

MR. DEVIZES. By the way, we don't know the lady's name.

ROBERT. Observe me finding it out.

MR. DEVIZES. Is she married or single?

ROBERT. I'll know at a glance. And mark me, if she is married, it is our nervous gentleman who has come between her and her husband; but if she is single it is little Wet Face who has come between him and his wife.

MR. DEVIZES. A Daniel!

(*A young man and woman are shown in: very devoted to each other, though* ROBERT *does not know it. Yet it is the one thing obvious about them; more obvious than his cheap suit, which she presses so carefully beneath the mattress every night, or than the strength of his boyish face. Thinking of him as he then was by the light of subsequent events one wonders whether if he had come alone something disquieting could have been read in that face which was not there while she was by. Probably not; it was certainly already there, but had not yet reached the surface. With her, too, though she is to be what is called changed before we see them again, all seems serene; no warning signals; nothing in the way of their happiness in each other but this alarming visit to a lawyer's office. The stage direction might be 'Enter two lovers.' He is scarcely the less nervous of the two, but he enters stoutly in front of her as if to receive the first charge. She has probably nodded valiantly to him outside the door, where she let go his hand.*)

ROBERT (*master of the situation*). Come in, Mr. Ross (*and he bows reassuringly to the lady*). My partner—indeed my father. (MR. DEVIZES *bows but remains in the background.*)

PHILIP (*with a gulp*). You got my letter?

ROBERT. Yes—yes.

PHILIP. I gave you the details in it.

ROBERT. Yes, I have them all in my head. (*Cleverly.*) You will sit down, Miss—I don't think I caught the name. (*As much as to say, 'You see, Father, I spotted that she was single at once.'*)

MR. DEVIZES (*who has also formed his opinion*). You didn't ask for it, Robert.

ROBERT (*airily*). Miss—?

PHILIP. This is Mrs. Ross, my wife. (ROBERT *is a little taken aback, and has a conviction that his father is smiling.*)

ROBERT. Ah yes, of course; sit down, please, Mrs. Ross. (*She sits as if this made matters rather worse.*)

PHILIP (*standing guard by her side*). My wife is a little agitated.

ROBERT. Naturally. (*He tries a 'feeler.'*) These affairs—very painful at the time—but one gradually forgets.

EMILY (*with large eyes*). That is what Mr. Ross says, but somehow I can't help— (*the eyes fill*). You see, we have been married only four months.

ROBERT. Ah—that does make it—yes, certainly. (*He becomes the wife's champion, and frowns on* PHILIP.)

PHILIP. I suppose the sum seems very small to you?

ROBERT (*serenely*). I confess that is the impression it makes on me.

PHILIP. I wish it was more.

ROBERT (*at a venture*). You are sure you can't make it more?

PHILIP. How can I?

ROBERT. Ha!

EMILY (*with sudden spirit*). I think it's a great deal.

PHILIP. Mrs. Ross is so nice about it.

ROBERT (*taking a strong line*). I think so. But she must not be taken advantage of. And of course we shall have something to say as to the amount.

PHILIP (*blankly*). In what way? There it is.

ROBERT (*guardedly*). Hum. Yes, in a sense.

EMILY (*breaking down*). Oh, dear!

ROBERT (*more determined than ever to do his best for this wronged woman*). I am very sorry, Mrs. Ross. (*Sternly.*) I hope, sir, you realise that the mere publicity to a sensitive woman—

PHILIP. Publicity?

ROBERT (*feeling that he has got him on the run*). Of course for her sake we shall try to arrange things so that the names do not appear. Still—

PHILIP. The names? (*By this time* EMILY *is in tears.*)

EMILY. I can't help it. I love him so.

ROBERT (*still benighted*). Enough to forgive him? (*Seeing himself suddenly as a mediator.*) Mrs. Ross, is it too late to patch things up?

PHILIP (*now in flame*). What do you mean, sir?

MR. DEVIZES (*who has been quietly enjoying himself*). Yes, Robert, what do you mean precisely?

ROBERT. Really I—(*he tries brow-beating*). I must tell you at once, Mr. Ross, that unless a client gives us his fullest confidence we cannot undertake a case of this kind.

PHILIP. A case of what kind, sir? If you are implying anything against my good name—

ROBERT. On your honour, sir, is there nothing against it?

PHILIP. I know of nothing, sir.

EMILY. Anything against my husband, Mr. Devizes! He is an angel.

ROBERT (*suddenly seeing that little Wet Face must be the culprit*). Then it is you.

EMILY. Oh, sir, what is me?

PHILIP. Answer that, sir.

ROBERT. Yes, Mr. Ross, I will. (*But he finds he cannot.*) On second thoughts I decline. I cannot believe it has been all this lady's fault, and I decline to have anything to do with such a painful case.

MR. DEVIZES (*promptly*). Then I will take it up.

PHILIP (*not to be placated*). I think your son has insulted me.

EMILY. Philip, come away.

MR. DEVIZES. One moment, please. As I did not see your letter, may I ask Mr. Ross what is your business with us?

PHILIP. I called to ask whether you would be so good as to draw up my will.

ROBERT (*blankly*). Your will! Is that all?

PHILIP. Certainly.

MR. DEVIZES. Now we know, Robert.

ROBERT. But Mrs. Ross's agitation?

PHILIP (*taking her hand*). She feels that to make my will brings my death nearer.

ROBERT. So that's it.

PHILIP. It was all in the letter.

MR. DEVIZES (*coyly*). Anything to say, Robert?

ROBERT. Most—ah—extremely—(*he has an inspiration*). But even now I'm puzzled. You are Edgar Charles Ross?

PHILIP. No, Philip Ross.

ROBERT (*brazenly*). Philip Ross? We have made an odd mistake, father. (*There is a twinkle in* MR. DEVIZES's *eye. He watches interestedly to see how his son is to emerge from the mess.*) The fact is, Mrs. Ross, we are expecting to-day a Mr. Edgar Charles Ross on a matter—well—of a kind— Ah me. (*With fitting gravity.*) His wife, in short.

EMILY (*who has not read the newspapers in vain*). How awful. How sad.

ROBERT. Sad indeed. You will quite understand that professional etiquette prevents my saying one word more.

PHILIP. Yes, of course—we have no desire— But I did write.

ROBERT. Assuredly. But about a will. That is my father's department. No doubt you recall the letter now, father?

MR. DEVIZES (*who if he won't hinder won't help*). I can't say I do.

ROBERT (*unabashed*). Odd. You must have overlooked it.

MR. DEVIZES. Ha. At all events, Mr. Ross, I am quite at your service now.

PHILIP. Thank you.

ROBERT (*still ready to sacrifice himself on the call of duty*). You don't need me any more, father?

MR. DEVIZES. No, Robert; many thanks. You run off to your club now and have a bit of lunch. You must be tired. Send Surtees in to me. (*To his clients.*) My son had his first case to-day.

PHILIP (*politely*). I hope successfully.

MR. DEVIZES. Not so bad. He rather bungled it at first, but he got out of a hole rather cleverly. I think you'll make a lawyer yet, Robert.

ROBERT. Thank you, father. (*He goes jauntily, with a flower in his button-hole.*)

MR. DEVIZES. Now, Mr. Ross. (*The young wife's hand goes out for comfort and finds* PHILIP'S *waiting for it.*)

PHILIP. What I want myself is that the will should all go into one sentence, 'I leave everything of which I die possessed to my beloved wife.'

MR. DEVIZES (*thawing to the romance of this young couple*). Well, there have been many worse wills than that, sir.

(EMILY *is emotional.*)

PHILIP. Don't give way, Emily.

EMILY. It was those words, 'of which I die possessed.' (*Imploringly.*) Surely he doesn't need to say that—please, Mr. Devizes?

MR. DEVIZES. Certainly not. I am confident I can draw up the will without mentioning death at all.

EMILY (*huskily*). Oh, thank you.

MR. DEVIZES. At the same time, of course, in a legal document in which the widow is the sole—

(EMILY *again needs attention.*)

PHILIP (*reproachfully*). What was the need of saying 'widow'?

MR. DEVIZES. I beg your pardon, Mrs. Ross. I unreservedly withdraw the word 'widow.' Forgive a stupid old solicitor. (*She smiles gratefully through her tears.* SURTEES *comes in.*) Surtees, just take a few notes, please. (SURTEES *sits in the background and takes notes.* The facts of the case, as I understand, Mrs. Ross, are these: Your husband (*Quickly*)—who is in the prime of health—but knows life to be uncertain—

EMILY. Oh!

MR. DEVIZES. —though usually, as we learn from holy script itself, it lasts seven times ten years—and believing that he will in all probability live the allotted span, nevertheless, because of his love of you thinks it judicious to go through the form—it is a mere form—of making a will.

EMILY (*fervently*). Oh, thank you.

MR. DEVIZES. Any details, Mr. Ross?

PHILIP. I am an orphan. I live at Belvedere, 14 Tulphin Road, Hammersmith.

EMILY (*to whom the address has a seductive sound*). We live there.

PHILIP. And I am a clerk in the employ of Curar and Gow, the foreign coaling agents.

MR. DEVIZES. Yes, yes. Any private income?

(*They cannot help sniggering a little at the quaint question.*)

PHILIP. Oh no!

MR. DEVIZES. I see it will be quite a brief will.

PHILIP (*to whom the remark sounds scarcely worthy of a great occasion*). My income is a biggish one.

MR. DEVIZES. Yes?

EMILY (*important*). He has £170 a year.

MR. DEVIZES. Ah.

PHILIP. I began at £60. But it is going up, Mr. Devizes, by leaps and bounds. Another £15 this year.

MR. DEVIZES. Good.

PHILIP (*darkly*). I have a certain ambition.

EMILY (*eagerly*). Tell him, Philip.

PHILIP (*with a big breath*). We have made up our minds to come to £365 a year before I—retire.

EMILY. That is a pound a day.

MR. DEVIZES (*smiling sympathetically on them*). So it is. My best wishes.

PHILIP. Thank you. Of course the furnishing took a good deal.

MR. DEVIZES. It would.

EMILY. He insisted on my having the very best. (*She ceases. She is probably thinking of her superb spare bedroom.*)

PHILIP. But we are not a penny in debt; and have £200 saved.

MR. DEVIZES. I think you have made a brave beginning.

EMILY. They have the highest opinion of him in the office.

PHILIP. Then I am insured for £500.

MR. DEVIZES. I am glad to hear that.

PHILIP. Of course I would like to leave her a house in Kensington and a carriage and pair.

MR. DEVIZES. Who knows, perhaps you will.

EMILY. Oh!

MR. DEVIZES. Forgive me.

EMILY. What would houses and horses be to me without him!

MR. DEVIZES (*soothingly*). Quite so. What I take Mr. Ross to mean is that when he dies—if he ever should die—everything is to go to his —his spouse.

PHILIP (*dogged*). Yes.

EMILY (*dogged*). No.

PHILIP (*sighing*). This is the only difference we have ever had. Mrs. Ross insists on certain bequests. You see, I have two cousins, ladies, not well off, whom I have been in the way of helping a little. But in my will, how can I?

MR. DEVIZES. You must think first of your wife.

PHILIP. But she insists on my leaving £50 to each of them. (*He looks appealingly to his wife.*)

EMILY (*grandly*). £100.

PHILIP. £50.

EMILY. Dear, £100.

MR. DEVIZES. Let us say £75.

PHILIP (*reluctantly*). Very well.

EMILY. No, £100.

PHILIP. She'll have to get her way. Here are their names and addresses.

MR. DEVIZES. Anything else?

PHILIP (*hurriedly*). No.

EMILY. The convalescent home, dear. He was in it a year ago, and they were so kind.

PHILIP. Yes, but—

EMILY. £10. (*He has to yield, with a reproachful, admiring look.*)

MR. DEVIZES. Then, if that is all, I won't detain you. If you look in to-morrow, Mr. Ross, about this time, we shall have everything ready for you.

(*Their faces fall.*)

EMILY. Oh, Mr. Devizes, if only it could all be drawn up now, and done with.

PHILIP. You see, sir, we are screwed up to it to-day.

(*'Our fate is in your hands,' they might be saying, and the lawyer smiles to find himself such a power.*)

MR. DEVIZES (*looking at his watch*). Well, it certainly need not take long. You go out and have lunch somewhere, and then come back.

EMILY. Oh, don't ask me to eat.

PHILIP. We are too excited.

EMILY. Please may we just walk about the street?

MR. DEVIZES (*Smiling*). Of course you may, you ridiculous young wife.

EMILY. I know it's ridiculous of me, but I am so fond of him.

MR. DEVIZES. Yes, it is ridiculous. But don't change; especially if you get on in the world, Mr. Ross.

PHILIP. No fear!

EMILY (*backing from the will, which may now be said to be in existence*). And please don't give us a copy of it to keep. I would rather not have it in the house.

MR. DEVIZES (*nodding reassuringly*). In an hour's time. (*They go, and the lawyer has his lunch, which is simpler than* ROBERT'S: *a sandwich and a glass of wine. He speaks as he eats.*) You will get that ready, Surtees. Here are the names and addresses he left. (*Cheerily.*) A nice couple.

SURTEES (*who is hearing another voice*). Yes, sir.

MR. DEVIZES (*unbending*). Little romance of its kind. Makes one feel quite gay.

SURTEES. Yes, sir.

MR. DEVIZES (*struck perhaps by the deadness of his voice*). You don't look very gay, Surtees.

SURTEES. I'm sorry, sir. We can't all be gay. (*He is going out without looking at his employer.*) I'll see to this, sir.

MR. DEVIZES. Stop a minute. Is there anything wrong? (SURTEES *has difficulty in answering, and* MR. DEVIZES *goes to him kindly.*) Not worrying over that matter we spoke about? (SURTEES *inclines his head.*) Is the pain worse?

SURTEES. It's no great pain, sir.

MR. DEVIZES (*uncomfortably*). I'm sure it's not—what you fear. Any specialist would tell you so.

SURTEES (*without looking up*). I have been to one, sir—yesterday.

MR. DEVIZES. Well?

SURTEES. It's—that, sir.

MR. DEVIZES. He couldn't be sure.

SURTEES. Yes, sir.

MR. DEVIZES. An operation—

SURTEES. Too late, he said, for that. If I had been operated on long ago there might have been a chance.

MR. DEVIZES. But you didn't have it long ago.

SURTEES. Not to my knowledge, sir; but he says it was there all the same, always in me, a black spot, not so big as a pin's head, but waiting to spread and destroy me in the fulness of time. All the rest of me as sound as a bell. (*That is the voice that* SURTEES *has been hearing.*)

MR. DEVIZES (*helpless*). It seems damnably unfair.

SURTEES (*humbly*). I don't know, sir. He says there's a spot of that kind in pretty nigh all of us, and if we don't look out it does for us in the end.

MR. DEVIZES (*hurriedly*). No, no, no.

SURTEES. He called it the accursed thing. I think he meant we should know of it and be on the watch. (*He pulls himself together.*) I'll see to this at once, sir.

(*He goes out.* MR. DEVIZES *continues his lunch.*)

The curtain falls here for a moment only, to indicate the passing of a number of years. When it rises we see that the engraving of Queen Victoria has given way to one of King Edward.

ROBERT is discovered, immersed in affairs. He is now a middle-aged man who has long forgotten how to fling cards into a hat. To him comes SENNET, a brisk clerk.

SENNET. Mrs. Philip Ross to see you, sir.

ROBERT. Mr. Ross, don't you mean, Sennet?

SENNET. No, sir.

ROBERT. Ha. It was Mr. Ross I was expecting. Show her in. (*Frowning.*) And, Sennet, less row in the office, if you please.

SENNET (*glibly*). It was these young clerks, sir—

ROBERT. They mustn't be young here, or they go. Tell them that.

SENNET (*glad to be gone*). Yes, sir.

(*He shows in Mrs. Ross. We have not seen her for twenty years and would certainly not recognize her in the street. So shrinking her first entrance into this room, but she sails in now like a galleon. She is not so much dressed as richly upholstered. She is very sure of herself. Yet she is not a different woman from the EMILY we remember; the pity of it is that somehow this is the same woman.*)

ROBERT (*who makes much of his important visitor and is also wondering why she has come*). This is a delightful surprise, Mrs. Ross. Allow me. (*He removes her fine cloak with proper solicitude, and EMILY walks out of it in the manner that makes it worth possessing.*) This chair, alas, is the best I can offer you.

EMILY (*who is still a good-natured woman if you attempt no nonsense with her*). It will do quite well.

ROBERT (*gallantly*). Honoured to see you in it.

EMILY (*smartly*). Not you. You were saying to yourself, 'Now, what brings the woman here?'

ROBERT. Honestly, I—

EMILY. And I'll tell you. You are expecting Mr. Ross, I think?

ROBERT (*cautiously*). Well—ah—

EMILY. Pooh. The cunning of you lawyers. I know he has an appointment with you, and that is why I've come.

ROBERT. He arranged with you to meet him here?

EMILY (*preening herself*). I wouldn't say that. I don't know that he will be specially pleased to find me here when he comes.

ROBERT (*guardedly*). Oh?

EMILY (*who is now a woman that goes straight to her goal*). I know what he is coming about. To make a new will.

ROBERT (*admitting it*). After all, not the first he has made with us, Mrs. Ross.

EMILY (*promptly*). No, the fourth.

ROBERT (*warming his hands at the thought*). Such a wonderful career. He goes from success to success.

EMILY (*complacently*). Yes, we're big folk.

ROBERT. You are indeed.

EMILY (*sharply*). But the last will covered everything.

ROBERT (*on guard again*). Of course it is a matter I cannot well discuss even with you. And I know nothing of his intentions.

EMILY. Well, I suspect some of them.

ROBERT. Ah.

EMILY. And that's why I'm here. Just to see that he does nothing foolish.

(*She settles herself more comfortably as Mr. Ross is announced. A city magnate walks in. You know he is that before you see that he is Philip Ross.*)

PHILIP (*speaking as he enters*). How do, Devizes, how do. Well, let us get at this thing at once. Time is money, you know, time is money. (*Then he sees his wife.*) Hello, Emily.

EMILY (*unperturbed*). You didn't ask me to come, Philip, but I thought I might as well.

PHILIP. That's all right.

(*His brow had lowered at first sight of her, but now he gives her cleverness a grin of respect.*)

EMILY. It is the first will you have made without taking me into your confidence.

PHILIP. No important changes. I just thought to save you the—unpleasantness of the thing.

EMILY. How do you mean?

PHILIP (*fidgeting*). Well, one can't draw up a will without feeling for the moment that he is bringing his end nearer. Is that not so, Devizes?

ROBERT (*who will quite possibly die intestate*). Some do have that feeling.

EMILY. But what nonsense. How can it have any effect of that kind one way or the other?

ROBERT. Quite so.

EMILY (*reprovingly*). Just silly sentiment, Philip. I would have thought it would be a pleasure to you handling such a big sum.

PHILIP (*wincing*). Not handling it, giving it up.

EMILY. To those you love.

PHILIP (*rather shortly*). I'm not giving it up yet. You talk as if I was on my last legs.

EMILY (*imperturbably*). Not at all. It's you that are doing that.

ROBERT (*to the rescue*). Here is my copy of the last will. I don't know if you would like me to read it out?

PHILIP. It's hardly necessary.

EMILY. We have our own copy at home and we know it well.

PHILIP (*sitting back in his chair*). What do you think I'm worth to-day, Devizes?

(*Every one smiles. It is as if the sun had peeped in at the window.*)

ROBERT. I daren't guess.

PHILIP. An easy seventy thou.

EMILY. And that's not counting the house and the country cottage. We call it a cottage. You should see it!

ROBERT. I have heard of it.

EMILY (*more sharply, though the sun still shines*). Well, go on, Philip. I suppose you are not thinking of cutting me out of anything.

PHILIP (*heartily*). Of course not. There will be more to you than ever.

EMILY (*coolly*). There's more to leave.

PHILIP (*hesitating*). At the same time—

EMILY. Well? It's to be mine absolutely of course. Not just a life interest.

PHILIP (*doggedly*). That is a change I was thinking of.

EMILY. Just what I have suspected for days. Will you please to say why?

ROBERT (*whose client after all is the man*). Of course it is quite common.

EMILY. I didn't think my husband was quite common.

ROBERT. I only mean that as there are children—

PHILIP. That's what I mean too.

EMILY. And I can't be trusted to leave my money to my own children! In what way have I failed them before?

PHILIP (*believing it, too*). Never, Emily, never. A more devoted mother— If you have one failing it is that you spoil them.

EMILY. Then what's your reason?

PHILIP (*less sincerely*). Just to save you worry when I'm gone.

EMILY. It's no worry to me to look after my money.

PHILIP (*bridling*). After all, it's my money.

EMILY. I knew that was what was at the back of your mind.

PHILIP (*reverently*). It's such a great sum.

EMILY. One would think you were afraid I would marry again.

PHILIP (*snapping*). One would think you looked to my dying next week.

EMILY. Tuts.

(PHILIP *is unable to sit still.*)

PHILIP. My money. If you were to invest it badly and lose it. I tell you, Devizes, I couldn't lie quiet in my grave if I thought my money was lost by injudicious investments.

EMILY (*coldly*). You are thinking of yourself, Philip, rather than of the children.

PHILIP. Not at all.

ROBERT (*hastily*). How are the two children?

EMILY. Though I say it myself, there never were better. Harry is at Eton, you know, the most fashionable school in the country.

ROBERT. Doing well, I hope.

PHILIP (*chuckling*). We have the most gratifying letters from him. Last Saturday he was caught smoking cigarettes with a lord. (*With pardonable pride.*) They were sick together.

ROBERT. And Miss Gwendolen? She must be almost grown up now.

(*The parents exchange important glances.*)

EMILY. Should we tell him?

PHILIP. Under the rose, you know, Devizes.

ROBERT. Am I to congratulate her?

EMILY. No names, Philip.

PHILIP. No, no names—but she won't be a plain Mrs., no sir.

ROBERT. Well done, Miss Gwendolen. (*With fitting jocularity.*) Now I see why you want a new will.

PHILIP. Yes, that's my main reason, Emily.

EMILY. But none of your life interests for me, Philip.

PHILIP (*shying*). We'll talk that over presently.

ROBERT. Will you keep the legacies as they are?

PHILIP. Well, there's that £500 for the hospitals.

EMILY. Yes, with so many claims on us, is that necessary?

PHILIP (*becoming stouter*). I'm going to make it £1000.

EMILY. Philip!

PHILIP. My mind is made up. I want to make a splash with the hospitals.

ROBERT (*hurrying to the next item*). There is £50 a year each to two cousins, ladies.

PHILIP. I suppose we'll keep that as it is, Emily?

EMILY. It was just gifts to them of £100 each at first.

PHILIP. I was poor at that time myself.

EMILY. Do you think it's wise to load them with so much money? They'll not know what to do with it.

PHILIP. They're old.

EMILY. But they're wiry. £75 a year between them would surely be enough.

PHILIP. It would be if they lived together, but you see they don't. They hate each other like cat and dog.

EMILY. That's not nice between relatives. You could leave it to them on condition that they do live together. That would be a Christian action.

PHILIP. There's something in that.

ROBERT. Then the chief matter is whether Mrs. Ross—

EMILY. Oh, I thought that was settled.

PHILIP (*with a sigh*). I'll have to give in to her, sir.

ROBERT. Very well. I suppose my father will want to draw up the will. I'm sorry he had to be in the country to-day.

EMILY (*affable now that she has gained her point*). I hope he is wearing well?

ROBERT. Wonderfully. He is away playing golf.

PHILIP (*grinning*). Golf. I have no time for games. (*Considerately.*) But he must get the drawing up of my will. I couldn't deprive the old man of that.

ROBERT. He will be proud to do it again.

PHILIP (*well satisfied*). Ah! There's many a one would like to look over your father's shoulder when he's drawing up my will. I wonder what I'll cut up for in the end. But I must be going.

EMILY. Can I drop you anywhere? I have the greys out.

PHILIP. Yes, at the club.

(*Now* MRS. ROSS *walks into her cloak.*)

PHILIP. Good-day, Devizes. I won't have time to look in again, so tell the old man to come to me.

ROBERT (*deferentially*). Whatever suits you best. (*Ringing.*) He will be delighted. I remember his saying to me on the day you made your first will—

PHILIP (*chuckling*). A poor little affair that.

ROBERT. He said to me you were a couple whose life looked like being a romance.

PHILIP. And he was right—eh, Emily?—though he little thought what a romance.

EMILY. No, he little thought what a romance.

(*They make a happy departure, and* ROBERT *is left reflecting.*)

The curtain again falls, and rises immediately, as the engraving shows, on the same office in the reign of King George. It is a foggy morning and a fire burns briskly. MR. DEVIZES, SENIOR, *arrives for the day's work just as he came daily for over half a century. But he has no right to be here now. A year or two ago they got him to retire, as he was grown feeble; and there is an understanding that he does not go out of his house alone. He has, as it were, escaped to-day, and his feet have carried him to the old office that is the home of his mind. He was almost portly when we saw him first, but he has become little again and as light as the schoolboy whose deeds are nearer to him than many of the events of later years. He arrives at the office, thinking it is old times, and a clerk surveys him uncomfortably from the door.*

CREED (*not quite knowing what to do*). Mr. Devizes has not come in yet, sir.

MR. DEVIZES (*considering*). Yes, I have. Do you mean Mr. Robert?

CREED. Yes, sir.

MR. DEVIZES (*querulously*). Always late. Can't get that boy to settle down. (*Leniently.*) Well, well, boys will be boys—eh, Surtees?

CREED (*wishing* MR. ROBERT *would come*). My name is Creed, sir.

MR. DEVIZES (*sharply*). Creed? Don't know you. Where is Surtees?

CREED. There is no one of that name in the office, sir.

MR. DEVIZES (*growing timid*). No? I remember now. Poor Surtees! (*But his mind cannot grapple with troubles.*) Tell him I want him when he comes in. (*He is changing, after his old custom, into an office coat.*)

CREED. That is Mr. Dev—Mr. Robert's coat, sir.

MR. DEVIZES. He has no business to hang it there. That is my nail.

CREED. He has hung it there for years, sir.

MR. DEVIZES. Not at all. I must have it. Why does Surtees let him do it? Help me into my office coat, boy.

(CREED *helps him into the coat he has taken off, and the old man is content.*)

CREED (*seeing him lift up the correspondence*). I don't think Mr. Devizes would like you to open the office letters, sir.

MR. DEVIZES (*pettishly*). What's that? Go away, boy. Send Surtees.

(*To the relief of* CREED, ROBERT *arrives, and, taking in the situation, signs to the clerk to go. He has a more youthful manner than when last we saw him, has* ROBERT, *but his hair is iron grey. He is kindly to his father.*)

ROBERT. You here, father?

MR. DEVIZES (*after staring at him*). Yes, you are Robert. (*A little frightened.*) You are an old man, Robert.

ROBERT (*without wincing*). Getting on, father. But why did they let you come? You haven't been here for years.

MR. DEVIZES (*puzzled*). Years? I think I just came in the old way, Robert, without thinking.

ROBERT. Yes, yes. I'll get some one to go home with you.

MR. DEVIZES (*rather abject*). Let me stay, Robert. I like being here. I won't disturb you. I like the smell of the office, Robert.

ROBERT. Of course you may stay. Come over to the fire. (*He settles his father by the fire in the one arm-chair.*) There; you can have a doze by the fire.

MR. DEVIZES. A doze by the fire. That is all I'm good for now. Once —but my son hangs his coat there now. (*Presently he looks up fearfully.*) Robert, tell me something in a whisper: Is Surtees dead?

ROBERT (*who has forgotten the name*). Surtees?

MR. DEVIZES. My clerk, you know.

ROBERT. Oh. Why, he has been dead this thirty years, father.

MR. DEVIZES. So long! Seems like yesterday.

ROBERT. It is just far back times that seem clear to you now.

MR. DEVIZES (*meekly*). Is it. (ROBERT *opens his letters, and his father falls asleep.* CREED *comes.*)

CREED. Sir Philip Ross.

(*The great* SIR PHILIP *enters, nearly sixty now, strong of frame still, but a lost man. He is in mourning, and carries the broken pieces of his life with an air of braggadocio. It should be understood that he is not a 'sympathetic' part, and any actor who plays him as such will be rolling the play in the gutter.*)

ROBERT (*on his feet at once to greet such a client*). You, Sir Philip.

PHILIP (*head erect*). Here I am.

ROBERT (*because it will out*). How are you?

PHILIP (*as if challenged*). I'm all right—great. (*With defiant jocularity.*) Called on the old business.

ROBERT. To make another will?

PHILIP. You've guessed it—the very first time. (*He sees the figure by the fire.*)

ROBERT. Yes, it's my father. He's dozing. Shouldn't be here at all. He forgets things. It's just age.

PHILIP (*grimly*). Forgets things. That must be fine.

ROBERT (*conventionally*). I should like, Sir Philip, to offer you my sincere condolences. In the midst of life we are— How true that is. I attended the funeral.

PHILIP. I saw you.

ROBERT. A much esteemed lady. I had a great respect for her.

PHILIP (*almost with relish*). Do you mind, when we used to come here about the will, somehow she—we—always took for granted I should be the first to go.

ROBERT (*devoutly*). These things are hid from mortal eyes.

PHILIP (*with conviction*). There's a lot hid. We needn't have worried so much about the will if—well, let us get at it. (*Fiercely.*) I haven't given in, you know.

ROBERT. We must bow our heads—

PHILIP. Must we? Am I bowing mine?

ROBERT (*uncomfortably*). Such courage in the great hour—yes—and I am sure Lady Ross—

PHILIP (*with the ugly humour that has come to him*). She wasn't that.

ROBERT. The honour came so soon afterwards—I feel she would like to be thought of as Lady Ross. I shall always remember her as a fine lady richly dressed who used—

PHILIP (*harshly*). Stop it. That's not how I think of her. There was a time before that—she wasn't richly dressed—(*he stamps upon his memories*). Things went wrong, I don't know how. It's a beast of a world. I didn't come here to talk about that. Let us get to work.

ROBERT (*turning with relief from the cemetery*). Yes, yes, and after all life has its compensations. You have your son who—

PHILIP (*snapping*). No, I haven't. (*This startles the lawyer.*) I'm done with him.

ROBERT. If he has been foolish—

PHILIP. Foolish! (*Some dignity comes into the man.*) Sir, I have come to a pass when foolish as applied to my own son would seem to me a very pretty word.

ROBERT. Is it as bad as that?

PHILIP. He's a rotter.

ROBERT. It is very painful to me to hear you say that.

PHILIP. More painful, think you, than for me to say it? (*Clenching his fists.*) But I've shipped him off. The law had to wink at it, or I couldn't have done it. Why don't you say I pampered him and it serves me right? It's what they are all saying behind my back. Why don't you ask me about my girl? That's another way to rub it in.

ROBERT. Don't, Sir Philip. I knew her. My sympathy—

PHILIP. A chauffeur, that is what he was. The man who drove her own car.

ROBERT. I was deeply concerned—

PHILIP. I want nobody's pity. I've done with both of them, and if you think I'm a broken man you're much mistaken. I'll show them. Have you your papers there? Then take down my last will. I have everything in my head. I'll show them.

ROBERT. Would it not be better to wait till a calmer—

PHILIP. Will you do it now, or am I to go across the street?

ROBERT. If I must.

PHILIP. Then down with it. (*He wets his lips.*) I, Philip Ross, of 77 Bath Street, W., do hereby revoke all former wills and testaments, and I leave everything of which I die possessed—

ROBERT. Yes?

PHILIP. Everything of which I die possessed—

ROBERT. Yes?

PHILIP. I leave it—I leave it—(*The game is up.*) My God, Devizes, I don't know what to do with it.

ROBERT. I—I—really—come—

PHILIP (*cynically*). Can't you make any suggestions?

ROBERT. Those cousins are dead, I think?

PHILIP. Years ago.

ROBERT (*troubled*). In the case of such a large sum—

PHILIP (*letting all his hoarded gold run through his fingers*). The money I've won with my blood. God in heaven! (*Showing his teeth.*) Would that old man like it to play with? If I bring it to you in sacks, will you fling it out of the window for me?

ROBERT. Sir Philip!

PHILIP (*taking a paper from his pocket*). Here, take this. It has the names and addresses of the half-dozen men I've fought with most for gold; and I've beaten them. Draw up a will leaving all my money to be divided between them, with my respectful curses, and bring it to my house and I'll sign it.

ROBERT (*properly shocked*). But really I can't possibly—

PHILIP. Either you or another; is it to be you?

ROBERT. Very well.

PHILIP. Then that's settled. (*He rises with a laugh. He regards* MR. DEVIZES *quizzically.*) So you weren't in at the last will after all, old Sleep by the Fire. (*To their surprise the old man stirs.*)

MR. DEVIZES. What's that about a will?

ROBERT. You are awake, father?

MR. DEVIZES (*whose eyes have opened on* PHILIP'S *face*). I don't know you, sir.

ROBERT. Yes, yes, father, you remember Mr. Ross. He is Sir Philip now.

MR. DEVIZES (*courteously*). Sir Philip? I wish you joy, sir, but I don't know you.

ROBERT (*encouragingly*). Ross, father.

MR. DEVIZES. I knew a Mr. Ross long ago.

ROBERT. This is the same.

Mr. Devizes (*annoyed*). No, no. A bright young fellow he was, with such a dear, pretty wife. They came to make a will. (*He chuckles.*) And bless me, they had only twopence halfpenny. I took a fancy to them; such a happy pair.

Robert (*apologetically*). The past is clearer to him than the present nowadays. That will do, father.

Philip (*brusquely*). Let him go on.

Mr. Devizes. Poor souls, it all ended unhappily, you know.

Philip (*who is not brusque to him*). Yes, I know. Why did things go wrong, sir? I sit and wonder, and I can't find the beginning.

Mr. Devizes. That's the sad part of it. There was never a beginning. It was always there. He told me all about it.

Robert. He is thinking of something else; I don't know what.

Philip. Quiet. What was it that was always there?

Mr. Devizes. It was always in them—a spot no bigger than a pin's head, but waiting to spread and destroy them in the fulness of time.

Robert. I don't know what he has got hold of.

Philip. He knows. Could they have done anything to prevent it, sir?

Mr. Devizes. If they had been on the watch. But they didn't know, so they weren't on the watch. Poor souls.

Philip. Poor souls.

Mr. Devizes. It's called the accursed thing. It gets nearly everybody in the end, if they don't look out. (*He sinks back into his chair and forgets them.*)

Robert. He is just wandering.

Philip. The old man knows. (*He slowly tears up the paper he had given* Robert.)

Robert (*relieved*). I am glad to see you do that.

Philip. A spot no bigger than a pin's head. (*A wish wells up in him, too late perhaps.*) I wish I could help some young things before that spot has time to spread and destroy them as it has destroyed me and mine.

Robert (*brightly*). With such a large fortune—

Philip (*summing up his life*). It can't be done with money, sir.

(*He goes away; God knows where.*)

Death of a Salesman [1]

ARTHUR MILLER

REQUIEM

CHARLEY. It's getting dark, Linda.

(LINDA *doesn't react. She stares at the grave.*)

BIFF. How about it, Mom? Better get some rest, heh? They'll be closing the gate soon.

(LINDA *makes no move. Pause.*)

HAPPY (*deeply angered*). He had no right to do that. There was no necessity for it. We would've helped him.

CHARLEY (*grunting*). Hmmm.

BIFF. Come along, Mom.

LINDA. Why didn't anybody come?

CHARLEY. It was a very nice funeral.

LINDA. But where are all the people he knew? Maybe they blame him.

CHARLEY. Naa. It's a rough world, Linda. They wouldn't blame him.

LINDA. I can't understand it. At this time especially. First time in thirty-five years we were just about free and clear. He only needed a little salary. He was even finished with the dentist.

CHARLEY. No man only needs a little salary.

LINDA. I can't understand it.

BIFF. There were a lot of nice days. When he'd come home from a trip; or on Sundays, making the stoop; finishing the cellar; putting on the new porch; when he built the extra bathroom; and put up the garage. You know something, Charley, there's more of him in that front stoop than in all the sales he ever made.

CHARLEY. Yeah, he was a happy man with a batch of cement.

LINDA. He was so wonderful with his hands.

BIFF. He had the wrong dreams. All, all, wrong.

HAPPY (*almost ready to fight* BIFF). Don't say that!

BIFF. He never knew who he was.

CHARLEY (*stopping* HAPPY'S *movement and reply. To* BIFF). Nobody dast blame this man. You don't understand: Willy was a salesman. And for a salesman, there is no rock bottom to life. He don't put a bolt to a nut, he don't tell you the law or give you medicine. He's the man way out there in the blue riding on a smile and a shoeshine. And when they start not smiling back—that's an earthquake. And then you get yourself a couple of spots on your hat, and you're finished. Nobody dast blame this man. A salesman is got to dream, boy. It comes with the territory.

---

[1] From *Death of a Salesman* (New York: The Viking Press, Inc., 1949).

BIFF. Charley, the man didn't know who he was.

HAPPY (*infuriated*). Don't say that!

BIFF. Why don't you come with me, Happy?

HAPPY. I'm not licked that easily. I'm staying right in this city, and I'm gonna beat this racket! (*He looks at* BIFF, *his chin set.*) The Loman Brothers!

BIFF. I know who I am, kid.

HAPPY. All right, boy. I'm gonna show you and everybody else that Willy Loman did not die in vain. He had a good dream. It's the only dream you can have—to come out number-one man. He fought it out here, and this is where I'm gonna win it for him.

BIFF (*with a hopeless glance at* HAPPY, *bends toward his mother*). Let's go, Mom.

LINDA. I'll be with you in a minute. Go on, Charley. (*He hesitates.*) I want to, just for a minute. I never had a chance to say good-by.

(CHARLEY *moves away, followed by* HAPPY. BIFF *remains a slight distance up and left of* LINDA. *She sits there, summoning herself. The flute begins, not far away playing behind her speech.*)

LINDA. Forgive me, dear. I can't cry. I don't know what it is, but I can't cry. I don't understand it. Why did you ever do that? Help me, Willy, I can't cry. It seems to me that you're just on another trip. I keep expecting you, Willy, dear, I can't cry. Why did you do it? I search and search and I search, and I can't understand it, Willy. I made the last payment on the house today. Today, dear. And there'll be nobody home. (*A sob rises in her throat.*) We're free and clear. (*Sobbing more fully, released.*) We're free . . . We're free . . . (BIFF *lifts her to her feet and moves up right with her in his arms.* LINDA *sobs quietly.* BERNARD *and* CHARLEY *come together and follow them, followed by* HAPPY. *Only the music of the flute is left on the darkening stage as over the house the hard towers of the apartment buildings rise into sharp focus, and*

THE CURTAIN FALLS

Brutus to the Roman People

FROM JULIUS CAESAR [1]

WILLIAM SHAKESPEARE

Romans, countrymen, and lovers! hear me for my cause; and be silent, that you may hear. Believe me for mine honor; and have respect to

[1] Act III, Scene ii.

mine honor, that you may believe. Censure me in your wisdom; and awake your senses, that you may the better judge. If there be any in this assembly—any dear friend of Cæsar's,—to him I say, that Brutus' love to Cæsar was not less than his. If, then, that friend demand why Brutus rose against Cæsar, this is my answer: Not that I loved Cæsar less, but that I loved Rome more. Had you rather Cæsar were living, and die all slaves, than that Cæsar were dead, to live all free men? As Cæsar loved me, I weep for him; as he was fortunate, I rejoice at it; as he was valiant, I honor him; but as he was ambitious, I slew him. There are tears for his love, joy for his fortune, honor for his valor, and death for his ambition. Who is here so base, that would be a bondman? If any, speak; for him have I offended. Who is here so rude, that would not be a Roman? If any, speak! for him have I offended. Who is here so vile, that will not love his country? If any, speak; for him have I offended. I pause for a reply. None? Then none have I offended. I have done no more to Cæsar than you shall do to Brutus. The question of his death is enrolled in the Capitol; his glory not extenuated, wherein he was worthy; nor his offences enforced, for which he suffered death. Here comes his body, mourned by Mark Antony, who, though he had no hand in his death, shall receive the benefit of his dying—a place in the commonwealth,—as which of you shall not? With this I depart: That, as I slew my best lover for the good of Rome, I have the same dagger for myself, when it shall please my country to need my death.

Hamlet's Soliloquy on Death

FROM HAMLET[1]

WILLIAM SHAKESPEARE

To be, or not to be: that is the question:
Whether 'tis nobler in the mind to suffer
The slings and arrows of outrageous fortune,
Or to take arms against a sea of troubles,
And by opposing end them? To die: to sleep;
No more: and, by a sleep to say we end
The heart-ache and the thousand natural shocks
That flesh is heir to, 'tis a consummation
Devoutly to be wish'd. To die, to sleep;
To sleep; perchance to dream: ay, there's the rub;
For in that sleep of death what dreams may come

[1] Act III, Scene i.

When we have shuffled off this mortal coil,
Must give us pause. There's the respect
That makes calamity of so long life;
For who would bear the whips and scorns of time,
The oppressor's wrong, the proud man's contumely,
The pangs of disprized love, the law's delay,
The insolence of office, and the spurns
That patient merit of the unworthy takes,
When he himself might his quietus make
With a bare bodkin? who would fardels bear,
To grunt and sweat under a weary life,
But that the dread of something after death,
The undiscover'd country from whose bourn
No traveller returns, puzzles the will,
And makes us rather bear those ills we have
Than fly to others that we know not of?
Thus conscience does make cowards of us all;
And thus the native hue of resolution
Is sicklied o'er with the pale cast of thought,
And enterprises of great pith and moment
With this regard their currents turn awry,
And lose the name of action.

Advice to the Players

FROM HAMLET [1]

WILLIAM SHAKESPEARE

Speak the speech, I pray you, as I pronounced it to you, trippingly on the tongue; but if you mouth it, as many of your players do, I had as lief the town-crier spoke my lines. Nor do not saw the air too much with your hand, thus, but use all gently; for in the very torrent, tempest, and, as I may say, the whirlwind of passion, you must acquire and beget a temperance that may give it smoothness. O, it offends me to the soul to hear a robustious periwig-pated fellow tear a passion to tatters, to very rags, to split the ears of the groundlings, who for the most part are capable of nothing but inexplicable dumb-shows and noise. I would have such a fellow whipped for o'erdoing Termagant; it out-herods Herod: pray you, avoid it. Be not too tame neither, but let your own discretion be your tutor: suit the action to the word; the word to the action; with this special observance, that you o'erstep not the modesty

[1] Act III, Scene ii.

of nature; for any thing so overdone is from the purpose of playing, whose end, both at the first and now, was and is, to hold, as 't were, the mirror up to nature; to show virtue her own feature, scorn her own image, and the very age and body of the time his form and pressure. Now this overdone, or come tardy off, though it make the unskilful laugh, cannot but make the judicious grieve; the censure of the which one must in your allowance o'erweigh a whole theatre of others. O, there be players that I have seen play, and heard others praise and that highly, not to speak it profanely, that, neither having the accent of Christians nor the gait of Christian, pagan, nor man, have so strutted and bellowed that I have thought some of nature's journeymen had made men and not made them well, they imitated humanity so abominably.

The Advice of Polonius

FROM HAMLET [1]

WILLIAM SHAKESPEARE

Give thy thoughts no tongue,
Nor any unproportion'd thought his act.
Be thou familiar, but by no means vulgar;
The friends thou hast, and their adoption tried,
Grapple them to thy soul with hoops of steel;
But do not dull thy palm with entertainment
Of each new-hatch'd, unfledg'd comrade. Beware
Of entrance to a quarrel, but being in,
Bear't that the opposed may beware of thee.
Give every man thine ear, but few thy voice;
Take each man's censure, but reserve thy judgment.
Costly thy habit as thy purse can buy,
But not express'd in fancy; rich, nor gaudy;
For the apparel oft proclaims the man,
And they in France of the best rank and station
Are most select and generous, chief in that.
Neither a borrower nor a lender be;
For loan oft loses both itself and friend,
And borrowing dulls the edge of husbandry.
This above all: to thine own self be true,
And it must follow, as the night the day,
Thou canst not then be false to any man.

[1] Act I, Scene iii.

Portia's Mercy Speech

FROM THE MERCHANT OF VENICE [1]

WILLIAM SHAKESPEARE

The quality of mercy is not strained;
It droppeth, as the gentle rain from heaven,
Upon the place beneath; it is twice blessed—
It blesseth him that gives, and him that takes.
'Tis mightiest in the mightiest: it becomes
The thronèd monarch better than his crown;
His sceptre shows the force of temporal power,
The attribute to awe and majesty,
Wherein doth sit the dread and fear of kings;
But mercy is above this sceptred sway,
It is enthronèd in the hearts of kings,
It is an attribute to God himself;
And earthly power doth then show likest God's
When mercy seasons justice. Therefore, Jew,
Though justice be thy plea, consider this—
That, in the course of justice none of us
Should see salvation: we do pray for mercy;
And that same prayer doth teach us all to render
The deeds of mercy. I have spoke thus much
To mitigate the justice of thy plea;
Which if thou follow, this strict court of Venice
Must needs give sentence 'gainst the merchant there.

Othello's Apology

FROM OTHELLO [2]

WILLIAM SHAKESPEARE

Most potent, grave, and reverend signiors,
My very noble and approved good masters,
That I have ta'en away this old man's daughter,
It is most true; true, I have married her:
The very head and front of my offending
Hath this extent, no more. Rude am I in my speech,
And little bless'd with the soft phrase of peace;

1 Act IV, Scene i.
2 Act I, Scene iii.

For since these arms of mine had seven years' pith,
Till now some nine moons wasted, they have used
Their dearest action in the tented field,
And little of this great world can I speak,
More than pertains to feats of broil and battle,
And therefore little shall I grace my cause
In speaking for myself. Yet, by your gracious patience,
I will a round unvarnish'd tale deliver
Of my whole course of love; what drugs, what charms,
What conjuration, and what mighty magic,—
For such proceeding I am charg'd withal,—
I won his daughter.

. . . . .

Her father loved me; oft invited me;
Still question'd me the story of my life,
From year to year,—the battles, sieges, fortunes,
That I have pass'd.
I ran it through, even from my boyish days,
To the very moment that he bade me tell it:
Wherein I spake of most disastrous chances,
Of moving accidents by flood and field,
Of hair-breadth scapes i' the imminent deadly breach,
Of being taken by the insolent foe
And sold to slavery, of my redemption thence
And portance in my travels' history:

. . . . .

This to hear
Would Desdemona seriously incline:
But still the house-affairs would draw her hence;
Which ever as she could with haste dispatch,
She'd come again, and with a greedy ear
Devour up my discourse: which I observing,
Took once a pliant hour, and found good means
To draw from her a prayer of earnest heart
That I would all my pilgrimage dilate,
Whereof by parcels she had something heard,
But not intentively: I did consent,
And often did beguile her of her tears,
When I did speak of some distressful stroke
That my youth suffer'd. My story being done,

She gave me for my pains a world of sighs:
She swore, in faith,'twas strange, 'twas passing strange,
'Twas pitiful, 'twas wondrous pitiful:
She wish'd she had not heard it, yet she wish'd
That heaven had made her such a man: she thank'd me,
And bade me, if I had a friend that loved her,
I should but teach him how to tell my story,
And that would woo her. Upon this hint I spake:
She loved me for the dangers I had pass'd;
And I lov'd her that she did pity them.
This only is the witchcraft I have used.

He Jests at Scars

FROM ROMEO AND JULIET [1]

WILLIAM SHAKESPEARE

ROMEO: He jests at scars, that never felt a wound.
(JULIET *appears above at a window.*)
But, soft! what light through yonder window breaks?
It is the east, and Juliet is the sun.
Arise, fair sun, and kill the envious moon,
Who is already sick and pale with grief,
That thou, her maid, art far more fair than she:
Be not her maid, since she is envious;
Her vestal livery is but sick and green,
And none but fools do wear it: cast it off.
It is my lady; O! it is my love!
O! that she knew she were!
She speaks, yet she says nothing: what of that?
Her eye discourses, I will answer it.—
I am too bold, 't is not to me she speaks:
Two of the fairest stars in all the heaven,
Having some business, do entreat her eyes
To twinkle in their spheres till they return.
What if her eyes were there, they in her head?
The brightness of her cheek would shame those stars,
As daylight doth a lamp; her eyes in heaven
Would through the airy region stream so bright
That birds would sing and think it were not night.

[1] Act II, Scene ii.

PART VII

Dramatic Monologues

My Last Duchess

ROBERT BROWNING

That's my last Duchess painted on the wall,
Looking as if she were alive. I call
That piece a wonder, now: Fra Pandolf's hands
Worked busily a day, and there she stands.
Will't please you sit and look at her? I said
"Fra Pandolf" by design: for never read
Strangers like you that pictured countenance,
The depth and passion of its earnest glance,
But to myself they turned (since none puts by
The curtain I have drawn for you, but I)
And seemed as they would ask me, if they durst,
How such a glance came there; so, not the first
Are you to turn and ask thus. Sir, 't was not
Her husband's presence only, called that spot
Of joy into the Duchess' cheek: perhaps
Fra Pandolf chanced to say "Her mantle laps
Over my lady's wrist too much," or "Paint
Must never hope to reproduce the faint
Half-flush that dies along her throat:" such stuff
Was courtesy, she thought, and cause enough
For calling up that spot of joy.
  She had a heart—how shall I say?—too soon made glad,
Too easily impressed; she liked whate'er
She looked on, and her looks went everywhere.
Sir, 't was all one! My favour at her breast,
The dropping of the daylight in the West,
The bough of cherries some officious fool
Broke in the orchard for her, the white mule

She rode with round the terrace—all and each
Would draw from her alike the approving speech,
Or blush, at least. She thanked men,—good! but thanked
Somehow—I know not how—as if she ranked
My gift of a nine-hundred-years-old name
With anybody's gift. Who'd stoop to blame
This sort of trifling? Even had you skill
In speech—(which I have not)—to make your will
Quite clear to such an one; and say, "Just this
Or that in you disgusts me; here you miss,
Or there exceed the mark"—and if she let
Herself be lessoned so, nor plainly set
Her wits to yours, forsooth, and made excuse,
—E'en then would be some stooping; and I choose
Never to stoop.
  Oh sir, she smiled, no doubt,
Whene'er I passed her; but who passed without
Much the same smile? This grew; I gave commands;
Then all smiles stopped together.
  There she stands
As if alive. Will 't please you rise? We'll meet
The company below, then, I repeat,
The Count your master's known munificence
Is ample warrant that no just pretence
Of mine for dowry will be disallowed;
Though his fair daughter's self, as I avowed
At starting, is my object. Nay, we'll go
Together down, sir. Notice Neptune, though,
Taming a sea-horse, thought a rarity,
Which Claus of Innsbruck cast in bronze for me!

The Patriot

An Old Story

ROBERT BROWNING

It was roses, roses, all the way,
  With myrtle mixed in my path like mad:
The house-roofs seemed to heave and sway,
  The church-spires flamed, such flags they had,
A year ago on this very day.

The air broke into a mist with bells,
  The old walls rocked with the crowd and cries.
Had I said, "Good folk, mere noise repels—
  But give me your sun from yonder skies!"
They had answered, "And afterward, what else?"

Alack, it was I who leaped at the sun
  To give it my loving friends to keep!
Naught man could do, have I left undone:
  And you see my harvest, what I reap
This very day, now a year is run.

There's nobody on the house-tops now—
  Just a palsied few at the windows set;
For the best of the sight is, all allow,
  At the Shambles' Gate—or, better yet,
By the very scaffold's foot, I trow.

I go in the rain, and, more than needs,
  A rope cuts both my wrists behind;
And I think, by the feel, my forehead bleeds,
  For they fling, whoever has a mind,
Stones at me for my year's misdeeds.

Thus I entered, and thus I go!
  In triumphs, people have dropped down dead.
"Paid by the world, what dost thou owe
  Me?"—God might question; now instead,
'Tis God shall repay: I am safer so.

Mia Carlotta [1]

T. A. DALY

Giuseppe, da barber, ees greata for "mash,"
He gotta da bigga, da blacka mustache,
Good clo'es and good styla an' playnta good cash.

W'enevra Giuseppe ees walk on da street,
Da people dey talka, "how nobby! how neat!
How softa da handa, how smalla da feet."

[1] From *Selected Poems of T. A. Daly.* By permission of Harcourt, Brace and Company, Inc.

He raisa hees hat an' he shaka hees curls,
An' smila weeth teetha so shiny like pearls;
O! many da heart of da seely young girls
He gotta.
Yes, playnta he gotta—
But notta
Carlotta!

Giuseppe, da barber, he maka da eye,
An' lika da steam engine puffa an' sigh,
For catcha Carlotta w'en she ees go by.

Carlotta she walks weeth nose in da air,
An' look through Giuseppe weeth far-away stare,
As eef she no see dere ees som'body dere.

Giuseppe, da barber, he gotta da cash,
He gotta da clo'es and da bigga mustache,
He gotta da seely young girls for da "mash,"
But notta—
You bat my life, notta--
Carlotta.
I gotta!

APPENDIX I

Novels Suitable for Readings

Allen, Hervey	*Action at Aquila; Anthony Adverse*
Allen, James Lane	*A Kentucky Cardinal*
Bachellor, Irving	*A Light in the Clearing; A Man for the Ages*
Benet, Stephen V.	*The Devil and Daniel Webster*
Benson, Sally	*Junior Miss*
Bowman, Peter	*Beach Red*
Bromfield, Louis	*Green Bay Tree*
Buck, Pearl	*The Good Earth; A House Divided*
Burress, John	*Little Mule*
Cather, Willa	*Lucy Gayheart; My Antonia; The Professor's House*
Churchill, Winston	*The Crisis*
Coatsworth, Elizabeth	*The Cat Who Went to Heaven*
Cobb, Irvin S.	*The Judge Priest Stories*
Cronin, A. J.	*The Citadel; The Green Years*
Day, Clarence	*God and My Father*
Deeping, Warwick	*Sorrel and Son; The Ten Commandments*
Dickens, Charles	*David Copperfield; Pickwick; Tale of Two Cities*
Douglas, Lloyd C.	*Green Light; Magnificent Obsession; Precious Jeopardy; The Big Fisherman; The Robe*
Eliot, George	*The Mill on the Floss; Silas Marner*
Ferber, Edna	*Cimarron; Show Boat; The Great Son*
Flannery, Lewis	*Brooks Too Broad for Leaping; Suns Go Down*

Attention is called to the condensations of current best sellers in such magazines as *Ladies' Home Journal, Omnibook,* and *Reader's Digest.*

Flavin, Martin	*Journey in the Dark*
Fontaine, Robert	*A Happy Time*
Gale, Zona	*Birth*
Garland, Hamlin	*Son of the Middle Border*
Hardy, Thomas	*The Return of the Native*
Gilbreth, F. B., and Ernestine Cary	*Cheaper by the Dozen*
Hardy, Thomas	*The Return of the Native*
Hemingway, Ernest	*Farewell to Arms; The Old Man and the Sea*
Hilton, James	*And Now Goodbye; Goodbye, Mr. Chips; Lost Horizon; The Story of Dr. Wassell*
Hough, Emerson	*The Covered Wagon; The Mississippi Bubble*
Hutchinson, A. S. M.	*If Winter Comes*
James, Marquis	*The Cherokee Strip*
Marquand, John P.	*B. F.'s Daughter; Point of No Return; So Little Time*
Maugham, W. Somerset	*The Maugham Reader*
Nathan, Robert	*Journey of Tapiola; The Portrait of Jennie*
Otis, James	*Toby Tyler*
Priestley, J. B.	*The Good Companions*
Rawlings, Marjorie Kinnan	*The Yearling*
Rice, Alice Hegan	*Mr. Opp; Mrs. Wiggs of the Cabbage Patch*
Saroyan, William	*My Name Is Aram*
Skinner, Cornelia Otis	*Our Hearts Were Young and Gay*
Spence, Hartzell	*One Foot in Heaven*
Steinbeck, John	*Cannery Row; East of Eden; Grapes of Wrath; Tortilla Flat; The Wayward Bus*
Suckow, Ruth	*The Folks*
Swinnerton, Frank	*Nocturne*
Van Dyke, Henry	*The Story of the Other Wise Man*
Walpole, Hugh	*Jeremy*
Wells, H. G.	*Tono Bungay*
Wolfe, Thomas	*You Can't Go Home Again*
Wouk, Herman	*The Caine Mutiny*

APPENDIX II

Plays Suitable for Readings

Anderson, Maxwell	*Anne of a Thousand Days; Both Your Houses; Elizabeth the Queen*
Anouilh, Jean	*Antigone*
Balderston, John	*Berkeley Square*
Barker, Granville	*Prunella*
Barrie, James M.	*Dear Brutus; Quality Street; The Admirable Crichton; The Will*
Beach, Lewis	*The Clod; The Goose Hangs High*
Besier, Rudolph	*The Barretts of Wimpole Street*
Bulwer-Lytton, Edward	*Richelieu*
Carroll, Paul Vincent	*Shadow and Substance*
Cohan, George M.	*A Prince There Was*
Congreve, William	*The Way of the World*
Connelly, Marc	*Green Pastures*
Davis, Owen	*Icebound*
Day, Clarence	*Life with Father*
Drinkwater, John	*Abraham Lincoln*
Eaton, Walter Prichard	*Twelve One-Act Plays*
Eliot, T. S.	*The Cocktail Party*
Ferber, Edna, and George Kaufman	*Minick; The Royal Family*
Feris, Walter	*Death Takes a Holiday*
Franken, Rose	*Another Language*
Gale, Zona	*Miss Lulu Bett*
Galsworthy, John	*Escape; Justice; The Pigeon; The Silver Box*
Glaspell, Susan	*Alison's House*
Goldsmith, Oliver	*She Stoops to Conquer*
Green, Paul	*In Abraham's Bosom*
Hankin, St. John	*The Cassilis Engagement*
Hart, Moss	*Winged Victory*
Hart, Moss, and George Kaufman	*You Can't Take It with You*
Hodges, H., and T. W. Percival	*Grumpy*

Howard, Sidney	*The Late Christopher Bean; The Silver Cord; They Knew What They Wanted*
Hughes, Hatcher	*Hell-bent for Heaven*
Ibsen, Henrik	*Hedda Gabler; The Doll's House*
Inge, William	*Come Back, Little Sheba*
Jeffers, Robinson	*Medea*
Jerome, Jerome K.	*The Passing of the Third Floor Back*
Kaufman, George, and Edna Ferber	*Dinner at Eight*
Kingsley, Sidney	*Darkness at Noon; Detective Story; Men in White*
Martin, A. L.	*Smilin' Through*
Masefield, John	*Tragedy of Nan*
McCullers, Carson	*The Member of the Wedding*
Millay, Edna St. Vincent . . .	*The King's Henchman*
Miller, Arthur	*All My Sons; Death of a Salesman*
O'Neill, Eugene	*Anna Christie; Beyond the Horizon; Ile; Strange Interlude; The Hairy Ape*
Osborn, Paul	*On Borrowed Time*
Pollock, Channing	*The Fool*
Rice, Elmer	*Counsellor at Law; Street Scene*
Shakespeare, William	*As You Like It; Hamlet; Julius Caesar; Macbeth; Merchant of Venice; Much Ado About Nothing; Taming of the Shrew; The Tempest; Twelfth Night*
Shaw, George Bernard	*Candida; The Devil's Disciple*
Sheridan, Richard B.	*The Rivals; The School for Scandal*
Sheriff, R. C.	*Journey's End*
Sherwood, Robert	*Idiot's Delight; The Petrified Forest*
Sierra, G. Martinez	*The Kingdoms of God*
Smith, Winchell	*Lightnin'*
Sophocles	*Antigone*
Tarkington, Booth	*Clarence; Seventeen*
Underhill, J. G.	*The Cradle Song*
Van Druten, John	*Young Woodley; I Remember Mama*
Webster, Jean	*Daddy Long Legs*

Wilde, Oscar . . . . *The Importance of Being Earnest*
Wilder, Thornton . . . . . . *Our Town*
Williams, Jesse Lynch . . . . *Why Marry?*
Williams, Tennessee . . . . . *A Streetcar Named Desire; The Glass Menagerie*
Zangwill, Israel . . . . . . *The Melting Pot*

APPENDIX III

Suggested Reading in the Field of Oral Reading

Abercrombie, Lascelles, *The Theory of Poetry* (New York: Harcourt, Brace and Company, 1926).

Allen, G. W., *American Prosody* (New York: American Book Company, 1935).

Andrews, C. E., *The Writing and Reading of Verse* (New York: D. Appleton and Company, 1929).

Barbe, Waitman, *Great Poems Interpreted* (New York: Hinds, Noble & Eldrege, 1914).

Bates, Gladys deSylvia, and Helena Kay, *Literature for Interpretation* (Boston: Expression Company, 1939).

Boleslavski, Richard, *Acting: The First Six Lessons* (New York: Theatre Arts, Inc., 1933).

Chase, Stuart, *Power of Words* (New York: Harcourt, Brace and Company, 1954).

Crafton, Allen, and Jessica Royer, *Self Expression Through the Spoken Word* (New York: Thomas Y. Crowell Company, 1928).

Crocker, C., V. Fields, and W. Broomall, *Taking the Stage* (New York: Pitman Publishing Corporation, 1939).

Cunningham, C. C., *Literature as a Fine Art* (New York: The Ronald Press Company, 1941).

Cunningham, C. C., *Making Words Come Alive* (Dubuque, Iowa: Wm. C. Brown, 1951).

Curry, S. S., *Imagination and Dramatic Instinct* (Boston: The Expression Company, 1896).

Daniels, Earl, *The Art of Reading Poetry* (New York: Farrar & Rinehart, Inc., 1941).

Dolman, John, Jr., *The Art of Play Production* (New York: Harper & Brothers, 1928).

Dudley, Louise, *The Study of Literature* (Boston: Houghton Mifflin Company, 1928).

Eastman, Max, *The Enjoyment of Poetry* (New York: Charles Scribner's Sons, 1918).

———, *Art and the Life of Action* (New York: Alfred A. Knopf, 1934).

Flesch, Rudolf, *The Art of Plain Talk* (New York: Harper & Brothers, 1946).

Fogerty, Elsie, *The Speaking of English Verse* (New York: E. P. Dutton Company, 1923).

Franklin, Miriam A., *Rehearsal,* 3rd ed. (New York: Prentice-Hall, 1950).

Hayakawa, S. I., *Language in Thought and Action* (New York: Harper & Brothers, 1949).

Herendeen, Jane, *Speech Quality and Interpretation* (New York: Harper & Brothers, 1946).

Hillyer, Robert, *First Principles of Verse* (Boston: The Writer, Inc., 1950).

Jackson, Holbrook, *The Reading of Books* (New York: Charles Scribner's Sons, 1947).

Krapp, George Philip, *Pronunciation of Standard English in America* New York: Oxford University Press, 1919).

Lee, Irving J., *Language Habits in Human Affairs* (New York: Harper & Brothers, 1943).

———, *The Language of Wisdom and Folly* (New York: Harper & Brothers, 1949).

Millett, Fred B., *Reading Poetry* (New York: Harper & Brothers, 1950).

Ryerson, Florence, and Colin Clements, *First Person Singular: A Book of New Monologues* (New York: Samuel French, Inc., 1938).

Santayana, George, *The Interpretation of Poetry* (New York: Charles Scribner's Sons, 1936).

Selden, Samuel, *A Player's Handbook* (New York: F. S. Crofts & Company, 1934).

Stageberg, Norman C., and Wallace L. Anderson, *Poetry as Experience* (New York: American Book Company, 1952).

Tallcott, Rollo, *Acting and Public Speaking* (Indianapolis: Dobbs-Merrill Company, 1922).

Thomas, Wright, and Stuart Gerry Brown, *Reading Poems* (New York: Oxford University Press, 1941).

Thonsson, Lester, and Elizabeth Fatherson, *Bibliography of Speech Education* (New York: H. W. Wilson Company, 1939).

Walpole, Hugh R., *Semantics, The Nature of Words and Their Meanings* (New York: W. W. Norton & Company, 1941).

APPENDIX IV

Suggested Reading in Radio and Television

Abbot, Waldo, *Handbook of Broadcasting* (New York: McGraw-Hill Book Company, 1950).

Barnhart, Lyle D., *Radio and Television Announcing* (New York: Prentice-Hall, Inc., 1953).

Bretz, Rudy, *Techniques of Television Production* (New York: McGraw-Hill Book Company, 1953).

Chester, Giraud, and Garnet R. Garrison, *Radio and Television: An Introduction* (New York: Appleton-Century-Crofts, Inc., 1950).

Ewbank, Henry L., and Sherman P. Lawton, *Broadcasting Project: Radio and Television* (New York: Harper & Brothers, 1953).

Greene, Robert, *Television Writing* (New York: Harcourt, Brace and Company, 1952).

Levenson, William B., and Edward Stasheff, *Teaching Through Radio and Television* (New York: Rinehart & Co., 1952).

Lindsley, Charles F., *Radio and Television Communication* (New York: McGraw-Hill Book Company, 1953).

Phillips, David C., John M. Grogan, and Earl H. Ryan, *Introduction to Radio and Television* (New York: The Ronald Press Company, 1954).

Seipman, Charles A., *Radio, Television, and Society* (New York: Oxford University Press, 1950).

Waller, Judith C., *Radio the Fifth Estate* (Boston: Houghton Mifflin Co., 1950).

Wentworth, Harold, *American Dialect Dictionary* (New York: The Thomas Y. Crowell Company, 1944).

Wylie, Max, *Radio and Television Writing* (New York: Rinehart & Co., 1950).

APPENDIX V

Suggested Reading in the Field of Choral Reading

Abney, Louise, *Choral Speaking Arrangements for High Schools* (Boston: Expression Company, 1937).

De Banke, Cécile, *The Art of Choral Speaking* (Boston: Baker's Plays, 1937).

Deplitch, Edith Martha, *Poems of Fun and Fancy* (Boston: Expression Company, 1942).

DeWitt, M. E., *Lilts for Fun; Let Us Recite Together; Choice Recitation with Group Movement* (Boston: Expression Company, 1934).

———, and others, *Practical Methods in Choral Speaking* (Boston: Expression Company, 1935).

Drew, Alfred, and Robinson Barry, *A Commentary on Prose and Verse Speaking* (Boston: Baker's Plays, 1935).

Enfield, Gertrude, *Verse Choir Technique* (Boston: Expression Company, 1937).

Gullan, Marjorie, *Choral Speaking* (London: Methuen & Company, Ltd., 1931).

———, *The Speech Choir* (New York: Harper & Brothers, 1937).

Hamm, Agnes Curran, *Choral Speaking Techniques* (Milwaukee: Tower Press, 1941).

Hicks, Helen G., *The Reading Chorus* (New York: Noble and Noble, 1939).

Keefe, Mildred Jones, *Choric Interludes* (Boston: Expression Company, 1942).

Keppie, Elizabeth, *The Teaching of Choric Speech* (Boston: Expression Company, 1931).

———, and others, *Speech Improvement Through Choral Speaking* (Boston: Expression Company, 1942).

Newton, Muriel B., *The Unit Plan for Choral Reading* (Boston: Expression Company, 1938).

Nichols, Wallace B., *The Speaking of Poetry* (Boston: Expression Company, 1937).

Rasmussen, Carrie, *Choral Speaking for Speech Improvement* (Elementary School) (Boston: Expression Company, 1939).

Rehner, Herbert Adrian, *The Dramatic Use of Oral Interpretation and Choral Speaking* (Chicago: Bruce-Howard, 1951).

Robinson, Marion P., and others, *Poetry Arranged for the Speaking Choir* (Boston: Expression Company, 1936).

———, *Poetry for Men to Speak Chorally* (Boston: Expression Company, 1939).

———, *Poetry for Women to Speak Chorally* (Boston: Expression Company, 1940).

Sutton, Vida R., *Seeing and Hearing America* (Boston: Expression Company, 1936).

Swann, Mona, *An Approach to Choral Speech* (Boston: Expression Company, 1934).

———, *Many Voices,* Parts I and II (Boston: Expression Company, 1934).

APPENDIX VI

Suggested Reading in the History of Oral Reading

Perusal of the following books will give a comprehensive view of the evolution in attitude toward Oral Reading from 1828 to the present.

Babcock, M. M., *Handbook for Teachers of Interpretation* (Chicago: University Publishing Company, 1930).

Bassett, L. E., *Handbook of Oral Reading* (Boston: Houghton Mifflin Company, 1917).

Boardman, Gail, *Oral Communication of Literature* (New York: Prentice-Hall, Inc., 1952).

Clark, S. H., *Interpretation of the Printed Page* (Chicago: Row-Peterson Company, 1898).

———, and Babcock, M. M., *Interpretation of the Printed Page,* Rev. Ed. (New York: Prentice-Hall, 1940).

Cumnock, R. M., *Choice Readings* (With Elocutionary Advice) (Chicago: A. C. McClurg, 1898).

Curry, S. S., *Lessons in Vocal Expression* (Boston: Expression Company, 1895).

Delaumosne, L., and Arnaud, A., *The Desarte System* (New York: E. S. Werner, 1887).

Emerson, Charles W., *Psycho-Vox, or the Emerson System of Voice Culture* (Boston: Emerson College, 1903).

Fulton, R. I., and T. S. Trueblood, *Practical Elocution* (Boston: Ginn and Company, 1893).

Hamill, S. S., *New Science of Elocution* (New York: Phillips, Hunt, 1886).

Hollister, R. D. T., *Literature for Oral Interpretation* (Ann Arbor, Michigan: Wahr, 1929).

Johnson, Gertrude E., *Modern Literature for Oral Interpretation* (New York: D. Appleton-Century Company, 1920).

———, *Dialects for Oral Interpretation* (New York: D. Appleton-Century Company, 1922).

———, *Studies in the Art of Interpretation* (New York: D. Appleton-Century Company, 1940).

Kerfoot, J. B., *How to Read* (Boston: Houghton Mifflin Company, 1916).

Lee, Charlotte I., *Oral Interpretation* (New York: Houghton Mifflin Company, 1952).

Lowrey, Sara, and Johnson, Gertrude E., *Interpretative Reading* (Techniques and Selections), Rev. Ed. (New York: D. Appleton-Century Company, 1953).

McLean, Margaret Prendergast, *Oral Interpretation of Literary Forms* (New York: E. P. Dutton and Company, 1936).

Murdoch, James E., *Analytic Elocution* (Cincinnati: Van Antwerp, Bragg, 1884).

Parrish, W. M., *Reading Aloud,* 3rd ed. (New York: The Ronald Press, 1953).

Phillips, Arthur Edward, *The Tone System* (Chicago: The Newton Company, 1909).

Robb, Margaret, *The Teaching of Oral Interpretation of Literature in the Colleges and Universities of the United States* (New York: H. M. Wilson Company, 1941).

Rush, James, *The Philosophy of the Human Voice* (Philadelphia: The Library Company, 1828).

Russel, William, *Orthophony or Vocal Culture* (Boston: Houghton Mifflin Company, 1882).

Shoemaker, J. W., *Practical Elocution* (Philadelphia: National School of Elocution, 1883).

Talcott, R. A., *Art of Acting and Public Reading* (Indianapolis: Bobbs-Merrill Company, 1922).

Tassin, Algernon, *Oral Study of Literature* (New York: F. S. Crofts & Company, 1930).

Tresidder, Argus, *Reading to Others* (Chicago: Scott, Foresman and Company, 1940).

Woolbert, Charles H., and Severina E. Nelson, *The Art of Interpretative Speech,* 3rd ed. (New York: F. S. Crofts & Company, 1945).

APPENDIX VII

Suggested Reading in the Field of Literary Criticism

Abbott, Charles D., *Poets at Work* (New York: Harcourt, Brace & Company, 1948).

Abercrombie, Lascelles, *The Theory of Poetry* (New York: Harcourt, Brace & Company, 1926).

Alden, Raymond M., *Critical Essays of the Nineteenth Century* (New York: Charles Scribner's Sons, 1921).

Anderson, Maxwell, *The Basis of Artistic Creation* (New Brunswick: Rutgers University Press, 1942).

Atkins, J. W. H., *Literary Criticism in Antiquity* (Cambridge, England: Cambridge University Press, 1934).

Bradley, A. C., *Oxford Lecture on Poetry* (New York: The Macmillan Company, 1926).

Brooks, Cleanth, *The Well Wrought Urn* (New York: Reynal & Hitchcock, 1947).

Buck, Philo Melvin, *Literary Criticism* (New York: Harper & Brothers, 1930).

Burke, Kenneth, *The Philosophy of Form* (Baton Rouge: Louisiana State University Press, 1941).

Coleridge, S. T., *Biographia Literaria,* ed. by Shawcross (Oxford: Oxford University Press, 1907).

Colum, Mary M., *From These Roots* (New York: Charles Scribner's Sons, 1937).

Devoto, Bernard A., *The Literary Fallacy* (Boston: Little, Brown & Company, 1944).

Eastman, Max, *The Literary Mind* (New York: Charles Scribner's Sons, 1931).

Eliot, T. S., *The Sacred Wood* (London: Methuen & Co., 1928).

Erskine, John, *The Literary Discipline* (New York: Duffield & Company, 1923).

Ghiselin, Brewster, *The Creative Process,* A Symposium (Berkeley: University of California Press, 1952).

Gilbert, Allan H., *Literary Criticism, Plato to Dryden* (New York: American Book Company, 1940).

Hamilton, Rostrevor, *Poetry and Contemplation* (Cambridge, England: Cambridge University Press, 1937).

Johnson, C. F., *Elements of Literary Criticism* (New York: Harper & Brothers, 1898).

Jordan, E., *Essays in Criticism* (Chicago: University of Chicago Press, 1952).

Langer, Susanne K., *Feeling and Form* (London: Routledge & Kegan Paul Limited, 1953).

Levin, Harry, *Perspectives of Criticism* (Cambridge: Harvard University Press, 1949).

Lowes, John Livingston, *Essays in Appreciation* (Boston: Houghton Mifflin Company, 1936).

Morris, Charles, *Signs, Language and Behavior* (New York: Prentice-Hall, Inc., 1946).

Peyre, Henry, *Writers and Their Critics* (Ithaca: Cornell University Press, 1944).

Poe, Edgar Allan, *Literary Criticism* (New York: Colonial Company, 1903).

Pound, Ezra, *ABC of Reading* (New Haven: Yale University Press, 1934).

Richards, I. A., *Practical Criticism, A Study of Literary Judgment* (New York: Harcourt, Brace & Company, 1929).

———, *Principles of Literary Criticism* (New York: Harcourt, Brace & Company, 1930).

Saintsbury, George, *Loci Critici* (New York: Ginn and Company, 1903).

Scott, Fred Newton, *Papers* (Chicago: University of Chicago Press, 1929).

Spender, Stephen, *World Within World* (London: Hamish Hamilton, 1951).

Spingarn, J. E., *Creative Criticism and Other Essays* (New York: Harcourt, Brace and Company, 1931).

Stallman, R. W., *Critiques & Essays in Criticism* (New York: The Ronald Press, 1949).

Wells, Henry, *The Judgment of Literature* (New York: W. W. Norton Company, 1928).

Wilson, Edmund, *The Intent of the Critic* (Princeton: Princeton University Press, 1941).

Zabel, Morton Dauwen, *Literary Opinion in America,* Rev. Ed. (New York: Harper & Brothers, 1951).

APPENDIX VIII

Suggested Cuttings from Shakespeare

Mark Antony's Oration . . .	*Julius Caesar,* Act III, Scene ii
Speech of Brutus in the Forum	*Julius Caesar,* Act III, Scene ii
Mark Antony on Caesar's Body	*Julius Caesar,* Act III, Scene i
Cassius Instigating Brutus . .	*Julius Caesar,* Act I, Scene ii
Marullus to the People . . .	*Julius Caesar,* Act I, Scene i
Brutus to Cassius	*Julius Caesar,* Act I, Scene ii
Brutus to Cassius	*Julius Caesar,* Act IV, Scene iii
Tamora's Plea for Her Son . .	*Titus Andronicus,* Act I, Scene i
Soliloquy of Lady Macbeth . .	*Macbeth,* Act I, Scene v
The Instigation Scene . . .	*Macbeth,* Act I, Scene vii
After the Murder	*Macbeth,* Act II, Scene ii
Lady Macbeth to Macbeth . .	*Macbeth,* Act III, Scene ii
Othello's Defense	*Othello,* Act I, Scene iii
Othello's Farewell to Happiness	*Othello,* Act III, Scene ii
Othello and Iago	*Othello,* Act III, Scene iii
Polonius to Laertes	*Hamlet,* Act I, Scene iii
Hamlet's Self-Condemnation .	*Hamlet,* Act II, Scene ii
Hamlet's Soliloquy on Death .	*Hamlet,* Act III, Scene i
Hamlet's Advice to the Players	*Hamlet,* Act III, Scene ii
Hamlet and His Mother . . .	*Hamlet,* Act III, Scene iv
Hamlet and the Ghost . . .	*Hamlet,* Act I, Scene v
Hamlet and Ophelia	*Hamlet,* Act III, Scene i
Queen Mab	*Romeo and Juliet,* Act I, Scene iv
Romeo to Juliet	*Romeo and Juliet,* Act II, Scene ii
Romeo and the Friar	*Romeo and Juliet,* Act II, Scene iii
Juliet and the Nurse	*Romeo and Juliet,* Act II, Scene v
Juliet and the Nurse	*Romeo and Juliet,* Act II, Scene ii
Coriolanius' Scorn of the People	*Coriolanus,* Act II, Scene ii
Cominius on Coriolanus . . .	*Coriolanus,* Act II, Scene ii

NESTOR ON ADVERSITY	*Troilus and Cressida,* Act I, Scene iii
ULYSSES ON THE GRECIAN FAILURE	*Troilus and Cressida,* Act III, Scene iii
ULYSSES ON MAN'S FORGETFULNESS	*Troilus and Cressida,* Act I, Scene iii
APPEAL OF QUEEN KATHERINE .	*Henry VIII,* Act II, Scene iv
WOLSEY ON HIS FALL	*Henry VIII,* Act III, Scene ii
CRANMER'S PROPHECY	*Henry VIII,* Act V, Scene v
BASSANIO AND THE CASKETS . .	*The Merchant of Venice,* Act III, Scene ii
LORENZO AND JESSICA	*The Merchant of Venice,* Act V, Scene i
PORTIA AND NERISSA	*The Merchant of Venice,* Act I, Scene ii
LAUNCELOT AND OLD GOBBO . .	*The Merchant of Venice,* Act III, Scene ii
SHYLOCK AND TUBAL	*The Merchant of Venice,* Act III, Scene i
TITANIA AND OBERON	*A Midsummer Night's Dream,* Act II, Scene i
PROSPERO ABJURES MAGIC . . .	*The Tempest,* Act V, Scene i
RICHARD'S FAITH	*Richard II,* Act III, Scene ii
RICHARD ON THE HOLLOWNESS OF POWER	*Richard II,* Act III, Scene ii
YORK ON BOLINGBROKE	*Richard II,* Act V, Scene ii
HOTSPUR'S FOP	*I Henry IV,* Act I, Scene iii
LADY PERCY'S CONCERN	*I Henry IV,* Act II, Scene iii
FALSTAFF ON HIS SOLDIERS . . .	*I Henry IV,* Act IV, Scene ii
KING HENRY ON SLEEP	*II Henry IV,* Act III, Scene i
THE KINGDOM OF THE BEES . .	*Henry V,* Act I, Scene ii
HENRY V BEFORE BARFLEUR . .	*Henry V,* Act III, Scene i
WARWICK AT BARNET	*III Henry VI,* Act V, Scene iv
GLOUCESTER'S SOLILOQUY . . .	*Richard III,* Act I, Scene i
THE DREAM OF CLARENCE . . .	*Richard III,* Act I, Scene iv
RICHARD'S DESPAIR	*Richard III,* Act V, Scene iii
RICHARD'S ADDRESS TO HIS SOLDIERS	*Richard III,* Act V, Scene iii
KATHERINE AND PETRUCHIO . .	*The Taming of the Shrew,* Act II, Scene i
ORLANDO AND ROSALIND	*As You Like It,* Act III, Scene ii
VIOLA AND THE CAPTAIN . . .	*Twelfth Night,* Act I, Scene ii

APPENDIX IX

Suggested Readings from the Bible[1]

I. The Twenty Great Short Stories of the Bible

The Bible is one of the greatest collections of short stories in the world. With *The Arabian Nights* and the *Decameron* it forms a literary heritage out of which the modern short story has developed. New Testament parables such as "The Good Samaritan" foreshadow the modern short story.

So rich is the Bible in literary treasure that any attempt to list the best stories in it leads to great differences of opinion. This list was compiled by James S. Stevens for his critical volume, *The English Bible:*

1. Joseph. Gen. 37–48.
2. Balaam and Balak. Num. 22–24.
3. The Capture of Jericho. Josh. 6.
4. The Wars of Gideon. Judg. 6–8.
5. Jepthah's Daughter. Judg. 11.
6. Samson. Judg. 14–16.
7. Ruth. (The whole book.)
8. David and Goliath. I Sam. 17.
9. David and Jonathan. I Sam. 18–20.
10. Elijah and the Prophets of Baal. I Kings 18.
11. Naboth's Vineyard. I Kings 21.
12. The Ascension of Elijah. II Kings 2.
13. Esther. (The whole book.)
14. The Three Hebrew Children. Dan. 3.
15. Daniel in the Lion's Den. Dan. 6.
16. Jonah. (The whole book.)
17. The Good Samaritan. Luke 10:25–37.
18. The Prodigal Son. Luke 15:11–32.
19. The Lame Man of Bethesda. John 5:1–9.
20. The Shipwreck of Paul. Acts 27.

[1] The student might enjoy reading Thomas H. Marsh, "Some Problems of Oral Bible Reading," *Quarterly Journal of Speech,* XXIII, 396.

II. Other Selections

1. Oration of Moses. Deut. 28.
2. The Great Arraignment. Isa. 1.
3. The Covenant with Death. Isa. 28.
4. The Destruction. Isa. 34.
5. The Restoration. Isa. 35.
6. The Sword of the Lord. Ezek. 21.
7. The Fall of Tyre. Ezek. 27.
8. The Sermon on the Mount. Matt. 5–7.
9. Paul Before Agrippa. Acts 26.
10. Charity. I Cor. 13.
11. The Argument for Resurrection. I Cor. 15.

APPENDIX X

Great Speeches for Oral Reading

Demosthenes	*On the Crown*
Cicero	*Second Oration Against Cataline*
Mirabeau	*Necker's Financial Policy*
Lord Chatham	*On American Affairs, May 30, 1777*
Edmund Burke	*On Conciliation with America*
Charles James Fox	*The American War*
William Pitt, The Younger . . .	*Abolition of the Slave Trade*
Thomas Erskine	*Defense of Stockdale*
Richard Brinsley Sheridan . . .	*Trial of Warren Hastings*
Daniel O'Connell	*Ireland Worth Dying For*
Henry Grattan	*A Declaration of Irish Right*
Oliver Cromwell	*At the Opening of First Protective Parliament*
Henry Brougham	*Parliamentary Reform*
Lord Chesterfield	*Against Licensing Gin Shops*
John Bright	*Free Trade*
Robespierre	*Against Granting the King a Trial*
William Wilberforce	*The British Slave Trade*
Bulwer-Lytton	*On the Crimean War*
Lord Macaulay	*Jewish Disabilities*
Sir Robert Peel	*On the Repeal of the Corn Laws*
William E. Gladstone	*Domestic and Foreign Affairs*
Lord Beaconsfield	*"Conservatism"*
Richard Cobden	*On the Corn Laws*
George Washington	*Farewell Address*
John Hancock	*The Boston Massacre*
Thomas Jefferson	*First Inaugural Address*
John Jay	*To the People of Great Britain*
Fisher Ames	*On the British Treaty*
Patrick Henry	*The Call to Arms*
Andrew Jackson	*Second Inaugural Address*

Alexander Hamilton	*Compromises of the Constitution*
Benjamin Franklin	*Dangers of a Salaried Bureaucracy*
Samuel Adams	*American Independence*
Henry Clay	*Sixty Years of Sectionalism*
Daniel Webster	*Reply to Hayne*
John C. Calhoun	*Compromise Measures*
Abraham Lincoln	*The Gettysburg Address*
Abraham Lincoln	*The Second Inaugural Address*
Abraham Lincoln	*Cooper Institute Address*
William Lloyd Garrison	*Encouragement to the Oppressed*
Rufus Choate	*The Age of the Pilgrims*
Edward Everett	*Character of Washington*
Wendell Phillips	*Murder of Lovejoy*
Stephen A. Douglas	*Speech at Freeport*
Robert G. Ingersoll	*The Liberty of Man, Woman and Child*
Theodore Parker	*The State of the Nation*
Henry Ward Beecher	*The Liverpool Address*
Charles Sumner	*The Crime Against Kansas*
Phillips Brooks	*Lord, Is It I?*
Henry W. Grady	*The New South*
William Jennings Bryan . . .	*The Cross of Gold*
Theodore Roosevelt	*The Muck-rakers*
Albert J. Beveridge	*The March of the Flag*
Eugene Debs	*On Receiving Sentence*
Woodrow Wilson	*The League of Nations*
William Edgar Borah	*Against the League of Nations*
Franklin D. Roosevelt	*The First Inaugural*
Adolph Hitler	*The Versailles Treaty*
Winston Churchill	*Blood, Sweat and Tears*

APPENDIX XI

Anthologies of Materials for Oral Reading

Adams, J. Donald, *The Treasure Chest* (New York: E. P. Dutton Company, Inc., 1946).

Angle, Paul M., *The Lincoln Reader* (New Brunswick, N.J.: Rutgers University Press, 1947).

Avon All-American Fiction Reader (New York: Avon Double Size Books, 1947).

Bates, Gladys DeSilva and Helena Kay, *Literature for Interpretation* (Boston: Expression Company, 1941).

Benet, Stephen Vincent, Selected Works of, 2 vols. (New York: Farrar and Rinehart, 1942).

Benet, W. R., and Conrad Aiken, *An Anthology of Famous British and American Poetry* (New York: Random House, 1945).

Brigance, W. N., *Classified Speech Models* (New York: F. S. Crofts, 1928).

Buck, Paul, and Gassner, John, *A Treasury of the Theatre* (New York: Simon & Schuster, 1940).

Burnett, Whit, ed., *This Is My Best* (New York: Dial Press, 1942).

Cerf, Bennett, *Sixteen Famous American Plays* (New York: Garden City Publishing Company, 1941).

Ciardi, John, *Mid-Century Poets* (New York: Twayne, 1950).

Clark, Thomas Curtis, ed., *Christ in Poetry* (New York: Association Press, 1952).

Cott, Ted, *Treasury of the Spoken Word* (New York: The Hermitage Press, 1949).

Compere, Moiree, ed., *Living Literature for Oral Interpretation* (New York: Appleton-Century-Crofts, 1949).

DeVries, Peter, *No, But I Saw the Movie* (Boston: Little, Brown & Company, 1952).

Felleman, Hazel, *The Best Loved Poems of the American People* (New York: Garden City Publishing Company, 1936).

Frankenburg, Lloyd, *Pleasure Dome* (New York: Houghton Mifflin Company, 1949). (This book has valuable bibliographies of principal American editions of many poets and of recordings.)

Fuess, Claude M., and Emory S. Basford, *Unseen Harvests* (New York: The Macmillan Company, 1947).

Gassner, John, *Best American Plays* (New York: Crown Publishers, Inc., 1952).

Glaspell, Susan, *Plays* (New York: Dodd, Mead and Company, 1931).

Herzberg, Max J., *This Is America* (New York: Pocket Books, Inc., 1951).

Kronenberger, Louis, *Reader's Companion* (New York: The Viking Press, 1945).

———, *Best Plays Series* (New York: Dodd, Mead & Company, Inc., annual).

Lowry, Howard, *An Oxford Anthology of English Poetry* (New York: Oxford University Press, 1940).

Luccock, Halford E., and Frances Brentano, *The Questing Spirit* (New York: Coward-McCann, Inc., 1947).

Maugham, W. Somerset, *Modern English and American Literature* (Philadelphia: The Blakiston Company, 1944).

Nichols, William, *Words to Live By* (New York: Simon & Schuster, 1948).

Pertwee, E. Guy, *More Scenes for Recital* (New York: Samuel French, 1947).

Quinn, Arthur Hobson, *Representative American Plays* (New York: Century Company, 1917).

Rodman, Selden, *100 American Poems* (New York: Penguin Signet Books, 1948).

Runyon, Damon, *Runyon First and Last* (Philadelphia: J. P. Lippincott Company, 1949).

Short, Raymond W., and Richard B. Sewell, *Short Stories for Study* (New York: Henry Holt and Company, 1941).

Smith, Logan Pearsall, *The Golden Shakespeare* (New York: The Macmillan Company, 1950).

Speare, M. E., *The Pocket Book of Short Stories* (New York: Pocket Books, Inc., 1946).

Stern, Philip Van Doren, ed., *A Pocket Book of Modern Short Stories* (New York: Pocket Books, Inc., 1943).

Stuber, Stanley I., *The Christian Reader* (New York: The Association Press, 1952).

Untermeyer, Louis, *Anthologies of British and American Poetry* (New York: Harcourt, Brace and Company, 1950).

Williams, Oscar, *A Little Treasury of Modern Poetry* (New York: Charles Scribner's Sons, 1950).

Woollcott, Alexander, *As You Were* (New York: Viking Press, 1943).

APPENDIX XII

Terms of Versification

SYLLABLE

A single or articulated vocal sound forming a word, or part of a word.

```
 /   x            x  /           /   x
pow/ er          de/ tail       Sun/ day
```

The syllable always contains a vowel sound, but not always consonants.

STRESS

Emphasis upon a certain syllable.

```
 /  x             x  /           /   x
pow er           de tail        Sun day
```

FOOT

The phonetic unit of a line of verse, consisting of two or more syllables.

```
 x    /     x   /     x    /       /      /  x  /
The lone/ and lev/ el sands/ stretch far/ a way.
```

The common kinds of feet are:

Iambic. Two syllables, the stress falling on the second.

```
 x    /     x    /     x   /     x   /    x  /
Till love/ and Fame/ to noth/ ing ness/ do sink
```

Anapestic. Three syllables, the stress falling on the third.

```
 x   x    /    x  x  /
And with God/ be the rest
```

Iambic and *anapestic* feet are said to be *rising* because the reader moves *toward* the stress.

Trochaic. Two syllables, the stress falling on the first.

```
 /   x   /   x   /   x   /
Life is/ but an/ emp ty/ dream.
```

Dactylic. Three syllables, the stress falling on the first.

```
   /    x   x     /     x   x    / x   x     /   x
Just  for  a/  hand  ful  of/  silver  he/  left  us,
```

Trochaic and *dactylic* feet are said to be *falling* because the reader moves *away from* the stress.

The *spondee* (//), two syllables, both stressed, and the *pyrrhic* (x x), two syllables, both unstressed, are mainly "substitutions" though now and then a line (or a rhythmical group) is characterized by these feet.

Spondaic.

```
 /    /      x     /      x     /      x      /        x    /
So  live/  that  when/  thy  sum/  mons  comes/  to  join
```

Pyrrhic.

```
  x     x      /      /       x     x      /     /      x    /
And  the/  firm  soul/  does  the/  pale  train/  de  fy
```

MEASURE (METER)

The pattern by which feet (of whatever kind) are arranged to form a line of verse. The common measures in English poems are:

Dimeter. Two feet to the line.

```
 x     /     x    /                      x    /    x    /
The light/ that lies                  The debt/ is paid,
 x   /    x     /                      x    /    x    /
In wo/ man's eyes.                    The ver/ dict said.
```

—RALPH WALDO EMERSON (1803–1882).

Trimeter. Three feet to the line.

```
x   /       x     /      x    /
A bird/ came down/ the walk:
 x   /     x    /    x  /
He did/ not know/ I saw;
```

—EMILY DICKINSON (1830–1886).

Tetrameter. Four feet to the line.

```
 x     /     x    /     x    /    x    /
Come live/ with me/ and be/ my love,
 x    /    x   /    x    /     x    /
And we/ will all/ the pleas/ ures prove.
```

—CHRISTOPHER MARLOWE (1564–1593).

Pentameter. Five feet to the line.

x / x / x / x / x /
'Were I/ as base/ as is/ the low/ ly plain,
x / x / x / x / x /
And you,/ my Love/ as high/ as heaven/ a bove,

—JOSHUA SYLVESTER (1563–1618).

Hexameter. Six feet to the line.
Septameter. Seven feet to the line.

CAESURA

Most long lines of poetry contain a pause somewhere near the middle. This is called the "caesura." Many four-stress lines have a caesura, and nearly all five- and six-stress lines have one; longer lines are likely to have more than one. This pause may be caused (1) by the punctuation of the line (a comma, most often), (2) by the thought, or (3) by the grammatical structure, such as the beginning of a new phrase or clause ("2" and "3" are likely to coincide).

If I/ have fal/tered // more or less
In my/ great task // of hap/ pi ness

—ROBERT LOUIS STEVENSON (1850–1894).

ENJAMBENT

Punctuation and thought also affect the end of the verse in a very important manner. If the line ends with a comma or a dash, we usually pause there in the reading. If the punctuation is a period or a semicolon, we make a decided pause, or a "full stop," in the reading. In either case, we say that the line is "end-stopped." But if there is no punctuation to cause a partial or a full stop at the end of the line, we say that it is "run-on," or *enjambed.* End-stopped lines are likely to be monotonous; enjambed ones less likely to tire the ear.

BREATH-SWEEP

The number of syllables pronounced with one breath between two pauses is called the breath-sweep. Enjambent prolongs the breath-sweep.

SOUND RECURRENCE

Besides the "metrical rhythms" there are also rhythms which depend upon the recurrence of similar sounds.

Masculine rime. If the rime involves only single syllables, it is called masculine rime.

Feminine rime. If the rime involves both an accented and an unaccented syllable, it is called a feminine rime. A line of iambic or anapestic feet with an extra unstressed syllable at the end is said to have a feminine ending, *singing, bringing.*

Double rime. If two accented syllables are involved (one of which may be a secondary accent), the rime is said to be "double."

Internal rime. If the rime-word occurs elsewhere than at the end of the line, it is called "internal rime."

Concealed rime. If the rime occurs at irregular intervals within the passage of poetry, it is called "concealed rime."

Alliteration. Recurrence of the same consonant sound or of vowel sounds initially in accented syllables of verse.

x / x / x / x / x /
The *p*lowman *h*omeward *p*lods *h*is *w*eary *w*ay

Assonance. A rhyming of one word with another in the accented vowel and those that follow, the consonants of the two words being unlike.

x / x / x / x /
And sh*o*wn n*o* gl*o*rious m*o*rning face.

Onomatopoeia. Use of a word whose sound suggests its sense, e.g., *buzz, kiss.*

The *moan* of doves in immemorial elms.

Blank Verse

Unrhymed iambic pentameter.

Alexandrine

Iambic hexameter with caesura after second, third, or fourth stress.

Free Verse

Irregular rhythms following no fixed metrical pattern.

Stanza

The arrangement of lines according to a fixed pattern, usually marked by end-rhyme.

The common stanza forms are:

Couplet. Stanza of two lines with end-rhyme.

Terza rima. Three-line stanzas rhyming *a b a,* in which the *b* rhyme becomes the *a* rhyme of the following stanza. *aba, bcb, cdc.*

Quatrain. Four-line stanza.

Ballad stanza. Quatrain of alternating four and three stress lines, rhyming *abcb* (sometimes *abab*).

Rhyme royal. Seven-line stanza of iambic pentameter, rhyming *ababbcc.*

Ottava rima. Eight-line stanza of iambic pentameter, rhyming *abababcc.*

Spenserian stanza. Nine-line iambic stanza of which the first eight are pentameter and the last is alexandrine, rhyming *ababbcbcc.*

Sonnet. A fixed verse form of Italian origin, consisting of fourteen lines, typically five-foot iambics, and treating, usually, a single emotion, sentiment, or reflection. Two standard types of sonnets varying in verse groupings and rhyming schemes, are recognized: (1) The Italian sonnet, also called the Petrarchan, or regular sonnet, in which the lines are grouped into an octave of two quatrains running on two rhymes (thus, *abba, abba*) and a sextet of two tercets on two or three rhymes, having more freedom of arrangement, but commonly running *cdc, dcd;* or *cde, cde.* (2) The English, Elizabethan, or Shakespearean sonnet, in which the lines are grouped into three quatrains and a couplet with rhyme scheme *abab, cdcd, efef, gg.* The Spenserian sonnet united the quatrains by interlacing the rhymes: *abab, bcbc, cdcd, ee.*

Rhetorical Rhythms

Sometimes the main rhythms in poetry cannot be analyzed by any of the methods which have been defined and described. This is true in the case of "parallelism," the main rhythmical principle of biblical poetry, Walt Whitman's verse, and much primitive poetry. Parallelism repeats similar thoughts. These repetitions affect the structure and sounds of the verse but it is impossible to scan these rhythms as is done in ordinary "metrical rhythms." Oratorical prose sometimes employs refrains, alliterations, and repetition of sentence structure, but these devices are not amenable to scanning as is poetry. But it is undeniable that these devices do help produce an oratorical rhythm.

APPENDIX XIII

The Notebook

Many teachers of Oral Reading require the student to keep a notebook as a record of the course. The written work and the oral work go hand in hand. These notebooks are called in periodically and checked for performance. The student may be required to write up one of the projects listed at the conclusion of each chapter in the book. The student may be required to do one project a week. He may also be asked to write up two book reports: one on another text in oral interpretation and another on literary criticism. Lists of these books are found in the appendices. But the chief purpose of the notebook is to record the analysis of the selections studied. When the student reads in class, he may hand the notebook to the instructor who will use it to make comments on the reading and to check the written work. Such a periodic check helps to keep the work from becoming slipshod.

In the analysis of a selection the following outline has been found useful in preparation for the platform. The paragraphs may be as long as necessary to cover the topic.[1]

1. Speaker
2. Audience
3. Occasion
4. Central idea
5. Climax
6. Key words and phrases
7. Paraphrases
8. Mood
9. Form
10. Is it a story? a ballad? a picture? an idea?

These ten points may be added to or subtracted from as the teacher or the student sees fit. But if the student will conscientiously answer these, he will have a fairly good grasp of the selection he is going to read.

[1] For another approach to analysis see Don Geiger, "A 'Dramatic' Approach to Interpretative Analysis," *Quarterly Journal of Speech,* XXXVIII, 189.

In order to show how this list of points may be utilized in the analysis of a poem, let us take Robert Frost's "Stopping by Woods on a Snowy Evening" and answer them in reference to that poem:

Stopping by Woods on a Snowy Evening [2]

ROBERT FROST

Whose woods these are I think I know.
His house is in the village though;
He will not see me stopping here
To watch his woods fill up with snow.

My little horse must think it queer
To stop without a farmhouse near
Between the woods and frozen lake
The darkest evening of the year.

He gives his harness bells a shake
To ask if there is some mistake.
The only other sound's the sweep
Of easy wind and downy flake.

The woods are lovely, dark and deep,
But I have promises to keep
And miles to go before I sleep,
And miles to go before I sleep.

Analysis

1. Speaker: Any nature lover.
2. Audience: He is talking to himself.
3. Occasion: Stopping in a woods on December 21.
4. Central Idea: The conflict between the beauty of nature and the duty of man is brought out in the poem.
5. Climax: The realization that there is a conflict between the joys of nature and the call of duty.
6. Key words and phrases: woods, snow, promises.
7. Paraphrases: "And miles to go before I sleep," is repeated for the second time. Is the speaker turning over in his mind what the

[2] From *The Collected Poems of Robert Frost* (New York: Henry Holt and Company). By permission.

promises are and what their significance is? Have these promises something to do with Christmas? The miles may be not geographical but psychological miles.

8. Mood: Quiet contemplation.
9. Form: Difficult rhyme scheme: *aaba; bbcb; ccdc; dddd.*
10. The poem is a picture.

The following analysis blank is suggested for students in the class to use in rating one another. This blank or a similar one [3] may be mimeographed by the teacher and distributed to the class. Then the ratings each student receives from his classmates can be pasted in his notebook. Check A, B, C, D, or F for each item.

I. Total Impression

	A	B	C	D	F
1. The reader was well prepared.					
2. The reader projected the central idea.					
3. The reader's interpretation was enjoyable.					
4. The reader was interested in the audience.					
5. The process of sharing was effective.					
6. The selection was suitable to audience and occasion.					

II. What I Heard

	A	B	C	D	F
1. The voice quality suited the selection.					
2. Vocal variety was employed to give meaning.					
3. Emphasis was brought out by the voice.					
4. Pauses were effectively employed.					
5. Change of pace aided the interpretation.					
6. The articulation was distinct.					
7. The voice reflected the mood of the selection.					
8. The reader was fluent.					
9. The reader was confident.					

[3] For another analysis blank see Clyde W. Dow, "A Literary Interpretation Analysis Blank," *Quarterly Journal of Speech,* XXV, 285. And for a philosophy of criticism the student is referred to S. S. Curry, "Criticism," in *Studies in the Art of Interpretation,* by Gertrude E. Johnson (New York: D. Appleton-Century Company, 1940). See also W. M. Parrish, *Reading Aloud* (New York: The Ronald Press Company, 1953) for an extensive list of criteria for the oral reader.

III. What I Saw

	A	B	C	D	F
1. The posture of the reader set the mood.					
2. The reader made us forget the book.					
3. The body was alive.					
4. The gestures aided the interpretation.					
5. Facial expression was adequate for the selection.					
6. Bodily movement suggested confidence.					

Here is another list of criteria which should aid the student to make a just appraisal of the good and bad points of a classmate's performance:

1. Did the reader read as if he were talking to you?
2. Did the reader pronounce his words correctly?
3. Did the reader seem to understand the meaning of the words?
4. Was the phrasing helpful to the understanding?
5. Were the right words emphasized so as to bring out the meaning?
6. Did the reader recognize the contrasts of the author?
7. Was the implication of the author clearly indicated?
8. Was the emphasis skillful?
9. Did the reader change his pace?
10. Was enough use made of the pause?
11. Did you get the mood the reader attempted to convey?
12. Did you agree with the attitude conveyed?
13. Did the reader seem to have the whole idea in mind?
14. Was the reader vivacious?
15. Did the reader succeed in making you aware of the imagery?
16. Was the reading sincere?
17. Was the physical response characterized by well-balanced enthusiasm?
18. Was there adequate bodily expression? hands? face?
19. Was the total pattern monotonous? or alive and interesting?
20. Was there variety in melody, timing, force, and quality?
21. Was there a nice balance between thought and rhythm?
22. Was the sing-song eliminated without ruining the music?
23. Did the mood change as the mood of the passage changed?
24. Did the voice seem well supported?
25. Were the sounds clearly formed?
26. Did the reader project his voice?
27. Was there sufficient resonance?
28. Did the reader steer a nice course between pedantic pronunciation and slovenly pronunciation?
29. Did the enunciation seem affected?
30. Did you ever feel that the reader was "caressing" his voice?
31. Were such figures of speech as asyndeton, alliteration, and assonance duly observed so as to bring out the sound values?
32. Was there a feeling of mutual give and take between the reader and the audience?
33. Was the audience dead to the attempts of the reader?
34. Did you feel that the reader was

reading within the pattern of his art?

35. Was there abandonment, yet restraint?
36. Did the reader succeed in suggesting more than he actually said?
37. Did the reader succeed in letting himself be the channel for the author?
38. Did you feel that the reading was intelligent, sympathetic, and moving?

Index

ABBOTT, LYMAN, 117
Abraham Lincoln (JOHN DRINKWATER), 210
Abstractions, 103–04
Accent, 35–36
Acres of Diamonds (RUSSELL H. CONWELL), 65, 74, 161
Acting:
  audience and, 55
  relationships, diagram, 54
  speaking, reading and, 52–53
ADAMS, J. DONALD (quoted), 20–21
Adjectives, 73–75
Adverbial modifiers, 73
Adverbs, 73
AESCHINES, 168
Aesthetic distance, composition factor, 46–48
Affricates, 131, 132
After Blenheim (ROBERT SOUTHEY), 32–33
AHERNE, BRIAN, 183
AIKEN, CONRAD (*Bread and Music*), 330
Alexandrine, 475
ALFANGE, DEAN (*My Creed*), 273
ALLEN, FRED, 226
Alliteration, 475
Anapestic feet, 472
ANDERSON, IDA LOU, 164
ANDERSON, MAXWELL (quoted), 250
ANDERSON, SHERWOOD, 14, 182
  I'm a Fool, 173, 393–402
Annabel Lee (EDGAR ALLAN POE), 367–68
Anticipatory attitude, listener, 257
Antiphonal reading, 217–18
Appreciation:
  reader's, 186–87
  tools of, *see* Tools of understanding and appreciation
Argumentation, 79–80
ARISTOTLE (*Poetics*), 27
ARLISS, GEORGE, 243
ARNOLD, MATTHEW, 245
  Dover Beach, 244, 260, 330–31
Ars Poetica (ARCHIBALD MACLEISH), 24–25
Articulation:
  problems, 133–38
    misplaced sounds, 135–36
    muscular movement, 133–34
  processes, 136–38
    assimilation, 137
    blending, 136–37
    gradation, 137–38
As I Walked Out One Evening (W. H. AUDEN), 331–33
Aspirate, voice quality, 128
Assertion, rhetorical device, 66–68
Assimilation, articulation, 137
Associations, 100
  making, 261–63
Aesthetic Attitude, The (H. S. LANGFELD), 46
Atlantic, The, 176, 225
Attention, fixing listener, 257–63
Attitude, 81–83
  developing, listener, 255–57
AUDEN, W. H. (*As I Walked Out One Evening*), 331–33
Audience:
  acting and, 55
  captive, 189–90
  listening, 191–92
  public speaking and, 55
  reader and, 176–77, 189–92
  reading and, 55–59
    dialogue, 58–59
    dramatic monologue, 59
    lyric poetry, 56–58
    prose, 55–56
  reading to, 15–16
  voluntary, 190–91
Author:
  reader's relation to, 181–85
    biographical approach, abuses, 183–85
    biographical material, value and use, 181–82
    relevancy, 183
  releasing, 225–27

Babbitt (SINCLAIR LEWIS), 22
BACON, FRANCIS (*Of Truth*), 159
Balance, composition factor, 31
Ballad of Trees and the Master, A (SIDNEY LANIER), 356–57
Ballad stanza, 476
Barrel Organ, The (ALFRED NOYES), 11
Barretts of Wimpole Street, The, 183, 200
Barrie, Sir James M. (*Will, The*), 27, 202, 203–04, 264, 413–32
BARRYMORE, JOHN, 243, 257
Barter (SARA TEASDALE), 381
Beach Red (PETER BOWMAN), 39
Beat! Beat! Drums! (WALT WHITMAN), 388–89
BEECHER, HENRY WARD (quoted), 51–52, 74, 76, 98, 251
  Liverpool Address, The, 256
  Yale Lectures on Preaching, 44–45, 145
Belief, reader's, 250
BENÉT, STEPHEN VINCENT, 243
  Devil and Daniel Webster, The, 172
BENÉT, WILLIAM ROSE (quoted), 84–85
  Jesse James, 216, 220–22
BENNY, JACK, 16, 226
Beyond the Horizon, 29, 31
BIBLE, THE:
  American Translation, An (JAMES GOODSPEED), 114–15
  Good Samaritan, The, 29, 153–54
  King James Version, 114
  One Hundred and Seventh Psalm, 334–35
  Philippians, 38
  Prodigal Son, The, 29, 31, 162–63, 291–92
  Revised Standard Version of the New Testament, 112, 115
  Romans, 31
  St. Matthew, 29–30
  Sermon on the Mount, The, 217–18
  Song of Songs, The, 265, 335–36
  Twenty-fourth Psalm, 139
  Twenty-third Psalm, 73, 333
  Weymouth translation, 115
Biographical material:
  abuses, 183–85
  value and use, 181–82
Birches (ROBERT FROST), 303–04
BLAKE, WILLIAM (*Tiger, The*), 336–37
Blank verse, 475
Blending, articulation, 136–37
Bodily action, 165–67
Bombardment, The (AMY LOWELL), 292–94
BOND, F. FRASER (quoted), 6
Boot and Saddle (ROBERT BROWNING), 41–42
Boots (RUDYARD KIPLING), 167
BOWMAN, PETER (*Red Beach*), 39
BOYER, CHARLES, 188
Boy Penrod, The (BOOTH TARKINGTON), 172
Bread and Music (CONRAD AIKEN), 330
Break, Break, Break (ALFRED LORD TENNYSON), 33, 81, 260, 381–82
Breathing, 123–25
Breath-sweep, 474
Bridge of Sighs (THOMAS HOOD), 73
BROOKE, RUPERT (*Soldier, The*), 337
BROOKS, PHILIP (quoted), 43
BROOKS, VAN WYCK (quoted), 41 fn.
Brooksmith (HENRY JAMES), 173
BROMFIELD, LOUIS, 172
BROUN, HEYWOOD (quoted), 76
BROWN, CHARLES REYNOLDS (quoted), 124
BROWN, JOHN MASON (quoted), 225
BROWN, ROLLO WALTER (quoted), 88–89
BROWNING, ELIZABETH BARRETT, 19, 183
  How Do I Love Thee? 27, 263
  Sonnets from the Portuguese, 162, 337–38
BROWNING, ROBERT, 17
  Boot and Saddle, 41–42
  dramatic monologue, 208
  Evelyn Hope, 167
  Home Thoughts from Abroad, 338–39
  How They Brought the Good News From Ghent to Aix, 70–72
  Incident of the French Camp, An, 302–03
  Love Among the Ruins, 45
  Meeting at Night, 83–84, 85
  My Last Duchess, 29, 107, 250–51, 441–42
  My Star, 57
  obscurity and the referent, 106–07
  Paracelsus, 245
  Parting at Morning, 339
  Patriot, The, 442–43
  Prospice, 339–40
  Ring and the Book, The, 28
  Up at a Villa—Down in the City, 102
BRYANT, WILLIAM CULLEN (*To a Waterfowl*), 340–41
BULLOUGH, EDWARD (quoted), 154
BUNNER, H. C. (*One, Two, Three*), 67
BUNYAN, JOHN (*Pilgrim's Progress*), 174

BURKE, EDMUND, 105–06
  Judgment of a Representative, The, 273
BURKE, THOMAS (*Chink and the Child, The*), 172
BURNS, ROBERT (*Honest Poverty*), 341–42
Business, oral reading in, importance, 1–3
BUTLER, NICHOLAS MURRAY (quoted), 10
BYRON, LORD (*To Thomas Moore*), 342–43

Cadence, preacher's, 158
Cadenced verse, 38–39
Caesura, 474
CALDWELL, ERSKINE, 172
Calvary (EDWIN ARLINGTON ROBINSON), 369
Camera, television:
  facing, 230–31
  fright, 227–28
Candida (GEORGE BERNARD SHAW), 99
Captive audience, 189–90
CARPENTER, F. B. (quoted), 82–83
CAWEIN, MADISON:
  Deserted, 343
  Man Hunt, The, 343–45
  Snow, 345
Celestial Surgeon, The (ROBERT LOUIS STEVENSON), 113
Characters:
  as human beings, 198
  differentiating, 201–03
  introducing, 204
  number, 198–99
Character story, 173–74
Chicago (CARL SANDBURG), 27, 161, 241, 260, 369–70
CHILD, PROFESSOR, 21
Chink and the Child, The (THOMAS BURKE), 172
Choir, choral reading, 213–14
Choral reading, 210–23
  antiphonal reading, 217–18
  choir, 213–14
  conductor, 212–13
  materials, 214–18
  reading in field of, suggested, 456–57
  reading in unison, 216
  selections, 218–22
  solo and chorus, 216–17
  values, 210–12
    dramatic effects, 210–11
    improved speech, 211
    social understanding, 211–12
Chorus, solo and, choral reading, 216–17
CHURCHILL, J. W., 48, 167
CHURCHILL, WINSTON (quoted), 15, 76
  Dunkirk, 274
Class discussion, nourishing, 20
Clearness, referent and, examples, 104–05
Climax, rhetorical device, 65–66
Cloak, The (NIKOLAI GOGOL), 172
CLOONEY, ROSEMARY (quoted), 262
COBB, IRVIN S., 177
COLERIDGE, SAMUEL TAYLOR (*Rime of the Ancient Mariner*), 15–16, 23
COLETTE, 23
Collections, 103
Columbus Citizen, The, 186
Communication, 25–26, 153–54
  mass media, 224–25
Comparison, composition factor, 28–31
COMPERE, MOIREE, 189
Composed upon Westminster Bridge (WILLIAM WORDSWORTH), 391
Composition:
  factors, 26–48
    aesthetic distance, 46–48
    balance, 31
    comparison, 28–31
    contrast, 28–31
    extrinsic, 42–48
    harmony, 27–28
    individuality, 43–44
    intrinsic, 26–42
    meter, 39–42
    proportion, 31
    rhythm, 32–39
    suggestiveness, 44–46
    unity, 26–27
    universality, 42
    variety, 28
  philosophies, 22–26
    communication, 25–26
    expression, 23–24
    imagination, 23
    impressionism, 24–25
    integration, 26
    realism, 22
Concealed rime, 475
Conductor, choral reading, 212–13
Congo, The (VACHEL LINDSAY), 11, 34, 81, 315–16
Connectives, 75
Connotation, 112–13
CONRAD, JOSEPH (*Lagoon, The*), 175
Consonants, 131–33
Constant Lover, The (SIR JOHN SUCKLING), 380
Context, definition by, 110
Continuants, 131, 132
Contrast, composition factor, 28–31
Convictions, reader's, 185–86

CONWELL, RUSSELL H. (*Acres of Diamonds*), 65, 74, 161
COPPÉE (*The Substitute*), 173
CORNELL, KATHERINE, 183, 253
CORSON, HIRAM (quoted), 6–7, 19, 107
CORWIN, NORMAN (*On a Note of Triumph*), 39
Cosmopolitan in a Café, A (O. HENRY), 173
COSTELLO, FRANK, 230
Couplet, 475
COWPER, WILLIAM (quoted), 155
CRANE, STEPHEN:
  Dark-Brown Dog, A, 172
  Red Badge of Courage, The, 260–61
CRAVEN, FRANK, 16
Cremation of Sam McGee, The (ROBERT W. SERVICE), 324–26
Critic, the, 267–68
Criticism, 78
  reading in field of, suggested, 460–62
CRONIN, A. J. (*Green Years, The*), 89
CROSS, MILTON, 143
Crossing the Bar (ALFRED LORD TENNYSON), 383
CROTHERS, SAMUEL M. (quoted), 159
CUMNOCK, ROBERT, 5
Cutting, problem, 199–201
  length, 199–200
  order of events, 200
  transitions, 200–01

Dactylic feet, 473
DALY, T. A. (*Mia Carlotta*), 443–44
DANIEL, HAWTHORNE, 255
D'ANNUNZIO, GABRIELE (*End of Candia, The*), 172
DANTE (*Inferno*), 23
Dark-Brown Dog, A (STEPHEN CRANE), 172
DARROW, CLARENCE, 82
DAY, CLARENCE, 177
Days (RALPH WALDO EMERSON), 349
Deacon's Masterpiece, The (OLIVER WENDELL HOLMES), 264–65
Dear Lord and Father of Mankind (JOHN GREENLEAF WHITTIER), 390–91
Death of a Salesman (ARTHUR MILLER), 433–34
Death of Socrates, The (PLATO), 294–96
Death of the Hired Man, The (ROBERT FROST), 28, 40, 43, 305–09
DEBS, EUGENE, 258
Declaration of Independence, 75
Definition, 109–11
  by context, 110
Definition (*Cont.*):
  by derivation, 110–11
  by examples, 111
  by negation, 111
DEFOE, DANIEL (*Life and Strange Adventures of Robinson Crusoe*), 23
DEMOSTHENES, 100, 168
DENNIS, RALPH B. (quoted), 252
Denotation, 112–13
DE QUINCEY, THOMAS, 112
Derivation, definition by, 110–11
Description, 79
  introductory material, 204–05
Deserted (MADISON CAWEIN), 343
Devil and Daniel Webster, The (STEPHEN VINCENT BENÉT), 172
DEWEY, THOMAS, 15
Dialogue:
  reading, audience and, 58–59
  stories with, 393–412
DICKENS, CHARLES, 12, 165, 177, 251
DICKINSON, EMILY:
  I Never Saw a Moor, 345
  rhythm and meter, 41 fn.
Diction:
  acceptable, 142–43
  voice and, 142–44
Dimeter, 473
Dirge (PERCY B. SHELLEY), 32
Discourse:
  types, 78–80
    argumentation, 79–80
    description, 79
    exposition, 78
    narration, 80
  units, 68–77
    adjectives, 73–75
    adverbial modifiers, 73
    adverbs, 73
    nouns, 68–69
    paragraph, 77
    parts of speech, 68–75
    sentence, 76–77
    thought connectives, 75
    vehicles of thought and emotion, 76–77
    verbs, 69–73
Discussion, class, nourishing, 20
Distinctness, 153
Distractions, 154
Dr. Keith's Letter to His Son Willie from The Caine Mutiny (HERMAN WOUK), 298–301
Doll's House, The (KATHERINE MANSFIELD), 172
Don Juan in Hell, 188
DOS PASSOS, JOHN R., 172
Double rime, 475

Dover Beach (MATTHEW ARNOLD), 244, 260, 330–31
Dramatic effects, choral reading, 210–11
Dramatic monologue, 207–08, 441–44
  reading, audience and, 59
DRAPER, RUTH, 59, 188, 191, 267
DREISER, THEODORE, 182
DRINKWATER, JOHN (*Abraham Lincoln*), 210
Dunkirk (WINSTON CHURCHILL), 274

Eagle, The (ALFRED LORD TENNYSON), 386
Education, general, oral reading in, importance, 3–4
EISENHOWER, DWIGHT D., 8
  Our Great Team Commander, the Symbol of Allied Victory, 274–77
Elegy in a Country Churchyard (THOMAS GRAY), 108
Elements of Rhetoric (RICHARD WHATELY), 5
ELIOT, T. S., 100, 182
  Hollow Men, The, 154, 346–48
EMERSON, RALPH WALDO, 42, 261
  Days, 349
  Self-Reliance, 278
Emotional ownership, 247–49
Emotions, interpreting, 167–68
Endymion (JOHN KEATS), 104–05, 182, 354
Enjambent, 474
Esquire magazine, 86
Essay on Criticism (ALEXANDER POPE), 17, 37
Essay on Man, An (ALEXANDER POPE), 368
Essays, speeches, reports, 273–90
Evaluation, 264–69
  critic, 267–68
  design, 264–65
  listenability, 266–67
  medium, 265–66
EVANS, MAURICE, 184, 225, 254, 257
Evelyn Hope (ROBERT BROWNING), 167
Events, order of, cutting, 200
Eve of St. Agnes (JOHN KEATS), 104
EVERETT, EDWARD, 27
Examples, definition by, 111
Excesses of God, The (ROBINSON JEFFERS), 353
Experience, language and, 94–102
  associations, 100
  imagery, 96
  symbols, 96–98
  total meaning, 99
  words and things, 101–02
Experience (*Cont.*):
  words and thought, 95–96
  world of words, 100–01
Explanation, 78
Exposition, 78
  criticism, 78
  explanation, 78
  interpretation, 78
Express, The (STEPHEN SPENDER), 28
Expression, philosophy of composition, 23–24

Fall of the House of Usher (EDGAR ALLAN POE), 175
Falsetto, voice quality, 128
FARRELL, JAMES, 172
FAULKNER, WILLIAM, 25, 42, 43, 76–77, 105, 172, 182
  Sound and the Fury, The, 45–46
Faust (GOETHE), 17
Feminine rime, 475
FERBER, EDNA:
  Gay Old Dog, The, 175
  Giant, 109
FIELDS, JAMES T. (quoted), 165–66
Flower in the Crannied Wall (ALFRED LORD TENNYSON), 382
FONTAINE, ROBERT, 177
Fool's Prayer, The (EDWARD ROWLAND SILL), 327–28
Foot, 472–73
FORBES-ROBERTSON, JOHNSTON, 184
Force, variety in, 163–65
For You, O Democracy (WALT WHITMAN), 389
FOSDICK, HARRY EMERSON, 82, 90
Fountain, The (JAMES RUSSELL LOWELL), 70, 359–60
Four Million, The (O. HENRY), 172
Frailty, Thy Name Is a Misnomer (OGDEN NASH), 318–19
FRANCIS, ARLENE, 8, 231
Free verse, 38–39, 475
Fricatives, 131, 132
FROST, FRANCES (*Storyteller, The*), 349–50
FROST, ROBERT, 7, 11, 31, 38, 42, 185, 238–39, 241, 243, 249, 250, 261
  Birches, 303–04
  Death of the Hired Man, The, 28, 40, 43, 305–09
  Home Burial, 167
  Pasture, The, 34, 305
  Stopping by Woods on a Snowy Evening, 66–67, 350, 478

GALE, ZONA (*Miss Lulu Bett*), 183
GALSWORTHY, JOHN (quoted), 248–49
  Once More, 173

GALSWORTHY, JOHN (*Cont.*):
Quality, 172
Told by the Schoolmaster, 402–06
Gay Old Dog, The (EDNA FERBER), 175
General Education in a Free Society, 3
General William Booth Enters into Heaven (VACHEL LINDSAY), 316–18
GENÊT (quoted), 23–24
Gettysburg Address (ABRAHAM LINCOLN), 27, 38, 43–44, 75, 100, 114, 287–88
Giant (EDNA FERBER), 109
GIBBS, WOLCOTT (quoted), 99
GIELGUD, JOHN, 257
GLASGOW, ELLEN (quoted), 13–14
Glides, 131, 132
GODFREY, ARTHUR, 9, 226
God's World (EDNA ST. VINCENT MILLAY), 361–62
Goethe (quoted), 92, 99
Faust, 17
GOGOL, NIKOLAI (*Cloak, The*), 172
Golden Bough (ELINOR WYLIE), 392
Good Samaritan, The (BIBLE), 29, 153–54
GOODSPEED, EDGAR (*American Translation, An*), 114–15
Gradation, articulation, 137–38
GRAHAM, BILLY, 42
Grapes of Wrath (JOHN STEINBECK), 257, 410–12
Grass, The (CARL SANDBURG), 39, 370
GRAY, THOMAS (*Elegy*), 108
Great Stone Face (NATHANIEL HAWTHORNE), 172
Green Years, The (A. J. CRONIN), 89
Grouping of words, 151–53
GUEST, EDGAR, 244
Guinevere (ALFRED LORD TENNYSON), 32
GUITERMAN, ARTHUR (*Lyric Laughter*), 214
Gunga Din (RUDYARD KIPLING), 309–11
Guttural, voice quality, 128

Hair Cut (RING LARDNER), 27, 173
HALE, EDWARD EVERETT (*Man Without a Country, The*), 172
Halstead Street Car (CARL SANDBURG), 22
HAMBURGER, PHILIP (*Men of Faith*), 238–39
HAMILTON, ALICE (*Words Lost, Strayed, or Stolen*), 118–21
Hamlet (WILLIAM SHAKESPEARE), 112, 172, 197, 198
Advice to Polonius, 437
Advice to the Players, 436–37
Soliloquy on Death, 435–36
HAND, LEARNED (*Preparation of Citizens for Their Political Duties*), 278–79
HAMPDEN, WALTER, 4, 162, 184
HARDWICKE, SIR CEDRIC, 188
HARDY, THOMAS, 11
Return of the Native, The, 96
HARKNESS, GEORGIA (*Toward Understanding the Bible*), 29
Harmony, composition factor, 27–28
Harper's, 176, 225
HARTE, BRET:
Outcasts of Poker Flat, The, 172
Uncle Jim and Uncle Billy, 173
HAVILAND, OLIVIA DE, 99
HAWTHORNE, NATHANIEL (*Great Stone Face*), 172
HAYES, HELEN, 253–54
HEARN, LAFCADIO, 11
HEMINGWAY, ERNEST, 76, 172
Old Man and the Sea, 23
HENLEY, WILLIAM ERNEST (*Invictus*), 350–51
HENRY, O.:
Cosmopolitan in a Café, 173
Four Million, The, 172
Romance of a Busy Broker, 173
Service of Love, A, 406–09
Henry V (WILLIAM SHAKESPEARE), 90–91
HERRICK, ROBERT (*To the Virgins to Make Much of Time*), 351
Hexameter, 474
Hiawatha (WILLIAM WADSWORTH LONGFELLOW), 33–34
HIGDON, BARBARA (quoted), 191–92
HILLYER, ROBERT (quoted), 259
Night Piece, 286
On Reading Verse Aloud, 280–86
Historical introduction, 205–06
HOFFENSTEIN, SAMUEL (*Poems in Praise of Practically Nothing*), 214
Hollow Men, The (T. S. ELIOT), 154, 346–48
HOLMES, OLIVER WENDELL (*Deacon's Masterpiece, The*), 264–65
Home Burial (ROBERT FROST), 167
HOMER, 171
Home Thoughts from Abroad (ROBERT BROWNING), 338–39
Honest Poverty (ROBERT BURNS), 341–42

HOOD, THOMAS:
Bridge of Sighs, 73
I Remember, I Remember, 351–52
HORACE, 100
House Beautiful, The (ROBERT LOUIS STEVENSON), 379–80
HOUSMAN, A. E.:
Shropshire Lad, A, 84
When I Was One-and-Twenty, 352
How Do I Love Thee? (ELIZABETH BARRETT BROWNING), 27, 263
How They Brought the Good News From Ghent to Aix (ROBERT BROWNING), 70–72
Human need, oral reading in meeting, importance, 7–8
Humble Remonstrance, A (ROBERT LOUIS STEVENSON), 174

Iambic feet, 472
Ideas, rhetorical devices:
central, 62–63
main and subordinate, 63–65
I Hear America Singing (WALT WHITMAN), 389–90
Iliad, 171
I'm a Fool (SHERWOOD ANDERSON), 173, 393–402
Imagery, 85–91, 96
Imagination, 23
using, 263
Implication, rhetorical device, 66–68
Impressionism, 24–25, 45
Incident of the French Camp, An (ROBERT BROWNING), 302–03
In Distrust of Merits (MARIANNE MOORE), 363–65
Individuality, composition factor, 43–44
I Never Saw a Moor (EMILY DICKINSON), 345
Inferno (DANTE), 23
Inflection, 139–42, 156
INGERSOLL, ROBERT GREEN (quoted), 36, 82
Liberty of Man, Woman, and Child, 65, 258
In Memoriam A. H. H. (ALFRED LORD TENNYSON), 69–70, 383–85
In Railway Halls (STEPHEN SPENDER), 376
Integration, 26
Internal rime, 475
Intellectual ownership, 247–49
Interpretation, 78
Interpretative listening, 263–64
Introductory material, recital, 204–06
characters, 204
descriptions, 204–05
Introductory material (*Cont.*):
getting acquainted, 204
historical introduction, 205–06
setting, 205
Invictus (WILLIAM ERNEST HENLEY), 350–51
I Remember, I Remember (THOMAS HOOD), 351–52
IRVING, HENRY, 184
It is a Beauteous Evening, Calm and Free (WILLIAM WORDSWORTH), 391–92

JAMES, HENRY (*Brooksmith*), 173
JAMES, WILLIAM (*Social Value of the College-Bred, The*), 286–87
Jaw, 134
JEFFERS, ROBINSON (*Excesses of God, The*), 353
JEFFERSON, JOSEPH, 15, 198
Jesse James (WILLIAM ROSE BENÉT), 216, 220–22
John Brown (VACHEL LINDSAY), 313–15
JONSON, BEN (*Song to Celia*), 353
Judgment of a Representative, The (EDMUND BURKE), 273
Julius Caesar (WILLIAM SHAKESPEARE), 67, 161
Brutus to the Roman People, 434–35

KALLEN, H. M. (quoted), 20
KALTENBORN, H. V., 102, 158
KEATS, JOHN, 42, 112–13
clearness and the referent, 104–05
Endymion, 104–05, 182, 354
Eve of St. Agnes, 104
Ode to a Grecian Urn, 68, 260
Thing of Beauty Is a Joy Forever, A, 354
When I Have Fears that I May Cease to Be, 355
King James Version (BIBLE), 114
KINGSLEY, CHARLES (*Young and Old*), 355
KIPLING, RUDYARD, 98, 103
Boots, 167
Gunga Din, 309–11
Namgay Doola, 173
Only a Subaltern, 173
Recessional, The, 31
Tommy, 311–13
KIRK, GRAYSON (quoted), 3

Labels, classes, 102–04
abstractions, 103–04
collections, 103
names, 102–03

Lady, A (AMY LOWELL), 358–59
Lady of Shalott, The (ALFRED LORD TENNYSON), 11
Lagoon, The (JOSEPH CONRAD), 175
L'Allegro (JOHN MILTON), 40–41, 363
LAMB, CHARLES (*Old Familiar Faces, The*), 356
Lament (EDNA ST. VINCENT MILLAY), 260, 362
LANGFELD, H. S. (*Aesthetic Attitude, The*), 46
Language, experience and, 94–102
  associations, 100
  imagery, 96
  symbols, 96–98
  total meaning, 99
  words and things, 101–02
  words and thought, 95–96
  world of words, 100–01
LANIER, SIDNEY (*Ballad of Trees and the Master, A*), 356–57
LARDNER, RING, 172
  Hair Cut, 27, 173
LATHAM, A. J. (quoted), 232
LAUGHTON, CHARLES, 7–8, 90, 188–89, 191, 225, 226
  How to Read Aloud at Home, 269
Lay of the Last Minstrel, The (SIR WALTER SCOTT), 371
Leadership, developing, 18–19
Lectures on Elocution (THOMAS SHERIDAN), 5
Length, recital, 195–96
  cutting, 199–200
LETTS, WINIFRED M. (*Spires of Oxford, The*), 357–58
LEWIS, FULTON, JR., 102
LEWIS, SINCLAIR, 172
  Babbitt, 22
  Main Street, 22
LEWIS, SIR WILMOTT, 162
Liberty of Man, Woman, and Child, The (ROBERT G. INGERSOLL), 65, 258
Life and Strange Adventures of Robinson Crusoe (DANIEL DEFOE), 23
Life magazine, 86
LINCOLN, ABRAHAM:
  Gettysburg Address, 27, 38, 43–44, 75, 100, 114, 287–88
  Private Enterprise, 289–90
  Second Inaugural Address, 64, 288–89
  study of Shakespeare, 82–83
Lincoln, the Man of the People (EDWIN MARKHAM), 360–61
LINDSAY, VACHEL:
  Congo, The, 11, 34, 81, 315–16
LINDSAY, VACHEL (*Cont.*):
  General William Booth Enters into Heaven, 316–18
  John Brown, 313–15
  Negro Sermon: Simon Legree, 218–20
Lips, 134
Listenability, 266–67
Listening, 253–70
  anticipatory attitude, 257
  associations, making, 261–63
  attention, fixing, 257–63
  attitude, developing, 255–57
  audience, 191–92
  evaluation, 264–68
  for rhetorical devices, 257–60
  imagination, using, 263
  interpretative, 263–64
  learning situation, 255–57
  references to your experiences, 260–61
  retention, 268–69
  skill, 253–55
Literary composition, *see* Composition
Literary criticism, reading in field of, suggested, 460–62
Liverpool Address, The (HENRY WARD BEECHER), 256
London, 1802 (WILLIAM WORDSWORTH), 392
LONGFELLOW, WILLIAM WADSWORTH:
  Hiawatha, 33–34
  Rainy Day, The, 358
Love Among the Ruins (ROBERT BROWNING), 45
LOWELL, AMY, 11, 90
  Bombardment, The, 292–94
  Lady, A, 358–59
LOWELL, JAMES RUSSELL (quoted), 43
  Fountain, The, 70, 359–60
LUCCOCK, HALFORD E. (quoted), 155
LUCE, CLARE BOOTH, 230
Lyric Laughter (ARTHUR GUITERMAN), 214
Lyrical poetry, 330–92
  reading, audience and, 56–58

Macbeth (WILLIAM SHAKESPEARE), 13, 40, 198, 210–11
MACLAREN, GAY (quoted), 166
MACLEISH, ARCHIBALD, 243–44
  Ars Poetica, 24–25
Main Street (SINCLAIR LEWIS), 22
Make-up, use, 183–84
Man Hunt, The (MADISON CAWEIN), 343–45
MANSFIELD, KATHERINE (*Doll's House, The*), 172
MANSFIELD, RICHARD, 184
MANTELL, ROBERT, 184

Man Without a Country, The (EDWARD EVERETT HALE), 172
Man With the Hoe (EDWIN MARKHAM), 260
MARKHAM, EDWIN:
Lincoln, the Man of the People, 360–61
Man With the Hoe, The, 260
Markheim (ROBERT LEWIS STEVENSON), 172
Marmion (SIR WALTER SCOTT), 320–21
MARSHALL, JOHN (quoted), 44
MARX, GROUCHO, 226
Masculine rime, 474
MASEFIELD, JOHN, 182
Mass media of communication, 224–25
Mateo Falcone (PROSPER MÉRIMÉE), 172
MATTHEWS, BRANDER, 11
MAUGHAM, W. SOMERSET:
P & O, 172
Summing Up, The, 108
MAUPASSANT, GUY DE (*Piece of String, The*), 173
MCNAMEE, GRAHAM, 143
Meaning:
changes, 111–12
total, 99
Measure, *see* Meter
MEDINA, HAROLD R., 255
Meeting at Night (ROBERT BROWNING), 83–84, 85
MELVILLE, HERMAN (*Moby Dick*), 257–58
Men of Faith (PHILIP HAMBURGER), 238–39
Men Show Devotion to a Loved Officer (ERNIE PYLE), 296–98
Merchant of Venice, The (WILLIAM SHAKESPEARE), 197, 198, 201, 262–63
Portia's Mercy Speech, 438
MEREDITH, BURGESS, 184
MEREDITH, ROY (*Mr. Lincoln's Camera Man: Mathew B. Brady*), 74
MÉRIMÉE, PROSPER (*Mateo Falcone*), 172
Merry Men, The (ROBERT LOUIS STEVENSON), 175
Meter, 32, 473–74
composition factor, 39–42
Metonymy, 30
Mia Carlotta (T. A. DALY), 443–44
Microphone:
facing, 228–30
fright, 227–28
MILLAY, EDNA ST. VINCENT, 11, 151, 182, 185
God's World, 361–62
MILLAY, EDNA ST. VINCENT (*Cont.*):
Lament, 260, 362
MILLER, ARTHUR (*Death of a Salesman*), 433–34
MILLET, 27
MILTON, JOHN:
L'Allegro, 40–41, 363
obscurity and the referent, 105–06
Paradise Lost, 23
When I Consider How My Light Is Spent, 363
MINER, WORTHINGTON (quoted), 231
Miniver Cheevy (EDWIN ARLINGTON ROBINSON), 319–20
Misplaced sounds, 135–36
Mission to Moscow, 183–84
Miss Lulu Bett (ZONA GALE), 183
Mr. Lincoln's Camera Man: Mathew B. Brady (ROY MEREDITH), 74
Moby Dick (HERMAN MELVILLE), 257–58
MOLEY, RAYMOND (quoted), 101
Monologue, dramatic, 207–08, 441–44
reading, audience and, 59
Monotony, 146
MONTGOMERY, ROBERT, 8
Mood, 81–83
Moonlight (JOHN V. A. WEAVER), 386
MOORE, MARIANNE (*In Distrust of Merits*), 363–65
MOORE, THOMAS:
Oft, in the Stilly Night, 366
Orator Puff, 141–42
MOOREHEAD, AGNES, 188, 191
MORLEY, CHRISTOPHER (*To a Post-office Inkwell*), 366–67
MOTT, JOHN R., 90
Mumbling, 146–47
MURROW, EDWARD R. (quoted), 164, 227
Muscular movement, 133–34
jaw, 134
lips, 134
tongue, 133–34
Mutual Broadcasting Company, 98
My Creed (DEAN ALFANGE), 273
My Last Duchess (ROBERT BROWNING), 29, 107, 250–51, 441–42
My Star (ROBERT BROWNING), 57

NADEL, NORMAN (quoted), 186
Names, 102–03
Namgay Doola (RUDYARD KIPLING), 173
Narration, 80
Narrative poetry, 302–29
Narrative prose, 291–301
reader and the audience, 176–77
reading, 171–80
story:

Narrative prose, story (*Cont.*):
sharing, 177–79
type, 173–75
story telling impulse, 171–72
unified effect, 175–76
Nasal:
consonants, 131
voice quality, 128
NASH, OGDEN (*Frailty, Thy Name Is a Misnomer*), 318–19
National Association of Teachers of Speech, 162
Naturalness:
concept, 51–52
training vs., 50–51
Negation, definition by, 111
Negro Sermon: Simon Legree (VACHEL LINDSAY), 218–20
NEIHARDT, JOHN, 191–92
New York Times, The, 255, 256
Book Review, 20
Night Piece (ROBERT HILLYER), 286
NORDINE, KEN, 9–10
Normal, voice quality, 128
Notebook, student, 477–81
Nouns, 68–69
Novels:
list of, for reading, 447–49
recitals, 196–206

Obscurity, referent and, examples, 105–07
O Captain! My Captain (WALT WHITMAN), 388
Occasion, reader's relation to, 192–93
O'CONNOR, WILLIAM VAN (*Tangled Fire of William Faulkner, The*), 182
Ode to a Grecian Urn (JOHN KEATS), 68, 260
Odyssey, 171
Of Old Sat Freedom on the Heights (ALFRED LORD TENNYSON), 385
Oft, in the Stilly Night (THOMAS MOORE), 366
Of Truth (FRANCIS BACON), 159
Old Familiar Faces, The (CHARLES LAMB), 356
Old Man and the Sea, The (ERNEST HEMINGWAY), 23
OLSON, ELDER (*Poetry of Dylan Thomas*), 106
Onomatopoeia, 475
On a Note of Triumph (NORMAN CORWIN), 39
Once More (JOHN GALSWORTHY), 173
One, Two, Three (H. C. BUNNER), 67
One Hundred and Seventh Psalm (BIBLE), 334–35
Only a Subaltern (RUDYARD KIPLING), 173
On Reading Verse Aloud (ROBERT HILLYER), 280–86
Open Road, The (WALT WHITMAN), 163
Oral reading, *see also* Reading
anthologies of materials for, 469–71
choral, *see* Choral reading
function, 17–20
history of, suggested reading in, 458–59
importance, 1–11
nature, 11–17
practicality, 11–12
reading in field of, suggested, 453–54
speeches for, 467–68
thinking the thought, 12–14
Oral voice quality, 128
Orator Puff (THOMAS MOORE), 141–42
Order of words, 108–09
Originality, 241–44
Orotund, voice quality, 128
OSLER, SIR WILLIAM, 251
Othello (WILLIAM SHAKESPEARE), 30–31, 112
Othello's Apology, 438–40
Ottava rima, 476
Our Great Team Commander, the Symbol of Allied Victory (DWIGHT D. EISENHOWER), 274–77
Our Town (THORNTON WILDER), 16
Outcasts of Poker Flat, The (BRET HARTE), 172
Out of the Cradle Endlessly Rocking (WALT WHITMAN), 72–73
Overtones, voice, 240–41
Oxford Book of Ballads, The (SIR ARTHUR QUILLER-COUCH), 216
Ozymandias (PERCY BYSSHE SHELLEY), 260

P & O (W. SOMERSET MAUGHAM), 172
Pace, change, 162–63
Pantomimes, 166–67
Paracelsus (ROBERT BROWNING), 245
Paradise Lost (JOHN MILTON), 23
Paragraph, the, 77
PARKER, THEODORE (quoted), 44
Parting at Morning (ROBERT BROWNING), 339
Parts of speech, 68–75
Pasture, The (ROBERT FROST), 34, 305

Patriot, The (ROBERT BROWNING), 442–43
Pause, 160–62
Pectoral, voice quality, 128
Pentameter, 474
PERKINS, MAX, 27
PERRY, BLISS (quoted), 48, 127, 167
Personal limitations, 199
Personal magnetism, reader's, 250–51
Peter Quince at the Clavier (WALLACE STEVENS), 377–79
PFAFF, PAUL L., 7
PHELPS, WILLIAM LYON, 21, 244, 263
PHILLIPS, HAROLD COOKE (quoted), 2–3
Philosophies of composition, 22–26
  communication, 25–26
  expression, 23–24
  imagination, 23
  impressionism, 24–25
  integration, 26
  realism, 22
Philosophy of Composition, The (EDGAR ALLAN POE), 26, 81
Philosophy of the Human Voice, The (JAMES RUSH), 5
Phonation, 125–26
Phrasal patterns, 113–17
Phrases, 38
Piece of String, The (GUY DE MAUPASSANT), 173
Pilgrim's Progress (JOHN BUNYAN), 174
PILLSBURY, WALTER B. (quoted), 268–69
Pitch:
  monotony due to sameness in, 146
  steps and slides, 156
PLATO (*Death of Socrates, The*), 294–96
Plays, 413–40
  list of, for reading, 450–52
  recitals, 196–206
Plosives, 131
Plot:
  interesting, 197
  story, 174–75
POE, EDGAR ALLAN, 176
  Annabel Lee, 367–68
  Fall of the House of Usher, 175
  Philosophy of Composition, 26, 81
  Raven, The, 28, 81, 210
  Telltale Heart, The, 172
  To Helen, 37
Poems in Praise of Practically Nothing (SAMUEL HOFFENSTEIN), 214
Poetics (ARISTOTLE), 27
Poetry:
  lyrical, *see* Lyrical poetry
Poetry (*Cont.*):
  narrative, *see* Narrative poetry
Poetry of Dylan Thomas (ELDER OLSON), 106
POPE, ALEXANDER:
  Essay on Criticism, 17, 37
  Essay on Man, An, 368
Preacher's cadence, 158
Preparation of Citizens for Their Political Duties, The (LEARNED HAND), 278–79
Prisoner of the Sand (ANTOINE DE SAINT EXUPÉRY), 175
Private Enterprise (ABRAHAM LINCOLN), 289–90
Prodigal Son, The (BIBLE), 4, 29, 31, 162–63, 291–92
Professions, oral reading in, importance, 1–3
Pronunciation drills, list of words for, 149
Proportion, composition factor, 31
Prose:
  narrative, *see* Narrative prose
  reading, audience and, 55–56
Prospice (ROBERT BROWNING), 339–40
Psalms:
  One Hundred and Seventh, 334–35
  Twenty-fourth, 139
  Twenty-third, 73, 333
Psychological means, 81–91
  imagery, 85–91
  mood and attitude, 81–83
  sound and sense, 83–85
Public recital, *see* Recitals
Pusey, Nathan M. (*Religion's Rôle in Liberal Education*), 115–16
PYLE, ERNIE, 177
  Men Show Devotion to a Loved Officer, 151–53, 296–98
Pyrrhic feet, 473

Quality (JOHN GALSWORTHY), 172
Quality, voice, 127–28
Quatrain, 476
QUILLER-COUCH, SIR ARTHUR (*Oxford Book of Ballads*), 216

Radio and television reading, 224–39
  broadcast, the, 231–34
  camera:
    facing, 230–31
    fright, 227–28
  mass media of communication, 224–25
  microphone:
    facing, 228–30
    fright, 227–28
  oral reading in, importance, 8–10

Radio and television reading (*Cont.*):
  recordings, use, 235–36
  releasing the author, 225–27
  suggested readings, 455
  suggestions, practical, 234–35
Rainy Day, The (HENRY WADSWORTH LONGFELLOW), 358
RANDALL, CLARENCE BELDEN, 2
Range, speaking voice, 155–56
Rate, changes in, 148
RATHBONE, BASIL, 191
Raven, The (EDGAR ALLAN POE), 28, 81, 210
RAYBURN, SAM, 230
RAYMOND, HENRY, 256
Reader:
  appreciation, 186–87
  audience and, 176–77
  author relations, 181–85, 189–92
    biographical approach, abuses, 183–85
    biographical material, value and use, 181–82
    relevancy, 183
  belief, 250
  convictions, 185–86
  listening to selection, 187–88
  make-up, use, 183–85
  occasion relations, 192–93
  originality, 241–44
  overtones of the voice, 240–41
  ownership, intellectual and emotional, 247–49
  personality, effacing, 184–85
  personal limitations, 199
  personal magnetism, 250–51
  responsive materials, choosing, 188–89
  selection relations, 185–87
  self-conceit, avoiding, 245–46
  speech background, 246–47
  taste, 244–45
Reader's Digest, The, 161, 241
Reader's Guide to Periodical Literature, 182
Reading:
  aloud at home, how to, 269
  antiphonal, 217–18
  as if speaking, 14–15
  audience and, 55–59
    dialogue, 58–59
    dramatic monologue, 59
    lyric poetry, 56–58
    prose, 55–56
  choral, *see* Choral reading
  choral reading field, suggested, 456–57
  history of oral reading, suggested, 458–59
Reading (*Cont.*):
  in unison, 216
  literary criticism, field of, suggested, 460–62
  narrative prose, 171–80
  novels suitable for, list, 447–49
  oral, *see* Oral reading
  oral reading field, suggested, 453–54
  plays suitable for, list, 450–52
  province of, 53–55
  radio and television, *see* Radio and television reading
  radio and television field, suggested, 455
  relationships, diagram, 54
  skill in, 150–51
  speaking, acting and, 52–53
  to audience, 15–16
Realism, 22
Recessional, The (RUDYARD KIPLING), 31
Recitals, public, 195–209
  dramatic monologue, 207–08
  length, 195–96, 199–200
  miscellaneous, 195–96
  plays, novels, stories, 196–206
    choice, criteria governing, 197–99
    cutting, problem, 199–201
    differentiating characters, 201–03
    introductory material, 204–06
    mechanics, 203–04
  unity, 196
Recordings, use, 235–36
Red Badge of Courage, The (STEPHEN CRANE), 260–61
Referent, the, 102–07
  abstractions, 103–04
  clearness and, examples, 104–05
  collections, 103
  labels, classes, 102–04
  names, 102–03
  obscurity and, examples, 105–07
Relaxation, 138–39
Relevancy, 183
Religion's Rôle in Liberal Education (NATHAN M. PUSEY), 115–16
Reports, essays, speeches, 273–90
Resonance, 126–27
Responsive materials, choosing, 188–89
Retention, 268–69
Return of the Native, The (THOMAS HARDY), 96
Revised Standard Version of the New Testament, 112, 115
REYNOLDS, QUENTIN, 177
Rhetorical devices, 62–68
  assertion, 66–68
  central idea, 62, 63

Rhetorical devices (*Cont.*):
climax, 65–66
implication, 66–68
listening for, 257–60
main and subordinate ideas, 63–65
Rhetorical rhythms, 476
Rhyme royal, 476
Rhythm:
composition factor, 32–39
rhetorical, 476
Richard Cory (EDWIN ARLINGTON ROBINSON), 216, 258
RICHARDS, I. A. (quoted), 25–26
Rime of the Ancient Mariner, The (SAMUEL TAYLOR COLERIDGE), 15–16, 23
Ring and the Book, The (ROBERT BROWNING), 28
Rip Van Winkle, 198
ROBINSON, EDWIN ARLINGTON:
Calvary, 369
Miniver Cheevy, 319–20
Richard Cory, 216, 258
Romance of a Busy Broker (O. HENRY), 173
Romantic Movement, 23
Romeo and Juliet (WILLIAM SHAKESPEARE), 440
ROOSEVELT, FRANKLIN DELANO, 15, 38, 184–85
clearness and the referent, 105
ROOSEVELT, THEODORE, 127
ROSS, DAVID, 237
ROSSETTI, CHRISTINA (*Song*), 56–57
RUSH, JAMES, 5

SAINT EXUPÉRY, ANTOINE DE (*Prisoner of the Sand*), 175
St. Matthew (BIBLE), 29–30
Salute to the Flag, 212
SANDBURG, CARL, 182
Chicago, 27, 161, 241, 260, 369–70
Grass, The, 39, 370
Halstead Street Car, 22
Saturday Evening Post, 86, 111, 176
Saturday Review, 225
SCHLESINGER, ARTHUR M., JR. (quoted), 74–75
SCOTT, SIR WALTER, 174
Lay of the Last Minstrel, The, 371
Marmion, 320–21
Second Inaugural Address (ABRAHAM LINCOLN), 64, 288–89
Selection:
listening to, 253–70
reader's, 187–88
reader's relation to, 185–87
Self-conceit, avoiding, 245–46
Self-development, oral reading in, importance, 5–7
Self-Reliance (RALPH WALDO EMERSON), 278
Sense, sound and, 83–85
Sentence, the, 76–77
Septameter, 474
Sermon on the Mount, The (BIBLE), 217–18
SERVICE, ROBERT W.:
Cremation of Sam McGee, The, 324–26
Shooting of Dan McGrew, The, 321–34
Service of Love, A (O. HENRY), 406–09
Setting:
introductory material, 205
story, 175
SHAKESPEARE, WILLIAM, 144
cuttings from, suggested, 463–66
Hamlet, 112, 172, 197, 198
Advice to Polonius, 437
Advice to the Players, 436–37
Soliloquy on Death, 435–36
Henry V, 90–91
Julius Caesar, 67, 161
Brutus to the Roman People, 434–35
Macbeth, 13, 40, 198, 210–11
Merchant of Venice, The, 197, 198, 201, 262–63
Portia's Mercy Speech, 438
Othello, 30–31, 112
Othello's Apology, 438–40
Romeo and Juliet, He Jests at Scars, 440
Sonnets, 371–74
Taming of the Shrew, The, 199–200, 205–06
universality, 42
SHAW, GEORGE BERNARD, 188
Candida, 99
SHELLEY, PERCY BYSSHE:
Dirge, 32
Ozymandias, 260
Threnos, 40
To a Skylark, 374–76
SHERIDAN, RICHARD BRINSLEY, 5
SHERIDAN, THOMAS, 5, 13
SHERROD, ROBERT (*Tarawa*), 109
Shooting of Dan McGrew, The (ROBERT W. SERVICE), 321–24
SHRINER, HERB, 226
Shropshire Lad, A (A. E. HOUSMAN), 84–85
SILL, EDWARD ROWLAND (*Fool's Prayer, The*), 327–28
SITWELL, EDITH, 185

SKINNER, CORNELIA OTIS, 59, 191
Slides, 156
SMITH, LILLIAN (*Strange Fruit*), 96
Snow (MADISON CAWEIN), 345
Snow Story, The (CHAUNCEY THOMAS), 175
Social understanding, choral reading, 211–12
Social Value of the College-Bred, The (WILLIAM JAMES), 286–87
Soldier, The (RUPERT BROOKE), 337
Solo and chorus, choral reading, 216–17
Song (CHRISTINA ROSSETTI), 56–57
Song of Songs, The (BIBLE), 265, 335–36
Song to Celia (BEN JONSON), 353
Sonnet, 476
Sonnets (WILLIAM SHAKESPEARE), 371–74
Sonnets from the Portuguese (ELIZABETH BARRETT BROWNING), 162, 337–38
SOTHERN, E. H., 184
Sound:
  misplaced, 135–36
  recurrence, 474–75
  sense and, 83–85
Sound and the Fury, The (WILLIAM FAULKNER), 45–46
SOUTHEY, ROBERT (*After Blenheim*), 32–33
Speaking, public:
  audience and, 55
  reading, acting and, 52–53
  reading as if, 14–15
  relationships, diagram, 54
  writing and, unite in oral reading, 10–11
Speech, 128–39
  articulation, 133–38
    misplaced sounds, 135–36
    muscular movement, 133–34
    processes, 136–38
  background, 246–47
  consonants, 131–33
  improved, choral reading, 211
  improving, 18
  patterns, 156–58
  relaxation, 138–39
  vowels, 128–31
Speech education, oral reading in, importance, 4–5
Speeches:
  essays, reports, 273–90
  for oral reading, 467–68
Speech Monographs, 5
SPENCER, HERBERT, 182
SPENSER, EDMUND (quoted), 247
Spenserian stanza, 476
SPENDER, STEPHEN (quoted), 19
  Express, The, 28
  In Railway Halls, 376
Spires of Oxford, The (WINIFRED M. LETTS), 357–58
Splendor Falls, The (ALFRED LORD TENNYSON), 124
Spondaic feet, 473
Spondee, the, 473
STALLINGS, SYLVIA (*What Word for Spring?*), 376–77
Stanza, 475–76
STEINBECK, JOHN (quoted), 172, 178–79
  Grapes of Wrath, 257, 410–12
  Sweet Thursday, 45
Steps, 156
STEVENS, WALLACE (*Peter Quince at the Clavier*), 377–79
STEVENSON, ADLAI, 127
STEVENSON, ROBERT LOUIS, 183
  Celestial Surgeon, The, 113
  House Beautiful, The, 379–80
  Humble Remonstrance, A, 174
  Markheim, 172
  Merry Men, The, 175
STOKES, THOMAS L. (quoted), 86–88
Stopping by Woods on a Snowy Evening (ROBERT FROST), 66–67, 350, 478
Stories:
  character, 173–74
  dialogue, 393–412
  plot, 174–75
  recitals, 196–206
  setting, 175
  sharing, 177–79
  types, 173–75
Storyteller, The (FRANCES FROST), 349–50
Storytelling impulse, 171–72
Strange Fruit (LILLIAN SMITH), 96
Stress, 35, 472
Substitute, The (COPPÉE), 173
SUCKLING, SIR JOHN (*Constant Lover, The*), 380
Suggestiveness, composition factor, 44–46
SULLIVAN, ED, 227
Sweet Thursday (JOHN STEINBECK), 45
SWING, RAYMOND GRAM, 143–44
Syllable, 472
Symbols, 96–98
Sympathies, enlarging your, 19
Synecdoche, 31

Taming of the Shrew, The (WILLIAM SHAKESPEARE), 199–200, 205–06

Tangled Fire of William Faulkner, The (WILLIAM VAN O'CONNOR), 182
Tarawa (ROBERT SHERROD), 109
TARKINGTON, BOOTH (*Boy Penrod, The*), 172
Taste, 244–45
  forming, 17–18
TEASDALE, SARA (*Barter*), 381
Television reading, *see* Radio and television reading
Telltale Heart, The (EDGAR ALLAN POE), 172
Tempo, variety in, 158–63
  change of pace, 162–63
  pause, 160–62
TENNYSON, ALFRED LORD, 11
  Break, Break, Break, 33, 81, 260, 381–82
  Crossing the Bar, 383
  Eagle, The, 386
  Flower in the Crannied Wall, 382
  Guinevere, 32
  In Memoriam A. H. H., 69–70, 383–85
  Of Old Sat Freedom on the Heights, 385
  Splendor Falls, The, 124
  Ulysses, 240–41, 382–83
Terza rima, 475
Tetrameter, 473
Thing of Beauty Is a Joy Forever, A (JOHN KEATS), 354
Thirty Seconds Over Tokyo, 184
THOMAS, CHAUNCEY (*Snow Story, The*), 175
THOMAS, DYLAN, obscurity and the referent, 106
THOMAS, LOWELL, 14, 102, 225, 231, 246–47
  clearness and the referent, 105
Thought, words and, 95–96
Threnos (PERCY BYSSHE SHELLEY), 40
THURMAN, HOWARD (quoted), 251
Tiger, The (WILLIAM BLAKE), 336–37
Time magazine, 9, 86, 233
Times Weekly Review, The, 267
To a Post-office Inkwell (CHRISTOPHER MORLEY), 366–67
To a Skylark (PERCY BYSSHE SHELLEY), 374–76
To a Waterfowl (WILLIAM CULLEN BRYANT), 340–41
To Helen (EDGAR ALLAN POE), 37
To the Virgins to Make Much of Time (ROBERT HERRICK), 351
To Thomas Moore (LORD BYRON), 342–43
Told by the Schoolmaster (JOHN GALSWORTHY), 402–06
Tommy (RUDYARD KIPLING), 311–13
Tongue, 133–34
Tools of understanding and appreciation, 61–93
  discourse:
    types, 78–80
    units, 68–77
  psychological means, 81–91
  rhetorical devices, 62–68
Total meaning, 99
Toward Understanding the Bible (GEORGIA HARKNESS), 29
TRACY, SPENCER, 184
Training, naturalness vs., 50–51
Transitions, in cutting, 200–01
TREVELYAN, G. M. (quoted), 255–56
Trimeter, 473
Trochaic feet, 472
TRUEBLOOD, THOMAS C., 5
TUNNEY, GENE, 244
TWAIN, MARK, 11, 177
TWEED, GEORGE R. (quoted), 241–43
Twenty-fourth Psalm, The (BIBLE), 139
Twenty-third Psalm (BIBLE), 73, 333

Uncle Jim and Uncle Billy (BRET HARTE), 173
Uncle Tom's Cabin, 198
Ulysses (ALFRED LORD TENNYSON), 240–41, 382–83
Understanding, tools, *see* Tools of understanding and appreciation
Unity, composition factor, 26–27
Universality, composition factor, 42
Up at a Villa—Down in the City (ROBERT BROWNING), 102

Values, choral reading, 210–12
  dramatic effects, 210–11
  improved speech, 211
  social understanding, 211–12
VAN VOORHIS, WESTBROOK, 232–34
Variety, 155–65
  composition factor, 28
  in tempo, 158–63
  in vocal method, 155–58
  in volume and force, 163–65
Verbs, 69–73
VERGARA, ALLYS DWYER (quoted), 187
Versification, terms, 472–76
VIERICK, PETER, 191
Vocalism (WALT WHITMAN), 387
Voice, 123–28
  agreeable, 143–44
  breathing, 123–25
  correcting:
    heaviness, 147

Voice (*Cont.*):
  correcting (*Cont.*):
    lack of flexibility, 147
    lack of sense of rhythm, 147–48
    lifelessness, 147
    monotony due to sameness in pitch, 146
    mumbling, 146–47
    too loud, 147
    too rapid rate, 148
    too slow rate, 148
    weak thin, 146
  diction and, 142–44
  overtones, 240–41
  phonation, 125–26
  quality, 127–28
  range, 155–56
  resonance, 126–27
Voice and Spiritual Education (HIRAM CORSON), 6–7
Volume, variety in, 163–65
Voluntary audience, 190–91
Vowels, 128–31

WALLACE, LEW, 166
WARREN, LEONARD, 82
WEAVER, JOHN V. A. (*Moonlight*), 386
WEBSTER, DANIEL (quoted), 44, 114
WHARTON, EDITH, 140
WHATELY, RICHARD, 5, 12
What Word for Spring? (SYLVIA STALLINGS), 376–77
When I Consider How My Light Is Spent (JOHN MILTON), 363
When I Have Fears that I May Cease to Be (JOHN KEATS), 355
When I Was One-and-Twenty (A. E. HOUSMAN), 352
WHITMAN, WALT:
  Beat! Beat! Drums! 388–89
  For You, O Democracy, 389
  I Hear America Singing, 389–90
  O Captain! My Captain, 388
  Open Road, The, 163
  Out of the Cradle Endlessly Rocking, 72–73
  Vocalism, 387
  Wound-Dresser, The, 328–29
WHITTIER, JOHN GREENLEAF (*Dear Lord and Father of Mankind*), 390–91
Who's Who in America, 255
WILDE, OSCAR, 127
WILDER, THORNTON (quoted), 257–58
  Our Town, 16
Will, The (SIR JAMES M. BARRIE), 27, 202, 203–04, 264, 413–32
WILLKIE, WENDELL, 53
WILSON, GARFF B. (quoted), 4
WILSON, WOODROW, 256
WOLFE, JULIA ELIZABETH, 182
WOLFE, THOMAS, 27, 182
Words:
  associations, 100
  changes of meaning, 111–12
  connotation, 112–13
  definition, 109–11
  denotation, 112–13
  grouping, 151–53
  imagery, 96
  language and experience, 94–102
  order, 108–09
  phrasal patterns, 113–17
  pronunciation drills, list for, 149
  referent, the, 102–07
  symbols, 96–98
  things and, 101–02
  thought and, 95–96
  total meaning, 99
  world of, 100–01
Words, Lost, Strayed, or Stolen (ALICE HAMILTON), 118–21
WORDSWORTH, WILLIAM, 183
  Composed upon Westminster Bridge, 391
  It Is a Beauteous Evening, Calm and Free, 391–92
  London, 1802, 392
  World Is Too Much With Us, The, 62, 69, 260
World Is Too Much With Us, The (WILLIAM WORDSWORTH), 62, 69, 260
WOUK, HERMAN (*Dr. Keith's Letter to His Son Willie* from The Caine Mutiny), 298–301
Wound-Dresser, The (WALT WHITMAN), 328–29
Writing, speaking and, unite in oral reading, 10–11
WYLIE, ELINOR (*Golden Bough*), 392

Yale Lectures on Preaching (HENRY WARD BEECHER), 44–45, 145
Young and Old (CHARLES KINGSLEY), 355